From Nowhere

Artists, Writers, and the Precognitive Imagination

Eric Wargo

Anomalist Books
Charlottesville, Virginia

An Original Publication of Anomalist Books
From Nowhere: Artists, Writers,
and the Precognitive Imagination
Copyright © 2024 by Eric Wargo
ISBN: 978-1-949501-33-9

Book design: Seale Studios
Cover photograph by HTO, Wikimedia Commons. Replica of the
painting from the Chauvet cave, in the Anthropos Museum, Brno,
South Moravia, Czech Republic.

Anomalist Books
3445 Seminole Trail #247
Charlottesville, VA 22911

CONTENTS

PART THREE: ALIENATED MAJESTY

For Emily, May, and Laura

Really these premonitions of a book—states of soul in creating—are very queer and little apprehended.
—Virginia Woolf, *Diary* (1929)

What I pretend to be past is all in the future. Yet to you, reading this, it's over. All very confusing …
—Virginia Woolf, letter to Vita Sackville-West (1927)

Acknowledgments

I began my research for this book in 2019, when my daughter Emily (then three) was just learning to draw. Her first recognizably figurative picture was a crayon rendering of "Grandma" as a kind of lozenge shape transected by two lines (legs? Arms?). Her drawings quickly grew in complexity—more lines transecting the lozenges, which appeared in strange groups crisscrossed with squiggles—and the stories she emphatically told about these shapes were in some cases mind-bogglingly complex. There was a large and complex scribble that she called "A Pond with Whales Jumping and a Fish with Fins with a Reindeer Who Can't Get out of His Tent Because It's an Arslarf House." When pressed for further explanation, she explained that an Arslarf was a kind of tuna that swims in circles looking for ice cream. Emily has come a long way since then; and now, as this project sees the light of day, her little sister May is beginning her art career, with similar verve. The house their mom Laura and I share with them is awash with brilliant art from God-knows-where.

Emily and May are the people I thank the most—first, for their patience. When they are old enough to enjoy my favorite movie, *Alien*, they will probably note an alarming similarity between their writer dad and the "Space Jockey," H. R. Giger's ancient fossilized star pilot, permanently staring into a viewscreen and fused with its couch. They and Laura, whom I also sincerely thank, have been very patient with my obsessions, piles of books and papers, and need for solitude on weekends over the past several years. But I also thank my daughters for their influence: If I'm right in my conclusions, they are probably my biggest. Somehow, in ways I'll never fully know, they are now transmitting to me things they will learn in their futures even after I am gone. This is the way I suspect prophecy works as a cultural system. (If you make it to the end of this book, you'll see what I mean.)

I also express deep gratitude to Jeffrey Kripal, another influence. Jeff's whole body of work offers a conceptual framework for approaching the paranormal as a profoundly important factor in human culture. His pair of books over a decade ago now, *Authors of the Impossible* and *Mutants and Mystics*, directly inspired my research project that led to this book. And Jeff, personally, has been a great friend and enthusiastic champion of my work. I could not have embarked on nor completed this project without that support and encouragement. He read an early draft and his comments were invaluable.

Also crucial to my thinking (and my mental health) has been the rogue's gallery of weirdos I have come to know in one way or another because of my precognition research, in some cases through symposia at Esalen and events at Rice University that Jeff has invited me to. I can't mention them all by name, but David Metcalfe has been a particularly valuable friend and co-investigator of weird and liminal cultural realms. I also thank super-precog Tobi Watari, who has contributed greatly to my thinking about precognition and dreams over the years. Annoyingly, she has even made me change my mind on a few occasions. And as always, I thank Patrick Huyghe, who has ever been a patient and supportive editor and friend.

While they are credited throughout the book and in the endnotes, I also want to acknowledge here at the outset a few scholars, independent researchers, and bloggers, most of whom I don't know personally, who documented some of the coincidences and cases of artistic prophecy (although not necessarily described as such) with which I have built my arguments: Layla Alexander-Garrett, Pierre Bayard, Julia Briggs, Julie Kane, Christopher Knowles, Dominic Kulcsar ("wmmvrrvrrmm"), Anthony Peake, Philippe Refabert, James Valentini, and Slavoj Žižek.

Lastly, I must also thank the pair of intelligently behaving orange orbs I saw fly over the Philadelphia Museum of Art on the evening of July 4, 2009. Long story. Unlike Roy Neary in *Close Encounters*, I didn't get a sunburn from these anomalous objects—they were too high up and far off—but I really don't know what they were, and I think they had a lot to do with this book.

Move Along, Nothing to See Here

*Art discloses our own mystery even as it lays bare the
mystery of consciousness and the mystery of the world. It
is* paranormal*, an anomaly casting doubt upon our own
most cherished certainties about the nature of reality.*
—J. F. Martel, *Reclaiming Art in the Age of Artifice*
(2015)

"Where do you get your ideas?"
Artists and writers famously cringe when they hear
this question in interviews or are asked it in casual
conversation. It is annoying because it is so often unanswerable.

Novelists sometimes deliver prepared wisecracks. Sci-fi writer
Harlan Ellison used to tell people he got his ideas from a mail-order
idea service in Schenectady, for example. Those who are more indulgent
may allow themselves to speculate about the unconscious. Stephen
King has credited the "boys in the basement" with the premises of his
scary bestsellers.[1]

It is also common for creative people to deflect the question of the
origins of their ideas with some recitation of the truism that what really
matters in an art career is not the psychologically discredited notions
of inspiration or genius but simple hard work and persistence—the
practice, practice, practice that gets you to Carnegie Hall. Reminding
you of Thomas Edison's famous quip that genius is "one percent
inspiration, and ninety-nine percent perspiration," they may talk about
their self-discipline and the long years they have put into perfecting
their craft.

Until about 300 years ago, answering the question, "where do you
get your ideas?", wouldn't have been as hard, nor the common answers
so uninspiring. Evidence from Paleolithic painted caves in Europe

and Southeast Asia hint strongly that the first artists got their ideas in visionary states like trances and dreams. Their ideas—at least, some of them—came from spiritual realms and from supernatural experiences. The earliest cultures to write down their myths and religious texts were explicit about ideas originating elsewhere than in a person's head and life. Novelty and innovation have not always been valued everywhere and at all times—it is mainly with modernity that people have come to place such a premium on the new. But even in antiquity, the inventive Greeks placed a high value on novelty,[2] and they too thought their new ideas came as gifts of the muses, the gods, or the personal divine oracle they called the *daimon*. Later, in the Christian medieval world, it was normal for poets and craftspeople to credit their works entirely to the Lord.

The idea that creative genius was a gift of contact with the divine retained its force in the novelty-loving Renaissance, even as a new, more modern, psychological paradigm was quietly taking shape. The first art historian, Giorgio Vasari, affirmed that the geniuses of his time, such as his friend Michelangelo, were divinely inspired. But his 1550 book, *Lives of the Most Eminent Painters, Sculptors, and Architects*, also marked a shift toward localizing creativity in the individual artist's body and mind, their gift of contact with the divine coming frequently at the cost of singular quirks of personality and character. It is largely from Vasari that we got our cultural category of artist as a breed apart from mere craftspeople cleaving conservatively to some taught tradition. His book also enshrined many of the stereotypes that we now regularly associate with artists, such as difficult personalities and eccentricity, and even in some cases mental illness.

The artist as a solitary heroic genius remains a kind of archetype, but among critics and psychologists who study creativity, it is one that is no longer believed in. The artist's fall from grace began with the Enlightenment. Natural scientists in Isaac Newton's day rejected any physical causation that was not naturalistic and mechanistic, and philosophers extended this to cultural causation, invention, poetic brilliance. A kind of thermodynamic, billiard-ball psychological model reduced creation to the reshuffling and reassembly of prior influences: Old ideas recombine to form new ideas. Even the Romantic poets rebelling against the Enlightenment's reductions at the turn of the 19th century felt compelled to naturalize and humanize the assembling property, the Imagination. It partook of the divine, but it was also intrinsically human and obeyed psychological laws—a two-mindedness that produced some of the most interesting and culture-changing works of the imagination that also happened to be, figuratively if not literally, *about* the imagination. Samuel Taylor Coleridge's *Kubla Khan* and Mary Shelley's *Frankenstein* are the best-known examples. Both came to the authors initially in dreams.[3]

By the turn of the 20th century, psychologists had adopted the Romantics' metaphors of interiority (caves and subterranean rivers) to explain and express the constancy (William James) and hiddenness (Sigmund Freud) of the mind's inventive powers, but those powers were increasingly located in the brain. Interest in the occult has always lurked in the background for many of the most profound thinkers about the imagination, but naturalism—or what we nowadays call materialism—generally has a way of trumping that interest, forcing the occult to remain occult.

Fast forward another century, and the ability to actually observe what happens in the brain when people make decisions, solve problems, and have creative insights has resulted in triumphal statements that the ancient mysteries of creativity have finally been solved. "For the first time, we can see the source of imagination, that massive network of electrical cells that lets us constantly form new connections between old ideas," wrote Jonah Lehrer in his 2012 book *Imagine*.[4] It's quite simple: "The source of every new idea is the same. There is a network of neurons in the brain, and then the network shifts."

When it was discovered that Lehrer had invented quotes from Bob Dylan and other creative case studies to support his claims, it became clear that his particular network of electrical cells was doing more than forming new connections among old ideas. *Imagine* was recalled by the publisher and he was fired from his positions at *The New Yorker* and *Wired* for his creative invention. I don't know, but I suspect Lehrer's falsifications slipped past his editors because everything in his book sounded so sure, so sciencey, so savvy. It reflected the kind of counterintuitive-but-not-too-counterintuitive just-so story that today's science publicity machine is skilled at selling and that an increasingly science-literate public is primed to consume in TED talks and podcasts like Radiolab (where Lehrer was a frequent contributor).

Imagine's argument is simplistic and, I think, pretty unimaginative, but it reflects a zeitgeist. Pick up most any academic or pop-scientific article or book on creativity, and you will find a better-supported, less glib version of the same basic assertion: that inspiration in its divine or semi-divine sense—and with it, genius—is a quaint old myth. Authors will authoritatively cite the latest psychology studies seemingly debunking any notion of some "sacred river" (Coleridge's term) whence our best and most original ideas issue as though from nothing. What really matters, they generally agree, is the computational ability of the brain to assemble data from past experience and transform it into some novel solution to a technical or aesthetic problem.[5] They will certainly try to inspire you a little with the astonishing recombinatory properties of human cognition,[6] our ability to see things from new perspectives, the ability to "bisociate" or make oddball nonintuitive juxtapositions, and so on.[7] They will also helpfully emphasize specific personality traits that contribute to flashes of insight, the habits known to cultivate them, and the laborious work—the perspiration—that is usually needed to turn those cortical twitches into something having cultural value.[8] They will especially underscore the importance of the very real but invisible laborers (and social-economic contexts) making creative work possible—not spirits, not figurative boys in some unconscious basement, but real collaborators and helpers and long-suffering partners, people with their own brilliant, ever-shifting neural networks, whose contributions typically get overlooked and obscured by relations of class, gender, and race.

All these things—disposition, effort, the brain's recombinatory powers, and social contexts—are undeniably important, and I don't think they are at all in doubt. But there is a limiting presumption inherent in all this, one that follows naturally from that mechanistic physics of the Enlightenment. It is that what comes first in creation are the materials already found lying around, the billiard balls already on the table, moving with their own specific momentum in predictable trajectories—those "old ideas." Old ideas can come in the form of inherited traditions and cultural influences (other past or present artists or the giants on whose shoulders scientific discoverers famously stand) or the stock of life experience called memory, or some mix. But creative causation is nearly always described as causally unilinear: It flows from the past, even if that past stuff is remixed and rearranged in seemingly unpredictable and even irreducible ways.

This may seem so commonsensical as to be beyond question, steeped as we are in the presumptions of Newtonian physics that causes only flow in a single direction in time. But it requires that we ignore myriad weird and even unsettling anomalies in the arts and literature and popular culture that look very much as though a creator was somehow reaching into their future, not the past—and what's more, doing it effortlessly.

Believe It or Not

When writing about what I will call for convenience *artistic prophecy*, it is hard not to sound like Ripley's Believe It or Not!, the American franchise started in 1919 exploiting the strange and curious as fodder to sell newspapers, books, and other products. But believe it or not, paintings, films, novels, poems, TV shows, and other forms of high and mass culture very often foreshadow future events with an accuracy that is more than uncanny.

The best-known and most-debated example is an 1898 novel called *Futility* by a popular turn-of-the-century sea-adventure writer named Morgan Robertson. *Futility* tells the story of an alcoholic seaman working aboard the largest ocean liner ever built, the *Titan*, which hits an iceberg on an April night in the North Atlantic on a run between New York and Liverpool, killing nearly everyone on board due to a shortage of lifeboats. Fourteen years later, the 51-year-old writer, having hit bottom after a lifetime of alcohol addiction, would have been nearly as stunned as his fellow New Yorkers by the April 15, 1912 *New York Times* headline reporting that the Liverpool-based RMS *Titanic*, bound for New York and with close to the same stats as his fictitious *Titan*, had carried most of its passengers to a watery grave under nearly identical circumstances to those in his novel. It was the *Titanic*'s maiden voyage, on a route that was nearly a mirror image of *Titan*'s.[9]

But *Futility* is just the tip of an enormous iceberg, so to speak. Here are a handful of other examples.

In 1951, after a long creative struggle with a story that felt perpetually unrealistic to him, New York novelist Norman Mailer published *Barbary Shore*, about a writer like himself living and working in a Brooklyn Heights rooming house with a colorful mix of artist neighbors, one of whom turns out to be a KGB spy. A few years later, after a stint in Hollywood, Mailer returned to New York, to Brooklyn Heights, where he rented a room in a building to work on his next novel. One day he was stunned to encounter a *New York Times* headline about a top KGB Colonel named Rudolf Abel who had just been caught running a massive spy ring out of the same building Mailer was then using for his office. Mailer only knew the spy as "Emil Goldfus," the "guitarist" who worked in the room directly one floor down from his.[10] *Barbary Shore* is regarded as Mailer's worst novel … but prophecy is unrelated to quality, or lack thereof. *Futility* is terrible too, in case you were tempted to pick up a copy.

Don DeLillo's definitely not-terrible 1985 novel *White Noise* centers on an "airborne toxic event"—the result of a chemical spill—that forces the evacuation of a small college town and acquires an almost metaphysical significance for the story's death-obsessed protagonist, professor of Hitler Studies Jack Gladney. *White Noise* was published a mere month after the gas cloud from a horrific chemical spill at a Union Carbide plant in Bhopal, India, took the lives of as many as 8,000 people and injured over half a million more—still one of the worst industrial disasters ever recorded. DeLillo obviously wrote his novel several months or more before that disaster.[11] Most reviewers dutifully remarked on this incredible coincidence with a sort of perplexed shrug, as one of those things, perhaps the effect of a postmodern world where those sorts of dread-inducing news stories are now the norm. Few seriously considered the possibility that the prescience was more than coincidental.[12]

Michel Houellebecq is regarded as a literary *enfant terrible* in France, where he has aroused criticism for occasionally right-wing and anti-Islamic views. He has also been called prophetic for his 2001 novel *Platform*, about a middle-aged French sex tourist in Thailand, culminating with a terrorist attack at a Thai resort. In the novel, Islamic extremists drive a van filled with fertilizer explosive into a nightclub, killing 200 people, including the narrator's lover. A year later, in October 2002, a real Islamic extremist group called Jemaah Islamiya set off a car bomb between two popular nightclubs in Bali, Indonesia, killing 202 people. Although it was in a different Southeast Asian locale, the attack was very similar to the one in Houellebecq's novel, and with a strikingly similar death toll. (Houellebecq said he had chosen the "200" number for his novel arbitrarily.) Thirteen years later, the French satirical weekly *Charlie Hebdo* ran a cover story on Houellebecq to accompany the publication of a new book, *Submission*, about a democratically elected Muslim president who imposes Sharia law on France. The title on the cover was "The Predictions of Sorcerer Houellebecq," next to a Nostradamus-like caricature of the author.[13] Apparently coincidentally, the same week, and on the very day of the publication of the novel, two French Muslim brothers, Saïd and Chérif Kouachi, entered the *Charlie Hebdo* offices wearing masks and killed 12 staff and injured many more. Among those killed at the magazine offices was a friend of Houellebecq, columnist Bernard Maris.[14]

In November 2009, the poet and artist Frankétienne, known as the "father of Haitian letters," wrote an absurdist play called *Melovivi* or *The Trap*, about two unnamed persons trapped in rubble following an unspecified disaster. The 73-year-old Frankétienne had for decades spoken of chaos and destruction as necessary precursors to creation ("the womb of light and life," as he put it in a 2011 interview[15]), and his works in various media—novels, songs, poems, paintings—were often on apocalyptic themes. At 4:53 p.m. on January 12, 2010, just minutes after Frankétienne had finished a rehearsal of his new play in the yard of his home, a magnitude 7.0 earthquake struck the already impoverished island, displacing nearly 900,000 people and killing a still-unknown number (estimates ranged from 92,000 to 316,000[16]). Thousands were trapped in rubble, just as in his play. Although his home in the capital Port-au-Prince was partly destroyed, Frankétienne survived the damage and has no doubt that his play was a premonition—"The voice of God spoke to me."[17] Two days before the quake, a disembodied voice had told the artist to obtain a medallion of Saint Andrew, and his driver went to the neighboring city Léogâne, where Andrew is the Patron Saint, to obtain one.[18] Léogâne turned out to be the quake's epicenter.

As I was writing this book, readers of my previous books emailed me about apparent literary prophecies of the COVID-19 pandemic. The most widely cited is a novel called *The Eyes of Darkness* by thriller writer Dean Koontz. Koontz first published the novel in 1981 under a pseudonym; it centered on secret experiments involving a viral bio-weapon developed at a lab near Gorki, Russia, called Gorki-400. But after the collapse of the Soviet Union in 1989, Koontz republished it, this time under his own name, and changed the location of the lab to Wuhan, China. The lethal virus is called Wuhan-400 in the reissued version. In both editions, the novel is set in 2020. The SARS-CoV-2 virus originated in Wuhan province in late 2019 and was declared a worldwide pandemic in 2020; much popular speculation centered on the possibility that it had been accidentally or deliberately released from China's major virology lab in Wuhan. Somewhat lessening the uncanniness, perhaps, is that Koontz clearly chose that province after researching the locales of the bioweapons labs of the U.S.'s likely post-Cold War adversaries ... but still.[19]

It is a truism that science fiction writers often are accurate in foretelling the future. As amazing as some cases seem—H. G. Wells describing radiation-contaminated battlefields in his 1914 novel *The World Set Free*, for instance,[20] or many now-commonplace technologies, including something like the internet, described by Jules Verne in his 1863 draft *Paris in the Twentieth Century*[21]—it is these writers' job to extrapolate from existing science and predict future technological and social trends. That makes many such cases ambiguous as evidence of anything paranormal or preternatural. Prediction—extrapolation from prior trends and, often, envisioning of worst-case scenarios—is different from precognition.

What should we make, for instance, of Martin Caidin's 1968 novel *Marooned*, about an Apollo mission malfunction requiring round-the-clock help from ground control? Two years later, a strikingly similar scenario unfolded aboard Apollo 13 after one of the capsule's oxygen tanks exploded en route to the moon.[22] Caidin, who had an interest in psychic phenomena, thought he had prophesied the disaster. Yet, a crisis involving America's space program might have been an obvious topic for a techno-thriller writer, especially during the buildup to the moon landings. Space disasters even found their way into popular songs of the period, most famously David Bowie's 1968 "Space Oddity." Even for believers in literary prophecy, cases like *Marooned* are necessarily, let's say, marooned in a limbo of uncertainty. However, it is also true that many writers in the SF genre have a knack of foretelling seemingly unpredictable historical twists, as well as totally unpredictable turning points in their own lives.[23]

Philip K. Dick is a much-discussed case of an SF writer seemingly gifted with special foresight.[24] To cite just one of many examples, in 1962, while living in Northern California, he wrote a story about entrepreneurs building an android simulacrum of Abraham Lincoln. He couldn't find a publisher, so the story languished unread in his desk drawer. But then two years later, Disneyland unveiled with considerable fanfare what became one of its most popular exhibits, their animatronic Abraham Lincoln. When he read about it in the newspaper, Dick clipped the article as proof that he was a "precog" straight out of one of his stories. But what is stranger, Dick's story had centered on one of the inventors' obsessive relationship with a young woman assistant hired to bring verisimilitude to the Lincoln simulacrum, for instance by applying makeup to its face late at night. About a decade later, Dick found himself living in Orange County, in an apartment building near Disneyland, and discovered that one of his neighbors worked at the park. The young woman's job? Putting makeup on the animatronic Lincoln late at night after the park was closed.[25] What are the odds?

Cases like these are frequently dismissed as "random" isolated one-offs. But as we will see throughout this book, creative people who do this at all may do it repeatedly. Books have been written just about Dick's bizarrely precognitive life.[26] Morgan Robertson too was constantly experiencing weird coincidences—what later would come to be called synchronicities—connected with his writing, and he even appears to have attributed his creative muse to some supernormal power before that memorable night in 1912 confirmed his prophetic gift. One of the returning protagonists in his earlier fiction was an alcohol-addicted seaman named Finnegan who somehow had a sixth sense for perils in the water ahead, constantly perplexing his more sober, rationalistic shipmates—clearly a self-portrait. It's why I said Robertson' would have been only "nearly" as stunned as his contemporaries by the loss of the *Titanic*. It might not actually have seemed all that surprising after a life of weird brushes with fate.[27]

Our sample of claimed artistic prophecy is particularly large in the world of letters. It is not because writers are especially precognitive compared to artists in other media, but because by the very nature of their work they tend to leave a significant and easily studied paper trail. Apart from their creative output, they also have a habit of keeping diaries, penning memoirs, and doing interviews where they talk in detail about their lives. It is like attaching a printer directly to the phenomenon of interest. But creative people in all media act as seismographs for history- and life-quakes ahead.[28]

The archetypal shipwreck in a cold Northern ocean, for instance, is Caspar David Friedrich's *The Sea of Ice*. Painted sometime in 1823 or 1824, it is one of the most iconic and recognizable paintings of the Romantic period, depicting a roughly pyramidal heap of ice in a bleak arctic twilight. Nowadays it is ubiquitous on book covers and in textbooks as practically the ur-example of the sublime mood in art. Barely visible, unless you look closely, is the aft end of an unlucky ship, just disappearing below the water. The Dresden painter told a visitor to his studio that the ship was meant to be HMS *Griper*, one of two vessels that Admiral William Edward Parry had taken in search of the Northwest Passage in a storied 1819-20 expedition. Friedrich had evidently read Parry's 1821 book about that adventure (translated into German in 1822) or at least read excerpts from it that appeared in German papers.[29] However, in reality, both the *Griper* and the lead vessel, HMS *Hecla*, returned safe and sound after spending a cold winter above the Arctic Circle—so Friedrich's depiction was pure artistic license … unless we regard it as prophecy. In 1824, on a subsequent expedition, the HMS *Fury*, the ship that replaced *Griper* because it had had trouble keeping up with *Hecla* on the first voyage, was wrecked in the frigid waters off the West coast of Baffin Island.

In 1930, a Romanian surrealist painter living in Paris named Victor Brauner painted a realistic self-portrait in which he was blinded in one eye (*Self-portrait with Enucleated Eye*). The theme of displaced or injured eyes came to obsess Brauner in his work, and over the subsequent years he made several more paintings of figures with one occluded or injured eye, including a 1931 painting of a decapitated head with one bleeding eye (*The Head of Benjamin Fondane*) and a 1934 painting of Adolf

Hitler with a dagger in the eye. Many of his other paintings centered on ghostly eyes and an obsession with vision. Astonishingly, in 1938, Brauner interceded to break up a fight between two Spanish surrealists, Oscar Dominguez and Esteban Francés. A glass thrown by Dominguez struck Brauner instead of its target, causing him to lose his left eye. Thus a major theme in Brauner's art prefigured a major, calamitous, and totally unpredictable—"random"—turning point later in his life.[30]

Artistic prophecy isn't all death, doom, and disaster. My absolutely favorite example centers on the funniest moment of one of the funniest movies ever made, Rob Reiner's 1984 mockumentary *This Is Spinal Tap*. I'm referring to the anticlimactic descent onto a concert stage of a miniature Stonehenge model that had been made to the wrong proportions—18 inches instead of 18 feet—because confused lead guitarist Nigel Tufnel (played by Christopher Guest, who also co-wrote, or really co-improvised, the movie) used a double apostrophe instead of a single one on the back of a restaurant napkin. The band watch in horror as the tiny monument, dwarfed even by two dwarves doing a jig around it, gets tangled in wires. Heavy metal insiders assumed that the filmmakers had based this scene on a real fiasco involving the band Black Sabbath that had occurred just six months before the film's release: That band had planned to include a Stonehenge model in their concert tour for their *Born Again* album (an instrumental on the album was called "Stonehenge"), but they were forced to shelve the idea at the last minute because the fake monument delivered to them was several times *too large*—a result of a failure of communication between the band and the company commissioned to make the prop. According to bassist Geezer Butler, the instructions were mistakenly delivered in meters instead of feet. Yet "impossibly," *Spinal Tap* had already been written and shot by the time of Black Sabbath's embarrassing mixup. An early version of the Stonehenge scene appears in a demo reel made for studio execs in 1981 or 1982. Thus, the filmmakers' idea for a hilariously mis-sized Stonehenge model preceded the real-life Black Sabbath mishap by a year or more.[31] Even more amazingly, the real-life Black Sabbath debacle involved a dwarf, painted to look like the devil, ridiculously jumping off the monument onto a pile of mattresses during an unintentionally laughter-provoking dress rehearsal.[32]

And to tragedy and comedy we must add the utterly surreal. The 2011 debut episode of Charlie Brooker's dystopic Channel 4 series *Black Mirror*, entitled "The National Anthem," centered on a fictitious British Prime Minister being blackmailed by terrorists to have sex with a pig on live television. The episode focused specifically on the role of social media in compelling the leader to carry out the deed in front of the nation. Four years later, in 2015, a storm erupted on social media when a new unauthorized biography of UK Prime Minister David Cameron alleged that he had, during an initiation ritual for a dining club at Oxford in the 1980s, inserted "a private part of his anatomy" in the mouth of a dead pig. Cameron, of course, denied the allegations. Beyond what it revealed about the secret rituals of England's ruling elite, this scandal was also a hilariously obvious and uncanny permutation of the by-then-famous *Black Mirror* episode. I hope this is the only scenario from that dark series that comes true.

You get the idea.

This kind of thing is so prevalent that some intelligence agencies have begun paying attention. In 2018, the German defense ministry enlisted the help of specialists in comparative literature at the University of Tübingen to plug plots of novels from around the world into a computer in an effort to predict the next areas of regional conflict and "black swan" events like 9/11.[33] Project Cassandra, as it was called, was successful in predicting the 2019 social unrest in Algeria two years before it occurred, using tremors in that country's literary scene. In naming their effort, the project's directors were referencing East Germany's literary superstar Christa Wolf, who in 1983 penned a retelling of the fall of Troy from the prophetess Cassandra's point of view. Her novel *Kassandra* seemed to foretell the demise of her own country at the end of that decade, after the fall of the Berlin Wall. It so happens that, like Phil Dick and Morgan Robertson, Wolf was no stranger to paranormal and synchronistic events, and she often took inspiration from her dreams and hypnagogic experiences—a common trait of visionary writers and artists (and shamans).[34] It may not be accidental that she was drawn to the subject of the perpetually disbelieved Trojan prophetess for what became her most famous novel.

We have been indoctrinated in our culture against taking alleged evidence of psychic phenomena seriously. So, when people discover bizarre coincidences between art and life like those I've mentioned, they will chuckle uneasily, maybe be a bit "weirded out," as Charlie Brooker said he was about the whole pig business,[35] or rehearse some cognitive-dissonance prophylactic like the skeptics' "law of large numbers," and then forget it soon afterward. It doesn't occur to anybody—besides the German defense ministry, apparently—to actually keep a tally. Nor does the more radical possibility occur to us: that these apparent anomalies in the world of culture might be giving us an important clue that there is more to the oldest of mysteries, the origins of ideas, than what centuries of post-Enlightenment psychology have led us to believe.

Synopsis

The hypothesis I will be advancing in the following chapters reflects a very old-fashioned assumption about creativity—an assumption more than 40,000 years old, in fact. It is that the most original ideas, the nuclei of novels and songs and sculptures and paintings and films—if not always the perspiration-inducing sanding and polishing that make these nuclei presentable—do have what could be called a supernormal or paranormal origin, just as creators have often intuited. The best art and literature do not arise merely from some hammering-together of available influences and cultural raw materials on some inner cognitive workbench. However, the real origin of new ideas may not be exactly what the ancient Greeks or the hyperancient Paleolithic cave painters supposed. I won't be arguing for a spirit world that literally breaks through a cave wall or canvas and guides the painter's hand. And I stand with modernity in saying that the Lord isn't a very helpful explanatory term either.

When the masses of evidence, including (believe it or not) abundant scientific evidence, are fairly considered, the existence of precognition cannot reasonably be denied anymore or explained away as self-delusion or the result of faulty reasoning about the odds of coincidence.[36] It seems in fact to be incredibly common. In my book *Time Loops*, I made the case that precognition is probably an intrinsic but still scientifically uncharacterized component of ordinary cognition, one that represents a fascinating and probably vast future frontier for psychology. Moreover, multiple scientific currents of just the last couple decades are converging on a plausible physical and even biological framework to explain how it might work. Sensitivity to future experiences doesn't defy known physical principles, as was always claimed by skeptics. It simply defies our assumptions—that is, three-century-old Enlightenment assumptions—about the unilinear flow of physical and mental causation. We are entering a brave new world where concepts like retro-(that is, backwards-) causation and time travel are thinkable things, and a new science of precognition I believe will be part of that.

Like Superman and humble journalist Clark Kent, precognition and creative inspiration are seldom seen in the same room together—which is to say, these topics have in the past belonged to traditionally separate areas of inquiry (and mostly, non-inquiry, in the case of precognition).

But as we will see in Part One, there are striking convergences between how precognition is most often experienced by people in nighttime dreams and waking visions and how inspiration has always been experienced and described by creative artists, scientists, and inventors. Both strike experiencers as something "out of nowhere"—suggesting a hidden, secret kinship or even a secret identity. Could Clark Kent really be Superman?

To answer that question, we will begin in Chapter 1 with a close look at Jamaican-American sculptor Michael Richards, who seems to have predicted his death on 9/11 in an astonishing body of work in the last years of the millennium. I will examine Richards' sculptures and other apparent artistic prophecies of that day's events in the context of contemporary theories of psychic phenomena and the emerging currents in the physical sciences that are giving precognition a new kind of scientific plausibility. We will then shift gears in Chapter 2 to look at two striking, older cases of psychic inspiration—one of them from the great American writer Mark Twain and another from Mary Craig Sinclair, the writer wife of Upton Sinclair. Both believed their best ideas came to them from other people, telepathically. But a fascinating study of precognitive dreams by an early 20th-century aeronautical engineer named J. W. Dunne will help us recast their inspiration in more plausible, precognitive terms: I think they got their ideas from their future selves.

Chapter 3 will examine the principles that would cause precognition to manifest obliquely, indirectly, and symbolically in creators' lives, and what this has to do with the unconscious. Sigmund Freud is both a key theorist and a key case study here. Despite not believing in precognition, the 1895 dream that gave him his famous theory that dreams are the disguised fulfilment of repressed wishes seems, with the benefit of hindsight, to have really been a premonition of a life-altering health crisis he experienced nearly three decades later, when he was in his sixties. Despite his own disbelief in such possibilities, I argue that Freud's theory of the unconscious—or what is sometimes called his metapsychology—is really a readymade theoretical framework for understanding precognition. I will recruit Freud's framework to make the case that spontaneous, seemingly "foreign," alien, or novel-feeling thoughts may be the biosignature of precognition in action. *From nowhere* may be what it feels like when a new idea actually arises from a loop between the artist's or writer's present and their future.

Some of the most famous precognitive artworks, like the most commonly reported precognitive dreams, center on calamities or destruction of some sort. Chapter 4 will examine premonitions of disaster in Werner Herzog's 1972 masterpiece *Aguirre, the Wrath of God* and Freud's 1920 book *Beyond the Pleasure Principle*, as well as a small handful of artistic prophecies of the famous "Face on Mars" photographed by one of the Viking orbiters in 1976. After its discovery, that Martian feature was imagined by some people as a remnant or reminder of an ancient interplanetary war. Precognition's seeming focus on destruction counterintuitively reveals that it homes in on situations and discoveries (whether real or fictional) where we can imagine *surviving* some existential peril, or at least a crushing blow to our egos. It is an expression of our "life instinct."

Art has been intertwined with religion for as long as we can see back in human time—they are twin strands of culture's double helix. And from the start, they have both been linked to the impossible. The first artists were shamans, visiting other worlds in dreams and other altered states. Artists continue to be popularly compared to shamans, but it is a comparison that many social scientists resist due to the whiff of the supernatural—or, superstitious belief in the supernatural—that is associated with shamanism. In Part Two, I will try to persuade you that the magic is very real.

As we will see in Chapter 5, themes and motifs in Paleolithic cave paintings provide hints that the supernormal nature of creativity was taken for granted by the first artist-shamans forty millennia ago. Dreams, trance states induced by drugs or sensory deprivation, and other methods used by shamans then and now to access nonordinary realities, are believed by some parapsychologists, and many experiencers, to give access to the future. The paintings Ice Age shamans made on the walls of caves like Chauvet and Lascaux in France could be showing us the very roots of prophecy as a cultural tradition. Then in Chapter 6 we will fast-forward to the 20th-century to examine the modernist shaman Virginia Woolf, whose 1925 novel *Mrs. Dalloway* seems to have been born from a premonition of its real-life model's death, possibly from suicide. Appropriately or coincidentally enough, Woolf's novel strikingly anticipated Carl Jung's theory of meaningful coincidence, synchronicity. Synchronicity was a mid-20th-century framing for impossible experiences that had as much to do with the emerging medium of cinema as it did with the emerging science of quantum physics. These were cultural and scientific currents that also fascinated Woolf, whose 1931 *The Waves* could be considered the first quantum novel; and it, too, seems to have had a precognitive origin.

Another modern shaman/prophet is Russian director Andrei Tarkovsky, the subject of Chapter 7. Tarkovsky's 1979 masterpiece *Stalker* prophesied not only the Chernobyl disaster a few years later but also a series of personal tragedies, including his own terminal cancer, that was probably caused by shooting that film in a highly toxic location. Sometimes the future causes the past, which causes the future: The terrible consequences of making *Stalker* were what inspired Tarkovsky to make *Stalker* in the first place, an example of what I call a time loop. A similarly time-looping (and shaman-like) artist was the American abstract painter Cy Twombly. I will show in Chapter 8 that while Twombly's psychic antennae were sometimes drawn to very public calamities like the JFK assassination, some of his works seem to have prophesied the later responses of his audience to the works themselves. The works of Tarkovsky and Twombly illustrate probably the most radical entailment of my argument in this book: The most ingenious products of the human imagination may sometimes have *no* rationally or causally determinable backstory, since they originate solely from loops in the creator's life, bootstrapping themselves into existence.

This, to me, is perhaps the most exciting implication of the precognitive imagination: Creators—and, really, *anyone*, insofar as we create—are sometimes like God in Genesis, creating literally *ex nihilo*. The title, *From Nowhere*, is meant to signal both the out-of-nowhere quality of precognitive inspiration and the fact that, in a world where causal loops could actually be the rule, there really might be no original author of *any* idea: From nowhere=from nothing=from nobody. If there is a spiritual agenda or subtext in all this, it is the message preached by one 17th-century Zen master, Bankei: Our search for past causal origins of things is ultimately futile. New ideas, like the fundamental material building blocks of the physical world as revealed by quantum physics, ultimately arise from nothing, from what Bankei called the Unborn.

Part Three shifts gears again, to consider some of the larger cultural implications of the from-nowhere and from-nothing nature of the precognitive imagination, beginning with questions of artistic influence and intellectual property. The literary scholar Harold Bloom wrote of writers' overriding psychological need to be original as the motor of poetic creation; and French critic Pierre Bayard wrote of "plagiarism by anticipation"—the idea that artists may be influenced precognitively by other artists they have yet to encounter. In their attempts to distinguish themselves from past artists and forge new creative ground, inspired creators sometimes draw inadvertently from their encounters with artists in their future, helping explain many perplexing cases of simultaneous literary creation and apparent (but "impossible") borrowing.

Chapter 9 applies this framework to look, first, at works by the great Prague writer Franz Kafka and the prophetic Los Angeles SF novelist Octavia Butler. The author of *The Metamorphosis* and *The Trial* weirdly seems to have borrowed ideas and images from soon-to-be-published works by his contemporary, Freud, in some of his stories. And Butler's 1979 time-travel masterpiece *Kindred* includes a key plot element she could only (I argue) have gotten from a popular movie,

James Cameron's *The Terminator*, that she saw five years later. We will also reconsider the perplexing late-19th-century plagiarism case of Helen Keller, who was accused of copying an already-published story in a fairy tale that she wrote for her school's literary journal when she was 11. She had no recollection of encountering the supposedly plagiarized story until the similarity was shown to her during the stressful tribunal at her school. Could some cases of alleged plagiarism really be precognition, unrecognized?

Without grasping that the imagination is often (if not always) a precognitive imagination, it can seem like creators are drawing from a common wellspring of ideas such as Jung's collective unconscious. As we will see in Chapter 10, while Jung was open to precognition and even experienced it himself on several occasions, he underestimated its pervasiveness in his clinic and in his intellectual milieu, and his theory of the collective unconscious may have reflected that. It goes by many names; the American filmmaker David Lynch calls it the "unified field," and his ideas about artists' common creative source may have been informed by a baffling precognitive collision with the Swiss painter H. R. Giger early in his career. Lynch's surreal 1977 debut feature *Eraserhead* seems to have precognitively anticipated some of Giger's designs for Ridley Scott's *Alien* two years later; and Giger's designs for *Alien* seem to have precognitively anticipated aspects of Lynch's second feature film, *The Elephant Man*. These artists, who admitted deeply admiring each other, were psychically bound—a possibility that leads me to introduce a very serious and important critical framework called the *precognitive-synchronistic clusterfuck* or PSC. Chapter 11 then looks at another arguable PSC from the same time period in California, involving two highly precognitive writers, Phil Dick and the ufologist Jacques Vallée. There is striking evidence that Dick's semi-autobiographical masterpiece *VALIS* was precognitively inspired by *The Invisible College*, a nonfiction book on nearly identical themes that Vallée published a year after Dick first drafted his novel. And it is possible that Vallée's ideas about the UFO phenomenon as a nonhuman control system may have been precognitively influenced by Dick, in turn.

Lastly, in Chapter 12, we will zoom out to consider the larger implications of retrograde influence for culture in the wider, anthropological sense of the word. Mystical and paranormal experiences, including apparent synchronicities, are the seeds from which religions spring. If those experiences are sometimes precognitive, it turns religions themselves into *tesseracts*, conveying information backward through time via the storytelling and pictorial traditions that have always accompanied religious traditions. Mythological and iconographic motifs, including what Jung called archetypes, may not reside in some static, phylogenetically ancient reservoir of symbolism, but may instead come from our collective future. They could even play a role in our survival and success as a species, drawing us subtly and very generally toward optimal historical outcomes—survival—the same way precognition likely works in the life of the individual.

This book is an invitation to think in a new way about creativity—one that I find exciting, and I hope you will agree. Needless to say, most of what I am arguing will be controversial, and parts of the argument have to remain speculative. Some of the cases of creative prophecy that I cite may be more convincing to you than others—subjectivity always enters into our judgments where the impossible is concerned, and I encourage readers to draw their own conclusions from the evidence I provide. Hardcore pseudoskeptics, if they bother to read these chapters, may scoff at most or all of my suggestions. But history very often shows hidebound retrograde minds of any era to be wrong, and there's no reason for our era to be any different. We are fast approaching a paradigm shift, a turning point in academic acceptance of many paranormal subjects (UFOs being a prominent example), and precognition is going to be one of them. There's just too much evidence, and too many real people experience it, sometimes daily. After more than a decade of researching precognition, not to mention observing it frequently in my own life, I am quite confident it can't be reduced to human bias and self-delusion. In the Afterword, I describe some of my own precognitive-creative experiences that led to this book.

A few disclaimers and clarifications: Although I briefly touch on experimental evidence in the first couple chapters, this book is not mainly about the science of psychic phenomena. Experimental evidence is in fact abundant, and readers interested in it can find it described at much greater length elsewhere, including my *Time Loops*. But to be perfectly honest, I don't think the scientific method, with its reliance on measurement and quantification and replication, is best poised to provide all the answers. The most interesting precognitive experiences are spontaneous and unpredictable—scientific psychology doesn't do well with such things. And more importantly, they are intimately associated with matters of *meaning*. They are the kinds of things the humanities are generally better equipped to study. This book is about the psychic as a factor in culture, the province of art historians and literary biographers and critics. My project would fit into what my friend Jeffrey Kripal, a historian of religions at Rice University, has recently named the *Superhumanities*: a reinvigorated and reimagined humanities that takes the super seriously instead of bending to the unspoken rule among many academics that "the truth must be depressing."[37]

It is important to be clear what I do *not* mean by de-privileging science. The argument I make in these pages will obviously be seen as a challenge to the most reductive versions of Enlightenment materialism. But it is also a challenge to a reflexive and I think knee-jerk anti-materialism that has tended to dominate the conversation around paranormal topics in recent years. Some popular writers and many experiencers assert that the reality of phenomena like ESP, UFOs, near-death experiences, and so on means that materialism is bankrupt, that any science that does not somehow privilege consciousness is destined for the dust-heap. But a one-sided reductionism can be just as suffocating when it comes from idealists as when it comes from a distinguished (elderly) scientist promoting some dismal materialist picture of the physical world and its limitations. There are fascinating and exciting ways to interpret phenomena like ESP that do not require us to take a side in philosophical debates over the fundamental nature of consciousness or reality (or that allow us to hold multiple views). As will become clear in these pages, the specific phenomenon of precognition does not, oddly enough, have much to do with consciousness at all, at least in its narrower colloquial sense of being awake and aware. Like inspiration, it is a phenomenon in and of the dark nowhere realm of the unconscious. That, to me, is why these topics—which may be the same topic—are so interesting.

For the most part, this book does not dwell on artists' precognitive or other paranormal experiences that are not directly associated with their creative process. Artists are overrepresented among people claiming or expressing psychic abilities, and biographies and memoirs of artists are full of psychic or psychic-seeming experiences of one sort or another.[38] The novelist and anthropologist Zora Neale Hurston, to cite just one example, reported a stunning childhood vision of twelve highly singular life events, all of which eventually came true, leaving her with the belief that she possessed a unique spiritual gift.[39] If I'm right about the precognitive imagination, this kind of thing likely played a role, probably an important role, in her fiction writing, but I am not enough of a Hurston expert to know how. In *Time Loops*, I described precognitive experiences in the lives of other creative people including Kurt Vonnegut, Vladimir Nabokov, and actor Alec Guinness, but again, not in direct connection to their creative work.[40] Here, I am focused more narrowly on the question of whether specifically creative inspiration can be understood as literally, not just figuratively, prophetic. Plenty of artists have expressed a suspicion that this is the case. In his wonderful 2015 book, *Reclaiming Art in the Age of Artifice*, J. F. Martel writes that "at the deepest level artists have always worked by the light of stars yet unborn."[41] But to my knowledge this hypothesis has never been examined or explored in a sustained way, using real evidence, and informed by a more or less coherent theory of how psychic phenomena, especially precognition, may operate.

This book is also not about psychic or precognitive *themes* in fiction and art—for instance, sci-fi stories or movies about prophesying the future or comic books involving prophetic superpowers. That's a huge topic—and again, one that I have addressed somewhat in my previous books and on my blog *The Nightshirt*—but it does not directly address precognition's possible involvement in the creative process. An artist's explicit interest in precognition does not necessarily equate to its playing a demonstrable role in their inspiration. Sometimes it does—Phil Dick would be an example—but most precognitive artists do not know or believe they are precognitive, and some, if asked, would likely express skepticism.

I have been asked why, in a book about creativity, I look mainly at artists and writers, not inventors, and only a few scientists. My strong hunch is that the hypothesis I am advancing in these pages would apply to many if not all creative endeavors. Scientists and inventors often describe their experiences of creative inspiration in the same terms, and with the same metaphors, that artists do.[42] But a case for precognition's role in creativity is best made when a creative product is somehow representational—that is, involves some image or story that can actually be compared to some later event or experience. That's possible with a novel or a poem or a painting or a film, the same way it is possible with a dream. It is less easy with a patent or a scientific discovery. Nonrepresentational arts like music or abstract painting share the same difficulty: My T-rex handful of potentially precognitive songs in this book focuses on lyrics, not melodic or other purely musical qualities. My look at Cy Twombly focuses mainly on his classical-historical subjects and themes, not the formal qualities of his mostly nonfigurative canvasses.

Another disclaimer: The concept of genius is not a popular one nowadays, due among other things to its implicit elitism.[43] Vasari's narratives of innately gifted young white men being discovered, nurtured, and tutored by older white men implicitly excluded the majority of humanity from artistic promise. My occasional use of the term genius in this book is assuredly not meant to uphold an elitist view of creativity. People like Freud, Woolf, or Lynch may be geniuses, but so are countless other people who haven't had the good fortune to be recognized for their art or thought. For most humans on this planet, creative potential remains undeveloped or untapped, or life circumstances get in the way of expressing it for the public or posterity. The figures I focus on simply created lasting works that can serve as case studies of what, I strongly suspect, all of us everywhere do when we think or create and are engaged in the daily artistry of living.

My subjects here are drawn largely from the very skewed and unrepresentative pool of prominent creators I already happened to like and knew a good deal about even before beginning my research. Thus, there is no claim to ethnic or national representativeness: With a couple partial exceptions, all are European or American. A higher percentage are male than I would wish. And I have deliberately limited myself to figures whose works are readily accessible to the reader via a quick Google search or a visit to the public library. Psychic deconstruction requires knowing the creator's life context, so it matters that we have biographies, autobiographies, letters, memoirs, and published accounts by people who knew them that we can draw upon, to compare their works to their lives. Biographies are something we unfortunately just don't have for the vast majority of the unsung geniuses who have ever walked our earth. As I have written and spoken on the subject of precognition over the past several years, I have heard many, many amazing accounts of artistic prophecy from lesser-known and amateur artists and writers, but those will have to wait for perhaps another book.

As Martel argues, the fact that art is so often in our late capitalist age subordinated to the ends of advertisement and propaganda leads non-artists to minimize the mystery at the heart of (super)human creativity. Concern over the fate of art may be as old as art itself, and for over a century, artists themselves have consciously explored the death of art and its fate in the age of mechanical—and now electronic—reproduction. As I write these words, the sudden eruption of artificial intelligence (AI) tools for generating texts, pictures, videos, music, and so on threatens to erode creativity's mystique even further. There is widespread anxiety—well founded—that people already only eking out a precarious living in many creative fields could soon have their jobs replaced by software. While the AI-generated art of the early 2020s is often more comical than profound, the capabilities of this technology are improving by rapid leaps, and that will only accelerate over the coming years.

While I do worry for our livings, I don't worry—at all—about the essential and inimitable humanity of art made by real people, and thus the eternal value of what flesh-and-blood artists create, as compared with what machines can generate. If I am right in my hypothesis about the real nature of the artistic imagination, then AI art, which relies solely on the machine equivalent of past experience, old ideas, will *always* lack the precognitive special sauce of true creativity. Just as previous artistic revolutions like photography that seemed threatening at first actually ended up liberating artists in new and unexpected ways, I like to think that the era of AI art could end up revealing the essential humanness of real artistic creation. I'm very confident it will ultimately prove to be just another instrument in an expanding artists' toolkit for creating amazing and world-changing works. It takes humans to be superhuman.

PART ONE

PRECOGNITION AND INSPIRATION

We are crucified on one plane, while the world is many-dimensional. We are aware of that and are tormented by our inability to know the truth.
—Andrei Tarkovsky, Diary entry (January 5, 1979)

Sculptor of the Impossible
Michael Richards, 9/11, and the Science of Precognition

"It's a poor sort of memory that only works backwards,"
the Queen remarked.
—Lewis Carroll, *Through the Looking-Glass* (1871)

After the World Trade Center was completed and opened for business in 1973, the Port Authority of New York and New Jersey had trouble filling the more than 13 million square feet of office space in its enormous towers. It was something of a scandal in the Manhattan real estate world—even after a controversial decision was made to subsidize the rents, there were still many vacancies. In 1997, the Port Authority saw an opportunity to support the arts in the city by granting the Lower Manhattan Cultural Council (LMCC) permission to use some of those unused offices as studios for artists, for what became the LMCC's World Views artist-in-residence program.

Every year, two cohorts of artists from all over the world—one in the summer and fall, one in winter and spring—occupied "studios in the sky" on the 91st and 92nd floors of the North Tower (Tower One) with breathtaking views nearly a quarter mile above lower Manhattan. Then, near the end of their five-month stay, they opened their studios to visitors for a final exhibition. These popular semi-annual events became, for a brief period around the turn of the millennium, a staple of the New York art scene.[1]

The 15 artists who moved their materials into their aerial studios in May of 2001 included people working in diverse media and representing 12 nationalities.[2] Perhaps unsurprisingly, some took the towers themselves, their occupants, and their open spaces as subjects for their works during their residencies.[3] For instance, Austrian graphics, video, and performance artist Carola Dertnig's 2001 project, . . . *but buildings can'talk*, is a cartoon series in watercolor depicting the towers, One and Two, as twin sisters leaning against each other and twisted in various yoga poses. "One … has a splinter in its back from a bombing attack in 1993. They both survived, but since then One feels insecure and old. After this incident they both started power yoga."[4] Tower One is glumly focused on attaining inner peace, while the more extroverted sister, Two, is in love with nearby Elisa Islanda (Ellis Island), "a cool dancer and singer, who looks a little like Kim Gordon from Sonic Youth."[5]

In early September, Dertnig and other Summer 2001 World Views artist cohort were working hard to complete their projects for their mid-October viewing. Unlike most of her fellows who worked in less portable media, Dertnig had been in the habit of bringing her drawings back to her apartment at the end of the day, rather than leaving them in her studio. This is why her drawings were among the small handful of works created by the group to survive the calamity that occurred in the early morning of September 11.[6]

Another in the group, Colombian video artist Monika Bravo, saved her work-in-progress because of a spontaneous impulse that she found inexplicable, "weird," in hindsight. She had spent the day before the attacks filming the view from her studio on the 92nd floor. She was getting such beautiful footage of a thunderstorm in the city that evening that she considered staying the night to create a 24-hour time-lapse of the weather over lower Manhattan, but her boyfriend persuaded her to stop filming and come home because she hadn't eaten. She usually left her tape in her camera if she wasn't done with a project, but this time she took it with her when she left. It became her short film *September 10, 2001, Uno Nunca Muere la Víspera*—another of the exceptional works saved from destruction. [7]

At 8:46 a.m. on September 11, just as the building was filling with employees at its hundreds of businesses, shops, and restaurants, American Airlines flight 11 flew into Tower One on its North side at an angle, between the 94th and 98th floors. The two floors with World Views studios were right on the border between survivability and oblivion.

Scottish painter Vanessa Lawrence had just stepped off the 91st floor elevator to begin work in her studio when the Tower shook from the jet's impact. This was the highest floor from which anyone escaped the building. She was able to descend via a smoke- and water-clogged stairwell, leaving the building just as the South Tower next door was collapsing.[8] (Although the second plane had hit the South Tower 17 minutes after the North Tower was struck, the South Tower was the first to fall.)

Lots of artists are night owls and late risers, so unlike their corporate counterparts in the surrounding offices, most of the World Views group had not yet arrived at their studios. Iranian sculptor Mahmoud Hamadani was still at home in Greenwich Village when the attacks began. He joined his neighbors out in the street to watch horrified as the buildings burned and then collapsed. "As soon as I looked up I knew that our studios were all gone," he recalled. "My first thought was the craziest thing: 'Oh my God, I left my glue gun on last night and it set the building on fire.'"[9]

The only one of the artists to lose his life in the attacks was such a night owl that he was still in his 92nd floor studio from the night before. Jamaican-American sculptor Michael Rolando Richards was in the habit of working late into the night and often slept there, rather than make an early morning two-hour subway commute back to his apartment in the Queens neighborhood of Rosedale. It was easier that way, since he had to be up again at 8:00 a.m. to make it to his day job at the Bronx Museum of the Arts.

Born in 1963 in Brooklyn, Richards had been raised in Kingston, Jamaica—his father was Jamaican and his mother Costa Rican—but he returned to New York to attend Queens College, where he got his BA in 1985. He then went to NYU for his MA, and afterward participated in a series of increasingly prestigious art programs and residencies during the 1990s. At the turn of the new millennium, he was just becoming recognized as a brilliant new voice in the art world, notable for an impressive, rapidly growing body of arresting work focusing on Black identity, anti-Black violence, and as he put it, "the doubt and discomfort which face Blacks who wish to succeed in a system which is structured to deny them access."[10] He turned 38 in August, 2001.

Most of Richards' sculptures incorporated themes of flight, such as planes, feathers, and aviators. He was fascinated by flying, having had vivid flying dreams even as a child. His excitement at being accepted into the LMCC's World Views program was partly from the fantasy of flight that his southwest-facing studio afforded him, a spectacular aerial view of New York Harbor with Ellis Island and the Statue of Liberty off in the distance. The idea of flight in his sculptures partly "references the Black church, the idea of being lifted up, enraptured or taken up to a safe place—to a better world," as he told one friend.[11] But the promise of escape through flight is always subverted in Richards' work: His planes, for instance, are typically shown crashing or descending or trapped in tar or barbed wire, "abandoned signs of hope and promise" as he put it.[12]

On the afternoon of September 10, Richards attended an art opening at the Grey Art Gallery in Washington Square Park, where he had worked as a preparator while at NYU. He then stopped to lift weights at the gym before arriving at his studio at 9:00 p.m. As he arrived, he greeted fellow artist Jeff Konigsberg, who was just finishing up and leaving for the night (their studios were diagonally across from each other). Later, just after snatching that tape from her camera, video artist Bravo remembered saying goodnight to Richards on her way to the elevators—he had just finished watching his New York Giants lose to the Denver Broncos on *Monday Night Football*. He then called his fiancée on his cellphone to let her know he was staying the night in his studio.

Little is known about the experiences of anybody on the 92nd floor or above from when the first plane hit the tower until its collapse 102 minutes later. Richards would likely have been awake and dressed, getting ready to leave for his job, when the plane hit the building on the opposite (northeast-facing) side a few floors up.[13] Attempts to reach Richards on his cellphone failed, as was the case for most who were trapped in the upper floors of both towers. The stairwells on Richards' 92nd floor and above were inaccessible. If he survived the initial impact and was trapped in his studio, he would have had a clear view from his southwest-facing studio of United Airlines flight 175 approaching and hitting the South Tower … but we can only speculate.

After the events of that day, Richards was quickly apotheosized into something much more than an up-and-coming Black artist lost too soon. He became an icon of "9/11 prophecy" because of how amazingly his work over the previous decade had foreshadowed the tragedy that took his life.

For example, a 1998 piece by Richards called *Air Fall I (His eye is on the sparrow, and I know he is watching me)* consists of 50 small airplanes suspended from a disk on the ceiling as they nosedive towards a circular mirror on the floor. The planes and the disk they descend from are covered in black hair, which Richards often incorporated in his pieces to represent how people judged him for his appearance.[14] In addition to being a sculptor, Richards was also a talented draftsman and incorporated his own poetry into his works. A series of works on paper that Richards created between 1996 and 2000 called *Escape Plan* includes images of parachutes and burning buildings accompanied by handwritten texts on themes of anxiety and dread.[15]

On the night before the attacks, Richards had probably been working on one of two sculptures that had already made an impression on friends and fellow artists who visited his studio and that struck them as especially uncanny in hindsight. One, according to Jeff Konigsberg, was of a Tuskegee Airman riding a burning meteor.[16] Through the 1990s and into the new millennium, Richards made a series of sculptures of the Black aviators who distinguished themselves in World War II but who still could not escape the racism of their country. These figures also necessarily called to mind the atrocious Tuskegee experiment conducted by the U.S. Public Health Service beginning in the early 1930s, in which Black patients with syphilis were given a placebo instead of penicillin to study the natural progression of the disease. Richards always used himself as his model in his sculptures, casting the molds from his own face and body, so the meteor-riding aviator was almost certainly a self-portrait.

Another piece that Richards' friends reported he had been working on in his World Views studio was a life-sized self-portrait of his own torso with wings on the back, one of them broken, called *Fallen Angel*.[17] This and his self-portrait riding a meteor are of course among those many lost works of the 2001 World Views program. But Richards created several striking works on similar themes in the mid-1990s and around the turn of the millennium that help us imagine the lost pieces.

While a fellow at the Socrates Sculpture Park in Long Island City, NY, Richards used the biblical motif of Jacob's Ladder to address the punishments awaiting people who attempt to transcend their condition. In Genesis, the trickster-cum-patriarch Jacob rests while fleeing from his brother Esau's wrath; taking a rock for a pillow, he dreams of angels ascending and descending a ladder to heaven, with God promising that the land he is sleeping on shall be his. The 1994 piece *Climbing Jacob's Ladder (He Lost His Head)* is a stack of slab-like ledges with disembodied heads around its base. Another sculpture Richards created for the sculpture park, called *Free F'All*, depicts himself as a Tuskegee Airman standing 16 feet in the air on a small landing, contemplating diving into a tiny bucket on the ground—a target that is obviously too small. His body is pierced with hundreds of small nails, invoking the wooden nail-pierced Nkisi N'kondi figures of the Kongo healing tradition, which informed much of Richard's work.

In 2000, Richards created another sculpture on a similar theme for the Franconia Sculpture Park near Minneapolis. *Are You Down?* depicts three life-sized Tuskegee Airmen (again, himself as the model for each) having parachuted from the sky and missed their target in the center of a circle of heavy black tar-like sand. They sit in a triangle, each dejectedly, backs to the small bulls-eye they had all three missed—another too-small target for an enormous leap or fall.

The story of Br'er Rabbit and the Tar Baby is a motif that Richards incorporated into many of his works to express the entwined ideas of escape and entrapment. In this narrative from the African oral tradition passed down in slave folklore and later incorporated in Joel Chandler Harris's Uncle Remus stories (and the 1946 Disney film *Song of the South*), the crafty Br'er Fox entraps Br'er Rabbit with a figure made of tar, but the rabbit wins his freedom by tricking his captor with the plea not to throw him in a nearby briar patch. Figuring Br'er Rabbit must really be afraid of it, Br'er Fox cruelly throws him in, only to have the rabbit escape, since he is perfectly at home in briar patches. A 1996 piece called *Brer Plane in the Briar Patch*, created while Richards was artist-in-residence at the Studio Museum of Harlem in 1995-96, depicts a tar-covered airplane entangled in barbed wire.

The story of Br'er Rabbit is also signaled in the piece that made Richards famous after 9/11, *Tar Baby vs. St. Sebastian*. Another sculptural self-portrait, it was created in 1999 while he was at the Art Center/ South Florida in Miami (now called Oolite Arts) and is now in the permanent collection of the North Carolina Museum of Art in Raleigh. Richards appears again in the flight suit and helmet of a Tuskegee Airman, standing placidly erect like a stiff board or, indeed, tower, all shining brightly in gold. He is suspended a little off the ground as if he is levitating, and his body is pierced by a multitude of planes, much the same way the early Christian martyr St. Sebastian, patron saint of soldiers and athletes, is depicted in Renaissance art as a pincushion of arrows. The impaled figure also calls to mind the Nkisi N'kondi figures that inspired Richards.[18]

Tar Baby vs. St. Sebastian is an arresting sculpture, even if you know nothing of the artist or how he lost his life. When you do know these details, that he and nearly 2,800 other people in the Twin Towers were literally martyred by planes, *Tar Baby vs. St. Sebastian* becomes altogether more … something.

What is the word? Impossible?

Yes. Michael Richards was a sculptor of the impossible.[19]

What Are the Odds?

In a new era dominated by discussions of race and racist violence, there is a growing number of retrospective articles and exhibition reviews of Richards' work. He is being rediscovered after having been largely forgotten for nearly two decades. But writers and curators still don't know what to make of the amazing coincidence that he died on 9/11 in a manner depicted in some of his sculptures. It prompts poetic musings about irony and loss, but few "go there" in speculating about what could really have been behind the artist's inspiration. Noncommittally, they will say his work was prescient and leave it at that.

What *you* make it will depend on your preconceptions about causality and the paranormal. If your worldview makes a place for premonitions and miracles, then you may have no problem believing, and even assuming, that Richards somehow intuited his tragic fate and worked it into his art during the years, months, and weeks leading up to that day. If on the other hand you are a university-educated, scientifically literate information consumer of the first quarter of the 21ˢᵗ century, there will likely be a part of you, maybe a big part, that harbors a knee-jerk skepticism. Not that anybody is lying—everything I've just written is well-documented, and you can go online and see the sculptures yourself. But you might assume or suspect that any connection between these works and the events of 9/11 must surely be coincidence, since prophecy or precognition are impossible and "go against science."

These debates—I have immersed myself in them for more than a decade now—quickly descend into "what are the odds" games of citing statistics. When debunking artistic and literary prophecies, the standard skeptical move is to invoke the law of large numbers. There is the undoubtedly true fact that the majority of works produced by artists leading up to 9/11 did not concern terrorism or burning buildings or martyrdom by planes. In hindsight, the argument goes, some small handful will seem to have been prophetic, but when we restore that lost denominator, the thousands or millions of other works that mostly bear no obvious connection to the tragedy, then the uncanniness of those one or two or three examples fades to statistical vapor.

At least, that's how it's supposed to work. In reality, it's not so simple.

Even if few of them are as astonishing as *Tar Baby vs. St. Sebastian*, seemingly prophetic artworks are not rare, either in the larger scope of art or in the context of specific major world events and disasters. I already mentioned Morgan Robertson's novel *Futility*, which seemed to predict the *Titanic* disaster. Skeptics have dismissed it as one of those chance one-offs that dissolve like an ice cube in the vast ocean of probability—except it isn't. Several other writers of the day also wrote stories that appeared to predict a major ocean-liner disaster similar to that of the *Titanic*, even if they didn't get the name of the ship right. One of them was prominent London journalist and editor W. T. Stead. Stead wrote of the danger of ocean liners having too-few lifeboats and in 1892 even wrote a story (later turned into a novel) about a fictional boat's collision with an iceberg and the rescue of its passengers by a real ship, the *Majestic*, captained by the real Edward J. Smith. Smith later became captain of the *Titanic* and stoically went down with his ship. What are the odds of that? Stead also recorded a premonition in which he would die in a press or throng of people, although he didn't connect this premonition to an ocean-liner disaster—he thought it might be a war or revolution. But, you guessed it, Stead was on the *Titanic* and died in the pandemonium of passengers who could not find a place in its too-few lifeboats.[20] Scores of ordinary people also reported dreams and other premonitions of that event, even if they did not translate those dreams into literature or art.[21] Among them was the five-year-old future novelist Graham Greene, who later wrote in a memoir that he dreamed of a shipwreck on the night of April 14, 1912, with a vivid image of a wave crashing over one of the crew.[22] It was the first of several disaster dreams he had in his life that came true, he said.

Probably abetted by 21st century media, the halo of recorded premonitions around 9/11 is bigger by orders of magnitude than that surrounding the sinking of the *Titanic*. With a quick internet search, you can see for yourself that cultural ephemera from the years and months prior to the attacks in New York and appearing to depict its events are myriad. A writer named John Valentini compiled numerous examples in a 2011 book called *Imagining 9/11*, and some of what he presents in its pages is rather stunning.[23] In 1997, for instance, fantasy artist Boris Vallejo painted a scene called *Eahnah's Window*, in which a nude woman reclines dreamily in front of a circular window showing one of the Twin Towers on fire, strikingly similar to what we all saw on CNN four years later just before the second plane hit. Vallejo's text explains: "Eahnah—called a witch by some, master scientist by others—has perfected a device that she calls a 'window.' The 'window' is near the weak place in the space-time fabric..."[24] The March 4, 2001, pilot episode of an *X-Files* spinoff series called *The Lone Gunmen* centered on a plot by the U.S. Government to fly remote-controlled jets into the Towers—later helping fuel post-9/11 paranoia that al-Qaeda had not been the true culprits.

Attacks on the towers were a weirdly common motif in comic books over the whole three-decade lifespan of the towers, but especially in their final years. The most amazing example, because of its proximity to the disaster, is Issue #596 of *The Adventures of Superman*, which was released the day after the attacks, on September 12, but had been written and drawn months earlier. After a rampage by villains Imperiex and Braniac 13, the world's capitals are in ruins, and Superman watches the twin "LexCorp" towers (obviously modeled on the Twin Towers) burn—a vision incredibly like what really happened a day before. DC Comics promptly recalled the issue, which of course turned it into a collector's item. ("Reality has eclipsed fantasy," one of the artists, Mike Wieringo, told an interviewer.[25])

A number of magazine, book, and CD covers from the months before 9/11 depicted planes converging on or destroying the towers, or the towers standing in ruins, or other ominous foreshadowings. For instance, the March 12, 2001, cover of *New York* magazine bore the headline, "Real Estate 2001—Is There Life Beyond the Boom?" over a picture of the towers, next to a wide-eyed woman clutching her face in terror. In June, Oakland, California, hip hop group The Coup designed a cover for an upcoming CD called *Party Music* depicting the Twin Towers exploding. After the events that September, they delayed their CD release so they could design a new cover.

Other examples have been sent to me by readers of my book *Time Loops*. On September 10, 2001, for instance, artist Jim Woodring drew a cartoon of Death (as a skeleton) piloting a plane into a proudly strutting frog fancily attired as an old-time robber baron. He captioned the drawing "Hell's a Poppin'" and sent it off to a Seattle paper that was regularly publishing his work.[26] The events of the following day would have rendered it tasteless, so he was able to pull the frame prior to publication. And an example that particularly haunts me is a 2000 music video for the song "We Haven't Turned Around" by the band Gomez. A man flees terrified through the streets of Manhattan, gesticulating wildly at oblivious or annoyed passersby to warn them of something terrible happening or about to happen up in the sky. In the last shot we see that he is at the plaza of the World Trade Center.

And Michael Richards was not even the only World Views artist whose works provoke puzzlement in light of 9/11. I already mentioned

Carola Dertnig's cartoons of the Towers, One and Two, bent over and twisted into power-yoga poses and grappling with their anxieties about the future. The drawings are eyebrow-raising, at the very least. And during a residency in 1999, new-media artists Jennifer and Kevin McCoy created a website and advertising banners for a fictional company called Airworld, parodying American corporate culture at the turn of the millennium. The banners bore absurd corporate-sounding slogans like "I Am Going: Circulate" or "Welcome We Are Air," and they all bore the ominous-in-hindsight Airworld logo: a pair of jets, joined at the wing, flying in opposite directions.[27]

Life very commonly seems to imitate art. I have spoken and corresponded with artists and writers who privately share experiences of depicting or describing things in their work that later played out in the news or in their own lives with uncanny exactness. But there are difficulties assessing such anecdotes with anything approaching scientific precision, and this is what has kept artistic prophecy beyond the pale for most serious scholars or academics. Writing of the alleged *Titanic* prophecies, skeptic Martin Gardner pointed out that there is no way of calculating the odds of an artwork or piece of literature corresponding to a subsequent event because there is no way of knowing the probabilities of any of the relevant variables.[28] He's absolutely right. Given the nearly infinite number of those variables, the likelihood or unlikelihood of the *Titanic* being named *Titanic* or of it colliding with an iceberg in April, so similar to a novel published fourteen years earlier, is really impossible to calculate and could, for all we know, be greater than we imagine.

An oft-cited case of literary prophecy that is similarly difficult to assess is Edgar Allen Poe's 1838 novel *The Narrative of Arthur Gordon Pym of Nantucket*. In the novel, four desperate shipwreck survivors in a lifeboat draw lots to decide which one should die and be cannibalized by the remaining three. The loser who suffers this grisly fate is a cabin boy named Richard Parker. Forty-six years after Poe's book was published, three survivors of a wrecked English yacht named *Mignonette* killed and drank the blood of a fourth survivor, the 17-year-old cabin boy, Richard Parker, while adrift in the south Atlantic. This incident, which led to a precedent-setting court case, is surely a head-scratcher. On the other hand, as skeptics have pointed out, Richard Parker was about as common a name as they come, in a century when shipwrecks and even cannibalism at sea were common occurrences.[29] How likely or unlikely was it that it would eventually happen to a real Richard Parker, given nearly half a century?[30]

Similarly, we don't know how likely or unlikely it was that the World Trade Center was going to be attacked by plane-flying terrorists in September 2001. There had already been a bomb attack in 1993—precisely what gave Dertnig's "One" such mortality-anxiety—and clearly, for whatever reason, many artists had imagined the destruction of the towers already by the time it happened in real life. Could some of their works have inspired the attacks, rather than vice versa? Nor do we know how many artworks there were in total or how many unreported or unnoticed others may have also somehow foreshadowed 9/11. Moreover, how do you delimit these things in time? A sculpture of jets flying into the World Trade Center made on September 10, 2001, by a New Yorker would probably seem amazing to most anyone (I'm not aware of such a work). A short story by a Japanese writer about a small plane crashing into a Tokyo bank on some random date in the 1950s, undoubtedly less so (I'm not aware of one of those either). But what about a Londoner painting the destruction of the Twin Towers following a vivid dream on the morning of September 11, 1996?

It happened. A 68-year-old former university art teacher living in London's Sudbury Hill suburb named David Mandell awoke from a dream exactly five years before the attacks, in which he saw the two towers crashing into each other and collapsing. He painted it in watercolor. Over the subsequent months he had a series of further dreams about the same event, one of which included planes crashing into the buildings—which he also painted. Each time he had such a dream, he had himself photographed under the clock at his local Barclays bank holding the picture he made to establish date and time. He knew from a lifetime of precognitive dreams about calamities like plane crashes, IRA bombings, and the like that these extremely vivid dreams might come true somehow. He told filmmakers for a British TV documentary that he was "shuddering and shaking" when he watched the attacks unfold in New York five years to the day after his first dream about the collapsing towers.[31]

Time Tunnels

The idea that people can sometimes feel, know, or dream the future is accepted in virtually every culture except our own, and it goes back to the earliest cultures of which we have written record. The ancient Greeks took divination of future events in dreams, visions, and other modalities—including what we now call ordinary intuition—very seriously.[32] Divination's possible mechanisms were the subject of learned inquiry and debate.[33] In the pre-Socratic period, shamans visited caves to learn the future from spirits of the dead. Since they lacked physical bodies, the dead were believed to see the future better than the living.[34] Later, after caves went out of fashion and started to be associated more with unreason (Plato's famous cave parable, etc.), Aristotle still included final causes in his breakdown of the types of causation, with the implication that somehow where we are headed may influence us right now. He also wrote a treatise on precognitive dreams, *On Divination in Sleep*. He dismissed most cases as coincidence—but only because they tended to be reported by lower-class people rather than the noble types he believed the gods should prefer to communicate with.

The idea of causation from the future, or *teleology*, remained largely unquestioned until the Enlightenment, when it was rejected from the then-coalescing scientific worldview because it smacked of the divine. At that time, the only teleology that scientists like Newton could imagine was one that somehow reflected God's divine plan, and the new principle in science was that it was unfair bringing God into the equation. The mechanistic picture of natural processes that resulted from this no-teleology rule transformed the world and gave us most of the scientific and technological boons we now take for granted, and the biomedical boons that have extended life expectancy. We all owe a deep debt to the reductive, mechanistic language for describing and controlling the natural world, the language glossed as materialism. But even materialism (at least in its current incarnation) is a paradigm, and as the historian of science Thomas Kuhn famously argued in his 1960 book *The Structure of Scientific Revolutions*, when enough unaccounted-for anomalies accumulate, paradigms ultimately have to shift. There may be a painful period of crisis that precedes that shift.

In the last two decades, the assumption that teleology has no place in natural law has been breaking down. Physicists are now talking about retrocausation—backwards causation, of a non-divine sort—as an explanation for some of the mysteries in quantum mechanics that have eluded explanation for a century. For instance, experimenters at the University of Rochester in 2009 subjected two halves of a split laser beam to different sequences of measurements. The results seemed to show that a certain type of final measurement amplified one of the halves of the beam *in its past*, compared to the other half of the beam that got a different final measurement.[35] It's hard to wrap our heads around the idea of affecting some physical system or object "in its past," but a very interesting argument is being made that the randomness or uncertainty that for nearly a century has been believed to govern the world of tiny particles really reflects yet-unknown causes flowing, interaction-to-interaction, backwards in time.[36] Einstein never liked that randomness—he famously complained in a 1926 letter to his colleague, physicist Max Born, that "*He* [God] does not play dice."[37] It is looking more and more like Einstein was right. The unpredictable part of a particle's behavior—for instance, the famous inability to precisely determine the position of an electron if you know its velocity, and vice versa—could reflect something about the *next* thing the particle is going to interact with. It means a kind of naturalistic teleology, at least at the smallest scales in nature.

It is possible that in special situations where multiple particles like electrons are entangled, the basis of quantum computers, that micro-scale teleology could be scaled up, made relevant to our world of medium-sized objects and people. Several research teams have lately shown that the temporal sequence of a computation can be reversed in a quantum computing circuit;[38] it suggests that such devices may have time-defying properties and might one day be used as predictive tools or even communication devices across time. In William Gibson's novel (and later TV series) *The Peripheral*, a near-future video gamer in a rural town in the American South communicates with scientists and hackers in 21st-century London via a quantum computer server, using a spooky (but real) quantum phenomenon called tunneling. This process even enables her to "visit" future London using an android avatar.[39] Gibson, who had famously predicted cyberspace and virtual reality in his 1984 novel *Neuromancer*, may again be anticipating the next revolution in information as well as communications technology. Besides faster, more powerful data-crunching, it is conceivable that quantum computing could lead to a kind of informational time travel, communication between different users—or even the same user—across time.[40]

More pertinently for my argument in this book, the spooky quantum effects underlying quantum computation are now being found to underlie many features of living systems, from photosynthesis to bird navigation to the ability of enzymes to break down other molecules.[41] Suggestive evidence that the brain is a biological quantum computer is already mounting;[42] and if that's the case, then something like the informational time travel predicted in *The Peripheral* may already be operative in our own nervous systems. Donning a futurist hat in my book

Time Loops, I prophesied (but really, just predicted) that our brains will turn out to be four-dimensional information processors, reaching across time in both directions as they coordinate our actions in the present. If so, it would suddenly make super-but-natural sense of countless ordinary people's "psychic" experiences as well as decades of research on ESP phenomena that, until now, have seemed to lack much physical plausibility and thus have been ignored by most mainstream psychologists. Quantum neurobiology may soon bridge the three-century chasm between mechanistic scientific psychology and the eternal testimony of human superexperience.

In fact, abundant evidence for the reality of precognition has been gathered over the past half century by parapsychologists, as well as by psychotherapists and dream researchers mostly working outside the conservative confines of academic psychology departments. A meta-analysis of five decades' worth of so-called "forced choice" card-guessing tasks, conducted by various parapsychology laboratories using strict experimental controls, showed astronomical significance for precognition.[43] People can guess what card will be drawn from a deck significantly better than chance would predict, although the effect sizes in such experiments tend to be small and people's performance declines over time as they tire of boring tasks. Not being boring matters—we'll come back to this. Similarly, participants are sometimes able to accurately draw or describe the contents of hidden or distant scenes (as assessed by independent judges), even when targets have not been chosen yet by the experimenter. An extensive body of research on this ability, sometimes called precognitive remote perception, resulted in similarly statistically overwhelming support.[44]

The most interesting body of ESP research over the past three decades has been on unconscious physiological and behavioral pre-sponses to imminent stimuli. In the mid-1990s, engineer Dean Radin pioneered the study of the retro-influence of arousing (versus boring) pictures on changes in skin conductance, heart rate, and blood flow to the fingertips. There is now a large and growing body of research on bodily forewarnings of imminent surprising, rewarding, or aversive stimuli measurable in those responses and others like eye movement and brainwave activity—in most cases, fractions of a second or as much as a few seconds prior to the unpredictable stimulus. Meta-analyses of these studies, again, show statistically very significant support for what is often called *presentiment* or "future feeling."[45] And it's not just a human thing. Experiments also hint that animals as complex as dogs and as simple as planarian worms behaviorally pre-spond to imminent aversive stimuli and rewards.[46]

In 2011, an eminent and not controversy-shy Cornell psychologist, Daryl Bem, published findings from several large experiments he conducted with a large participant pool of Cornell undergraduates showing that their behavior in various familiar psychological paradigms like priming or word-recall tasks was influenced by stimuli they would be exposed to *after* they made their responses.[47] For instance, participants were more accurate than chance at guessing which curtain on a computer screen would reveal a picture if the to-be-revealed picture was erotic. They performed no better than chance when the to-be-revealed pictures were boring. (Pictures were randomly determined after the mouse click—there was not "already" a picture behind the curtains.) In another variant of a familiar type of memory experiment, participants were shown a word list and then tested for their memory of what words had been on the list. "Impossibly," they performed better for words that they were then shown later on a refresher, *after* taking the test—what Bem called "retroactive facilitation of recall." Bem's results have since been replicated by numerous independent researchers and laboratories.[48]

Besides a few small laboratory studies, evidence for the most famous if not common manifestation of precognition—precognitive dreams—remains largely anecdotal due to notorious difficulties objectively studying idiosyncratic dream content as it relates to unique life events. But between a third and a half of people report having had such dreams, and again, ours is the only culture on Earth, ever, that doesn't officially admit that such things exist. Whereas experiencers once felt isolated and silenced by skeptical authorities and skeptical family members, the internet now allows large numbers of dreamers to share their experiences, a citizen-science research tool unavailable in previous eras.[49] The Himalaya-sized mountains of anecdotes gathered and examined by a growing number of researchers, including myself, paint a clear and consistent picture that precognitive dreams are normal. (I no longer even attach "para-" to this adjective, when it comes to precognitive dreams.) I suggest that precognition will turn out to be an ordinary part of human cognition, likely an aspect of memory rather than perception (as the term ESP or "extrasensory perception" leads people to assume). The fact that precognition is so associated with dreams could be consistent with what mainstream sleep scientists now believe is dreaming's role: to form or consolidate long-term memories.[50]

It's just that, if large numbers of dreamers are right, our memories go both directions in time. It's an idea having huge implications, and we'll explore them more in the next few chapters.

As with dreams, evidence of possible precognition or prophecy in art and literature cannot be assessed with the kind of rigor that scientists prefer. Since works of art are unique, like dreams, every case is a one-off, an anecdote. So unless they have experienced precognition in their own lives, someone only interested in evidence that can be weighed with significance tests and effect sizes will never be swayed, even by the most stunning cases like Richards' *Tar Baby vs. St. Sebastian*. But most things in life are not amenable to such tests. We go through life making judgments on imperfect evidence, and there is always some margin of uncertainty. No two situations are exactly alike, thus history has no control group. Consequently, I argue that we are compelled, like the philosophers of old, to use *reason* in our assessments of the evidence: How reasonable is a given case? The position of skeptics like Gardner, that precognition is a-priori impossible and thus never can account for the kinds of examples I've discussed so far, is no longer reasonable, given the abundant evidence supporting its existence and even the rudiments of a physical theory that could explain how it works.

Still, being reasonably certain that precognition exists only gets us so far. We still cannot say—and I definitely would not say—that every apparent similarity between an artwork and a subsequent event is evidence of it. There are still many unknowns. At this point, we don't know how pervasive precognition may be as a feature of our minds and lives. We don't know how "strong" it is, or whether its influence varies between individuals. If the evidence gathered from dreams and real-world application of psychic ability, for instance in the military's storied Star Gate psychic spying program that ran from the late 1970s until its closure and declassification in the mid 1990s is any indication, generalized psychic ability or "psi" varies a lot between persons. On the other hand, it also appears to be trainable; and it makes sense that if it exists as a capacity of the brain, then everybody likely expresses it to some degree, but that people may express it in different ways depending on differences in personality and cognitive style.[51] That especially makes sense if precognition is a part of memory. Just as some people have extraordinary memories, some have extraordinary precognition—and interestingly, in some well-studied psychics, those qualities are found together.[52]

We also don't know whether precognition has a range limitation in time. Evidence from individuals who keep strict dream records to check against later events in their lives suggests that people frequently have dreams about significant experiences years later—very often, as in David Mandell's first dream about the Twin Towers collapsing, on the same date of the year as the much later event. I suggested in my book *Precognitive Dreamwork and the Long Self* that precognitive dreaming may be part of a process that constructs our internal chronology by keeping close track of dates and associating long-term episodic (auto-biographical) memories with those dates.[53] A certain date of the year may be enough to cue the dreaming brain to symbolically pre-present a significant event on the same date a year or multiple years ahead in the individual's future, similar to the way anniversaries remind us, some-times subliminally or unconsciously, of important events that occurred on the same date in our past.

If your mind is not already bent by this, here is where it may begin to buckle. What I have just said implies a future, even a distant future, that already exists, such that it may not only be "seen" somehow (or more appropriately, "pre-membered") but also actually compared with the present. But in fact, an already-existing future is actually the least controversial claim I've made so far in this discussion.

After Einstein published his first paper on special relativity in 1905, a flurry of papers by other physicists and mathematicians worked out some of its incredible implications. Einstein's math teacher Hermann Minkowski grasped that, if what his former student wrote was true, then time and space are all part of the same continuum, and that the universe must really be a four-dimensional block, our lives in fact worldlines snaking several decades (ideally) through that block. A host of experi-ments, such as various iterations of the famous Michelson-Morley ex-periment, confirmed Einstein's predictions. And his later general theory of relativity described how mass literally converts space into time, by bending it: A heavy object actually slows time in its gravity well. The massive Earth's slight bending of space into the time dimension is the "force" that keeps you mostly glued to the floor.

The spacetime continuum is sometimes colloquially called a *block universe*. Since it is virtually impossible to visualize four-dimensions, you are permitted to sacrifice one of the spatial dimensions and picture a universe-sized brick or block whose length is time. Go ahead and make it a glass block so you can see inside it. In his novel *Jerusalem*, the comic-book writer and mage Alan Moore called it a "glass football" to show the universe's presumed expansion from nothing in the Big Bang and later collapse in a Big Crunch.[54] Objects in that glass block/football are actually worm- or snakelike forms, wending and twisting their way for some distance through the block. We ourselves are really four-dimensional serpents, but at any given time we only experience a slice or cross-section of that serpentine life. The particles our bodies are made of trace worldlines billions of years long, coalescing to make much more transient bodies and objects and then unwinding and coalescing in different patterns again and again through the cosmos's vast history.

Even today, few physicists or cosmologists question that we live in that block universe of Einstein and Minkowski. And conveniently, it is the reality that effectively makes precognition possible. Even if our consciousness seems to travel only forward across our long worldline from birth to death, some of the information carried by the particles that constitute our bodies and brains seems to propagate in temporal retrograde, from our future toward our past. Yet somehow, our conscious awareness seems to scroll, like a cursor across a video-editing timeline, in a single, forward direction through our serpentine life. Why we are only aware of a tiny brief segment of our "long self" at any given moment is a mystery. I certainly won't offer an explanation, although I do strongly suspect that the scientific study of precognition in coming years could get us closer to an answer.

If Einstein was right, this seemingly unshakeable fact about consciousness, that it is confined to a single moment and travels in a single direction, really belongs in the realm of other perceptual illusions studied by psychologists. Near the end of his life, Einstein famously wrote to the family of a recently departed friend, Michele Besso:

> Now he has departed from this strange world a little ahead of me. That means nothing. People like us, who believe in physics, know that the distinction between past, present and future is only a stubbornly persistent illusion.[55]

Whether it happens in five years, fifteen, or fifty, I expect that a major coming revolution in the sciences will be a radical reframing of our understanding of causation both at the fundamental level of quantum reality and in the living systems (and artificial quantum computers) that scale it up. I suggest that our brains will turn out to be information tunnels across time, bringing us news about our futures the same way it retains or helps us reconstruct information about our pasts.

However exactly precognition works—we still don't have anywhere near a complete answer—the bottom line is that it is no longer a supernatural topic. Superhuman, yes, but not supernatural. And here's an important point: If it exists at all, then it is no longer reasonable to still treat precognition as a great rarity or as an anomaly on those occasions when it happens to rise to our awareness. Our ease or difficulty of imagining a phenomenon has zero bearing on how common or rare that thing is in nature. If precognition exists at all—and obviously I think it does—then we should be looking for it everywhere, including right under our noses, hiding in the gaps of commonsensical but obsolete assumptions about consciousness and causation, the way we think and the way things go.

We Live in Loops

People who take precognition seriously often see it as a scientific frontier, a frontier of psychology and physics, but it is as much a frontier of the humanities. The humanities in our day have modeled themselves on science, bowing to materialism, not venturing beyond the bounds set by those who study and work with the measurable. Yet what matters in the humanities is not matter as measure, but matter as meaning—things that matter to thinking beings, and what Jeffrey Kripal calls "consciousness encoded in culture."[56] While things psychical have never *not* been an acknowledged factor for most cultures on Earth, in ours they have, until recently, been relegated to the cultural gutters, to "low" art, marginal literary genres like science fiction and comic books, dime-store paperbacks on ESP, and New Age spirituality. That's changing, though. There's a thaw happening. One sign of that thaw is that the topic of psychic and specifically precognitive experiences is now being discussed more openly, not only by some bold scientists but also by academics in other fields, as well as by artists and writers in the mainstream media, where it was once taboo. I mean *New York Times* bestselling authors on NPR, not just self-published writers on paranormal podcasts or late-night radio.

In Ayad Akhtar's acclaimed 2020 novel *Homeland Elegies*, about life as an American Muslim in the aftermath of 9/11, the narrator, a thinly fictionalized version of the author, describes his lifelong dreamwork practice, including a history of precognitive dreams.[57] In an interview on NPR's *Fresh Air*, the interviewer Dave Davies (filling in for regular host Terry Gross) asked Akhtar point blank if the dreams in the book were his real experiences. Davies expected Akhtar to evade answering, as he had remained cagey about the reality of other situations in the novel (such as whether his dad had been Donald Trump's cardiologist, as the novel's narrator's father is). But on the subject of his dreams, Akhtar was eager to talk: The dreams were all true—including a premonition of 9/11 that he had written into the novel.

> [Y]es, I had that dream. That was a dream that I had. And it was a terrifying dream, and I didn't understand it at the time. It was this, you know, terrible attack on the center of New York. And everybody was running around like insects that had lost a colony, like ants losing a colony—a sort of frenzied activity. And I woke up in a panic and a sweat. And two days later, you know, it was September 11, 2001. ... What is that about? ... When it happens often enough, you just start wondering—something's going on that we don't understand.[58]

Akhtar also told an interviewer for *The New Yorker* that it was a premonitory dream "in which he tried to escape an evil fog that was smothering the world" that induced him and his fiancée to move out of Manhattan when the first cases of COVID-19 were reported in that city in February 2020.[59]

Two years later, novelist and memoirist Dani Shapiro told NPR's *Weekend Edition* host Scott Simon of the precognitive roots of her new novel *Signal Fires*, which centers on a friendship between a retired doctor, Ben Wilf, and the lonely 11-year-old boy Waldo Shenkman who lives across the street from him. Shapiro didn't use the word "precognitive," but it was precognitive: She said the novel began in her head in 2007 as a single image of an older man, a doctor, standing at the window of his home, watching the astronomy-obsessed boy across the street look up at the sky. She wrote parts of the novel around these characters but set it aside before returning to it over a decade later. She told Simon:

> I'll tell you one very extraordinary and mystical thing ... which is that I began the book 15 years ago, and then about seven years later, I discovered that my dad, who raised me, had not been my biological father.

I created the character of Ben Wilf, seven or eight years *before* I made that discovery. He is just like my biological father. He has the same medical profession. He looks like him. He very much has his nature. What does that mean that I imagined and conjured this fully-fleshed-out character that was not something in any way based on someone that I knew existed?[60]

Simon responded: "Now I have chills." Welcome to the world of precognition, retrocausation, and time loops, Mr. Simon.

These are exchanges that I suspect would not have been found in mainstream media outlets even a decade ago. The chill-causing loopiness of life is something people in our rapidly transforming world are finally, perhaps, ready to awaken to and discuss. As Shapiro writes of her main character, a literary premonition of the biological father looming in her future: "Ben Wilf has come to believe we live in loops rather than one straight line."

Steampunk Connection
Extraordinary Inspiration
and the Empire of Meanwhile

*[T]he most arousing among our own thoughts are
foreign thoughts that use our heads.*
—Peter Sloterdijk, *After God* (2020)

"You see, son, here time becomes space."
—Richard Wagner, *Parsifal* (1882)

The American journalist and novelist Mark Twain was an assiduous
observer of events in his own life that we would now call paranormal. In 1891, he submitted an essay to *Harper's* magazine in which he
listed several examples of peculiar and coincidental experiences, such
as thinking of a friend and then running into them on the street, or
the then-familiar phenomenon of letters between friends "crossing" in
the mail—the kind of thing many nowadays would call synchronicities
but which Twain gave the name "mental telegraphy." Mental telegraphy
was this great American writer's unique and fascinating answer to the
question "Where do you get your ideas?" He believed he got them from
other people, psychically. And implicitly—and, he hoped, even more
often—other people might get them from him, directly and unmedi-
ated by the clumsy worldly technologies of moveable type and printing
presses and publishing.[1]

Twain's prime autobiographical example of mental telegraphy, an
experience that he described as the "oddest thing that ever happened
to me," was an idea that came to him all of a sudden one morning
while he was "idly musing" in bed—"suddenly a red-hot new idea
came whistling down into my camp," he wrote, "and exploded with

such comprehensive effectiveness as to sweep the vicinity clean of rubbishy reflections and fill the air with their dust and flying fragments." It was an idea for a book that demanded to be written immediately and would, he was sure, command wide attention, "to wit, a book about the Nevada silver-mines. The 'Great Bonanza' was a new wonder then, and everybody was talking about it."[2]

Alas, this pure-gold (or silver) idea wasn't a book Twain himself was really in a position to write, living as he did 3,000 miles away from the action, in Hartford, Connecticut. But he knew immediately who should write it: Mr. William H. Wright, a Nevada journalist he had worked with over a decade previously when he had been living in that Western state. Wright had been a fellow writer at the frontier rag *Territorial Enterprise*, but they were not close enough to have kept in touch in the 11 years after Twain moved back East. On the March morning when he had this great inspiration, Twain did not even know whether Wright was still alive. But the idea was so good that Twain immediately wrote Wright a letter outlining his idea:

> I began by merely and modestly suggesting that he make such a book; but my interest grew as I went on, and I ventured to map out what I thought ought to be the plan of the work, he being an old friend, and not given to taking good intentions for ill. I even dealt with details, and suggested the order and sequence which they should follow.[3]

But, Twain recalled, just as he was about to send the letter, he realized that he should find a willing publisher for the idea first, before he put his old colleague through a lot of work only to find that nobody was interested. So he held off on sending the letter and wrote to his own publisher instead, asking for a meeting to discuss the idea. His publisher was out of town, though, so the letter to Wright languished for a few days, during which time he more or less forgot the whole matter. Then, a week after he had had his great brainstorm, the mailman brought to his house a thick letter whose envelope was superscripted in a hand he dimly recognized—that of his old colleague, Wright.

With what must have been a sly twinkle in his eye, Twain announced to a relative who was visiting:

"Now I will do a miracle. I will tell you everything

this letter contains—date, signature, and all—without breaking the seal. It is from a Mr. Wright, of Virginia, Nevada, and is dated the 2d of March—seven days ago. Mr. Wright proposes to make a book about the silver-mines and the Great Bonanza, and asks what I, as a friend, think of the idea. He says his subjects are to be so and so, their order and sequence so and so, and he will close with a history of the chief feature of the book, the Great Bonanza."[4]

Twain thereupon opened the letter, and read it aloud. It was exactly as he had just described.

Mr. Wright's letter simply contained what my own letter, written on the same date, contained, and mine still lay in its pigeonhole, where it had been lying during the seven days since it was written. … Wright's letter and the one which I had written to him but never sent were in substance the same.[5]

This could be no accident of chance, Twain reasoned, as the parallels were too numerous and too specific. Moreover, the idea had come to him as something alien, "foreign":

The subject was entirely foreign to my thoughts; I was wholly absorbed in other things. Yet this friend, whom I had not seen and had hardly thought of for eleven years, was able to shoot his thoughts at me across three thousand miles of country, and fill my head with them, to the exclusion of every other interest, in a single moment. He had begun his letter after finishing his work on the morning paper—a little after three o'clock, he said. When it was three in the morning in Nevada it was about six in Hartford, where I lay awake thinking about nothing in particular; and just about that time his ideas came pouring into my head from across the continent, and I got up and put them on paper, under the impression that they were my own original thoughts.[6]

Stick a pin in Twain's phrase, "foreign to my thoughts." A common feature of psychic experiences is that they are experienced as uncaused or alien, a phenomenological quality they share with moments of artistic or literary inspiration. We'll be coming back to this.

Telegraphs and Chronophones

The idea of an occult mind-to-mind connection was of course not original to Twain. A century earlier, a German doctor named Anton Mesmer had promoted the idea of "animal magnetism." Using his hands to conduct what he believed were invisible magnetic-like currents within and around the bodies of people with various afflictions, Mesmer claimed to cure and even to see into their bodies. Mesmerism, as it was called, evolved into what we now call hypnosis, although in Mesmer's day that word connoted an occult mind-to-mind connection as well as a subtle physical connection, not simply making a person receptive to verbal suggestion.

In his *Harper's* article, Twain was riffing on (and also acknowledged his debt to) a Cambridge Classics teacher named Frederic W. H. Myers, whose work had boosted the scientific legitimacy of mesmeric-like emotional connection at a distance. In the 1880s, Myers had coined the term *telepathy* to describe a supernormal connection between people across great distances, especially during times of crisis—for example, awakening to a vision of a dripping-wet friend who, many miles away, had just drowned (an example from Myers' posthumously published book *Human Personality and its Survival of Bodily Death*). Myers supposed that when people were experiencing strong emotions like pain or fear, or undergoing the ultimate crisis of dying, these strong emotions could transmit long distances and be received by friends or loved ones, especially when in a receptive state like sleep. Myers and his colleagues, psychologist Edmund Gurney and skeptic Frank Podmore, collected hundreds of uncanny experiences like this and published them in a compendious 1886 volume, *Phantasms of the Living*.

We make sense of the unknown via the known, and marvels at the cutting edge of technology have for the past two centuries provided the main metaphors people use to help understand the inexplicable.[7] In the mid and late 19th century, it was new electrical telecommunications technologies that made a range of what we would now call paranormal experiences newly thinkable (if not always believable) by an increasingly science-literate and technology-using public.[8] Myers' concept was based on the metaphor of the telegraph, a bright, shiny telecommunications revolution that was uniting the world for the first time—the first information superhighway. Some of the earliest telepathy researchers even worked in the nascent field of telegraphy.[9] Telepathy was the core concept of the emerging field of psychical research that would evolve, about fifty years later, into what we now know as parapsychology.

Telepathy as Myers theorized it and as Twain imagined it—a kind of simultaneous, telegraph-like transmission of feelings or thoughts between persons—does not seem to be a culturally universal idea. Many or most cultures do have a belief in some sort of "extraordinary knowing," as psychotherapist Elizabeth Lloyd Mayer called it [10]—including knowing of the deaths of family members and friends before news reaches them, a very common experience. But there are other ways of imagining how that might work. To cite just one example, an Australian parapsychologist, Richard Rose, who worked among that country's indigenous peoples in the 1950s, found that such intimations were believed to be mediated by people's clan totems: They would see their totem animal in a dream or vision, or just notice the animal in real life, and know that a member of their clan had died.[11] The totemic relationship was both the medium and the message. The closest ancient-world parallel to Myers' theory may be that of the Greek philosopher Democritus, who believed that the soul was composed of atoms and that vivid images could be projected by a person in a state of excitement and received by a dreamer elsewhere, via pores in the skin. But while belief in the separability of the soul and/or spirit from the body is a universal idea—more on which later—the idea that some mental experiences by themselves can be transmitted person to person like a message or signal seems to be purely an invention of the Victorian age.

Twain's steampunk term, mental telegraphy, put a more writerly spin on Myers' concept—shifting from feeling (-pathy) to writing (-graphy).[12] There was, to be sure, no intense affection linking Twain to his old colleague Wright—they'd just been hard-drinking colleagues in a frontier newsroom, even semi-rivals, and hadn't kept in touch. But they were writers, and writers no matter how far apart and no matter how rivalrous, might be expected to share a bond. In a letter to Wright, Twain explained the thought-transmission he imagined had occurred as a matter of "mesmeric currents" flowing between them, harkening back also to the ideas of Mesmer that were a precursor to Myers' telepathy concept and that remained popular as a way of accounting for seeming telepathic experiences.[13]

Twain's experience with Wright was particularly striking, but he asserted in his article that crossed correspondence of one sort or another was so common in his experience that he had even started opting to save on postage by just writing letters and not sending them, since he was sure to receive replies anyway. That part sounds like a typically Twainian embellishment for color. But given the frequency of what he interpreted as mesmeric or telepathic thought transmission between himself and his creative friends, he also asked, quite seriously, whether this mental sharing may not be the real force shaping culture and knowledge, for instance helping account for so many nearly simultaneous inventions and discoveries in the history of science and technology: "[C]onsider for a moment how many a splendid 'original' idea has been unconsciously stolen from a man three thousand miles away!" He wrote:

> If one should question that this is so, let him look into the cyclopedia and con once more that curious thing in the history of inventions which has puzzled every one so much—that is, the frequency with which the same machine or other contrivance has been invented at the same time by several persons in different quarters of the globe. The world was without an electric telegraph for several thousand years; then Professor Henry, the American, Wheatstone in England, Morse on the sea, and a German in Munich, all invented it at the same time. The discovery of certain ways of applying steam was made in two or three countries in the same year. Is it not possible that inventors are constantly and unwittingly stealing each other's ideas whilst they stand thousands of miles asunder?

Twain went on in his article to list further examples, most famously the coincidence that both Charles Darwin and Alfred Russel Wallace hit on the idea of natural selection at exactly the same time, at opposite ends of the earth. We'll come back to that interesting case later.

In fact, Twain's experience of mind-to-mind contact with journalist Wright was not the oddest thing that had ever happened to him. There were a lot of odd things, really, but the oddest was certainly one of Twain's dreams, from a time when he was still merely Samuel Clemens, a 23-year-old apprentice pilot on a Mississippi River steamboat named the *Pennsylvania*. It was so odd that he left it out of his "Mental Telegraphy" manuscript, as it just couldn't fit that explanatory rubric. It was also far too personal and still, decades after the fact, too painful. And on occasions when he had told the story to people in private, he had gotten eye-rolls and disbelief, the chilling effect that often keeps experiencers of the super in the closet.

In 1858, Samuel had gotten a job for his 19-year-old brother Henry on the same boat as a "mud clerk." This was before the days when low-level jobs were dignified with impressive-sounding labels. A mud clerk literally facilitated loading and unloading cargo at muddy landing sites without proper docks—an unskilled and unpaid position. One day between runs, when the brothers were staying with their older sister and her family in St. Louis, Clemens dreamed vividly of Henry lying dead in a metal coffin wearing one of his own (Samuel's) suits. He said that the dream seemed so real that he went outside to collect himself after he awoke, before viewing the body, only then realizing it had only been a dream. The latter may be another storyteller's embellishment—his niece reported that he had the dream while napping in the afternoon and promptly reported it to his family when he came out of his room.

Whatever the case, the brothers then made the run south to New Orleans aboard the *Pennsylvania*, but Samuel was made to stay ashore in New Orleans after a fight with the boat's pilot. He then got the awful news that a boiler explosion had killed or injured many on the *Pennsylvania* on its run back north, near Memphis. Samuel made it to Memphis aboard another boat and was able to be with his severely burned brother after he arrived, but Henry then died from an overdose of morphine given by inexperienced doctors. The next morning, Samuel visited the "dead room" in the Memphis Exchange, where the bodies were laid out in caskets, and was stunned to find the scene from his dream: All the dead but Henry were in pine boxes, but some nurses, impressed with young Henry's stoicism and the beauty of his youthful, miraculously unburned face, had pitched in to buy him a metal one. Henry lay in the box in a suit he had borrowed from Samuel without Samuel's knowledge. Other details, too, were exactly what Samuel had dreamed.[14]

Late in his life, Twain dictated the story to his stenographer as part of his *Autobiography*. He explained that he had told his dream one night in 1885 at a dinner club he belonged to in Hartford, and that his companions had been skeptical. One of the gentlemen, echoing an argument that is still commonly used to debunk prophetic-seeming dreams, assured him that dreams morph in memory with each retelling, to conform more closely to supposedly foretold events. Twain said that thereafter he avoided telling the story—effectively, he was scared off, fearing further distorting his dream memory but also fearing the inevitable debunking arguments that can rain down on an experiencer's head.

It was probably the same trepidation that delayed Twain from submitting his accounts of mental telegraphy for publication—they too smacked of something supernatural or occult, and thus he knew they would not be taken seriously by some readers and could perhaps damage his reputation. He said in his introduction that it was the courageous work of Myers' Society for Psychical Research (SPR) that had done enough to legitimize such experiences that it gave him a kind of permission. But the vivid dream of Henry's dead body in a metal coffin a short time before the same scene played out in reality would have been less easy to fit into a steampunk rubric like telepathy or mental telegraphy. There simply was not in Twain's or Myers' day anything like a "chronophone" that could help explain how information from a terrible scene in his future could be transmitted several days back in time and be received in a dream.

Radio Days

At the end of the 19th century and the first half of the 20th, the next big advance in telecommunications, wireless technology, produced an even more apt metaphor for ostensible human psychic transmission: *mental radio*. In 1930, the socialist novelist and activist Upton Sinclair used that for the title of a book in which he put his muckraker reputation on the line in defense of the existence of telepathy, based on a series of fascinating experiments he both witnessed and participated in with his writer wife, Mary Craig Sinclair (née Kimbrough).[15] Craig, as she was known, is a fascinating, mostly unsung hero of psychical research, and she would have completely agreed with Twain's assessment about the true origins of ideas—that they may, more often than we know, come from somewhere else than our own head.[16]

Hailing from a family of lawyers in Mississippi, Craig called herself a Southern Belle but she was totally unlike the wilting, histrionic stereotype. She fiercely supported her husband's socialist causes while amassing a library of religious and philosophical works. Although she regarded spirituality with repugnance after childhood exposure to evangelical Christianity and was skeptical of psychic claims, she had always had experiences that challenged the materialistic givens of science. She was, as Twain had been, an avid follower of the interesting psychical research being conducted in Europe and America. She wondered whether there were really untapped potentials that could serve as a force for human betterment and rival the economic and political solutions that obsessed her husband:

> There were powers, only glimpsed by researchers in that field [psychical research], which might revolutionize the whole of human life. ... I couldn't rest without knowing whether they were real and usable. When I said that to my husband, he would answer, 'Let us compete. You find these powers before I work myself to death getting poverty out of the way.'[17]

So in the late 1920s, while Upton busily took on the oil companies (*Oil!*) and the unjust American judicial system (*Boston*, on the recently tried and executed Italians Sacco and Vanzetti), Craig embarked on telepathy experiments. Initially she partnered with a Polish medium and stage hypnotist but didn't trust his honesty, so she sought someone to work with who was of a more "hard-boiled materialistic-thinking" disposition. She initially found such a person in her sister's businessman husband, Robert L. Irwin, "whose philosophy of life does not include any 'mysticism' or unconscious knowledge."[18] "Bob" lived in Pasadena, California, some 40 miles' drive away from her and Upton's residence in Long Beach, and he was then housebound because of worsening tuberculosis. That unfortunate state of affairs enabled him to devote some time each day for their telepathy experiments. In her own account of these experiments appended to a later edition of her husband's book, Craig described Bob's role as follows:

> Each day at one o'clock, an hour which suits the convenience of both of us, he sits at a table in his home and makes a drawing of some simple object, such as a table-fork, or an ink-bottle, a duck, or a basket of fruit. Then he gazes steadily at his drawing, while he concentrates his mind intently on "visualizing" the object before him. ... When he has finished the fifteen minutes of steady concentration on one object, he dates his drawing and puts it away, until the time

when we are to meet and compare our records.[19]

For her part, Craig simply, as we would now say, meditated, with a paper and pencil, at the same appointed hour:

> At the end of the "wireless," I have done a different mental stunt. I have reclined on a couch, with body completely relaxed and my mind in a dreamy, almost unconscious state, alternating with a state of gazing, with closed eyes, into gray space, looking on this gray background for whatever picture, or thought-form may appear there. When a form appears, I record it at once ... At the end of fifteen minutes ... I date my drawing and file it until the day comes to compare notes with my brother-in-law.[20]

Every three or four days, the Sinclairs drove to visit Bob and compare notes, and the results they got were compelling: A significant proportion of her drawings matched those Bob had made and sent "on air" at the appointed time. But Bob's failing health—and Craig's increasing depression, which she suspected she was telepathically catching from Bob—compelled her to cease the experiment with Bob and continue with her writer husband instead. They did their drawings in separate rooms of their home, behind closed doors, but otherwise following the same protocol. Upton often selected his telepathy targets from magazines. And the results were striking—at least, for those of an open mind.

Upton reproduces many of the experiments in his book—Bob's or his own drawing side by side with Craig's written description or sketch. According to Upton, many of Craig's drawings or notes—about a quarter—exactly matched what the "sender" had drawn: a table fork, a knight's helmet, a tree, and so on. About a quarter, Upton admitted, were complete misses. The larger proportion, he said, captured some essential flavor of Bob's or his own drawing without being exactly right. The curiously sensible way in which the almosts deviated from their targets is nearly as compelling as the exact hits. For instance, on July 29, 1928, Sinclair recorded drawing "a cigarette, with two little curls of smoke, each running off like a string of the letter 'eeeee'..." Craig, he wrote "got the curls but not the cigarette," drawing "a curly capital S, several other half circles twisted together, and three ??? one inside the other. She added the following words: 'I can't draw it, but curls of some sort.'"[21] Both Upton and Craig chalked these distortions up to Upton's inability to keep his mind focused while he was supposed to be "sending." In this case, he said he was distracted by trains of mental association such as images of "the odious advertising now appearing in the papers."[22]

The results the Sinclairs reported resemble those of other, sometimes more formal telepathy experiments using drawings—including experiments conducted by the SPR in the previous century, as well as experiments conducted in France in the 1940s by parapsychologist René Warcollier.[23] Later researchers also noted something distinctly impressionistic about psychically acquired information, something fragile and fragmentary, keying in on forms but not meaning. One of Upton's drawings is a simple depiction of a conical volcano billowing black smoke from the top at an angle, while Craig saw in her mind's eye an angular beetle with two antennae facing downward—but the drawings are virtually identical.[24] A drawing by Upton of a bird's nest almost exactly matches a drawing by Craig of what she interpreted as "Inside of rock well with vines climbing on outside."[25]

Mental Radio was well-received. Sinclair sent a draft to his friend Albert Einstein, who in fact had witnessed some of the experiments firsthand at the Sinclairs' home, and the physicist wrote a glowing introduction for a planned German edition.[26] Predictably, psychic debunkers were less impressed. The aforementioned Martin Gardner dismissed the many matched drawings as guesswork on the part of an intuitive wife who could somehow anticipate each of her husband's picture choices and might have been able to see his hand movements.[27] Which ignores the fact that the trials were explicitly described as being conducted in separate rooms with a closed door between them and the similarly high rate of hits with Craig's brother-in-law in a separate town. As Sinclair put it in a preface to a later edition, "the learned gentleman didn't want to believe, and hadn't taken the trouble to go back and study the book."[28]

To be fair, part of the subject's implausibility to the science-minded is that there wasn't then, and still isn't, any known way for information to travel across space that doesn't use measurable electromagnetic radiation. Nothing like Twain's mesmeric currents have ever been detected that could link two minds together in the manner assumed by proponents of telepathy. Later in the 20th century, American and Soviet parapsychology researchers used Faraday cages and deep seawater (i.e. in submarines), both of which block such radiation, to assess whether it had any impact on psychics' performance, and it didn't. Nor does distance. And I see all the hands waving in the front row from readers who want to tell me, here in your past, about quantum entanglement. Tiny particles can be made to act in unison at a distance—it's the basis for quantum computing and other emerging technologies. But for reasons that have been well-explored by physicists, you can't use entanglement to send a signal.[29] It's a fun and evocative metaphor, as is "mental radio," but when all you have are metaphors, skeptics are allowed, indeed have a duty, to be at least a bit skeptical.

While Upton, less interested in these theoretical subtleties, explicitly described the drawings Craig made as records of mental contact between her and himself—"mind reading," as he repeatedly puts it—an extraordinary experience strikingly similar to Twain's allegedly telepathic inspiration for a book on the Nevada silver mines caused Craig to suspect that whatever it was they were investigating, simple broadcasting of ideas from a sender (Bob or Upton) to her, the receiver, could not be the whole story, if it was even any of the story.

The Black Magician

These days, *Mental Radio* is remembered, when it is remembered, only as a record of an interesting 1920s telepathy experiment, but it is much more than that. It is really a series of touching and humorous domestic vignettes about a busy, distracted husband and his writer wife trying to get his attention—and succeeding—via the expression of psychic abilities. It is psychic romance, not psychic science, and that is in fact its great strength and value. The element missing from most parapsychology is the dimension of meaning, including emotion—real human connection. These are the things novelists and storytellers are better at capturing than scientists are, and in this case the rich narrative captured by two professional writers (Craig wrote fiction and poetry, and Upton later said she was *Mental Radio*'s co-writer even though only his name appears on the spine) enables us to perform some detective work on what was really happening in their psychic experiments.

One morning in 1928, Craig was suddenly, out of the blue, seized with an idea for a story about an expert in hypnosis using his powers for ill, to manipulate and seduce. It came to her in a flash and seemed so excitingly original that she set aside everything else to get it down on paper. She proceeded to write a synopsis while her husband was at his office, and she was too excited to stop writing or talk to Upton when he came home to have his lunch. "Let me alone," she said, "I am writing a story." So off he went to quietly eat by himself in the next room—but not before depositing on her writing desk two light blue volumes that he had just received in the mail at his office.

As a famous author, Upton received many unsolicited books from writers all over the world, most of which were not interesting to him, yet some fell under the categories of Craig's library ("philosophy, psychology, religion, and medicine"). On this day, he had received a two-volume novel called *Patricia: A South African Romance* from a writer in Johannesburg named Marcus Romondt. It seemed to him, from his cursory glance at the first page, to concern religious cults in that country, so he brought them home for Craig.[30] She did not even glance at the volumes when he set them down on her desk, as she was too busy getting her thoughts about her story down on paper.

When she was at a stopping point some time later, she told Upton, "Oh, I have had the most marvelous idea for a story! … Something just flashed over me. Something absolutely novel—I never heard anything like it. I have a whole synopsis. Do you want to hear it?"

"No," Upton replied, "you had better go and eat." He quipped that it was his job "to try to keep her body on earth."

"I can't eat now," Craig said, "I am too excited."[31]

To calm herself down from her creative frenzy, Craig idly picked up the first volume of *Patricia* … and was stunned at what appeared on the page she randomly opened to: the capitalized words THE BLACK MAGICIAN at the bottom of page 192.[32] Amazed, she flipped a few pages back to the beginning of the chapter (XXI) and began reading. This chapter was about a sinister and furtive middle-aged hypnotist stalking the novel's beautiful young Dutch protagonist in London, contriving to make her fall in love with him using his mind-control talents. The details and setting were different, but it was substantially the occult premise she had just spent her morning writing about!

Craig's excitement over "her" most marvelous idea deflated as she read Romondt's chapter, but excitement was replaced by intense curiosity. It seemed like another one of the adventures in psychical experimentation she had been involved in with her husband—but this time wholly accidental, and much more puzzling. She went to Upton, who was finishing his lunch, and showed him the phrase she had taken as her theme: "Did you ever hear of that idea?"

Upton had to admit that he *had* heard of black magicians.

"Well, I never did," Craig said. "I thought it was my own. It is the theme of the 'story' I have just been writing. I have made a synopsis of the whole chapter in this book, and without ever having touched it!"[33]

She ascertained from her husband that he had not penetrated the book any farther than its first paragraphs and thus really knew nothing of what was inside. Thus she could not have gotten the phrase THE BLACK MAGICIAN or the themes of her story from Upton telepathically or "on air." She guessed therefore that it must have been a matter of clairvoyance or psychometry—somehow receiving the idea from the book itself, directly.

Clairvoyance, from the French for "clear-seeing," refers to an ability to mentally see or discern what is hidden, invisible, or at a distance in space, and implicitly requires no other person as a mental broadcast station. Like telepathy, the psychical sense of the term, originally associated with mesmerism and Spiritualism, was legitimized by the sciences of the late-19th century. The discovery of X-rays, for instance, made thinkable the idea that there are worlds beyond the visible, and that the unseen could be seen in special circumstances or with yet-unknown faculties of perception.[34]

The BLACK MAGICIAN episode was a paradigm shift for Craig. Afterward, she dispensed with the mental "sending" part of her experiment with Upton. From then on, her husband made his drawings at his leisure (or in a few cases, had his secretary make them) and put them in envelopes for her to clairvoyantly view at will. It was essentially the same procedure as would later be used by ESP researchers when developing clairvoyance as a psychic spying modality during the Cold War. The results were not affected—still approximately the same proportion of hits, misses, and almosts. Craig also conducted further experiments on her own in which she attempted to mentally divine the contents of randomly selected books from Upton's library. "She did it on so many occasions," Upton writes, "that she would sit and stare at me and exclaim, 'Now what do you *make of that?* She would insist that I sit and watch the process, so as to be able to state that she never had the book in her line of vision."[35]

But here's the thing: Clairvoyance cannot really explain any better than telepathy how Craig's consciousness, or her unconscious mind, could have alighted on the words THE BLACK MAGICIAN in *Patricia*, which at the time she began writing was at Upton's office and then in his briefcase. How or why did she psychically "see" that one phrase out of all the hundreds of thousands of other words and phrases pressed together in its pages? Although "black magic" and "black magician" appear on several pages, only once does it appear in all-caps, and *that was the very first page she opened the book to*. Invoking clairvoyance as an explanation requires the supplement of impossible coincidence, or perhaps a divine guiding hand.[36]

Craig didn't quite make the connection, but like Twain before her, she really seems to have been on the receiving end of a chronophone call from her future self.

Meanwhile

In his now-classic study of the rise of national movements in the Victorian era, *Imagined Communities*, historian Benedict Anderson argued that the most important word in the modern vocabulary, from the standpoint of politics and culture at least, is the word "meanwhile."[37] The sense of simultaneity across space that was created by the press and by the modern literary form of the novel in the 18th and 19th centuries was decisively important for the creation of national consciousness: a sense of collective unity and even togetherness among people widely dispersed in space, yet living their lives in parallel, co-located in time. Before novels and newspapers, people could not as readily imagine themselves as part of such a collective. The telegraph and wireless, seemingly negating the spatial distances between widely separated people, only reinforced and intensified this sense of simultaneity as the Victorian era ceded to the Edwardian. We today have trouble grasping how new and exciting the sense of meanwhile was for people in the 19th century and early 20th century, both for modern urban people enjoying the fruits of world-spanning empires and for those on the margins and in the hinterlands of those empires trying to imagine their way to independence by rewriting their own histories and cultures, imagining new nations. Indeed, the world was becoming "wired" just as the Empire was beginning to fall apart. This space-reimagining, space-conquering steampunk world, with its imperial anxieties and nationalist dreams, was the crucible of telepathy.[38] Victorian technology and that idea of meanwhile made instantaneous transmission of thoughts and feelings at a distance thinkable.

Having a believably sciencey rubric for previously homeless supernormal experiences made it more permissible, in a conservatively materialist world, to talk about such experiences and collect them and begin to study them, as Myers and his SPR colleagues did. But thinkability, as research on the metaphoric structuring of thought has long shown, is never innocent or unbiased.[39] The technologies and techno-metaphors of the times may be as constraining and even distorting of the supernormal imagination as they are revelatory. In this case, the Victorian tele-rubric imposed a distinctly spatial framing on phenomena that may have much more to do with bridging distances in time.[40]

In the first decades of the century, a soldier-turned-aeronautical engineer named John William Dunne—like Myers, working in the heart of the Empire of Meanwhile, in England—was actively exploring and trying to understand exactly the kind of interself messaging system that could parsimoniously explain phenomena like Twain's dream about his brother Henry, not to mention many of the kinds of experiences and feats being studied by psychical researchers under the rubric of telepathy.

Since his youth, Dunne had experienced frequent dreams that came to be confirmed shortly thereafter. Some were about personal experiences soon to happen to him, although most were about interesting stories he was soon to read in the news. In 1901, for example, while recuperating on the Italian Riviera after a stint fighting in the Boer War in South Africa, Dunne dreamed he was in a village near the Sudanese capital, Khartoum, and met three South African colonists who looked deeply tanned from being a long time out in the sun. The next morning, he read a news story of the first cross-continent trek by a group of colonists from the southern tip of the continent to Khartoum. The following year, while camped out in the South African bush with his regiment, Dunne dreamed of being on a French volcanic island about to blow and that 4,000 people were about to die. A few days later, the latest issue of the *Daily Telegraph* arrived with a shipment of mail, bearing a headline about the death of 40,000 people in the May 8, 1902 eruption of Mount Pelée on the French Caribbean island of Martinique. He misread the headline as saying 4,000, the figure that appeared in his dream. On another occasion in 1904, he dreamed of seeing people pressed against a balcony railing amid billowing black smoke. That afternoon he read a news story about a factory fire in Paris that had killed many female workers who had attempted to escape the flames onto a balcony.[41]

Some of Dunne's dreams were about tragedies hitting closer to home. Around 8:00 on the morning of September 10, 1912, for example, Dunne had a long nightmare involving a series of terrible plane crashes. By that point, he was one of the foremost innovators in the nascent British aerospace industry, and such dreams were very common for him—there was much at stake in the safety of the novel tailless monoplanes he was then designing and building, so stress seemed to cause calamitous dreams. But one of the accidents in this dream stood out from the rest. He wrote:

> I dreamed that I was standing in a very large meadow, situated in a landscape which I did not recognize. In this meadow a monoplane landed, crashing rather badly some fifty yards away. Immediately afterwards I saw B. coming to me from the direction of the wreck. I asked if much damage had been done. He replied, "Oh no, not much," and then added, "It's all that beastly engine; but I've got the hang of it now."[42]

"B." in Dunne's dream was a pilot named Bettington he had recently met at a military airplane competition in Salisbury Plain in England.[43] Shortly thereafter he had departed for Paris to supervise the construction of one of his new planes, which is where he had this dream. He awoke to find a French servant pouring his tea, and thought no more of his nightmare until two days later, when he read a news story about the death of Lieutenant Bettington, along with another pilot he did not know, in a monoplane crash (not one of Dunne's, fortunately) in a meadow near Oxford. The crash had occurred between 7:00 and 8:00 on the morning he had had his dream.

Dunne was examining his dreams in an era when dreams and the unconscious were increasingly of popular interest due to Sigmund Freud's writings. Freud himself dismissed any real possibility of getting glimpses of the future—he reinterpreted his patients' alleged premonitory dreams as hindsight memory distortion[44]—yet his work alerted readers to the possibility that their dreams were not just senseless productions of the nocturnally deranged mind either. In his 1927 book *An Experiment with Time,* Dunne took no issue with Freud's basic premise that dreams may be the disguised fulfilment of repressed wishes, but he proposed that the dreaming brain sometimes reaches into the individual's future as well as their past to construct those wish-fulfilling dream-edifices.[45] (We'll circle back to Freud's ideas, and his refusal of precognition, in the next chapter.)

In forensically investigating his dream about Bettington, Dunne was able to discern that some details of the dream corresponded to what he *believed* about the crash at the time he got the bad news, not what really happened. He assumed the crash had probably been caused by engine trouble, because the pilot had expressed exactly such a concern to Dunne's sister and she had relayed it to him at some point—so in the dream, the pilot walked away from the crash and blamed the "beastly engine." But Dunne later learned that what had really caused the accident was a lift wire that snapped during flight—a fact that would have been utterly clear to the pilot as his plane was plummeting out of control. Nor did Dunne consider the coincidence of the time of the dream as particularly relevant, since he had airplane-related nightmares commonly at that hour.

His investigation pointed to the fact that the dream was not plausibly a telepathic connection to the unlucky Lieutenant Bettington but a preview of his own thoughts upon reading the bad news about the crash two days later. Those thoughts included suppositions supplied by his own imagination that did not prove to be true. His volcano eruption dream showed the same principle: The real death toll from the Mont Pelée eruption ultimately turned out to be around 36,000, not a 4 and multiple zeroes as he had dreamt, suggesting that he was precognizing his own reading of the news story, not the real occurrence that unfolded halfway around the world. And in his numerical dyslexia, he was, as he wrote, "out by a nought"—he wrote that he only realized his mistake about the number of zeroes years later when looking at the clipping in order to tell the story in his book. His dream conformed to what he *thought* he read in the paper, in other words, not what was actually printed. So it wasn't clairvoyance—reading the paper from afar—either.

Dunne's discoveries are consistent with what later researchers on precognition have also found to be the case: Our dim and fragmentary impression of future experiences in dreams and other altered states is supplemented with a healthy dose of imagination. This makes quite a lot of sense if, as several parapsychological theorists have argued over the years, precognition is really just a kind of memory—one that, as Lewis Carroll's White Queen suggests to Alice, goes forward as well as backward.[46] Psychologists now recognize that ordinary memories are largely ad hoc imaginative creations, not faithful recordings of events, and that should be true of precognition as well.

Although he is mostly remembered for his study of dreams, Dunne also tried experiments in his waking life, such as divining the contents of unopened books. It is exactly like what Craig Sinclair did, and he met with similar success, except that he was guided by the assumption that his successes were the result of the same principle operative in his dreams: a connection to his own future. The fact that he was going to see it, as soon as he opened the book, provided a better, simpler, and more coherent explanation for his correct guess than any mental reaching across space.

Dunne's discoveries about precognition offer a counterintuitive but ultimately compelling way to reread our two cases of psychic inspiration. First, there is nothing in Twain's account of his idea for the book on the Great Bonanza to substantiate his assumption, born of nothing more than a newfangled communications-technology metaphor, that the coincidence between his own unsent letter and the letter he received from his friend was the result of a spontaneous transmission of thoughts on March 2 from Mr. Wright (whom he hadn't seen in over a decade) to himself in Hartford, Connecticut, via mesmeric currents or any other similar broadcast modality. What seems much more likely is that it was instead a "retromission" from the journalist in Hartford on March 9 to the very same journalist—himself—a week earlier. In other words, what he imagined must be mental telegraphy was much more probably something like a chronophone call from Twain to Twain, a message from his future self—in this case, his *excited* future self, as he opened the envelope from Wright and found his amazing intuition confirmed.

We can thank Twain's writerly ego for supporting this precognitive reframing. When he first received Wright's letter, Twain wanted to know one thing: In which direction had the presumed thought-transmission occurred? Although he had no intention to write the book on the Nevada silver mines and was glad to gift the idea to his former colleague, Twain nevertheless would have liked to be the one who came up with it first, and thus to have been the psychic transmission station and not merely the telegraphist on the receiving end. (There's a very Freudian psychosexual subtext to questions of creative influence, by the way, as we'll see in Part Three—jealously original creators like to influence, not be influenced.) So Twain wrote to Wright, asking for details, and he must have been a little disappointed to read the reply: Wright "had had his book in mind some time."[47] So Twain was forced to concede priority of the idea to Wright. The mesmeric currents, he conceded, "travel from west to east, not from east to west."[48] But really, if Wright had already been thinking of the idea for some time, then it makes much less sense of the notion that it was any kind of mind-to-mind mesmeric transmission at all, unless those thought-waves travel ridiculously slowly. It would have been the same time-defying rather than space-defying cognitive mechanism that had brought him a preview of seeing his brother Henry in a steel coffin all those years earlier in St. Louis.

We can reread Craig Sinclair's moment of inspiration in exactly the same way. It never occurred to Craig or her husband, steeped as they were—and as most people still are—in Enlightenment assumptions about the one-way arrow of mental causation, that her subsequent discovery of the phrase THE BLACK MAGICIAN in Chapter XXI of *Patricia* could have been what inspired her an hour or two *earlier* when the "most marvelous idea" came over her for a story about an evil hypnotist. Nor did it occur to the Sinclairs that this mechanism could potentially explain *all* the successes in their experiments. What she took to be telepathy or clairvoyance was more likely precognizing the emotional reward of seeing her husband's (or Bob's) drawings and comparing them to her own, along with the fascinating, exciting, or funny interaction that often ensued.[49] Craig's remarkable hits seem very much like premonitions of exciting interactions with her distracted husband, sometimes involving tokens of their intellectual partnership in the form of shared books. Here as in Twain's case, the energy for this retromission of information would have been exactly what Myers' supposed—heightened emotion—but it was her own (future) emotion she was picking up on, not that of Bob or Upton.

Just two years after Upton Sinclair published *Mental Radio*, botanist J. B. Rhine established his laboratory at Duke University to study the collection of putative abilities (telepathy, clairvoyance, and precognition) that came to be collectively branded ESP or extrasensory perception. His objective was to remove the messy human factor as much as possible in the quest for scientific objectivity. In experiments he and his wife Louisa Rhine conducted using cards with simple symbols (Zener cards), participants displayed ESP ability initially but with diminishing effect over time as the tasks quickly became boring.[50] The support for the existence of such abilities, after years of work with thousands of participants, remained statistically highly significant—it is a body of research that simply cannot be ignored. But minus the human dimension, minus the romance, minus (sometimes) the pain or even trauma of the kinds of experiences that especially attract psychic attention, the results were hardly inspiring or, for most people, all that persuasive. You need novelists and sculptors and poets and filmmakers and musicians to get at the super-dimensions of the human. Art is all about anecdote, and those anecdotes often reveal the flaws in our collective assumptions about science, as well as about the impossible. One of the weaknesses of science is that it is often only as good as the metaphors that inform its hypotheses, whereas art frequently reaches beyond the existing metaphors and supplies new ones. *Mental Radio* reveals that there is a crucial human dimension to psychic phenomena, however we frame or understand them. This is what makes these phenomena particularly elusive once laboratory methods are brought in to study them.

Even if Craig remained largely within the telepathy framing that Dunne had ruled out, she was a brilliant observer of her own mental process, and she noticed how her own associative unconscious embellished and distorted what she saw in her mind's eye—it is a familiar feature of ordinary memory that also seems to characterize precognition.[51] Upton includes the following explanation of one of their fascinating almosts: He had drawn a simple (American) football with laces at the top; her drawing was essentially the same—the same laces and band around the middle—except the shape was that of a fat calf with stubby legs and head jutting off:

> Consider, for example, a little drawing—one of nearly three hundred which this long-suffering husband has made for his witch-wife to reproduce by telepathy: a football ... neatly laced up. In her drawing Craig gets the general effect perfectly, but she puts it on a calf. Her written comment was: "Belly-band on calf."
>
> While Craig was making this particular experiment, her husband was reading a book: and now, wishing to solve the mystery, she asks, "What are you reading?" The husband replies, wearily: "DeKruif's *Hunger Fighters*, page 283." "What does it deal with?" "It is a treatise on the feeding of cows." "Really?" says Craig. "Will you please write that down for me and sign it?"
>
> But why did the cow become a calf? ... Says Craig: "Do you remember what I used to tell you about old Mr. Bebb and his calves?" ... Old Mr. Bebb made his hobby the raising of calves by hand, and turning them into parlor pets. He would teach them to use his three fingers as a nursing bottle, and would make fancy embroidered belly-bands for them, and tie them up in these. So to the subconscious mind which was once little Mary Craig Kimbrough of Mississippi, the idea of a calf sewed up like a football is one of the most natural in the world.[52]

Just as Dunne's dream of Lieutenant Bettington was a hybrid of the real crash he was going to read about two days later and what he was going to wrongly assume had caused it based on limited prior knowledge, Craig's image was an amalgam of the simple football image she would find her husband had drawn and her own free associations to the book he told her he had been reading at the time. Effectively, she was precognizing everything about this interaction, including her associations to things her husband told her about what he was reading, not just the drawing he had made.[53] The fact that Upton's main emotion during his experiments with Craig seemed to be bemusement at his "witch wife" further supports the idea that Craig was really a precog and not a telepath, since mild bemusement and distraction are not exactly the kinds of extreme emotionality that Myers had theorized is needed to power some psychic broadcast mind-to-mind.[54]

Further supporting the precognition-as-future-memory hypothesis, the side-by-side drawings Upton reproduces in the book, like those of other ostensible telepathy experiments utilizing drawings, strongly resemble memory experiments, such as those Jean Piaget later conducted with children in his studies of cognitive developmental milestones. The deviations between the drawings Upton made and those Craig made sometimes resemble the kinds of fragility of memory that brief exposure, long intervening time, or incomplete understanding may produce.

The BLACK MAGICIAN episode also reveals something else, though—another dimension of the phenomenon that, like an X-ray, illuminates all the other episodes in *Mental Radio* too, as well as many of the cases we're going to examine throughout this book. The theme of Romondt's chapter XXI, capturing another person's desire via a kind of psychic ability, was exactly what Craig was constantly doing with Upton, albeit in a less secretive way and with less sinister intent than the hypnotist Philip Ravenna in *Patricia*. I wonder if Craig noticed this formal resonance between her situation and that of the character. There is what I have called elsewhere a kind of "fractal geometry of prophecy," a tendency of psychically divined situations and objects to uncannily mirror the larger context in which they arise, similar to the recursiveness or self-similarity of fractal-geometric forms in mathematics.[55] Stories about impossible or psychic phenomena somehow magnetize the psychic mind. We precognize precognition. Like a fragment of a hologram containing a low-resolution version of the entire image, these specific instances of future-divining have a funny way of reflecting the larger contours of the precognitive individual's long self.

In anecdotes of psychic phenomena, a pattern recurs like a refrain: Someone has a dream or a vision or a flash of insight about some impossible-to-know state of affairs, and that state of affairs is shortly thereafter confirmed by a reading experience or a conversation with another person. Or, someone suddenly, randomly thinks about a person and shortly finds out an important piece of news about that person. Maybe the news is serious, like a death. A man thinks he glimpses an old college friend out the window and goes outside to find him—he's not there—but then comes inside, picks up a newspaper, and reads that friend's obituary (another example from one of Myers' books[56]). But it happens around other kinds of upheavals, and can manifest in other ways, including creativity: A comic book artist writes a story about his protagonist's mate being held at gunpoint by a hooded intruder, only to go into his kitchen to find his wife being held at gunpoint by a hooded intruder—a true, terrifying story that happened to *Planet of the Apes* artist Doug Moench in the late 1970s, related by Jeffrey Kripal in *Mutants and Mystics*.[57]

Those "scenes of confirmation"—when the accuracy of the experience is learned, often with some powerful emotion like surprise or shock—are typically overlooked by experiencers, who may not think to question their assumptions that some mind-to-mind (or perhaps, soul to soul) transmission or projection of thoughts has occurred. But details sometimes provide tracers showing that people are really precognizing those confirmatory moments or encounters. They may be profoundly meaningful experiences.[58] The beguilement of telepathy—that handy concept, still perhaps one of the few words in the average person's vocabulary of the psychic, with its tele- (spatial distance) implication—prevents us from contemplating that the individual has more likely foreseen, fore-felt, or imaginatively pre-experienced an important learning experience or real-world encounter ahead in their own future.[59]

Parapsychologists are not immune to the human tendency to turn complex and loopy temporal relationships into less intimidating spatial ones, even as further technological and social transformations have provided new metaphors for the phenomena they study. The rise of television in the second half of the 20th century greatly enhanced the thinkability of clairvoyance (versus telepathy) for instance, and it is no accident that in the TV age it was this psychic modality that came to dominate the interest of ESP researchers. In the 1970s, CIA-funded researchers in California rebranded clairvoyance as remote viewing—literally, tele-vision—developing and training this ability for intelligence-gathering purposes. But like early studies of telepathy, remote viewing experiments may often have been testing participants' precognition of the feedback they would receive subsequently, either when shown how well they had performed or even by reading the published papers and books of the researchers studying them.[60] Military remote viewers sometimes claim they didn't as a matter of course get feedback on their highly secret assignments, yet they often did learn informally when they were accurate, sometimes even in television news broadcasts.[61]

While subsequent advances in communications technology like the internet and virtual reality have further upped the metaphoric ante on the impossible,[62] none of them have helped move either the scientific or humanistic understanding of psychic phenomena beyond a mainly spatial framing. Even quantum entanglement, a popular metaphor of the last few decades, returns us to a spatial framing, as most people conceive of the "nonlocality" entanglement implies as a collapsing of spatial distances. In fact, some of the most interesting thinking about entanglement in physics is now suggesting that it may specifically be a time-related phenomenon having to do with retrocausation.[63]

Whether ESP is really "precognition only" is an ongoing debate in parapsychology, and there are interesting reasons why it would be very hard to distinguish between precognition and telepathy or clairvoyance in most cases. Yet again, when there are tracers of the sort that were forensically valuable to Dunne—such as discrepancies between a real event and how it is reported—they very often point to that less-easy-to-think precognition as the guilty party. However counterintuitive, it is really a simpler explanation and is also, oddly enough, more physically plausible than the alternatives. Science has never discovered mesmeric currents or any waves, fields, or energies that could carry information psychically mind-to-mind, but the body itself is a physical conduit connecting the individual to other points in their timeline, future as well as past. It's why I pin my hopes for the future of the super not on "nonlocal consciousness," a favorite of some New Age authors, but on that most maligned of meats, the body.

Explosion in a Shingle Factory

One of the bibles of the human potential movement is *The Future of the Body* by Michael Murphy, co-founder of the famous Esalen retreat in

Big Sur, California. The book is a massive compendium of research on human superabilities, including enhanced athletic performance and extraordinary psychic and spiritual experience. I've always liked Murphy's title, because of its emphasis on super-bodies, not just (as is typical in popular ESP writing) super-minds. The body is like a fiber-optic communications cable through the fourth dimension. It is literally a higher-dimensional object.

In the 1880s, contemporary with Myers' work on telepathy, two other English thinkers, mathematician Charles Howard Hinton and Cambridge theologian Edwin A. Abbott, tried to get people to imagine the world in four dimensions. Hinton's 1888 book *A New Era of Thought* described exercises to help readers mentally picture four-dimensional versions of familiar three-dimensional solids, such as the "hypercube."[64] The term he coined for higher-dimensional objects, *tesseracts*, later became a favorite of 20th-century science-fiction writers. Better remembered today, though, is Abbott's 1884 fable *Flatland*, which took a slightly more oblique, allegorical approach to his subject. In his story, a two-dimensional mathematician named A. Square is visited by a Sphere from three-dimensional Spaceland. A circle (a cross-section of the Sphere) is all A. Square's Flatlander senses can perceive of this visitor, and then it contracts to a point and vanishes. Appearing out of nowhere and disappearing again is behavior not unheard of in UFO reports of the following century, incidentally; and then in a scene uncannily like a UFO abduction, the Sphere lifts his frightened flat friend out of Flatland altogether to give him an awe-inspiring higher perspective: A. Square can then see inside closed buildings and has other "impossible" (or perhaps "clairvoyant") perceptions. When the Sphere returns A. Square to his flat world, nobody believes his account of what he experienced, and he is imprisoned as a heretic.

Because Einstein and relativity were still in their future, neither Hinton nor Abbott grasped that time itself was the fourth dimension they were searching for. It was Einstein's genius that pointed us to the fact that we ourselves, or at least our physical bodies, already occupy that higher dimension. The body is actually a hyperbody, a tesseract. Early in the 20th century, the French Surrealist painter and sculptor Marcel Duchamp was fascinated by theorizing about higher dimensions; Octavio Paz quoted him as saying, "Since a three-dimensional object casts a two-dimensional shadow, we should be able to imagine the unknown four-dimensional object whose shadow we are."[65] This idea informed Duchamp's unfinished 1923 masterpiece *The Large Glass*, but the first, and still the best, artistic representation of that four-dimensional hyperbody is the artist's 1912 painting *Nude Descending a Staircase, No. 2*. Inspired by Eadweard Muybridge's late-19th-century photographic studies of human and animal motion, it depicts in Cubist style a human figure walking down stairs, seemingly stretched through time, a bit like a long-exposure photograph. It is one of the most famous 20th-century artworks, and it almost singlehandedly secured Duchamp's place among the pantheon of great 20th-century artists, although at the time it scandalized people. When the painting was first exhibited in New York in 1913, one critic said it looked like an "explosion in a shingle factory."[66]

That unknown four-dimensional being hinted at by Duchamp's descending nude is what I refer to as the long self. Just extend that figure over the decades of a full human lifespan—not merely a worldline but a world-serpent of truly massive proportions, wending and twisting and snaking its way downstairs and upstairs, this way and that, through the block universe. It is that serpentine body, including (but not limited to) its nervous system, that not only carries information forward through time as memory but also carries it backward through time as what we call precognition. And it is almost entirely an *un*conscious thing—outside of, and for really interesting reasons we will be exploring throughout this book, actually *evading*, our conscious awareness.

Consciousness is mostly if not entirely 3-D, bound to the present moment, a mere cross-section of the long self, whereas our bodies are the 4-D entities that cause paranormal effects in the Flatland of consciousness. In other words, even though our bodies are long, our minds are flat. Instead of the body "descending" into that flat consciousness like a baffling UFO, as Abbott's visiting Sphere does, it is conscious awareness that is somehow compelled to traverse the elongated hyperbody in a single direction across time, like the cursor in a video-editing program or like the scan-bar in a Xerox machine moving slowly left to right across the lived text of the individual. Again, the reasons for this are a mystery—and it may in fact be an illusion—but better understanding precognition is probably a necessary step to unlocking it.

Even in altered states of higher or expanded "cosmic" consciousness, and even in the most vivid precognitive dreams and visions, other times in our biography appear transfigured and symbolically transformed, reduced or filtered through the conceptual frame of our narrow, flat, cursor-like present self. Our thoughts and feelings at other times are personified and embodied in human or human-like beings unrecognizable as ourselves, which we encounter and experience as

Other. We'll examine the very Einsteinian as well as Freudian reasons for this transfiguration in your very near future, Chapters 3 and 4. Suffice it to say, now, that if consciousness were "inflated" into something four-dimensional without gross reduction or simplification of the long self's contents, things would quickly get impossibly complicated and confused, not unlike the mashed-together density of text in a closed book … or an explosion in a shingle factory.

3

No Backstory
Precognition and the Unconscious

*[T]he future is more coherent than the present, more
animate and purposeful, and in a real sense, wiser.
It* knows *more, and some of this knowledge gets
transmitted back to us by what seems to be a purely
natural phenomenon. We are being talked to, by a very
informed Entity: that of all creation as it lies ahead of us
in time.*
—Philip K. Dick, Letter to Peter Fitting
(June 28, 1974)

In the problem space of this book, there is a Venn diagram with two
circles, Precognition and Inspiration. It is one thing to point to an
artwork or piece of literature and then to some subsequent event that it
supposedly prophesied and assume that it is a case where those circles
overlapped somehow. I suggest that with Mark Twain and Craig Sinclair, we have something more specific and valuable: two striking, well-
described instances in which the exotic, super, paranormal phenomenon
of precognition has been caught red-handed, so to speak, masquerading
as "mere" literary inspiration. The question then becomes: If it sometimes happens that inspiration is demonstrably precognitive, could it
often or even always be true? Are these two circles in fact the same
circle? Do they, like Clark Kent and Superman, share a secret identity?
These are the questions we will now examine more closely.

I think the famous "out of nowhere" quality of inspiration—the way
many of the best ideas come as foreign to one's thoughts (as Twain put
it)—could be an important clue. It is most often nowadays explained as
a submerged or subterranean unconscious, operating in parallel, busily
mulling some problem—those "boys in the basement" Stephen King

imagines solving creative problems behind the scenes. But this idea, and the psychoanalytic metapsychology at its root, may really be another of those "meanwhiles" living on like a revenant past the demise of aethers, mesmeric currents, and other relics of Victorian science. What if there is be *no backstory at all* to a truly new idea?

Although the unconscious has older roots than Sigmund Freud, it was his brilliant writing and theorizing around the turn of the last century in Vienna that made especially thinkable a basement with boys laboring in it. The main product of their labor, of course, was dreams, and it was a dream on the night of July 23-24, 1895, that gave Freud his breakthrough insight.

Freud was then a young maverick psychiatrist, attempting a brand-new, yet-unnamed approach to treating hysterics, but with only limited success. While on vacation at a rented house called Bellevue outside of town, he awoke from a remarkable dream in which he and some physician friends were examining one of his patients, a recently widowed childhood friend of his named Anna Hammerschlag, although he gave her the name "Irma" when writing about this dream. In the dream, Anna/Irma appeared reluctant or unable to open her mouth, as though she wore dentures. Then, inside her mouth, he observed white patches, scabs, and features resembling the turbinal bones in the nose. He determined that her malady was caused by an injection from a dirty syringe that one of his doctor friends, his family pediatrician Otto, had administered. The dream ended with the formula for an organic chemical, trimethylamine, in bold type.[1]

The dream excited Freud greatly, for he thought he could tell what it was about. Various forms of medical malpractice had lately been committed by his friends in the dream and, to a lesser extent, by himself. Moreover, he had just learned secondhand, from that pediatrician in fact, that Anna had not improved from her melancholy—she did not actually have the physical maladies he saw in his dream—despite his recent treatment of her. (His treatment included a suggestion that she somehow find a way to gratify her unmet sexual needs.) So his dream, he deduced, symbolically fulfilled his wish that he be blameless for her non-recovery—deflecting blame onto the other guilty doctors in the group, including Otto.

The dream of Irma's injection became what Freud called the "specimen" case of his new method of dream interpretation, the centerpiece of what became psychoanalysis. In the unconscious, he argued, we harbor unresolved complexes from childhood and morally and socially unacceptable desires and animosities. A censor in the mind keeps these thoughts and feelings out of our awareness, but they find oblique expression in neurotic obsessions and compulsions, in psychosomatic symptoms such as hysterical reactions, and in everyday forms of "psychopathology" like slips of the tongue, recurring mishaps, and irrational intrusive thoughts. And they especially find expression nightly in our dreams. Dreams meaningfully relate, Freud thought, to our repressed wishes, disguising them in a kind of symbolic code—a fact that could be discovered with the help of an analyst guiding the patient in the activity of *free-association*, getting the dreamer to state what each remembered element in a dream reminded them of.[2]

The governing principle of Freud's unconscious, at least as he formulated it in his earliest works, was pleasure. In accordance with the pleasure principle, and issuing from our most basic drives such as sex, dreams and other products of the unconscious flexibly and fluidly assemble mental associations based on life experience into images and scenarios that provide pleasure by imaginatively fulfilling our wishes. What he called *primary-process* thinking is an effortless and spontaneous—and undeniably ingenious—creative activity of the mind. Free association is essentially the primary process in reverse, decoding the dream by tracing the dream's images (the manifest content) back to their sources in the dreamer's unacknowledged or repressed thoughts and desires, via the same chains of mental association that the dreaming brain had used to concoct the dream in the first place (what Freud called the "dream-work"). For Freud, free-associating on our dreams was what he called the "royal road to the unconscious."[3]

The Interpretation of Dreams was written and published in 1899, but Freud was so sure his book would redefine psychiatry for the new century that he asked his publisher to put 1900 on it. It was truly ahead of its time, including in some ways Freud had not intended or hoped.

Nearly two and a half decades after Freud wrote his book, in 1923, his doctors discovered an oral cancer, the result of decades smoking his famous cigars. It manifested initially as a white patch (leukoplakia) at the back of his mouth, just like what he had seen in Anna's mouth in his dream almost three decades earlier. He was forced to undergo a series of terrible surgeries that left him with permanent scabs—again, like Anna—and, finally, the loss of his palate and part of his jaw. The removal of his palate would have meant that features in his nose (the turbinal bones) were visible from inside his mouth. In the last 15 years of his life he had to wear a monstrous denture that prevented him from opening his mouth or, for the most part, talking.[4]

For those who believe in dream precognition, as Freud did not, the conclusion is hard to avoid: The dream was a premonition. His friend and patient Anna seems to have been a stand-in, like a dream stunt double, for himself 28 years later. The dream even specifically contained what could be considered his own reproach at himself from that 28-year distance: "It's really only your fault," he told Anna, in the dream.[5] At the time he had the dream, he had just resumed smoking, against his friend Wilhelm Fliess's advice—Fliess was another of the doctors in the dream. In hindsight—because his 1923 doctors told him so—he knew full well that it was his cigar habit (symbolically, injection with a dirty syringe) that had given him cancer.

Although Freud himself didn't draw the connection, the final dream-image, the formula for an organic chemical in bold type, may have alluded to German chemist August Kekulé's then-recent, already-famous claim to have discovered the hexagonal-structure of the benzene molecule during a hypnagogic reverie of snakes eating their own tails, while he dozed in front of a fire. (Hypnagogic images are the brief, dreamlike scenes and situations glimpsed while falling asleep.) So this formula could be read as another precognitive element: Somehow, even before Freud awoke, his dream "knew," and was signaling to him, that it was to be the basis of his scientific glory, the same way Kekulé's hypnagogic reverie had been.[6]

Memory for Things Future

As we saw in the last chapter, J. W. Dunne brought to his study of precognitive dreams a keen forensic mind, testing and ruling out several then-common assumptions about why psychic dreams occur. His major insight has held up well in more recent research on the subject: Despite the beguiling metaphors based on the advanced telecommunications technologies of his era, dreams that seem, on the surface, like telegraph- or radio-like communication mind-to-mind, across space, are more likely to be chronophone calls from the dreamer's future self. It's an important distinction. It means, for one thing, that dreams do not bring us objective, accurate information about distant or future events. (A telephone caller can be mistaken or deceived, and so can the chronophone caller, oneself.) Rather, dreams seem to be previews of exciting or troubling experiences, including learning experiences, awaiting us—more akin to memory than perception, in other words, but running in reverse. Agreeing with this model, many parapsychologists have invoked Proust, describing precognition as "memory for things future."[7]

Like ordinary Proustian memory for things past, we seem to pre-cognize episodes in our future that affect us emotionally—episodes when we will be excited, scared, embarrassed, relieved, grateful, otherwise moved, or very often some mix of positive and negative emotions. Such episodes are exactly the sorts of things that get coded as memorable and retained in long-term autobiographical memory. One thing now known about ordinary memory is that what we remember of past experiences is really our memories of our memories, and that our memories gradually depart significantly from what really happened. It's likely that something like this happens in reverse with precognition: We pre-member our pre-membering of some future event, perhaps many future iterations of pre-membering, and thus should never expect a dream to any more closely resemble the real future experience, once we live through it, than we should expect a memory to resemble a real past experience as it may have been captured on some secret smartphone video. Memory is fluid and sometimes unreliable, and that is likely true whichever direction it goes in time.

That said, memories can sometimes be vividly clear and relatively accurate, especially if they center on something emotionally arousing, and especially if the emotion is negative. That could make sense of why published reports of vivid, accurate precognitive dreams tend to be pre-monitions of fearful or distressing events like terror attacks, assassinations, and plane crashes. A modern well-documented case of dreaming as clear future-memory involves Elizabeth Krohn, a Houston, Texas, mother and grandmother who began having accurate dreams about imminent disasters in the news, usually air crashes, after she was struck by lightning in the parking lot of her synagogue in 1988.[8] Similar to David Mandell, who authenticated his dream-watercolors by having himself photographed with them under his bank's clock showing the date, Krohn learned to send herself date- and time-stamped emails to authenticate her disaster dreams and verify that they preceded the foreseen news events.

On January 15, 2009, for instance, while on a trip to Israel, Krohn emailed herself a dream of an American jet making a water landing in New York and told her husband that the passengers were bizarrely standing on the wings. Six hours later, Chesley Sullenberger piloted his

US Airways jet to a safe landing on the Hudson River (the "Miracle on the Hudson"). Images of passengers lined up along the wings, awaiting rescue, flooded the media. On February 2, 2015, Krohn emailed herself a dream that a passenger plane with propellers, one wing straight up, crashed in Asia. A day and a half later, such a crash happened in Taipei, Taiwan, and a dashcam image of exactly what she had seen went viral on the internet. In another case, she dreamed of being on a flight from Buenos Aires to Barcelona that was about to crash in the Atlantic Ocean. In the dream, she comforted two Dutch passengers, a mother and her son. The crash that hit the headlines the next day matched her dream—there were no survivors—and the names of the passengers she had comforted were on the list of people killed. Researching the crash later, she read a human-interest story about the two passengers she had dreamed of comforting.[9]

As Dunne's theory would predict, Krohn's dreams closely corresponded to what she was going to see or read about the crashes, not necessarily the events themselves.[10] In the first two cases, her dream images visually matched viral photographs she and the world were about to see. Even more strikingly, the two Dutch passengers she encountered in her dream of the Atlantic crash were exactly the two she later read an article about—an impossible coincidence unless it was that article itself that was in fact the precognitive source of her dream. Like Dunne's dream about Lieutenant Bettington, Krohn's dream appears to have been supplemented by her imagination, based on her future reading.

Although most commonly reported to parapsychology researchers, premonitions about plane crashes and other tragedies are probably in the minority of precognitive dreams. Those who record their dreams and are alert for possible precognition in their journals find they dream with strange persistence about relatively mundane occurrences (a clogged sink, a frustrating situation at work, an interesting conversation with a friend) unfolding over the next few days. And like ordinary memory, precognition not only brings us foreshadowings of real situations we find ourselves in but also news stories as well as fictional stories or scenes in movies and TV shows.[11] The Russian-American novelist Vladimir Nabokov was fascinated by dreams, and by carefully recording his dreams on notecards, he successfully replicated Dunne's "experiment with time" over the course of a month in 1964. Among his precognitive "hits" were bizarre episodes that closely matched highly singular scenes in TV programs he would watch within days of the dream. In one case, he dreamed of being on a cliff by the ocean, which broke off the mainland to become an island-like ocean liner. It exactly matched a scene from a fantastical French children's cartoon he watched the next day.[12]

Dreams about big life events years and even decades in the future are also commonly reported, and that makes Freud's "specimen dream" far less unlikely-seeming as a premonition. For instance, long before he became a famous writer, the teenage Nabokov seemed set for a life of leisure when his uncle Vasily died and left him an estate outside St. Petersburg. But a year later, the 17-year-old Nabokov's estate and wealth were swept away, along with the old Tsarist order, by the Russian Revolution. He was forced into exile with his family. During this time, his dead uncle appeared in a dream and promised to return to him as "Harry and Kuvyrkin," names that the young Nabokov interpreted as circus performers (*kuvyrok*, the basis for Kuvyrkin, means "somersault"). But more than four decades later, then an émigré writer making a modest living teaching literature at Cornell University, Nabokov got the wonderful news that he was once again, for the first time since his youth, a wealthy man: *Harris and Kubrick* Pictures, Stanley Kubrick's production company, had bought the movie rights for his novel *Lolita* for a hefty sum. When anglicized, the circus performer Kuvyrkin in his dream would be Kubrick.[13] His wealthy benefactor had indeed, in some sense, returned to him.

When Dunne formulated his theory of dream precognition in *An Experiment with Time*, he humbly deferred to Freud by fitting his theory into that of the Viennese dream pioneer:

> Many people, I hear, suppose that there is some clash between serialism and the "wish-fulfillment" theory of dreams. There is none. "Wish-fulfillment" theories are concerned with explaining why the dreamer builds a particular dream edifice: I am interested in the quite different question of whence he collects the bricks.[14]

Dunne should have been less humble, I believe. It would be putting the cart before the horse to say that dreams perform the astonishing feat of reaching into our futures just to retrieve some symbolic "bricks" to help us disguise our current embarrassing wishes. If our dreaming mind is really able to retrieve information from the future, it reasonably must play some important psychological role, probably even a survival-related role. Precognition could be central to dreaming's function. Consequently, I like to flip Dunne's formulation: Instead of reaching into the future for the bricks to represent present wishes, dreams seem to pre-present future experiences and thoughts (including future wishes) using images and associations that are already available in memory, including memories of the past few days (Freud's "day residues"). A dream, I argue, is like a future tower assembled from the bricks of our immediate and more distant past.[15]

Freud's specimen dream for his vaunted dream theory is, I believe, an exquisite example of this principle. It consisted of people and situations already in his life in 1895, but these situations seem like characters and stage props helping depict a mixture of realizations, reproaches, and wishes he would harbor in his tumultuous early sixties, looking back on his blithe late 30s when he had the dream. I suggest the dream pre-presented not only the dreadful news of his illness and its progression after surgeries but also a self-reproach for his history of cigar use ("It's really only your fault"). And the dream-theory that he wove around this premonition—that dreams are just wish-fulfillments and not prophecies—was itself the fulfillment of a wish from that future vantage point: It effectively wished away his cancer as well as imaginatively preserved his conscience from any self-doubt that he had missed something essential about the nature of dreaming.[16]

Freud can be forgiven for not believing in dream precognition. We saw how Frederic Myers' telepathy theory was the dominant framing of psychic phenomena around the turn of the century and in the first several decades of the 20th century. Precognition as we now conceive it was not readily thinkable with the metaphors provided by the technologies of the telegraph and radio eras. Probably for that reason, Freud, like most scientists, refused to believe it was a possibility, even though he was open to telepathy and even wrote on what he called "thought transference" late in his career. Freud never publicly acknowledged any relationship between his 1895 dream and his 1923 cancer and surgeries, and we can only speculate whether he noticed the connection and felt any misgivings or doubts about his own dream theory as a result.

But one thing that the study of precognition shows is that we are not necessarily meant to consciously understand the precognitive content of our dreams. If precognition prepares us somehow for future experiences, such as perhaps preparing us for surprises and cushioning us against traumas—a reasonable hypothesis worth exploring and testing—then it is probably sufficient for it to operate largely in the background, outside of conscious awareness. In fact, the commonly heard idea that precognitive dreams always feel special or "numinous," or that they are especially vivid and memorable (as famous psychic Ingo Swann asserted[17]), is wrong.[18] So is the familiar assumption that premonitions are always warnings that we fail to notice or heed at our peril. The latter idea in fact may be inconsistent with both logic and physical law. The physical rules governing time travel—including time-traveling information—can help explain why.

Einsteinian physics allows for the extreme bending of the fabric of spacetime, bringing two distant points, even two distant times, into contact. Sometimes depicted in science diagrams as coffee-mug-handle-like tubes connecting two distant regions, wormholes are really the somewhat harder to visualize overlap of those two locations (the wormhole "mouths"), the fabric of spacetime being drawn together like a folded piece of paper or the wrinkled cloth of a dress. The latter was the image used by Madeleine L'Engle in her classic 1962 young-adult novel *A Wrinkle in Time*.[19] The term *wormhole* had not yet been coined, so she used Charles Howard Hinton's Victorian term *tesseract* to describe such a fold.[20] It's a notion that remained mostly speculative for decades, but in the early 1980s, thanks to growing interest in things like warp drives and hyperspace in then-recent science fiction, physicists in the U.S. and U.S.S.R. started exploring the real possibilities of rapid travel between distant points in spacetime via such exotica. They made an interesting, in fact crucial discovery about a problem that had always supplied fodder for pulp science fiction writers: the possibility of traveling into the past and causing a so-called "grandfather paradox" by changing history. That is, if you go in a time machine and kill your grandfather when young, there's no possibility of you being born … so who could have gone back in time to kill your grandfather?

Appropriately enough for the investigation of causation and retrocausation, these physicists—including the famous Kip Thorne, who worked with director Christopher Nolan designing the black hole and wormhole in the movie *Interstellar*—modeled the problem using billiard balls shot through wormholes to collide with themselves in the past. They found something reassuring: Shooting a billiard ball back in time to deflect its younger self off course, away from the wormhole mouth, always fails. The math shows that the ball always deflects itself *toward* the wormhole instead, ensuring that history is undamaged and that the universe is self-consistent.[21] It may be this law, known as the Novikov self-consistency principle (after Russian physicist Igor Novikov), that makes retrocausation (a form of informational time travel) hard to detect, even if it is ubiquitous. Any flow of information from the future into the past will always influence the past in such a way that the future is exactly the same. No paradoxes occur. Causation includes retrocausation; the two are inextricable.

Prophecies, by such a law, must always be self-fulfilling, and this has amazing implications for the understanding of dreams: *You are never going to have a completely accurate and clear precognitive dream about an outcome you would and could intercede to prevent.* It's not that the causality police will swoop down in their flying saucers to stop you; it's just that, from a future vantage point farther along your world-line in the block universe, it didn't happen. No amount of searching in hindsight will find spent causal arrows for an impossible event. *Things that couldn't happen, never did.*

According to this view, premonitions of dangers averted don't represent those dangers per se but, rather, the troubled thoughts and emotions experienced in the aftermath of a close call. For instance, in a case recorded by parapsychologist Louisa Rhine in her book *Hidden Channels of the Mind*, a woman in Washington State had a vivid dream in which her baby was crushed to death by a chandelier that had been hanging over the crib, with the clock on the bureau reading 4:35. Defying her husband's urging to just ignore the dream and go back to sleep, she went and got their baby and brought her into their bed to sleep. Two hours later, they were awakened by a loud crash in the nursery. The chandelier had indeed crashed into the crib, and the clock on the bureau read (of course) 4:35.

Had the mother's dream accurately showed her an event in a possible future, "a timeline not taken"? I really doubt there's some other, parallel universe where the woman's baby was in the crib when the chandelier fell, and that this is what the mother's dream keyed into. Parallel universes and timelines are special pleading that don't really help us understand precognition—nor, despite claims to the contrary, is there any empirical evidence for them.[22] Instead, it is simplest to think that the dream accurately showed the dreamer her own horrified imagining of a terrible possibility, a "what if" (what if she'd ignored her dream) that the fall of the chandelier would provoke in her a couple hours later. Thankfully, because this terrible mental image refluxed in time and caught her awareness earlier, and she acted on it, her baby was with her and not in the nursery when the chandelier fell. Because of her action, her dream became part of a causally circular "time loop" formation in the block universe. It is that circularity that throws people off, but time loops should really be inevitable in a universe that includes time travel and precognition.

We should not confuse our imagination, our ability to picture non-existent worlds and counterfactual realities (or our ability to picture the universe from an imagined vantage point outside history), with real perception. It's all a brain-generated hologram, a creation of the imagination. Information from the future is filtered through that imagination, just like memory and perception are.

Again, it is looking more and more like present reality arises from the intersection of causes propagating backward as well as forward in time, and that the blizzard of future-originating information carried backward along particles' worldlines, historically mistaken for "randomness," can be made coherent and scaled up in special exotic environments like quantum computers and tesseract brains.[23] But however coherent, retro-flowing information cannot travel in straight lines, bringing unambiguous video-quality previews of avoidable outcomes. The spacetime of the long self of a freely willed being is curved—not by massive objects like stars and black holes, but by existential perils as well as painful or just guilt-inducing situations that we would avoid or change if we knew about them. A kind of gravitational lensing bends information around these troubling psychosexual and existential vortices and prevents us from seeing them directly or interpreting them accurately.

I argue that it is this, and not Freud's "repression," that explains why the unconscious speaks in symbols. Those symbols are the obliquely aimed billiard balls shot back in time through wormholes from our older selves, deflecting us toward a future in which we graze grave or troubling outcomes but don't collide with them (usually). This in fact precisely describes Freud's story: He suffered for years as a result of his cancer, but he actually survived it, and even wrote some of his most important books during that last decade and a half when he could barely open his mouth. His genius flourished in the margin between truth and error, which was (for him, at least) also a margin between life and death. As weird as Freud's story seems, it appears to be a familiar pattern in the lives of creative people whose careers depend on their prophecies, even if they mistake their prophecies as insight or inspiration, as they are bound to. We'll see other examples of the same pattern.

What makes Freud's story doubly fascinating is the centrality of the story of Oedipus in his thinking. If all you knew of the Greek myth (and Sophocles' play *Oedipus the King*) was via Freud's "Oedipus complex," you'd think it was just a story about a man killing his father and marrying his mother. For Freud, the patricidal and incestuous dimensions were all that was important, and these were what his theory of repression focused on. But in the story, Oedipus commits those unspeakable crimes unknowingly because he is attempting to evade a prophecy that he will commit them. It is a story about fulfilling a foretold fate precisely by trying to evade it. For the Greeks, who believed in prophecy and divination (and in fact had some pretty sophisticated theories about it), this is precisely what could make a person's life tragic. And it is exactly what Freud did with the very dream that put him on the scientific map. You couldn't ask for a better, more Freudian irony than the irony that made Freud himself a tragic figure. That he seems to have ended his dream with a reference to Kekulé's dream-ouroboroses is only the "chef's kiss" capper of this perfectly loopy, specimen case of the essentially precognitive nature of dreaming.

Most people considering the evidence for precognitive dreams have continued to regard it as an occasional wonder of the dreamlife and have not bothered to ask: Why, if dreams occasionally do this, don't they always do it? It's a question that answers itself, I think: It's quite possible they *do* always do it and that we just don't notice. Precognition is so counterintuitive, and so "impossible" within at least our taken-for-granted Enlightenment assumptions about causation, that even people who are persuaded it can happen—perhaps because they have noticed it once or twice in their own dreams—still imagine it must somehow be a strenuous feat of nature, something reserved for rare occasions or big explosive disasters like 9/11 that are able to bend the fabric of spacetime with their awfulness. But it is a fallacy to suppose that something hard for us to imagine is therefore difficult for nature to accomplish.[24] If that were the case, most ubiquitous natural processes—the evaporation of water, DNA replication, or quantum entanglement—would be rarities too. Assuming there is a natural explanation forthcoming—and cupping my ear, I can hear it chugging down the tracks toward us already—then we can no longer think of precognition as a feat; it is simply a feature. The supposed or presumed rarity of precognition in dreams could be a function of the fact that people have never thought to look for it systematically and lacked the metaphors to help think about how it could be possible.

Dunne's *An Experiment with Time* was an important, indeed landmark step in the right direction. It was really a pioneering effort at what we would now call citizen science, recruiting the public to participate in an exciting new psychological frontier. How many readers performed his experiment by recording and looking for precognition in their own dreams will never be known. But we know that many prominent writers of the era, including C. S. Lewis, T. S. Eliot, and J. R. R. Tolkien, were fans of his book and that some writers, like Nabokov, actually carried out his experiment successfully. Like others who have followed Dunne's instructions, I have found in my own life and in my work with other dreamers that once ordinary, non-"psychic" people can be retrained to record their dreams and use their records to look for links to subsequent experiences, clear or at least highly suggestive instances of precognition appear commonly in their journals. Consequently, I hypothesize that precognition could be basic to dreams' functioning, hardly a rarity at all.

Here, I am suggesting that the same may be true of the arts, which have often been compared to public dreams.

In fact, precognition is much easier studied in the arts than in dreams. Dreams are intensely private affairs and are difficult to subject to objective scrutiny for a host of practical and logistical reasons. But works of art and literature almost by definition leave a public and more-or-less permanent trace. They can be compared to later events, reasonably if not exactly scientifically. And best of all, if we know anything about the artist's biography—as we often do when they are famous—then it is possible to examine the relationships between their works and their lives in much greater detail than is possible with most other kinds of claimed precognitive experiences. In other words, once our eyes are opened to it, art and literature could really be the privileged window into the hitherto hidden fourth-dimensionality of our minds, the precognitive imagination's royal road.

Unasked and Uninvited

There are few more nebulous, slippery, liminal, and powerful words than *imagination*. Among people who have had extraordinary, mystical, or supernormal experiences, there is a kind of natural distrust of this word, since it is so routinely used by skeptical authorities to invalidate such experiences, taking that term to mean "not real"—the product of mere hallucination or self-deception, or just failure to understand how the real world works. The condescending expressions that greet disclosures of UFO sightings or precognitive dreams are similar to the looks parents give to children reporting monsters in the closet or under the bed. For that reason, few sympathetic writers on paranormal topics have engaged meaningfully with the imagination, perhaps fearful of going down a path that opens the door to easy debunking. But as Jeffrey Kripal argues, it is via the imagination that supernormal experiences are, well, experienced. It's never not that way. "The imagination is the ultimate framework that makes any event plausible or implausible, possible or impossible."[25]

Kripal argues that Krohn's experiences, for instance, have been shaped by her own beliefs and expectations as well as by culturally available models and symbols.[26] Her life as a psychic dreamer began with a vivid and subjectively lengthy near-death experience after her lightning strike; although she came to after about 15 minutes, she spent what felt like two weeks in a lush extraterrestrial garden. UFO experiences similarly resemble and sometimes seem modeled on available imagery in popular culture—they are "mediated"—which, however, does not necessarily make these experiences any less real, since those pop-culture images were themselves based on earlier artists' and writers' real experiences, in turn.[27] Kripal describes the religious imagination, and the paranormal more generally, as the product of a "constant loop between Consciousness and Culture."[28]

When I set out to write this book on the precognitive powers of the imagination, I thought I'd be able, as part of it, to tell a compelling just-so story about our culture's progressive devaluing of the imagination relative to other kinds of thinking or ways of knowing.[29] But turns out, it's really not so simple. Imagination has always been problematic. Even in antiquity and the middle ages, it held associations of ignorance, illusion, and error and seems to have always been used the same way skeptics now use it, to diminish and debunk "wonders" that don't fit the writer's preferred story. Yet at the same time, imagination always (including today) has gone along with other capacities and functions of the psyche or soul as a necessary aid and even redeeming feature, pointing us beyond the limitations of the currently known and reasonable, supplementing, creating, and innovating. It has always "troubled" the boundaries between the internal and external world, the real and the illusory, and the established and the possible.[30] And there has never been a clear and coherent—or at least consensus—theory of it, even though many philosophers and psychologists and poets across the millennia have made attempts. The best anybody can ever do is theorize the imagination through what amounts to works of the imagination, the imagination imagining itself.[31]

Psychic experiences, too, are thoroughly mediated by the imagination, and on multiple levels. The way they are interpreted is shaped, as we've seen, by cultural models and framings, including metaphors taken from communications technology. And as Craig Sinclair and Dunne discovered, psychic information is supplemented by the psychic's own suppositions, which are products of the imagination too. What people precognize is often their own later waking thoughts, including thoughts about things they will read or learn about. One of the recurring—in fact, almost constant—themes in the study of precognitive dreams is how they can be pretty clearly "about" a very specific subsequent occurrence yet be visually unlike the occurrence, having an almost play-like quality with actors, scenes, and stage props drawn from the experiencer's prior memories and idiosyncratic associations.[32] Again, they are future towers built from past bricks.

Thus, in thinking through the imagination, I came to realize that it has all the boundary-crossing and boundary-weaving qualities of the most formidable tricksters of folklore, like Hermes, the god of interpreters and thieves. It is there at the bottom of reason and intellect, memory and judgment, perception and interpretation. You can't get behind it. The imagination always wins, despite our efforts to master or dominate it, and we are at its service. And one thing I think is clear: We don't yet know nearly enough about what is *not* imagination to draw any clear boundary around what *is* "just" the imagination.[33] For instance, dreams, those ultimate products of the unmoored imagination, often—I suspect always, though I could never prove it—relate at least in some symbolic or associative way to real future experiences.

Precognition manifests in waking states just as frequently. It can take the form of misperceptions, obsessions, and impulses—exactly the kinds of thing Freud catalogued as *parapraxes* in his second major book *The Psychopathology of Everyday Life*. It is common for psychics to report getting precognitive information from spontaneous intrusive thoughts (sometimes called "mind pops") and earworms—snippets of song lyrics that suddenly get stuck in one's head despite not having heard the song in a long time. For some people, precognitive information comes in the form of disembodied voices and visions. Dissociative states induced by drugs, meditation, illness, or trauma may also be liable to overlay information about the future onto present experience, almost like an augmented reality app. Many 21ˢᵗ-century technologies like immersive virtual simulations and the internet have provided writers with exciting new metaphors for supernormal phenomena, but I think augmented reality—in which additional information is superimposed on the camera's eye view of the surrounding environment—is a particularly apt metaphor to understand how precognition is experienced during waking states. We just need to imagine that the additional superimposed information comes from the future. It is an app on your i*Chrono*phone.

Psychics find that spontaneous visions, voices, or "random" thoughts may bear a direct or at least associative relationship to some imminent, often mundane event or learning experience, the same way dreams frequently do. Even if the experience is mundane, the precognitive imagination may render it dramatic. The connection may or may not be noticed by the experiencer immediately, and for those not paying attention (the vast majority of us), it probably never will be noticed. Again, it may not be necessary—and perhaps it's not even adaptive—for us to be consciously aware of precognition's guiding hand in our lives, at least not most of the time. But exceptionally clear and accurate visions anticipating tragedies, disasters, or accidents are a staple of the ESP literature, because they are so attention-getting. Like dreams, they are generally misinterpreted or not understood at all until the foreseen event comes to pass.

A few days after the *Titanic* disaster, for instance, a Vancouver woman named Mrs. Henderson was arrested by a sudden brief vision of her sister-in-law and niece in tears. She had not been thinking of them, and she did not yet know or even suspect that her brother (the husband of the woman in her vision) had perished in the disaster, believing at that point that he was working on another White Star liner. She didn't know he had been transferred to the *Titanic* in the days before the voyage. Mrs. Henderson's vision was just one of many reported *Titanic*-related premonitory experiences collected by parapsychologist Ian Stevenson in the 1960s.³⁴ Stevenson, working within the parapsychological models of his time, interpreted this as a case of telepathy and puzzled over why she should see her sister-in-law and niece and not her brother drowning. More plausibly, Mrs. Henderson was precognizing a mental picture of the grief her sister-in-law and niece were feeling, which would be sparked shortly by reading her sister-in-law's letter telling the bad news that her brother had been aboard the lost ocean liner. That is, it was another premonition of an emotionally impactful reading experience and the mental images it was about to evoke.

In late August, 2001, a North Carolina woman named Marie was vacationing in Washington, D.C., with her husband. They were in a car, and when they came into view of the Pentagon, she saw a column of thick black smoke rising from the building and was overcome with "such an intense, emotional feeling that she lost her breath."[35] Nearly hyperventilating, she experienced plunging into the Pentagon from above. "I truly felt like we were in danger," she said, and her scream startled and puzzled her husband, who (perhaps fortunately) was the one behind the wheel. Her experience was over in a few seconds, and she realized that in fact the Pentagon was not on fire and nothing was wrong. After the terror attacks two weeks later, Marie—who had had puzzling experiences before but never a vivid, evidently precognitive hallucination like this—reported her experience to Sally Rhine Feather, a parapsychology researcher at the Rhine Research Center in Durham, North Carolina, who included it in her book (with Michael Schmicker), *The Gift*. Feather is the daughter of Louisa Rhine and her parapsychologist husband J. B. Rhine.

Such waking precognitive visions are not rare occurrences—they are only rarely reported publicly. Since the publication of *Time Loops*, I receive regular emails from readers describing experiences like this. As I was writing this chapter, in fact, a woman named Holly emailed me about some of her precognitive dreams as well as a particularly striking driving-related premonition:

> Another instance is when I was scared to drive near "rock trucks" and would hurry to get around them. This was several years ago and came on me out of nowhere. I live in an area with many trucks like this on the road. I had all this anxiety about it and it lasted weeks. My husband was in the car with me one day and I was telling him about it. I said, "I don't know what is going on. I can just see a huge tire coming at me." Right as I am saying this the rock truck in front of me has a blowout and a huge piece of the tire comes right at my windshield. I calmly swerve so that we don't get hit … it was as if it was all in slow motion. My husband couldn't believe it! It is almost too incredible for me to believe! What is that? All I know is that once that happened, I was back to my normal driving self with no issues around those trucks.

Contrary to what debunkers often assert, people like Holly are not seeking attention. Holly is an elected official in a conservative Southern state, so the last thing she is looking for is publicity for an ESP experience. Most often, people share these stories seeking insight from an authority who will listen and perhaps provide insight rather than belittling or dismissing them.[36]

Psychic experiences are especially career killers in academia, helping to account for why there is such a cone of silence around the topic in the scientific and other fields that ought to be studying them. In his book *Comparing Religions*, Kripal relates a story told to him by an academic colleague on condition of anonymity. The woman had sent her young son to a petting zoo in care of a nanny and, suddenly, was arrested by a brief, terrifying vision of her son in his car seat, the car filling with white smoke after a crash. The time was 10:06 a.m. She called the nanny and asked that she bring her son home immediately, and to drive carefully. The nanny returned with the boy safe and sound. But upset that he hadn't gotten to pet the animals, the boy convinced his mom to bring him to the petting zoo herself the following day. On their way the next morning, another car swerved in front of hers and caused a crash. She turned and saw her son, terrified just as in her vision, and the car was filled with white "smoke"—actually dust from the successfully deployed airbags that may have saved their lives. The time of the woman's 911 call was 10:08—meaning the accident had occurred *exactly* a day after her vision, probably to the minute.[37]

The signature of these kinds of precognitive flashes, which distinguishes them from our more deliberate imaginative thought-stream, is that they are not only spontaneous but also surprising. Ordinary memories may sometimes be experienced as intrusive, arising at unwanted moments or in response to some cue (like a smell or a certain location), but they do not feel "foreign," like something introduced from elsewhere or outside. We recognize them as belonging to our past. In contrast, precognitive flashes more closely resemble the hallucinations experienced by people with psychosis or under the influence of psychedelic drugs. They feel externally generated, like something received—sometimes even like watching a movie. In clairvoyance exercises that were renamed remote viewing during the Cold War, psychics learned to be attentive to and rely *only* on those unexpected, foreign-feeling thoughts and images and to distrust interpretations (known as analytical overlay) that felt self-generated.

There may be a good reason for the out-of-nowhere quality of genuine precognitive information, helping to explain why it is so readily misrecognized as something arising externally: "Memories" from an individual's own future, refluxing backward in time, would be unsusceptible to a process that psychologists describe for ordinary memory and cognition, called *source-monitoring*. We often know (or at least, have some plausible even if not strictly accurate idea) how we know things we learned in our past. We recognize a memory as a memory because it fits into our biography. We can associate it with other memories. And in the same way, we recognize a thought as our own if it seems to flow from past thoughts we also recognize. But information from our future doesn't come with a graspable provenance, since it's not the future yet. We can't place it in our life. An analogy I sometimes use is a letter in our mailbox with no return address. Most people will simply throw out such letters, assuming they are junk mail. But professional psychics and mediums learn to pay attention to thoughts with no known origin, as that is where valuable, "impossible" information is liable to be found—albeit usually amid some real junk.

Which brings us back to the two circles of our Venn diagram, Precognition and Inspiration, and the question of whether they are more than simply overlapping circles. The peculiar phenomenological qualities of precognitive experiences—that they feel out of nowhere and uncaused—is one piece of evidence for a secret shared identity with inspiration, as that is exactly how inspiration is so often experienced and described. One of the things that comes through again and again in artists' memoirs is that their best ideas just happen. Whatever creativity is, cognitively or neurobiologically, phenomenologically it feels distinct from the ordinary stream of consciousness, from deliberate thought. Inspiration has that same foreign, alien, unaccounted-for quality that psychic information does. And like professional psychics and mediums, artists know to pay special attention when an idea comes out of nowhere.

Late one night in 1967, for instance, John Lennon was lying in bed, irritated after an argument with his then- (soon-to-be-estranged) wife Cynthia, who had fallen asleep next to him. Suddenly a phrase came into his mind unbidden: "pools of sorrow, waves of joy." Unable to sleep, he rose from bed, went downstairs, and started writing down what started pouring forth:

Words are flowing out like endless rain into a paper
cup
They slither wildly as they slip away across the
universe
Pools of sorrow, waves of joy are drifting through my
opened mind
Possessing and caressing me ...

Shortly before his death, Lennon told David Sheff in a *Playboy* interview that the resulting work, "Across the Universe," was one of his favorite songs as a Beatle. "I like the inspired stuff, not the created, clever stuff," he said.[38] "[The lyrics] were given to me as a *boom*! I don't own it, you know; it came through like that. I don't know where it came from ..."[39] Lennon explicitly compared it to mediumship:

It's not a matter of craftsmanship; it wrote itself. It *drove* me out of bed. I didn't want to write it, I was just slightly irritable and I went downstairs and I couldn't get to sleep until I put it on paper, and then I went to sleep. ... It's like being *possessed*; like a *psychic* or a *medium*. The thing *has* to go down. It won't let you sleep, so you have to get up, *make* it into something, and then you're allowed to sleep. That's always in the middle of the bloody night, when you're half awake or tired and your critical facilities are switched off.[40]

Artists and writers tapped into their muse often spontaneously supply metaphors of flowing and fluidity to describe the effortless profusion of the creative unconscious: rivers (Samuel Taylor Coleridge), oceans and tides (Virginia Woolf, David Lynch), bubbles blown through a pipe (Woolf again), and blazing, all-consuming fires. Physicist and writer Alan Lightman described moments of creative epiphany as feeling like smoothly riding or "planing" over the surface of water.[41] Franz Kafka likened his creative flow state to a blissful, riverlike ejaculation.[42] And many inspired art and literary works are auto-symbolically *about* that experience of inspiration, centered on those metaphors.[43] Coleridge's dream-inspired *Kubla Khan*, about a subterranean sacred river bursting out into the Mongol Khan's cedar-enfolded pleasure dome Xanadu, is only the most famous example. "Across the Universe," about words rushing out and overflowing Lennon's puny paper cup, is another. It could be called the fractal geometry of inspiration.

Although Freud went out of fashion with the turn to psychiatric medications in the latter part of the last century, neuroscientists have retained some version of his idea of the unconscious to account for many aspects of human behavior, although they will now often use different terms such as implicit processing. A standard neuroscience view of creative insight makes a space for the prehistory of the inspirational flash as a period of *incubation*: Aspects of a creative or scientific problem are assembled, set out side by side in some nonconscious mental workspace, and processing we're not aware of goes on, until voila, the curtain is drawn back on a solution.[44] We don't see the work, but the work gets done. We only see the result … and naturally, take the credit.

In his 1998 thriller *Bag of Bones*, Stephen King's writer-narrator articulates the superiority of the unconscious mind—it is the origin of his "boys in the basement" metaphor:

> So-called higher thought is, by and large, highly overrated. When trouble comes and steps have to be taken, I find it's generally better to just stand aside and let the boys in the basement do their work. That's blue-collar labor down there, non-union guys with lots of muscles and tattoos. Instinct is their specialty, and they refer problems upstairs for actual cogitation only as a last resort.[45]

Whether stated in Freud's psychodynamic terms or King's blue-collar labor scenario, it's a compelling way of thinking about the problem of inspiration. But Freud's critics have often seen the unconscious as paradoxical, and a cheat: If mind or consciousness is identical to brain processing (a problematic assumption to some, I realize, but let's grant it for the moment), then it is no fair invoking some invisible, un-felt layer of thought. This was Jean-Paul Sartre's objection to Freud's theory, for example: How could there be an agency inside us that is aware enough of what it is doing to engage in acts of selection, judgment, and censoring, yet that we consciously do not experience? It's really part of a larger problem: Historically, theories of mind have always been haunted by *homunculi*, deferring consciousness or agency onto a "mini-me" in the head. The Freudian unconscious is really just another (muscled, tattooed) homunculus.

One response has been to dismiss and devalue the unconscious—including instinct and intuition—altogether. Readers at all aware of mainstream psychological thinking in the past few decades will know about the famous "System 1" and "System 2" often associated with Princeton Behavioral Economist Daniel Kahneman and his 2011 book *Thinking Fast and Slow*. Kahneman won the Nobel Prize in 2002 (along with Vernon L. Smith) for research undermining the rational-actor presumption that had prevailed in economics pretty much since the beginnings of that field. The irrational and highly biased System-1 tends to win out in human behavior, leading generally (it is usually argued) to irrational, poorer choices than System 2. But instead of being a hidden domain or layer of thought, as in Freud's schema—the Freudian unconscious is often likened to the submerged portion of an iceberg—System-1 is just super-fast, automatic, knee-jerk, and basically shoddy. It's temporally "flat," and thus has no time to really weigh and consider problems with the needed care. Yet, while Kahnemann's schema might make sense for saving for retirement and taking care of one's health, I can think of plenty of writers, fighter pilots, and Chinese kung fu masters who would take issue with the superiority of System 2 over System 1 when it comes to many things that truly matter—including many high-stakes decisions. It is certainly not better at being original. After a few decades of being an outcast, our fast, from-the-gut intuition may be poised to make a comeback. I suspect precognition plays a huge role in System 1.[46]

In *The Mind Is Flat*, neuroscientist Nick Chater marshalled evidence from studies of perception and creative problem solving to argue that incubation and related crypto-Freudian ideas are an illusion. Instead, what happens, he argues, is that creative problems are really ruts in our thinking, cul-de-sacs in which a thinker runs in circles. All that is needed to provoke a eureka moment, quite often, is to step away from what you are working on. Then, in the shower or while taking out the trash or during a dream that night, processing is able to run in a different direction and often alights on the missing solution rather than that unproductive cul-de-sac. In his book *Imagine*, confabulist Jonah Lehrer invented Bob Dylan quotes to support this idea, that "Every creative journey begins with a problem … a feeling of frustration, the dull ache of not being able to find the answer,"[47] although he could have used real quotes from John Lennon (who actually wrote the song "Imagine") instead. Lennon described songs like "Nowhere Man" coming to him after stepping away:

I'd spent five hours that morning trying to write a song that was meaningful and good, and I finally gave up and lay down. Then "Nowhere Man" came, words and music, the *whole* damn thing as I lay down. The same with "In My Life"! I'd struggled for days and hours trying to write clever lyrics. Then I *gave* up and "In My Life" came to me. So letting it *go* is what the whole game is. You put your finger on it, it slips away, right? You know, you turn the lights on and the cockroaches run away; you can never grasp them.[48]

For Chater, there's no unfelt, unexperienced depth to the mind: It's all surface, all improvisation in the moment, even when the results suggest something more substantive, more "deep."[49] As reductive or eliminativist as it sounds on the surface, I find Chater's viewpoint compelling: While "the unconscious" often is useful as a heuristic or placeholder term, I don't believe there's literally a parallel, submerged portion of the mind thinking in secret, as Freud did. Icebergs are metaphors (except when they sink ships). But I also think Chater's argument does not go far enough. While it makes a nice, simple explanation for the common experience of solving a problem that one has banged one's head against for too long only after taking a needed break, it cannot really answer the larger question of inspiration and its nowhere-seeming origins.

Lehrer notwithstanding, many flashes of inspiration or insight are *not* experienced as solutions to problems. At least, the artist isn't aware of having posed any aesthetic question to their inner (or outer) oracle. Lennon was not trying to write a song when "pools of sorrow, waves of joy" came to him in his bed, for instance. He was trying to sleep. Craig Sinclair hadn't been problem-solving when she suddenly got the "most marvelous" idea for a book about a nefarious hypnotist. And Mark Twain was explicit that he wasn't looking for a book for himself—or anybody else—to write at the moment that his inspiration for a book on Nevada silver mines came to him. He was right in the middle of writing *Tom Sawyer*, in fact, and was busy enough with the problems that project was posing.[50] Whether it comes in a dream, a sudden flash of insight, in the flow state of doing one's craft, or just when trying to get some rest, artistic inspiration is indeed "out of the blue" as often as not, and quite often inconveniently so—a distraction and a trouble as often as it may be a long-awaited eureka.

The science of time travel can again come to our aid, here, in help-ing us understand why. Objects from the future, emerging through the open mouth of a wormhole, would have the same out-of-the-blue qual-ity. They would appear literally out of nowhere, unasked and uninvited, seemingly uncaused, because they have no backstory in the local past. Nothing leads up to their arrival—they just arrive. The same would be true of time-traveling information, such as "memories" traveling back from our future. This fact, along with the essentially paradoxi-cal nature of the unconscious as Freud originally formulated it and as many continue to use the term, is why I suggest that the unconscious is best thought of as *future* consciousness—or at least, future cogni-tion, literally pre-cognition—projected or superimposed onto present waking or dreaming thought, a kind of overlay of future situations, experiences, and feelings onto present experience. Information flowing back from our future feels out of the blue, comes unbidden, because it has no backstory. Beyond dreams and visions, precognition may simply skew or augment present sensory perceptions, actions, and decisions.[51] Whatever the case, if we are aware of it at all, it will feel unfamiliar, foreign, or externally imposed because it isn't the future yet—we have trouble recognizing this skewing factor as belonging to us. Same with inspiration, I suggest, and for the same reason. I obviously do suspect they really may be the same thing: Clark Kent really may be Superman.

The uncaused, alien, foreign quality of precognition would help explain the attributions given to creative insights before the Enlightenment or still today in nonwestern cultures. Ideas may be experienced as coming from gods, spirits, muses, or one's *daimon* in the classical Greek idiom.[52] In the first decades of the last century, the young Indian mathemati-cian-genius Srinivasa Ramanujan astonished his teachers and contem-poraries in his field by fast-forwarding past any mental labor in solving mathematical problems that were thought insoluble. It seemed to ev-eryone who worked with him that his thought processes were beyond the limits of reason, beyond genius, belonging to some supernatural, magical order. He himself credited his insights to his family goddess, Namagiri Thayar.[53] His solutions were given to him as divine gifts.

Or consider Kripal's experience: In November, 1989, after partici-pating in a multi-day celebration of the goddess Kali while doing re-search for his dissertation in Calcutta, the future historian of religions and the paranormal awoke in his bed paralyzed and experienced an intense surge of energy running through his body, as well as a download of information into his brain. He then felt like his consciousness was pulled out of his body as by some giant magnet.[54] At the time, Kripal compared his experience to the dead-but-sexually-aroused Shiva lying prostrate under Kali's feet in Indian religious iconography. But after decades of reading, writing, and reflection, he came to believe that in his download in Calcutta he precognitively received the books he went on to author about mysticism, the erotic, and the impossible—that his rapidly growing body of work *now* is the fulfilment of a time loop (or series of loops) that began *then*, on what he calls "that Night."[55]

Science and pop culture have provided apt new idioms for this kind of supernormal inspiration—including literal aliens. In her books *American Cosmic* and *Encounters*, University of North Carolina Wilmington religion scholar Diana Pasulka writes of modern scientists including AI and biotech innovators who believe that their novel and sometimes lucrative ideas come from the nonhuman intelligence or intelligences behind the UFO phenomenon.[56] The possibility that such intelligences shape our culture by interacting directly with human consciousness has been advanced and nuanced in different ways by contemporary UFO researchers like Jacques Vallée, horror novelist and UFO abductee Whitley Strieber, and multimedia artist Stuart Davis, host of the *Aliens and Artists* podcast.[57] Davis describes receiving a life-changing psychic download from a mantis-like entity who appeared to him one New Year's night while meditating during a fever. Whatever the reality or realities behind the phenomenon, Pasulka argues that belief in ongoing contact with nonhuman beings associated with UFOs is a new and rapidly evolving form of religiosity reflecting our digital age. It resembles the shamanic beliefs of many societies, that new ideas come from interactions with a world of more powerful and cleverer spirits, divinities, or the dead.

The belief that thoughts are being transmitted or downloaded into one's mind from some external, human or nonhuman source is of course famously common in people who have been diagnosed with schizophrenia-spectrum disorders. The psychiatric presumption is that such thoughts are simply the individual's own pathological, often persecutorial cognition that is not recognized as such due to a failure of source monitoring. Slightly less reductively, alien-seeming thoughts may be seen as meaningful but still largely unwelcome products of the Freudian unconscious bubbling up in waking life, as they do for non-schizophrenic people mainly in dreams. Serious mental illness and close encounters notwithstanding, the possibility that *some* alien thoughts may be a person's own future thoughts or perceptions displaced backward in time is only broached on the margins, even of paranormal research. But there is certainly anecdotal evidence, even in the psychiatric literature, that this may sometimes be the case.

People with schizophrenia often live in a world oppressively dense with coincidence (apophenia), and they sometimes experience intrusive thoughts or voices that seem to correspond to imminent events. In the early 1990s, a psychologist named Peter Chadwick published a first-person account of the onset of his schizophrenia, and he described it as a "step-ladder to the impossible."

> I found myself noticing colours, how intense, iridescent and significant they seemed to be. (This is a fairly common psychotic symptom.) I rushed up to my room, irrationally convinced that there would be a discussion on the radio which involved at least something on the hermeneutics of colour. There was. I sat in the park probing the evidence within for my own damnation. I dug deeper and deeper. My dog even began to dig, something she rarely did. Disturbed by this 'coincidence' I stood up and walked to another bench at the side of the main path. I wondered if there might actually be something in the mediaeval idea of possession and whether it might apply to me. A little girl walked past me with her mother, and after a brief glance my way she said to her, 'Mummy is that man possessed by The Devil?' Her mother also looked at me and replied, 'Yes dear'. Yet as far as I was concerned, all I looked was thoughtful. If it is possible to plunge a knife through a mind, those words did so.[58]

Our linear assumptions about causality dictate that even if reality is causally sensible, it should seldom conform to our thoughts. Consequently, we are a bit shocked when it does, and really shocked when it does again and again, as Chadwick experienced. Violations of our expectations are nowadays in neuroscience called *prediction errors*[59]— they come with a burst of dopamine to mark their importance. We predict that the world is, to an important extent, *un*predictable, so when that prediction is violated repeatedly in a storm of significant-feeling (dopamine-bursting) coincidences, it is not totally irrational to attribute it to some external, divine or alien intelligence or perhaps some nefarious government entity like the CIA. The oppressive piling up of uncanny coincidences, continually for days on end, led Chadwick to conclude- that "there was indeed an Organization of technological experts, informed by past enemies, the neighbors and maybe by newspaper personnel, out to monitor and predict my thoughts and then send in replies by the radio."[60] For Chadwick, this paranoid delusion was the only way to *de-weird* those coincidences. Of course, for parapsychologists, the kinds of error signals that lit up Chadwick's brain when he impossibly predicted the unpredictable raise hosts of interesting questions about possible overlaps between psychosis and "psi" phenomena such as precognition that mainstream psychology still denies.[61]

Coincidences can pile up for people without major mental illness too, of course. People in the throes of spiritual crisis, creative flow, or life transition may experience synchronicity storms, similar to (but less oppressive than) what Chadwick experienced. *Schizotypy* is a designation sometimes used for people who are highly creative and imaginative, and prone to occasional hallucinations or voice-hearing, but without the debility brought by schizophrenia.[62] Occasionally, voices from nowhere aid such people, even save their lives. For instance, as a young man, before beginning film school, the future director Andrei Tarkovsky spent a year prospecting for precious minerals in Siberia for a Soviet geology institute. Late one night, alone in his small cabin, he heard a disembodied voice ordering him to leave. The voice repeated until he finally obeyed, exiting the cabin. Just as he went outside, a tree fell and crushed the cabin.[63] In other instances, such voices may turn out to have some symbolic relationship to an imminent occurrence. Recall the voice that told Haitian playwright Frankétienne to obtain a medallion of Saint Andrew, patron saint of Léogâne, the epicenter of the earthquake that devastated his island two days later.

The bottom line: If you believe the necessarily always anecdotal evidence, when people see or hear things that aren't there, sometimes— again I stress, sometimes—they may be seeing or hearing things that *will be* there, superimposed on present reality. Or, they may be seeing or hearing things related, perhaps in some symbolic way, to forthcoming events, as seems to have happened with Frankétienne. Such possibilities seldom occur even to people who are open to psychic phenomena. Even now, almost a century after Dunne's pioneering work and despite substantial laboratory evidence and growing plausibility physics-wise, precognition remains so hard to conceive of—again, it is so counterintuitive—that it will be dismissed as mental aberration or, at best, the machinations of an archetypal universe governing our lives and thoughts. (We'll come back to synchronicity, and its major theorist Carl Jung, later.) I argue that some impossibly right ideas feel alien— that is, foreign and intrusive—because there's no return address, as they arise from a looping relationship to the thinker's own future, a place we haven't been to yet and thus can never recognize. The fact that those ideas come from the future would be *why* they are impossibly right.

In the aftermath of a profound mystical experience in early 1974, Philip K. Dick wrote in a letter to friend that the future is smarter, wiser, more knowledgeable than the present. Dick had been experiencing incredible synchronicities and downloads of ideas and insights that he attributed variously to a nonhuman intelligence or God, although as we will see later, the possibility that it was in fact his own future self that was bombarding him with information and mumbling to him in his half-awake states is an answer he repeatedly returned to.[64] The symbolic distortions that prevent time travel from causing grandfather paradoxes could even help explain why our future self so often appears to us in some mythological, archetypal, or other symbolic disguise.[65]

There are dazzling, even godlike implications of new ideas arising from misrecognized time loops in our biography. Spoiler alert: It makes the biblical feat of *creation ex nihilo* a thinkable, even necessary, part of our universe.

No Where, Man

As I was working on this book, the series *Get Back* was released—possibly the most significant document of creative brilliance ever put on film. In director Peter Jackson's restored and edited footage from the jam sessions and rehearsals that resulted in the Beatles' last-released album *Let It Be*, we get to watch as the 26-year-old Paul McCartney, noodling at the piano and bass, comes up and develops classic songs like "Let It Be" and "Get Back."[66] It is one thing to read an artist's account of how they came up with an idea, but another thing entirely to see it happen, in real time. If you grew up with that band and in awe of those songs, Jackson's series is overpowering, like an astonishing nine-hour-long primal scene. And the amazing—but on the other hand, totally obvious—thing is, there's really nothing to see. There's no frame you can pause on and see the moment of a song's conception, nor is there any deliberate and methodical hammering together of musical ideas as on some workbench or any mixing of musical ingredients in some alchemical laboratory (metaphors that reappear again and again in theories of the creative imagination). The songs seem to form themselves gradually, but from nowhere, while the fab four idly banter and play their instruments.

Get Back will provide psychologists who study creativity from a social cognition angle with abundant fodder. We do not see McCartney have some magical moment of solitary inspiration, but we do watch the songs come together with a little help from his friends, his bandmates, who introduce little ideas here and there that gradually fill out the evolving concepts. It seems like a perfect illustration of the mundane-ness as well as the sociality of art. Biographers will also remind us of the plain ordinary perspiration that had led to McCartney's facility with songwriting and his ability to just sit there and effortlessly *play*. By this point, in early 1969, he had been honing his craft for well over a decade, since his early teens, and then refining the additional skills of being a band member and collaborator, all the while managing the incredible pressures of fame with remarkable grace. But like anybody, he sometimes faltered. At this point late in the Beatles' existence, the vacuum left by the loss of producer Brian Epstein in 1967 and the growing disinterest of Lennon in the "job" of being a Beatle (as well as Lennon's visible heavy drug use and his greater preoccupation with Yoko Ono) had forced McCartney to assume the role of bandleader. As often happens, the creative dynamo leading the group sometimes alienated his bandmates by being too forceful in imposing his particular vision over theirs.

In light of this, there's another thing that *Get Back* revealed, which had mainly been known only by diehard Beatles fans because it had been left out of the original 1974 film *Let It Be* made from some of the same footage. Exactly three days after McCartney started to play around with the idea of a song exhorting some still-unknown person to "get back to where you once belonged," his bandmate George Harrison walked out—left the band—exasperated at the tensions among his bandmates and sick of getting little recognition or appreciation of his contributions by an increasingly bossy and controlling McCartney. It's the big cliffhanger ending of the first episode of Jackson's three-part series. The remaining Beatles met with Harrison twice over the following week, at Ringo Starr's Surrey mansion, to persuade the guitarist to, you know, *get back*. Adding to the irony of it all, the line "get back" actually came from a tune that *Harrison* had recently written, "Sour Milk Sea," about the imperative of getting out of unsatisfying situations.[67] McCartney took a line from Harrison's song, "Get back to where you should be," tweaked it slightly, and made it the basis of a new song that would ultimately be credited to him and Lennon.

Was the misguided lost soul who on the morning of January 10, 1969, had become *Jojo* (sounds like George) from *Arizona* (sounds like Harrison) none other than the disgruntled lead guitarist of the Beatles? There are often no smoking guns for artistic prophecy when we try to link an artwork or its themes to subsequent events in the creator's life. We are not, by a long shot, in the realm of the provable. But if the artistic imagination really is a precognitive imagination, then it would be perfectly reasonable to hypothesize that McCartney's minor musical obsession in the second week of January 1969 could have been a premonition of the situation that his own behavior was about to precipitate—another time-fractal in a world of time-fractals. Harrison left the band—opted to leave his sour milk sea—later that morning, the 10th, saying "See you 'round the clubs," not long after Lennon had spontaneously, and a bit uncannily, added a line to the new song: "But he knew it wouldn't last."[68] Harrison rejoined the band when they reconvened for rehearsals a week and a half later.

It's important to be clear: I am not suggesting any of this would have been intentional on McCartney's (or Lennon's) part. Especially in a society that doesn't literally believe in such things, precognition is almost always unconscious and unintended, expressed symptomatically in all the ways Freud thought neuroses were. In this case, it would simply have been the artist's unconscious seismograph reading out a faint signal of an impending life-quake in the form of an evolving song lyric, bending his songwriting toward a nebulous "Jojo" who for some reason was unhappy with his situation and temporarily left it.

Whether you find such a reading plausible or poppycock depends on how reasonable you regard the basic premise of this book: that the creative imagination indeed reaches into the artist's future for new ideas. Skeptics who cannot accept precognition on principle will roll their eyes. But here's where I think we should open our minds way, way wider. Having seen firsthand how true it is of dreams, I strongly suspect that we are simply blind to most artistic prophecy because we've lacked any metaphor (such as an iChronophone) to help us imagine how easy precognition could be for the imagination, rather than strenuous. And it certainly doesn't help that art and music historians and literary critics, academic authorities who may exert tremendous weight when students learn about the arts and literature in school, never alert people to the precognitive possibility. It's not on our cultural radar generally, and it is especially taboo in academia. In biographies and monographs of artists, odd resemblances between their works and subsequent events in their lives will be ignored (usually) or obfuscated in some way. And interpretation, more often than not, will proceed insistently along lines of influence connecting a work to past ideas of past artists and the individual's own prior life experiences. The very notion of artistic prophecy is foreclosed from the start, almost universally. Once you open your eyes and your mind, though, other exciting possibilities emerge.

4

Falling from the Sky
Trauma, Free Will, and the Prophetic Sublime

Artistic creation is by definition a denial of death.
Therefore it is optimistic, even if in an ultimate sense the
artist is tragic.
—Andrei Tarkovsky, Diary entry (February 3, 1974)

You never know what worse luck your bad luck has
saved you from.
—Cormac McCarthy, *No Country for Old Men*
(2005)

One day in the early 1960s, during Werner Herzog's years as a gymnasium student in Munich, the teenager was loitering in a friend's apartment, waiting for him to get off the phone with his girlfriend. The friend was a brilliant intellectual prodigy and had a sizeable book collection. The young future filmmaker idly drew a book from the bookshelf and read a paragraph that would change his life.

It was a book for young readers about historical discoverers like Columbus and Vasco de Gama, but what captivated Herzog was a brief description of the cruel and treacherous conquistador Lope de Aguirre. Scattered historical accounts tell a dark story: In 1560, Aguirre usurped the command of an expedition down the Amazon from Peru in search of the legendary El Dorado, "City of Gold." After murdering his own commanding officer, Aguirre killed the soldiers who were disloyal to him as well as many Indians, and eventually even killed his own daughter who had accompanied him. Calling himself "the wrath of God," Aguirre planned to overthrow the existing Spanish governments in the New World with his dwindling band of terrified followers—an insane

---

plan for which he was finally captured and executed.

Aguirre's Amazon adventure lingered in Herzog's thoughts for over a decade while he finished gymnasium, began his university studies, and embarked on his filmmaking career. Then, in early 1971, in a frenzied burst of inspiration while he was on a bus trip to Italy with his soccer team, the 29-year-old director banged out the screenplay for what became his masterpiece, *Aguirre, the Wrath of God,* on a portable typewriter perched uncomfortably on his lap. He later recalled that his teammates were all drunk and that the goalie sharing his seat vomited on his script, forcing him to throw out a few pages. He no longer remembers what was on them.[1]

Surviving the vomit, at the end of what Herzog wrote—which was only loosely based on historical fact—Aguirre, his daughter Flores, and the last few survivors of the doomed expedition are drifting down the Amazon on a log raft, the men nearly dead from fever, when they behold an astonishing sight: a ship, with sails and a canoe hanging from its prow, high in a tall tree, far higher than floodwaters could reasonably have carried it. It is an impossible, awe-inspiring vision. The men think they are hallucinating. In the script (though not in the film), Aguirre and a few men climb up and explore the impossible ghost ship.[2]

After writing his script, Herzog spent the next nine months preparing to shoot the film, casting his erratic friend Klaus Kinski in the lead role. He then shot the film on location in Peru over the course of five weeks at the end of 1971 and beginning of 1972, using a 35mm film camera he had stolen from a Munich film school (he said "I never considered in theft. … I had some kind of natural right to this tool"[3]). He claimed later that, while never having been to Peru before, every detail of the rainforest location he shot in was exactly as he had envisioned it on that bus trip with his soccer team earlier that year.[4] Hindsight claims like that don't count as evidence for precognition, but the end of his script, with its impossible boat in a tree, seems to have been a premonition of an incredible collision with fate—and a truly impossible survival story—that occurred during the tumultuous production.

Midway through filming *Aguirre* in December, the parents of the 15-year-old Peruvian girl, Cecilia Rivera, whom Herzog had cast to play the role of Aguirre's daughter Flores, withdrew their earlier permission, even though the girl was accompanied on the set by a chaperone. Starting over with a new actress would have been a disaster, so Herzog flew to Lima to persuade Ms. Rivera's parents to continue in her role. Herzog can be persuasive, and his mission to keep his actress was a success. Herzog, his wife, and members of his cast and crew were then booked on a December 21 flight from Lima back to the mountain town of Cusco to resume filming, but their flight was delayed due to repairs. The airline, Lineas Aéreas Nacionales Sociedad Anonima (LANSA), only had one serviceable plane that made multiple daily jaunts among all of Peru's inland routes. Because of the Christmas holiday, the Lima airport became a mob scene of people trying to get on the scarce flights to get home before the holiday. Herzog managed to bribe a LANSA employee for boarding passes for a Christmas Eve flight to Cusco, but at the last minute, the flight plan was changed—it would only go as far as the city of Pucallpa. So the filmmakers were again left stranded while the Lockheed L-188 Electra departed, packed with Pucallpa-bound passengers elated that they would be spending Christmas with their families.[5]

A half hour into the flight, the Electra disappeared from radar after entering a storm high in the air above the vast Amazonian rainforest. It never arrived at its destination. Herzog and his wife and crew, thanking their lucky stars, eventually made it back to the jungle to resume making their film, while authorities conducted a search for the missing plane. The search was called off after 10 days, and all 96 passengers and crew were presumed lost.

But then, astonishingly, 12 days after Flight 508 vanished, a 17-year-old girl in tattered clothes appeared at the edge of a camp of forest workers on a remote and uninhabited river, Rio Shebonya, looking like a demon because the whites of her eyes were solid red. She was a German girl named Juliane Koepcke. She had trekked all the way from where she had tumbled from the airplane after it broke apart, probably after a lightning strike, *nearly two miles* (3,000 meters) over the forest. She had been lucid during her descent in open air and could later describe the broccoli-like appearance of the forest canopy as she approached it before she lost consciousness. She awoke a day or two after the fall on the forest floor, covered in mud, next to the row of seats to which she had been buckled and that, somehow, had saved her life.[6]

People puzzled over Koepcke's miraculous survival of a two-mile fall and came up with a plausible explanation: Her row of seats had probably spun like a maple seed and was caught in a storm updraft that slowed her descent. Those seats are then thought to have *acted as a boat*, being caught by the forest canopy's dense net of lianas, which slowed her fall, bringing her to rest gently—or, gently enough—in the soft mud below.[7] Although bruised and battered (and with open wounds that became maggot-infested before she reached the men's camp), her only broken bone was her collarbone, and she recovered fully from her ordeal. She survived her trek out of the forest eating only a bag of candies in her pocket and following the local streams to where they joined a bigger river. Because she had grown up in the rainforest, the daughter of naturalists, she knew that a waterway would eventually take her to people. Herzog later learned that as he was filming *Aguirre*, Koepcke had been struggling alone to survive and reach civilization just a few rivers away from where they were shooting.[8]

Nearly three decades later, the dogged Herzog finally tracked Koepcke down—she had long since changed her name to avoid the unbearable publicity—and convinced her to let him make a documentary about her. Again, Herzog can be persuasive. In *Wings of Hope*, he and Koepcke (now a research biologist specializing in Amazonian bats) reminisce about the crowded airport where they were undoubtedly standing within a few feet of each other, and then retrace her path from the overgrown jungle wreckage of the obliterated Electra to the village where she had emerged, demon-like with bloodshot eyes, and reunite with one of the men who had aided her and brought her to civilization.

Herzog's script for *Aguirre, the Wrath of God* didn't include a plane or a row of plane seats caught in a tree—it was not set in the modern period, obviously—so it might not seem obvious to connect that ship seen by Aguirre and his fever-immobilized raft-mates to what happened to the ill-fated flight 508 and Juliane Koepcke, its miracle-survivor, caught by the trees in her falling seat like in a boat. By the time people saw Herzog's completed film, few outside of Peru remembered the crash of LANSA flight 508, and even if they did, they would not have known that Herzog himself was nearly on the same plane. Herzog himself doesn't seem to have drawn a connection between his *Aguirre* script and Koepcke—at least, he has not said so publicly. But I suggest that his script was a premonition. A ship caught in a tree at the end of a doomed mission (a single rowboat hanging down from it) and that mission's sole survivor prevailing by indomitable will, following the river out of the jungle (in the script though not in the film, Aguirre's raft carries him, alone, out into the Pacific Ocean) seems to have foreshadowed the impossible story of Juliane Koepcke: That sole survivor of the flight that nearly carried Herzog himself to his doom was caught impossibly by the trees in her row of seats and survived through another, less "mad" kind of indomitable will, by following a river, just miles from where

Herzog was filming.[9] It would be a symbolic transformation of a future emotionally impactful learning experience, exactly the way precognitive dreams most often seem to work.

Herzog claims that while he remembers few of his night dreams, he dreams vividly—"entire novels"—while awake.[10] I suggest the filmmaker was awake-dreaming when he saw his hallucinatory epic about Lope de Aguirre in his head and wrote his script. *Aguirre, the Wrath of God* seems very much like a precognitive dream-film. And if so, it was also a self-fulfilling prophecy, or what I call a time loop: He would not have nearly lost his life in the tragic-yet-slightly-miraculous crash of LANSA Flight 508, nor as a result have been nearly as captivated by the story of Juliane Koepcke afterword, had he not been artistically possessed, all those years earlier, by the story of that mad conquistador in a book that "seemed to stick out" from his friend's bookshelf.[11] It could also be significant that Herzog's close brush with that ill-fated flight occurred during his own quest to "rescue" his Flores, Cecilia Rivera, nearly the same age as Koepcke. The precognitive unconscious loves to home in on coincidences of various kinds, and I wonder whether Herzog's unconscious might have drawn a connection between the two young women.

Again, precognitive inspiration is always unconscious and unintended on the part of an artist, and Herzog himself would probably balk at the suggestion that he is literally psychic. Despite being regarded as a cinematic mystic and extolling artistic "ecstasy," he notoriously hates anything overtly smacking of the paranormal or New Age. He has ridiculed belief in UFOs, for instance, and told a *GQ* interviewer that there should be a holy crusade against yoga. ("It detours us from real thinking," he said.[12]) But he also says that coincidences have dogged him throughout his career, and he has described the fortuitous way his films often come together, and synchronicities associated with them.[13] We'll look at another example later.

Gone and There

There is something about destruction and desolation that acts as a magnet for the prophetic mind. We saw how 9/11 seemed to be precognized in so many artworks and dreams, as was the *Titanic* disaster before it. Fires, shipwrecks, plane crashes, and natural disasters like earthquakes have always dominated people's reports of spontaneous ESP experiences, just as they are prevalent in fictions about the paranormal.

Although it has mainly been considered an aesthetic and

philosophical category, *the sublime* encompasses many of the threatening but weirdly alluring circumstances and scenarios that magnetize premonitory experiences. Immanuel Kant used the term to describe the specific feeling evoked by landscapes and works of art that suggest immensity and destruction, or else the slow ravages of time.[14] Towering thunderclouds and storms at sea, scenes of massive destruction on a Biblical scale, and wild landscapes with ruins in them all fit into this category, as would most of Caspar David Friedrich's paintings, such as his prophetic *The Sea of Ice*. With his stories about individuals living in the wilderness or pushed to extreme circumstances, Herzog is sometimes seen as a modern heir of Friedrich. Experiences of the sublime are those that feel existentially threatening as well as threatening to the ego or its significance, causing us to feel our own being-there (*Da-sein*, as Heidegger called it) as virtual, like imaginatively putting ourselves in Schrödinger's catbox, testing what it is like to be there and not be there at the same time.

The roots of sublime existential exploration are found in early experiences of losing and finding the self or its familiar objects in play. In 1920, Sigmund Freud published what some consider to be his masterpiece, *Beyond the Pleasure Principle*. It is perhaps the least understood of Freud's works, but it is also one of the most read and the most memorable, in part because of the star of the show, Freud's 18-month-old grandson, Ernst. This grandson, Freud said, had a habit of tossing a spool over the side of his crib and savoring making it "gone" (in German, *fort*), with a long drawn-out "ooooooh." Every so often, he would give himself the more conventional reward of drawing it back on its string and exclaiming "there" (*da!*), although it seemed to be the gesture of throwing-away (or annihilation) that was more compelling to the child. When he was a little older, Ernst would play the same "fort-da" game with his own reflection in a mirror. Ernst liked to play gone with himself.

Freud's aim with his book was not to understand play behavior but to understand the baffling repetition-compulsions of survivors of trauma like war veterans, their habit of revisiting and reliving awful events in dreams and neurotic symptoms. The condition that came to named "shell shock" and that we now call PTSD seemed to fly in the face of his theory that, until that point, had been governed by an organism's seeking of pleasure. The repetition of the fort-da game was driven, Freud theorized, by a motivation beyond pleasure, what he called a "death drive," or *Thanatos*. Freud acknowledged the influence of Sabina Spielrein, a former psychoanalytic patient and protégé (and, some think, lover) of Carl Jung, who had written an essay in 1912 called "Destruction as the Cause of Coming-into-Being."[15]

Later thinkers in Freud's tradition developed the ideas in *Beyond the Pleasure Principle* in various interesting ways, such as emphasizing the rudiments of symbolic thought displayed in the fort-da game. It is possible to see such play as the stem cell of art: making some arbitrary object stand for or represent something not present. Symbolizing, in this view, arises from a kind of necessity. Little Ernst's casting away and recovering the spool was a way of gaining mastery over the comings and goings of his mother—a mother's increasingly frequent and lengthy absences being the first traumas a child must ordinarily confront in life. In the 1950s, child psychoanalyst D. W. Winnicott built an enduring theory of early development and creativity around the flickering appearing/disappearing role of children's first attachment objects, what he called transitional objects, and the liminal imaginal real-yet-unreal interzone in which play occurs. He suggested that the roots of symbolism, mythology, religion, and art are to be found in children's play with objects that are destined to be symbolically destroyed and then retrieved/rescued, although ultimately abandoned as the child matures.[16] The ability to play gone and there "scales up" in later life in aesthetic and spiritual feelings.[17]

The realm beyond pleasure also assumed centrality in the thinking of the French psychoanalyst Jacques Lacan, who was equipped with the perfect French word *jouissance*, meaning an excessive feeling that drives compulsion yet may be agonizing in its extremity. It is usually left untranslated or else translated as "enjoyment," with the asterisk that it may be an enjoyment that is not, on its face, all that enjoyable. Neurotics (and anybody insofar as they are neurotic) find themselves repetitively drawn to certain kinds of situations that enact a fantasized relationship to their original caregivers, including the traumas they may have inflicted. People often repetitively inflict traumas on themselves. Neurotic compulsions are well characterized in Lacan's terms, and in fact his theory of *jouissance* even maps quite well onto neurobiological mechanisms now known to underlie Pavlovian conditioning and substance use disorders.[18]

Freud's linkage of war neuroses to child's play in *Beyond the Pleasure Principle* was a very non-obvious equivalence to draw—indeed, it is "genius." Readers of Freud's text cannot but be struck by its genius, and the fertility of the theoretical ground he sowed with just that one anecdote about his grandson attests to it. But like other works of genius, there is something prophetic in the text that goes beyond its laying the groundwork for a theory of trauma as well as a whole domain of child psychology. After Freud had already drafted his book and shortly before it was published, his daughter Sophie Halberstadt, Ernst's mother, died from the Spanish Flu that had reached pandemic levels in war-ravaged Europe. Freud's friends and colleagues assumed—because the connection seemed obvious—that grief-stricken Freud had been inspired to write his great work on death, with a scene of a toddler innocently grappling with the traumatic absence of its mom, by this terrible loss—precisely that toddler's mother. Freud admitted that, if he didn't know better, he would likewise have assumed such a genesis. But the chronology was wrong, as he took pains to point out to everyone; it was largely written before that terrible event. (The "death drive," however, was added afterward.)

When chronologies in the world of genius are off in this way, it is a red flag for precisely the subject that interests the psychic deconstructionist. Was Freud's noticing of Ernst's game, and his seeing in it of a brilliant new way of looking at trauma and loss, a kind of premonitory augmentation of his perceptions and interests? Again, precognition often manifests in this way; it may even be the basis of what Freud considered to be neurotic symptoms and the perplexing deviations of perception and behavior (parapraxis) that he had described in his second major psychoanalytic book, *The Psychopathology of Everyday Life*.[19] I suggest that Freud's inspiration for *Beyond the Pleasure Principle* was, quite simply, a premonition of thoughts and emotions he would soon feel upon the loss of his daughter.[20] This kind of thing was not unusual for Freud, as we saw with his dream of "Irma's Injection." His life was punctuated with other similarly uncanny and puzzling episodes pointing to his unrecognized, indeed repressed, precognitive sensitivity.[21]

Precognitive dreams often contain traces or indicators of their impossible origins, in the form of anachronisms or what I call "time gimmicks," as well as other kinds of impossible objects.[22] It is a feature they share with prophetic works of literature or art, I believe. Herzog's boat in the tree would be one example. One type of time gimmick/impossible object is something that reverses cause and effect, for instance impossibly disappearing before appearing or paradoxically dying before being born—or being destroyed before coming into being. Citing MIT mathematician and cyberneticist Norbert Wiener, Lacan described a backward time-traveling object as coming into being by disappearing,[23] and this is exactly the logic of transitional objects. Fort comes before da; gone comes before there, and this is somehow the basis for their permanence. The spool at the heart of the fort-da game played by little Ernst, the most famous object in Freud's book, is, I suggest, a time gimmick, a visible trace of the book's premonitory inspiration.

Such objects, which seem to inhabit or emerge from a non-Euclidean dimension ruled by M. C. Escher, radiate UFO-like with an astonishing energy, beguiling and inspiring others—and indeed, defying time.[24] Precognitively birthed texts and artworks seem to have a way of inspiring others precognitively, almost like a virus that propagates in temporal retrograde. For instance, as we will see later, Franz Kafka, who was avidly interested in psychoanalysis, appears to have precognized the time-defying spool in *Beyond the Pleasure Principle* in a story he published a year before Freud's book came out. Impossible objects are so prevalent in the most prophetic texts and artworks, in fact, that I see them as a kind of biomarker of the precognitive imagination at work, the same way time gimmicks are in dreams.[25]

What Was Your Original Face on Mars?

Besides fiery or cataclysmic destruction, other things that evoke sublime experiences are juxtapositions of immensity and smallness, vast distance and proximity, and objects of great age. Among Kant's examples of the sublime was the appearance of the pyramids of Egypt to a still-distant traveler, looming on the far horizon—combining that sense of physical distance, contrast of scale, and immense antiquity. Sublime landscape paintings of the 18th century often had ruins in them, and landscapers creating sublime vistas for wealthy patrons often commissioned fake ruins, which to this day can be seen moldering in the grounds of English and Scottish country houses from the period. The literary critic Jonathan Culler, in a now-classic essay on tourism, wrote that the fantasy of civilization in ruins is a semiotic frame within which whatever survives amid those ruins appears particularly authentic—in other words, *really real*.[26] Ruins, and the archeological imagination more generally, are a fantasy screen or backdrop for whatever we want to elevate and redeem as genuine in this mostly fake and trivial world. In a sublime trope of his own, Freud famously likened the psyche to Rome, with modern buildings set amid archaeological ruins from different periods.[27]

There is a direct connection between the sublime in Romantic art and literature and the Waste Land of the Grail romances of earlier centuries, or the cursed heaths surrounding Hrothgar's kingdom in *Beowulf*. These were the original action-adventure epics, and like paintings of the sublime, they formed a backdrop for rugged men to stand out vividly and heroically. Their modern descendants include postapocalyptic sci-fi, which presents the same semiotic frame of a civilization in ruins and the fantasy of discovering something uniquely priceless and authentic amid them. In Walter M. Miller Jr.'s 1959 classic, *A Canticle for Leibowitz*, monks in a far-future, post-nuclear-war American Southwest find and preserve ancient engineering blueprints believed to have been created by their prewar defense contractor patron saint. The most iconic sublime object in this genre is the ruined Statue of Liberty jutting up from the sand of a far-future beach at the end of Franklin J. Schaffner's 1968 film *Planet of the Apes*.

Ever a projection screen for human hopes and fears, Mars has long been imagined as a sublime landscape filled with ancient ruins. A century before the Viking missions first sent pictures back from the surface of the Red Planet, features dimly viewable through Earth telescopes gave an impression of having been sculpted by alien hands (or machines) rather than by wind, dust, and water. The *canali* seen and drawn by Giovanni Schiaparelli inspired much speculation about an ancient desert civilization that had massively geoengineered its world to deliver precious water from the poles to the parched equatorial regions. Spiritualist mediums of the period claimed to be in contact with the planet's inhabitants.[28] But NASA's first orbital probes in the 1960s largely confirmed what scientists had by then surmised, that the planet was in fact desolate, crater-pocked, probably uninhabited and never lived in or on. I still remember vividly the first color photograph from the first Viking lander gradually, vertical strip by vertical strip, resolving on our RCA TV screen in 1976, revealing a desolate, boulder-strewn plain and pinkish sky. It was beautiful, and an incredibly exciting moment ... but the landscape was not an inviting one, nor one suggestive of life or civilization.

There was an all-too-sublime twist to the Mars story, though. Later that year, one of the Viking orbiters surveying the planet from above snapped something intriguing: a haunting, vaguely Egyptian-looking visage gazing up from a symmetrical plateau in the Cydonia Mensae region in the planet's northern hemisphere. A few days after the photo was taken, NASA released the image to the public, thinking (rightly, as it turned out) that it would stoke public interest in Mars exploration. They described the feature as a "huge rock formation ... which resembles a human head ... formed by shadows giving the illusion of eyes, nose and mouth." [29] Speculation abounded in the following years, and in certain corners of the internet, it continues. Some argued that the face and a set of nearby "pyramids" were erected either by human settlers in the distant past or by an indigenous Martian civilization that flourished many hundreds of millions of years ago, when that planet was blue and green.[30] It reawakened the kinds of fantasies about our nearest planetary neighbor that Schiapparelli's drawings of canals had nourished.

Mars is red for the same reason blood is: oxidized iron. Whether or not it is because of the planet's astrological significance and name, war and death have often played a big role in our Martian imaginings— H. G. Wells' *War of the Worlds* being the most well-known example. And among believers that the Face was artificial, the feature became the central icon in a narrative of ancient global destruction—perhaps nuclear war—that could have tragically rendered our nearest cosmic neighbor a dead world long ago.[31] The idea of ancient Martian Armageddon captured the imagination not only of the public but even of some scientists in an era gripped by nuclear fears.[32] The ever-skeptical Carl Sagan initially distanced himself from speculations about the Face, but in his 1980 PBS series *Cosmos*, he suggested that the pyramidal-looking features near it (the "Pyramids of Elysium") should be investigated, having earlier in his career suggested the possibility that we might find alien ruins in our solar system.[33] The dreadful possibility of our civilization destroying itself in a nuclear war was certainly one that was close to his heart as a disarmament activist. It happened to be Mars's dust storms that gave him his first model of nuclear winter, a frigid life-eradicating darkness that would ensue after multiple bomb detonations. In his last book, *The Demon-Haunted World*, Sagan, although still skeptical, acknowledged that the Face too deserved a closer look.[34]

To writers freer with their cosmic imaginings, that Face, created in a distant past and still staring out at the universe, seemed like it could be both a monument and a warning to our species. In that sublime space ruin—a kind of cosmic fort-da—humanity seemed to find, impossibly, its own reflection but also a distressing mirror of its own mortality on a distant world. So it is not surprising that multiple artists during the Cold War seem to have prophesied not only the Face on Mars but also its surrounding meme complex of planetary war.

The most famous member of the MFC, the Mars Face Club, is

Jack Kirby. Kirby, whom Grant Morrison called the "William Blake of comics,"[35] created or co-created most of the iconic superheroes for Marvel Comics in the 1960s, including the X-Men, the Fantastic Four, Iron Man, Thor, Black Panther, and the Hulk, among others.[36] But in 1959, before his creative heyday, he wrote a story (illustrated by Al Williamson) called "The Face on Mars," about astronauts to the Red Planet who discover a massive stone face and explore the ancient structure. The face is oriented vertically on a cliff face, rather than facing upward like the feature in the Viking photo. One of the team telepathically receives a hologram transmission showing an interplanetary war that laid waste the planet long in the past.

Comics researcher and blogger Christopher Knowles writes: "Starting in the late 50s, Kirby began receiving transmissions that seem to transcend the boundaries of time and space. He buried it all in allegory (read: 'wacked-out sci fi'), or rather, translated whatever he was picking up."[37] I don't know whether Kirby really experienced his inspiration as telepathic transmissions or downloads, like Philip K. Dick and other sci-fi peers of his generation. But Knowles notes that ancient astronauts, as well as interest in mysterious ancient monuments like the *mo'ai* of Easter Island, are recurring themes throughout Kirby's creative career.[38] His first explorations of these themes preceded the popular writings of Erich von Däniken and Zecharia Sitchin on ancient alien visitation, and may have influenced better-known fictional works of the 1960s like *2001: A Space Odyssey*. On his blog *The Secret Sun*, Knowles argues that Kirby's works also prophesied other developments in American culture, including the two Gulf Wars.[39] It is significant that Kirby not only seems to have anticipated a Martian face but also the war narrative around it—as well as seeming to have represented "fractally" the very fact of his own prophecy, given the fact that the story is about an astronaut *receiving a psychic vision* of the interplanetary war after he enters the eye of the ruin.

But Kirby wasn't the first. More than a decade earlier, in 1947, and almost three decades before the Face was imaged by Viking, the Japanese-American sculptor Isamu Noguchi created a one-foot-square sand model for a proposed gigantic face earthwork called *Sculpture To Be Seen from Mars* and took a photograph of his model. It was never built, and all we now have is that black and white photo in the archive of the Isamu Noguchi Foundation and Garden Museum in Long Island City, New York. It looks astonishingly like the Viking orbiter's photograph. The impassive facial expression is the same, and it is tilted in the artist's photo, similarly to how the Mars Face is often shown. (The familiar Face on Mars photograph was actually a close crop of a much larger image.) The proposed dimensions of Noguchi's earthwork, to be built in some "unwanted area" like a desert, were of an even grander scale than the Martian feature: Noguchi's face was to be ten miles long, its nose a mile in height.[40] The actual mesa on Mars is a little over a mile long.

As uncanny as the physical resemblance of Noguchi's proposed earthwork to the Viking photo (at least in the latter's cropped form) is its purpose as the sculptor envisioned it: to signal the human presence to the cosmos in the aftermath of our species' demise in a nuclear holocaust. Like Kirby's, Noguchi's face was associated with apocalyptic war, "a requiem for all of us who live with the atom bomb."[41] At the time, in 1947, shortly following the destruction of two Japanese cities by such weapons, Noguchi feared that such a world-ending conflict was inevitable.

In addition to being a memorial for humanity, bringing two planets and two ideas, the new and old, into juxtaposition, Noguchi's *Sculpture To Be Seen from Mars* may also have been meant as a monument to his father, Yone Noguchi, who had died that same year in Japan.[42] It could thus be that multiple immediate inspirations—grief over his father and fear for the possible demise of humanity—acted as a concrete nucleus "constellating" a sublime premonition of the Face on Mars and its surrounding interplanetary war meme three decades later.[43]

After the Apollo missions of the late 1960s and early 1970s, Noguchi explained that his unbuilt earthwork-sculpture had been consciously inspired partly by the so-called Nazca lines, linear animal forms in the Andes landscape theoretically viewable only from the sky, which supplied fodder for von Däniken when writing about ancient astronauts. Noguchi thought they were viewed astrally or out-of-body. He commented that the builders of the Andes configurations

> probably had some means of letting their imaginations travel to outer space . . . I don't think it's necessary to be corporeally or visually in outer space. I believe that one day we will find a way of letting our inner selves travel to the moon or beyond—instantly. Our imagination does travel. I mean, who hasn't been on Mars and seen it? To the artist, going to the moon was nothing new. I've been up there all the time.[44]

There is also a third, lesser-known member of the MFC: Ron Walotsky, an illustrator best known for his covers for the *Magazine of Fantasy and Science Fiction* as well as many SF paperback covers from the late 1960s through the end of the millennium. Six years before the Viking photo, Walotsky painted a cover for a 1970 Pyramid Books edition of Arthur C. Clarke's *Against the Fall of Night* showing a cracked desolate landscape with stone ruins in the foreground and an enormous upturned face earthwork dominating the horizon. It looks very much like what one imagines the Face in Cydonia Mensae would look like if viewed from the nearby Pyramids of Elysium.

Clarke's novel, originally written in 1953, is about a young man's journey outside his protected city on a far-future Earth, long since devastated by an interplanetary war. There is no face in the story like the one on the cover—Walotsky, in the tradition of other SF paperback illustrators of the period, was imaginatively embellishing. Yet the whole novel is clearly on the same themes as the Face on Mars meme: the contrast of ancient and futuristic, distance and intimacy, as well as dim memory of an ancient planet-devastating conflict. An ancient face gazing up at the stars seems to suggest a remnant of a civilization that once looked outward (and forward) but has long since withdrawn and stagnated. Revitalizing human civilization after untold years of stagnation in some protected enclave or a global dark age is, again, a common sublime motif in SF. Whether Walotsky was precognizing the Face on Mars when he did his cover for this novel or was simply inspired by somewhat similar images in then-recent SF, such as the Statue of Liberty on the beach in *Planet of the Apes*, is hard to say.

Kirby, Noguchi, and Walotsky were all active through the 1980s and would almost certainly have been aware of the Face on Mars, although none of them publicly mentioned it that I am aware of. Kirby was alive until 1994, and with his interest in ancient aliens, he almost certainly would have taken an interest in the Martian feature. Noguchi was intensely interested in science and technology all his life, right up to his death in 1988—nuclear weapons and space exploration both figured prominently in his work. One of his last sculptures, for example, was a Miami monument to the astronauts killed in the Challenger disaster. So I have little doubt that he would have been aware of and interested in the Viking missions as well as the resurgent concerns about nuclear war during the Reagan era, when the "Face on Mars as remnant of a destroyed Martian civilization" meme took shape. Less is known about Walotsky, who died in 2002, but his interest in space exploration can be inferred from the themes of his art. And there is a strong hint in his work that he was specifically a Sagan fan, so he certainly would have been aware of the Face and the controversies around it.

Walotsky's paintings are full of masks, and his most interesting fine-art works were real masks made from the shells of horseshoe crabs. He described that his initial inspiration for this series, which he called "Ancient Warriors of Lost Civilizations," came from staring at one of these shells on the beach one day, and it appeared to him like a face.[45] Walotsky honored this vision with his masks from the late 1980s up until his death, perhaps not consciously recalling the very real "source" for this idea: Sagan's *Cosmos* series. A segment in Episode Two was about the Heike crabs of the Inland Sea in Japan. The 1185 battle of the Heike clan against the Genji clan was fought on the shores of this sea, and a species of crab with a wrinkled carapace occasionally produced specimens that seemed face-like. These were preferentially saved from the fishermen's nets, tossed back into the water (fort-da again!). Consequently, an inadvertent selective breeding, over the centuries, led to a prevalence of crabs with a samurai grimace, believed in folk tradition to be ghosts of the Heike warriors. The Heike crabs, with their warrior faces, are more than a bit like the Face on Mars—living monuments of an ancient destructive war. But these "ghosts" have also been shaped, sculpted, precisely by generations of human selection, a subtle and accelerated Darwinian process, abetted by pareidolia and forgetting—just as Walotsky may have seen and forgotten a fascinating/haunting segment in a PBS series and taken inspiration from it in his art.

Since precognition is only ever confirmed in hindsight, skeptics will always argue that it is the retrospective view on the past, inevitably reframed by salient events, that produces seeming prophecies through the same kind of pareidolia—faces in the clouds of causality. Psychologists call it hindsight bias. The first task in the study of artistic prophecy, then, is establishing the extent to which our own activity in the present, scouring the past for precedents and selecting them out of a larger mass of irrelevancies, actually produces alleged coincidences instead of simply discovering them. Unfortunately, it's a judgment that ultimately depends on reason: How reasonable is the "it's just your imagination" argument? I leave it to the reader to decide about Walotsky's image, or Noguchi's proposed earthwork, or Kirby's comic—make of them what you will.

A related difficulty when studying artistic prophecy is separating possible backward-in-time transmission of information from ordinary, forward-going influence. It is unlikely that the Mars anomalists peering at low-resolution orbital photos knew about and could somehow have been biased by Noguchi's proposed earthwork, but they could potentially have been influenced by a childhood memory of Kirby's comic—which had appeared in September 1959, in issue #2 of a comic called *Race for the Moon*—or perhaps by Clarke's novel with its upturned face on the cover. There is no way of eliminating these as possibilities. Adding to the difficulty, in the world of time loops, an occurrence can be inspired by an artwork that precognized the occurrence (at some level, all prophecies are self-fulfilling). Nor of course can we ever eliminate the skeptics' eternal fallback of "just coincidence." But the fact that a Face associated with Mars specifically seems to have been prophesied by multiple artists begins to erode the law-of-large-numbers argument—the large numbers are supposed to be in the denominator, not the numerator.

Now, here's the thing: Later NASA photographs of the Face taken by new orbiters with much higher-resolution cameras in the late 1990s (after both Noguchi and Kirby had died) revealed greater erosion, less symmetry, and a much less human visage than Viking's low-res cameras had. The more it has been photographed by better cameras over the years, the less it looks even remotely artificial, least of all like a face. It is, almost certainly, just an irregularly eroded mesa—and the nearby "pyramids," just mountains.

No Face. No ancient planetary war.

There is a popular theory of psychic phenomena that real entropic events ripple across spacetime and are received by a "psychic retina."[46] Remote viewers during the Cold War were particularly accurate with "hot" targets like explosions, fires, nuclear reactors, rocket launches, and the like. But the fact that entropic scenes in fictional stories or movies burn similarly brightly in the psychic imagination suggests that it is not real entropy but the *signs* of entropy, or entropic cultural memes, that people detect psychically, entropic stories lying in wait in their future. Assuming some or all of the aforementioned works were really precognitive, the fact that, in the end, the Face on Mars is none but an idea, a fantasy, tends to support the latter interpretation.

The sublime is, as Culler wrote, a *semiotic* frame—it could even be defined as the semiotic (sign system) of entropy. The message it contains is, counterintuitively, a positive piece of news: "*I'm* still alive, *I* survived." The aesthetic response of the sublime is really our equivocal enjoyment of that "but I survived" signal. It accounts as much for our horrified fascination with accidents and tragedies—the way many Americans were glued to CNN watching and re-rewatching video clips of planes colliding with towers on 9/11, for example—as it does our appreciation of a painting by Friedrich, or a Herzog film. Interpreting a face-like Martian feature as a ruin helped space enthusiasts in the last decade of a terrifying arms race imagine and enjoy their survival, the same way cinematic visions like the half-buried Statue of Liberty in *Planet of the Apes* had done. I suggest it is this equivocal enjoyment of stimuli that, however ominous, remind us of our survival that often gets transmitted into the past in the form of premonitory dreams, visions, and artistic inspiration.[47]

Generally speaking, the curved spacetime of the long self tends to carry us past—but *just* past—existential perils. Consequently, many so-called premonitions of disaster are often really premonitions of the dreamer's own future survival of a close call. Survivor's guilt—the dark "luck" that, as Aristotle is supposed to have said, a soldier feels when it is his comrade-in-arms, maybe even his buddy, who gets hit with the arrow and not him—is the emotional core of many premonitory experiences.[48] (It is exactly those kinds of scenes, albeit nowadays involving more destructive technologies than arrows, that may dominate the repetitive dreams of war veterans with PTSD.) For Freud, and for anthropologist Ernest Becker who wove his brilliant and influential 1973 bestseller *The Denial of Death* around Freud's ideas, that Aristotelian luck reflects our basic narcissism;[49] but I prefer Lacan's reframing, centered on that not-enjoyable enjoyment *jouissance*. A state of affairs can only be represented through the oppositional signifiers of language: The only way we can see (and thereby savor) our aliveness is by witnessing (or ideally, just being able to vividly imagine) a calamity happening nearby or to others. It's not that we're bad, it's just a function of the symbolic way our minds make sense. But trauma is the price we pay for this fascination with our survival—and often, that trauma gets displaced backward in time.

Samuel Clemens' dream about his brother Henry is an illustrative example. Remember, he should have been on the riverboat that exploded, had it not been for his quarrel with the boat's pilot; then, in Memphis, he saw his dead brother wearing his (Samuel's) suit, which would have carried the message: *It should have been me, but wasn't.* Similarly,

Herzog would have had an enhanced sense of his aliveness thinking about the doomed LANSA flight he should have been on—that he had even bribed an airline official to be on—but for a twist of fate, that last-minute change of flight plan. Freud's dream of "Irma's Injection" was similarly prophetic of his own *survival* of his cancer and surgeries, despite how debilitating (and one imagines, existentially terrifying) they were. The Haitian playwright Frankétienne thought the voice telling him to obtain a medallion of Saint Andrew was that of God, but it could have been his future surviving self. Getting the medallion might even have been a sort of preemptive gesture of *gratitude* to the patron saint of the town he would come to learn was the quake's epicenter.

Arguably, we can even use this the same logic to reinterpret some artists' and writers' premonitions of their own deaths. Often, the premonition is really of a unique circumstance preceding dying, such as a terminal illness, not the death as such. Kafka could be cited here: In early 1924, he penned one of his most famous stories, "A Hunger Artist," about a man who fasts on stage as a form of theater—presented as a dying art (figuratively speaking) that people no longer appreciate. Kafka was suffering tuberculosis when he wrote the story, but this disease, which afflicts mainly the lungs, ordinarily does not prevent eating. He had no idea that, a few months later, the infection would spread to his throat—a rare but dreaded outcome—and prevented him taking food. His last days in a sanatorium near Vienna, where the 40-year-old writer was literally starving to death while he corrected the proofs for his last collection of short stories containing "A Hunger Artist," were witnessed by a physician friend who recorded Kafka's bafflement that he could have predicted the manner of his own death so eerily.[50] In Kafka's earlier, possibly also prophetic masterpiece *The Metamorphosis*, the unlucky bug-transformed Gregor Samsa is tortured by his own inability to enjoy food as he is dying from an infection.[51]

Becker could be cited here too. *The Denial of Death* argues that culture ultimately derives from our terror at our mortality—everything we do is an attempt to deny death or at least leave some legacy behind. It is one of the most influential and acclaimed books of the 1970s, winning its author a Pulitzer in 1974 and even making an appearance in Woody Allen's 1977 film *Annie Hall*. Sadly, Becker was unable to enjoy the acclaim, or even accept the Pulitzer. After completing the first draft of his book, the 48-year-old writer was diagnosed with colon cancer and died less than a year and a half later, right after the book's publication. (Asked in his final interview whether the book was a premonition, he dismissed such speculation, claiming that its themes were an organic development of his earlier research.[52]) Something similar happened to the Scottish writer Iain Banks—as Iain M. Banks, author of the well-known Culture series of SF novels. In early 2013, the 59-year-old novelist learned he had inoperable gallbladder cancer and would not survive the year. When he got this terrible news, he was already nearing completion of a novel called *The Quarry* … about a man with terminal cancer. He had no idea he was ill when he embarked on the project.

In a 2005 examination of literary prophecies, *Demain est écrit* (*Tomorrow Is Written*), French critic Pierre Bayard mentions several similar examples, such as the Belgian poet Emile Verhaeren, who died after accidentally falling under the wheels of a train on a crowded platform in Rouen, France, in 1916. Verhaeren's poetry had been full of ominous or gloomy images of trains, sometimes in association with death. Bayard also mentions the Russian poet and novelist Alexander Pushkin. In Pushkin's 1833 verse novel *Eugene Onegin*, the eponymous narrator reluctantly kills his former friend Vladimir Lensky in a duel after arousing Lensky's jealousy by dancing with his fiancée at a ball. Four years later, a jealous Pushkin died after a duel with his former friend, Baron Georges d'Anthès, who was rumored to be having an affair with Pushkin's wife, Natalia—a circumstance exactly mirroring the fate of Lensky in Pushkin's novel.[53] As we will see later, Andrei Tarkovsky, who loved Pushkin, uncannily prefigured the strange circumstances of his own death from cancer in his masterpieces *Stalker* and *The Sacrifice*.

Or recall *Titanic* passenger W. T. Stead's intuition that he would die in a press or throng of people. It proved eerily accurate, but if it was indeed a premonition, the circumstance he was seeing was not his death per se but the pandemonium on the deck of the *Titanic* as it sank. Like everyone else, he would at that point have been hoping for a place on a lifeboat or for rescue—the "life instinct" intensified to its utmost. As long as one is alive and hoping, that too is a kind of survival, a feeling of enhanced aliveness. This is what I imagine to be the case of Michael Richards, our sculptor of the impossible from Chapter 1, assuming he survived the impact of AA Flight 11 and found himself trapped on the 92nd floor of Tower One, hoping for rescue and aware that jets were being flown into the buildings. We don't know, of course, so can only speculate about that.

Br'er Rabbit in the Block Universe

By now, you may have already been asking the $64,000 question about Richards, but if not, I will ask it for you: If the sculptor was such a "precog," why didn't he have some presentiment to change his plans and be somewhere else than in his studio on the fatefully entropic morning? Is it some kind of special pleading to say he foresaw his death in his art without having an intuitive impulse to not be in his studio at all? Were the real precogs in this story all the people who called in sick that day for work in the World Trade Center or missed their flights on the hijacked planes—and Monika Bravo's boyfriend, who dissuaded her from staying the night in her studio filming the thunderstorm over Manhattan?[54] The answer is complicated, and it gets to the heart of some of the most interesting, science-fictional dimensions of the subject we are contemplating in this book.

We have already seen that people who display consistent precognitive ability seldom see future events literally with the quality of a closed-circuit video feed. A precognitive dream will typically be symbolically distorted in some way. And when dreams seem to be literal—like those dreams of David Mandell or Elizabeth Krohn—there are always crucial portions of that information missing: namely, the when and why and how. Over the decades, there have been attempts to create central registries for people to report their premonitions, with the idea that somehow this talent in the population can be pooled to avert or mitigate catastrophes like terror attacks and natural disasters.[55] But the patchiness of even the clearest-seeming precognitive dreams and visions has doomed such efforts. And that is not to mention that few public authorities would take seriously, or even be able to respond to, the imprecise warnings of one or two (or twenty or two hundred) dreamers and self-proclaimed psychics.

But there is a more fundamental reason that our intuitive idea that precognition could act as a "super-sense" to clearly scope the future landscape is not accurate, and it brings us back to the Oedipal ironies we discussed earlier with respect to Freud and his dream of Irma's Injection. It has to do with free will.

Precognitologists get asked about free will a lot. It's not as simple as saying we don't have such a thing, although some are happy to supply that answer and wash their hands of the whole issue. We do and we don't have free will—it depends on your perspective. From my present vantage point, my freely willed choice about 30 seconds ago, after some hesitation, to type the word "precognitologists" is now, after the fact, a done deal in the block universe. It is set in stone; it feels "determined." But from the vantage point of you, reading these words, even my still-freely-willed-feeling word choices as this sentence unfolds, such as the phrase I am about to write, "in your past," are in your past, fixed. If there is a future from which my current freely willed actions seem to be in the past and etched indelibly in the glass of the block universe, then by extension, even your freely willed reading of this sentence is "in the past" from another vantage point farther ahead. It means that any point in the future, even to the end of the universe, is just as fixed as the past is, all part of the block.

Our actions certainly contribute to the future, though. We help make the future with our actions. We are freely willed contributors to making the future out of the raw material of the present. But we can't directly *see* the real outcomes of our actions. Even with precognition, the future only appears as through a glass, darkly. Nor especially can we see alternative outcomes—a misleading, false claim made by many writers on ESP who claim that dreams show us "possible futures," counterfactual realities or timelines analogous to the "many worlds" of quantum physics. I argue that dreams show us, very unclearly, a single, already-existing future rather than clearly showing us alternative, yet-to-be-decided futures. But people find this idea troubling: The notion that one might foresee some awful outcome in a dream or vision yet be unable to prevent it—or just not recognize it—is a scary prospect. The idea that there is a single future ahead of us that might be foreseen feels somehow like physical confinement, as though a block universe means we are captives, bound and shackled, wanting to move or act in some certain way but restrained from doing so.

This is why Richards' continual return to the slave folk story of the Tar Baby in his sculptures is so fascinating and uncanny, given his seemingly stunning prophetic powers. The story is a classic conflict of two tricksters: Cunning predator Br'er Fox traps the rabbit with a baby made of sticky tar, holding the ever-evasive Br'er Rabbit fast. The Tar Baby is a lot like the block universe. In his life, Richards seems to have had a very unique perspective on free will, which can be thought of as a shorthand expression for our resolute human need to evade being pinned down and held captive by fate. Part of that captivity-fear is fear of being too-clearly seen and too-clearly known (including foreknown). The fear many people feel at the prospect of paranormal foresight could be an evolutionary legacy of having hidden from predators like Br'er

Fox long ago in our evolutionary past: We like to see—we like a good view from up high—but we don't like being seen, and thus feel conflicted at the thought of seeing our (future) self. When we *are* seen, we may imaginatively contort ourselves to prove that the seer was wrong—and it is true even when, especially when, the seer is oneself.

That is one way of framing Freud's still-valid core insight about the psyche: We are divided between a subjectivity that wants to know itself and an evasive, more object-like self that resists being known at all costs. It is why, despite Freud's own unseeing of its significance, his single archetype, Oedipus, is so important for the study of precognition.[56] Even when a course of action leads to some precognized future reward, and especially when that reward comes along with some negative emotion such as guilt—as rewards very often do[57]—then our constitutional evasiveness will lead us to want to do something different, take a different path ... even self-destructively. This tendency is only amplified when the precognitive brain detects some really calamitous iceberg in the waters ahead. In the Oedipus story, it was the hero's contortions to avoid his fate that ended up fulfilling his fate.

It's another way of stating why information about equivocal outcomes can *only* reach us in the present (for instance in dreams or some artistic inspiration) obliquely, indirectly, symbolically. Again, it can be thought of as a kind of gravitational lensing that inevitably distorts our perception of crises, catastrophes, and traumas: We never foresee them with the clarity that would enable us to avert them entirely, since that would be a paradox. This is why precognition guides us not in the manner of radar or some X-ray vision piercing the fog ahead, but more the way dark matter shapes the structure and spin of a galaxy—detectable mainly in life's perturbations and deviations, like a sudden artistic inspiration or a videographer's random urge to take her tape home as she left her studio on the evening before a terrorist attack. It takes different forms for everyone.

Before he died, Richards was celebrating a cluster of life achievements: an engagement, a newly "sculpted" body from lifting weights that gave him increased confidence,[58] and the increasing recognition that was opening new doors, such as getting accepted to the World Views program. Along with the prestige, the view of the Hudson with those icons of freedom and acceptance, Ellis Island and the Statue of Liberty, might have even seemed symbolic of his newfound success in the struggle that his work had chronicled over the previous decade: overcoming the extra obstacles placed in the path of an aspiring Black artist in a racist society and white-dominated art world.[59] He was feeling strong in his life and his career. But consider: It would have been the strength of precisely that inspired body of work, especially *Tar Baby vs. St. Sebastian*—which had been featured in a recent traveling exhibition called Passages: Contemporary Art in Transition[60]—that secured Richards a place in the World Views program in the first place. If we accept that that sculpture was precognitive, then this fact alone helps answer the question why Richards' precognition did not manifest as an urge to grab his things and go home to his fiancée after *Monday Night Football*. Had the sculptor not been in his studio on the morning of 9/11, he would not have created his most amazing and successful works. That would be a grandfather paradox. He would not have been there in that studio had it not been for what was going to happen to him.

If this seems like circular reasoning, it is.

Time travel and precognition in a self-consistent universe follow the tautological logic that physicists call closed timelike curves or causal loops. Again, a precognitive dream or artistic inspiration is like a billiard ball that was shot back in time through a wormhole from some future turning point in the individual dreamer or artist's life, deflecting them in just the right way that their actions lead them to that turning point. It is this, not repression, that really accounts for the obliquity or indirectness of precognitive dreams and art, the reason they tend to speak about the future in a symbolic language.[61] Our natural evasiveness—the sense in which we do have free will—demands it. In rare cases when the individual's worldly achievements or success are bound in a very direct way to some especially adverse fate, the effect is particularly strange, even uncanny, and occasionally tragic.

Richards seems to have intuited the stickiness and treachery of fate long before that fateful day in September 2001. Highly precognitive people often experience life as a perplexing landscape of synchronicity, and highly precognitive writers and artists frequently run into situations they had pre-presented in their art. Instead of being rewarding, there may be something tricksterish-feeling about it. It may feel like being stuck in a trap arranged by some slightly sadistic higher intelligence. I don't know, as no one has yet written a detailed biography of Richards, but I wonder if he experienced this in smaller doses throughout his life, as it seems to be the central intuition that he was struggling to find a way to express and depict in so many of his sculptures—almost like a Zen koan he kept revisiting from different angles and wrestling with.

Richards' success was a trap for him exactly the way Freud's was:

His work bound him to his fate, and his fate bound him to his work. The Tar Baby story that the sculptor continually returned to expresses this idea so brilliantly that I cannot believe his fixation on it was an accident. In the story, Br'er Rabbit ultimately outwits the fox, enticing him to throw him in the more escapable briar patch instead. Richards transforms the narrative into an Oedipal story: In that most astonishing retelling, the escape, the flight, the evasion, is somehow the real trap—as though hunters, shooting *symbols of evasion/escape* as weapons (planes), stood ready by the briar patch to finish the job, transforming Br'er Rabbit into the beautiful martyr St. Sebastian. Br'er Fox, in Richards' retelling, won. Just like Oedipus, Br'er Rabbit fulfills his fate by trying to evade it.

This career-long obsession with the entrapping subtext of liberation is what I find especially fascinating in Richards' sculptures, and what I find especially telling of his precognition—much more than the obvious physical similarity of that one sculpture, *Tar Baby vs. St. Sebastian*, to the 9/11 attacks. In a universe that includes time travel and tesseract brains, some things are just circular, and there's no way around that, pedantic logicians be damned. It's impossible, but it's the truth.

Postscript: Freeing the Captives

When I think of Michael Richards and his Tar Baby obsession, I can't help thinking of another sculptor, another Michael, whose sculptures depict with similar clarity, albeit less tragedy, the human predicament of being freely willed beings trapped in a block universe and whose free will is paradoxically part of what entraps us.

Michelangelo's *Four Captives* are muscular, larger-than-life-size figures who appear to be trapped by their marble matrix, struggling to get free.[62] It is often claimed that the sculptor made them this way deliberately, leaving them unfinished to express his unique methodology: liberating the forms that he felt already existed within the stone.[63] In a novel about the sculptor, Irving Stone had him say "I saw the angel in the marble, and carved until I set him free."[64] The real Michelangelo never actually said it so concisely, at least we don't have record of it, but his letters do confirm that this was more or less the way he thought about his art: He worked at a piece of marble systematically front-to-back, as though gradually unearthing something buried within the block. It would thus seem perfectly obvious that Michelangelo created his *Captives* to express his artistic truth, that creation is really a form of discovery, a kind of finding rather than making.

But it's not so. They were in fact unfinished works, their appearance of struggle a complete accident.

The figures began as part of a commission for a massive mausoleum for Michelangelo's patron, Pope Julius II. The project, begun in 1505, was intended to be the grandest tomb in Christendom, with more than 40 large figures arrayed on the triangular facades of an enormous four-sided pyramid. Supporting the saints, biblical figures, and allegorical figures of the arts and sciences in the middle and top tiers of the pyramid was to be a bottom layer of bound slaves, representing (as the sculptor's friend Vasari described) "all the provinces subjugated by the Pope and made obedient to the Apostolic Church."[65] But as often happens with lavish commissions, the money ran out. A year into the project, the pope had to tell his master-sculptor to stop work and come up with a much more modest design. There was no more need of the row of slaves, so these half-finished extras in Michelangelo's big-budget epic ended up back on his cutting-room floor, so to speak—that is, in his studio. He ended up finishing two of six captives that he had begun and gifted them to a fellow Florentine living in Rome, Roberto Strozzi. The aborted mausoleum also supplied other statues that became masterpieces in their own right, including the sculptor's famous Moses, now in the Rome church of San Pietro in Vincoli. But four of the unfinished captives became his constant companions in his work and remained in his studio. They were found by his nephew after his death.[66]

So, impossibly, Michelangelo's method, coupled with the vicissitudes of fate, conspired to produce four of his most haunting works, having taken on a specific meaning related to his expressed sense of the master's own art as liberating something imprisoned in a stone block. The question you are permitted to ask, although it is totally unanswerable from this historical distance, is: Was Michelangelo's original inspiration for those weight-bearing *slaves* as the foundation for a self-absorbed pope's tomb somehow a premonition of their ultimate abandonment and incompleteness, their destiny to be half-liberated *captives* of the marble, throughout eternity? Did their visible struggle, which appears like a struggle to free themselves, really have an unconscious precognitive inspiration? As with most things in the study of precognition, we can never know.

PART TWO

ARTISTS AND SHAMANS, SEPARATED AT BIRTH

To all appearances, the artist acts like a mediumistic being who, from the labyrinth beyond time and space, seeks his way out to a clearing.
—Marcel Duchamp, "The Creative Act" (1957)

What is the artist but the channel through which spirits descend—ghosts, visions, portents, the tinkling of bells?
—Isamu Noguchi, *A Sculptor's World* (1968)

5

"They Have Been Here!"
Cave Art and Long Superhumanity

*Time is not a straight line, it's more of a labyrinth, and
if you press close to the wall at the right place you can
hear the hurrying steps and the voices, you can hear
yourself walking past on the other side.*
—Tomas Tranströmer, "Answers to Letters" (1981)

*"One only understands the things that one tames," said
the fox.*
—Antoine de Saint-Exupéry, *The Little Prince* (1943)

There was something behind the wall. They could see its breath.
Like some shaman performing a private and obscure ritual, a
crouching figure slowly passed his incense—in fact, a steadily smolder-
ing mosquito coil—across and over the rubble in the deepest part of the
cramped niche. His two companions, bracing themselves against the
sloping stone, stood behind and watched his cautious movements. In
the light of their headlamps they saw it too: the pencil-straight smoke
smoothly rising and suddenly deflecting, becoming turbulent from the
rock's exhalation.

The Gorges de l'Ardèche, sometimes called the Grand Canyon of
Europe, is a network of canyons carved out of the limestone hills over
millions of years in southern France. More than 2,000 caves are known
to exist in the area, including some with artifacts showing human habi-
tation going back 300,000 years. The prospect of a big find—maybe
with an artifact trove or, even better, cave art—had driven park ranger
Jean-Marie Chauvet, vintner Eliette Brunel Deschamps, and technician Christian Hillaire for several years by the time they ventured into

this narrow grotto on a hillside overlooking a vineyard near a bend in the Ardèche River on an afternoon in late December 1994. Working mostly on weekends, the trio of lifelong cavers, bent over their little turbulent ribbons of smoke, had discovered several hidden caves in the area, and a few even had paintings, but none nearly as spectacular as the famous caves of the Dordogne region like Lascaux or other big-name caves that dot southern France and the Iberian Penninsula like the one at Altamira, Spain.

It was a few days before Christmas. They were just a stone's throw from one of the most popular sightseeing destinations in France, an impressive natural arch over the Ardèche river called Pont d'Arc. The late afternoon sun already cast lengthening shadows out in the valley, and it was dark and chilly in the narrow grotto where they suspected a deeper cave might be hiding. More crouching, muttering, reaching out of hands toward the rock. A cheek pressed close confirmed it—there was something behind the wall. They started pulling away rocks.

Their efforts over the next few hours exposed a passage that led deep into the hillside, just barely wide enough for a human to squeeze through. Because she was smallest, Eliette was the first to wriggle into the hole. She pressed through the tight, down- and then up-sloping passage and found that it opened out into a large dark gallery about three meters above a dirt floor dimly illuminated by her headlamp. Her companions followed, excitedly. The chamber was so big their lights barely pierced the darkness in front of them. Their voices echoed. They would need their rope ladder to climb down, and they went back to their car to retrieve it. It was now 9 p.m., dark outside.

On their return, Jean-Marie Chauvet led the way through the narrow entrance passage and was the first to descend to the floor of the interior chamber on the rope ladder. The others followed. Once on the cave floor, they advanced slowly, in single file, to disturb the setting as little as possible with their boots.

The chamber was so big that their headlamps didn't reveal much at first. All they immediately saw was that they had discovered a geological and biological treasure trove. They carefully skirted gorgeous, glistening, red-brown mineral formations, as well as large pits in the sediment that they recognized could be nests hollowed out tens of thousands of years ago by long-extinct cave bears. The floor was strewn with thousands of animal bones, including many bear skulls and skulls of ibexes that had also inhabited that landscape during the last Ice Age. The profusion of animal remains told them that this cave must have once had a more accessible entrance than the narrow fissure they had climbed in through. The bones were frosted with a glistening layer of hardened calcite, attesting to how long they had been resting there in the darkness, completely undisturbed.

Then, Eliette saw it first: a glimpse of red caught in the light of her headlamp resolved itself as the unmistakable head and hump of a woolly mammoth, painted in red ochre. "They have been here!" she cried out.[1]

Unable to speak now in their excitement, the trio proceeded farther into what they now realized was a kind of otherworldly (underworldly) cathedral, one that clearly rivaled the famous Lascaux Cave, 350 kilometers to the west. They found walls densely covered with animal images in red ochre and black charcoal—horses, bison, lions, wooly rhinos, aurochs, an owl, even a butterfly that looks an awful lot like Mothman. Other walls bore hand prints. A rock near what must have been the original mouth of the cave—long since blocked off from an ancient rock fall—was covered with red dots that were later discovered to be palm prints.

Standing in the silence, the three explorers felt an uncomfortable and uncanny sense of being watched by those who had painted the wild animals on the cave's smoothly contoured walls. They later described:

> [T]he emotion that gripped us made us incapable of uttering a single word. Alone in that vastness, lit by the feeble beam of our lamps, we were seized by a strange feeling. Everything was so beautiful, so fresh, almost too much so. Time was abolished, as if the tens of thousands of years that separated us from the producers of these paintings no longer existed. It seemed as if they had just created these masterpieces. Suddenly we felt like intruders. Deeply impressed, we were weighed down by the feeling that we were not alone; the artists' souls and spirits surrounded us. We thought we could feel their presence; we were disturbing them.[2]

Later scientific researchers—and filmmakers—reported the same unsettling experience.

Radiocarbon dating is difficult with pigments like red and yellow ochre that are mostly mineral-based. The artists in the cave that came to be named after Jean-Michel Chauvet used no binding medium. But the profuse charcoal used to make the blacks, and the traces of the fires the painters used to make the charcoal, enabled scientists to date some of the images to 32,000 years ago. More recent dating techniques have pushed back the age of the earliest charcoal traces to 37,000 years, more than twice the age of the paintings in Lascaux.[3] Until just a few years ago, the paintings in Chauvet Cave were the oldest representational images (pictures) known anywhere on the planet. A faint animal-headed "sorcerer" found on a rock slab in a cave near Verona, Italy, is probably as old.[4] Several recently discovered images in Southeast Asia, including a cattle-like animal painted on a cave wall in Borneo,[5] a wild pig on a cave wall on Sulawesi,[6] and an image of two human-like figures (one with a distinct bird beak) hunting water buffalo and pigs in a cave in Sumatra,[7] are older, having been dated at more than 40,000 years BP. The latter images are even older than the oldest anthropomorphic sculpture: a lion-headed man carved from mammoth ivory that was discovered in a German cave called Hohlenstein-Stadel in 1939. But Chauvet Cave remains the oldest sizeable assemblage of Paleolithic cave art, and even just on the internet, in documentaries, or in coffee-table books, some of it is quite stunning.

The styles in Chauvet and other caves may be as varied as you might expect to find in a modern art gallery. Some of the animals are realistic. Others resemble the spare but evocative drawings of Chinese calligraphers, conveying in just a few simple lines not just the form but also the unique personality, even humor, of a lion stalking its prey or a curious bear. Others are stylized or even cartoon-like. Some are distinctly contemporary in appearance, and some are even surreal. One mammoth on Chauvet Cave's Lion Panel has what appear to be wheels or balls for feet. Pablo Picasso was said to have visited Lascaux Cave and declared that "We have learned nothing in 12,000 years." It's a made-up story, unfortunately (and the timespan is wrong—it is now thought to be more like 17,000 years for that cave).[8] But many of the pictures Ice Age painters made, from whatever specific time period, do look more or less like something Picasso could have created at various points in his career. Art and music scholar Michael Tucker saw it as synchronistic that the most important painted caves were discovered simultaneously with the emergence of modernism in painting.[9]

Just try and wrap your head around art—sophisticated, modern, playful art—that is the better part of forty millennia old. How many generations, births and deaths, joys and sorrows, is that? It is possible that the last human being to set eyes on the paintings in Chauvet Cave before its 20th-century rediscovery was a ten-year-old child who strolled through with a torch and, amazingly, a wolf companion, 26,000 years ago.[10] The pair left clear, side-by-side tracks in cave sediment softened by water-seepage, and the child's torch-scrapings along the cave walls to keep it bright enabled researchers to date their walk. Some of the images were already as old when the child gazed at them as the first Neolithic settlements in the Fertile Crescent are to archaeologists to-day.[11] Interestingly, nearly all the human footprints in Paleolithic caves are from bare feet, suggesting that visitors routinely left their footwear at the entrance. There's no way of knowing if this was out of respect for the cave, respect for the paintings, or for some other reason. Whatever the case, a collapse of the cliff face completely sealed off the cave's only entrance about 5,000 years after the child and wolf visited, leaving it a perfect time capsule of a mindbogglingly distant epoch.

The world would have looked vastly different when the images in Chauvet Cave were created, even from space. Mile-high glaciers covered much of Northern Europe, and the shorelines of the continents would have reflected a sea that was 400 feet lower than it is now, with land bridges connecting mainland Europe to Britain and, on the other side of the world, Asia to North America. The people who created the paint-ings would have looked very different from their modern Europeans descendants too. They had dark skin, for one thing—gene variants for pale skin not having emerged in Europe until about 8,000 years ago, a mere eyeblink. Across the steppes and valleys of southern Europe, the dark-skinned and dark-eyed people of what is called the Aurigna-cian culture may have spent some of the year in small, widely scattered family groups, migrating to follow reindeer herds and other game, but coalescing into much larger, town- or city-like assemblages for por-tions of the year as well—an annual oscillation that has in recent years overthrown old, linear notions of social evolution.[12] Their societies may have been as complex, as varied, and as ever-changing as their art.

After their migration into Europe 40,000 years ago, the ancestors of the Chauvet Cave painters would sometimes have encountered and even mated with the similarly brainy, tool-using, probably lighter-skinned Neanderthals, who had lived in Europe for 300,000-400,000 years by that point. Most archaeologists now think that that branch of the hominin tree had gone extinct or been dissolved into ours before the oldest known European paintings were made. Still, the Neanderthals are important as a touchstone: They made tools and adorned themselves, they buried their dead,[13] and recent finds suggest they applied pigments to cave features,[14] but thus far there is scant evidence they ever made actual pictures. Many reasons have been proposed: One of many theories is that it is because they lacked an interest in or ability to remember their dreams.[15] That their brains differed from ours is clear, although what these differences meant for Neanderthals' cognitive abilities remains an open question. But because pictures like those in Chauvet Cave are so distinctive of *Homo sapiens sapiens*, it is sometimes said that they show us not only art's beginnings but even, as Werner Herzog romantically put it in his 2010 documentary, *Cave of Forgotten Dreams*, "the birth of the modern human soul."[16]

It's a great film—and possibly prophetic, as we will see—but I think Herzog is wrong. I think this art shows us something other than a birth, and something beyond the exactly human.

When People Turn into Bison

I admit that squeezing my ungainly writer's body into a womb-like Paleolithic grotto in search of the origins of ideas is driven partly by my constant quest for a good metaphor (and probably a bunch of Freudian reasons too—move on, nothing to see there). I'm hardly the first writer to abuse cave art that way. For moderns, caves are the ultimate metaphor for mystery and for the forgotten or repressed past. Caves preserve. Scary and science-fictional things might be lurking in them— evolutionary things. Pale things and things lacking senses. And for us, having the benefit of radiocarbon dating to tell us how truly old it all is, cave art evokes the mood of the sublime better than almost anything else. Humanity is immense, but we individual humans are truly puny. Check your ego at the door, with your shoes. But ancient and prehistoric people clearly attached a different range of meanings to caves. Animal stampedes around vulva-like niches in Chauvet Cave's deepest galleries are strongly suggestive of an association between the underworld and profusion or fecundity—the arrival of the new, not the burial and storage of the old. We know that in at least some ancient cultures, caves had counterintuitive associations with the future, not (or not only) the past, and it could have been true of Ice Age cultures as well.

Cave paintings are enchanting for a million reasons, but principally because they are the oldest direct traces of the human imagination— thinking about, mentally seeing, things that are not present. Humans are storytellers and, indeed, one of the very few things that can be said for certain about cave art, at a distance of over 37,000 years, is that the painters were not simply copying what they saw in front of their eyes, thumbs outstretched in front of nature.[17] Although it is pure projection, it is almost as if their situation, in the deepest, most inaccessible recesses, is meant to drive home this precise understanding: that we are looking at representations of things seen *only* in the mind's eye. But it's easy to be misled by that fact.

The birth of art was almost certainly not, as Herzog seems to suggest and as other writers like Graham Hancock have also suggested,[18] the birth *of* the imagination, the birth *of* storytelling, any more than the first writing in the Fertile Crescent 30 millennia later was the birth of speech. You can't build a fire, fashion a stone tool, collect berries for your elderly mother-in-law, or plan a hunt—things people had been doing for hundreds of thousands of years by that point—without imagining desired outcomes and without being able to perform the more complex imagining of what other people with other minds are thinking or experiencing. Stories about the world follow from this. Nor would you ceremonially bury a dead relative, which people had been doing for at least 80,000-100,000 years by that time, without imagining something like an afterlife or spiritual world. And more to the point, you can communicate all those imaginings in all kinds of transient ways: You can evoke mental images with words, "picture" in gesture, and act out real and mythological events. People had likely been telling and acting out stories and otherwise painting *mental* pictures for each other for aeons by the time they began to paint pictures on rock walls. Acting and song were the first arts, not painting. People likely also had been drawing and painting with less durable materials on exposed surfaces for a long time before they started doing it deep inside caves protected from the elements.

The so-called Great Leap Forward that occurred (by some estimates) around 50,000 years ago is no longer thought to have been some genetic flipped switch where storytelling and imagining and complex problem-solving suddenly came online.[19] It was specifically a cultural leap or set of cultural leaps—among other things, the beginnings of a durable visual art tradition. It would have had neurocognitive implications, though—cultural leaps always have neurocognitive implications. Pictures rewired us. And it's great news for us, here, now, because it is as if, for the first time in the 200,000- to 300,000-year history of *Homo sapiens*, a crude dot-matrix printer was finally plugged into the hyperdimensional quantum computer of the human brain, enabling us to see directly what *some* human beings were imagining, *some* of the time.

They were imagining animals, of course—great commotions of them. This fact is far more interesting than it seems at first glance, because it cannot be reduced to their lives as hunters. The most common animals painted on European cave walls are horses and bison, but those weren't the main game they hunted and ate. That realization disproved one of several longstanding theories about cave art, that it represented hunting magic—animal spirits being propitiated.[20] (As anthropologist Claude Lévi-Strauss put it in his 1962 book *Totemism*, "animals are good to think with," not just good to eat.[21]) But besides animals, Ice Age painters all over the world, from Spain to Sumatra, were also imagining *superhumans*: people with animal qualities—or animals with people qualities. There are disembodied hands and vulvas, but there are few ordinary people depicted in Paleolithic caves. Instead, there are distorted or stylized human-like beings, and mainly bison- or bird-headed or antlered humanoids. Most famously, in the deepest recesses of Lascaux Cave, there is a bird-headed man lying prone, with an erection, next to a bird-topped staff—more about that fellow momentarily.

One could not ask for a clearer illustration of Jeffrey Kripal's assertion in his 2022 book *The Superhumanities* that "we got to the superhuman before we got to the human. Way before."[22] The latter category and concern fits in a tiny lower right corner on the cosmic calendar of human thought. Most myth and religion over the millennia and tens of millennia is dominated by the themes seen on cave walls: extraordinary experiences, impossible physical transformations, contact with nonhuman beings, and superpowers.[23] Following the religion scholar Martin Reisebrodt, Kripal calls religion "legitimate science fiction."[24] Legitimate, because these themes *always* arise ultimately from real people's real (albeit "impossible") experiences—mystical experiences and paranormal experiences of all kinds. They are not just stories. Although paleoanthropologists had been very sluggish to acknowledge it, it is now widely held to be true of Ice Age cave painters as well—much of their art (not all) reflects extraordinary experiences, probably in what we now neutrally call altered states of consciousness.[25]

University of Witwatersrand rock-art scholar David Lewis-Williams has been one of the leading academic proponents of the shamanic hypothesis of cave art. Working and thinking in a cross-disciplinary vein sometimes called neurotheology, Lewis-Williams describes an "intensified trajectory of consciousness" characteristic of shamanic trance states and psychedelic experiences and found reflected in rock art from widely disparate cultures all over the world.[26] Everywhere, such art depicts what he calls "entoptic" phenomena (dots, zig-zags, etc.—*entoptic* meaning originating within the optical system rather than the environment), vortices or whirlpool-like tunnels, transformations into animals, and nonhuman beings.[27] It is a phenomenological trajectory familiar not only to people consuming psychedelics but also to lucid dreamers and other consciousness-spelunkers.[28] Until the 1990s, paleo-anthropologists had been reluctant to write or even speculate about Paleolithic shamanism—we just don't know enough about such a remote culture, went the refrain;[29] also, the subject of shamanism had such strong New Age and psychedelic overtones that it was anathema for many scientists. But in a series of articles and books, including his now-classic 2002 book *The Mind in the Cave*, Lewis-Williams wove a thick-enough "cable" of evidence, including neuroscience and hard-to-ignore cross-cultural comparisons, to persuade many in his field that Ice Age cave paintings—or many of them—were certainly made by shamans during or following experiences in nonordinary reality.[30]

Some of those shamans' beliefs can be inferred from their art. French paleoanthropologist Jean Clottes, the first authority to lead the scientific team studying Chauvet Cave, was an early convert to Lewis-Williams' ideas, and they collaborated in a 1996 book, *The Shamans of Prehistory*.[31] They argued that, much like the Greeks and other more recent cultures that we know attached spiritual significance to caves, Paleolithic people saw the seemingly solid material of a cave wall as a membrane or veil to the underworld that could be seen through and even penetrated.[32] Many images in caves seem to have been suggested by preexisting contours and cracks and embellished into animal figures. It is the artistic recruitment of pareidolia: the obsessively meaning-making mind's constant finding of patterns in natural features and "random" stimuli. Many modern artists have used the same trick—Salvador Dali called it his "paranoiac-critical method"—although in divinatory contexts it has many other names, including scrying. It's a fertile mode of accessing precognition, by the way—oops, but we're getting ahead of ourselves.

In some cases, images give the impression that the rock itself contained or was pregnant with animals or other beings. In Altamira Cave in Northern Spain, for instance, a doe as well as two possibly humanoid faces are seen to be pressing forward out of bulges in the wall.[33] Like rock artists today, the painters may have thought of themselves as midwives, using pigment to fix the images that dimly illuminated cave-wall features suggested to them. If so, it would also be consistent with the intuition of countless artists historically, that their actions were helping something into the world that they intuited was already there, latent—something found and not made. Many of the adumbrated, partial animal figures on cave walls give exactly the impression of Michelangelo's Captives, held somehow midway in the process of coming-into-being.

The prevalence in most caves of so-called negative handprints or hand stencils—outlines of hands made by blowing pigment through a tube onto a hand pressed against the rock—could support the idea of the cave wall's permeability. In Chauvet, several are found on two panels in what would have been the most accessible part of the cave during its roughly 10,000 years of human use, its Entrance Chamber. It is natural for us to see handprints as a kind of graffiti, an assertion that "I was here." But Clottes and Lewis-Williams point out the missing experiential dimension: The paint-covered hand pressed against paint-covered rock would have appeared in the dim torchlight to be penetrating it, entering it, like a hand reaching into water. They proposed that the negative handprints in Paleolithic caves are traces of a practice in which people were given a visual experience of reaching into the wall. There is no way to know for sure, but it is an elegant, intuitively compelling idea.[34] If true, it may be that everyone in the community had an opportunity to experience the impossible permeability of the rock. A 2022 survey of hand stencils in European caves showed that the hands belonged to people of all ages. A quarter of the international sample are the hands of children.[35] The same is true, incidentally, of footprints in Paleolithic caves—many are of children, sometimes but not always accompanied by adults.

In addition to permeability, Paleolithic art shows clear evidence that the painters believed in the fluidity of the world's creatures and objects, and especially the fluid boundaries of the (super)human. The most striking (and famous) image in Chauvet Cave is in its deepest recesses, the so-called End Chamber: what appears to be the vulva and thighs of a woman, resembling the various "Venus" figurines uncovered throughout Paleolithic Europe, either fused or juxtaposed with the upper body of a bison. It is painted on the back of a stalactite hanging into the chamber. It could represent a kind of divine copulation or rape, or it could be a hybrid being, or a human in the process of transformation or mutation—it is ambiguous. Paleoanthropologists forcefully resist drawing modern comparisons to the art of such a remote culture, but laypeople inevitably compare this image to the much-later Greek myth of the rape of Europa by Zeus in the form of a bull, as well as to the Minotaur kept captive by Europa's son, King Minos, in a subterranean labyrinth on Crete. The wanton nonacademic mind, as writer Gregory Curtis admits, goes immediately to Picasso's famous drawings of Minotaurs embracing women.[36] Whatever it may have originally represented, it has never been gazed on directly in modern times, as it cannot be seen from the terminus of the narrow metal walkway installed in the cave, which strictly follows the path taken by the three discoverers in their initial explorations. A researcher had to extend a small digital camera on a long pole to capture it.[37] Seems appropriate for a Holy of Holies.

The theme of human-animal mutation and hybridity is one that runs through all world folklore, myth, and imaginative literature. Images of human-animal hybrids or composites are nearly an iconographic universal—as close to an archetype as you can get.[38] According to art historian Louise S. Milne, hybrids go along with animal stampedes as a strangely persistent and widespread iconographic complex in art traditions everywhere, what she calls a visual "rhetoric of commotion" associated with dreams, madness, and ecstatic ritual.[39] It is all too tempting to see the riots of animals stampeding across the walls of Chauvet, Lascaux, and other European caves as a manifestation of this same "rhetoric"—but very likely, also *experience*—of commotion, what Milne calls "the storm in the head," in deepest time.

The animal commotions in Paleolithic caves resemble the river and oceanic images that erupt spontaneously for modern artists and writers during some of their most inspired states. Again, the fecundity of the creative, primary-process imagination when set free of its usual daily moorings, whether in dreams or in the ordinary trancelike flow state of doing one's craft, feels very much like wild things rushing out, unstoppable. Animals bursting out and across cave walls seem like another metaphor of flowing. Are those stampeding animals "spirits" or are they metaphors, and could those categories really, on some very deep level, be the same thing, or aspects of the same thing?

There are many ways to unmoor the imagination. Trance may be induced by drumming (auditory driving), drugs, fasting, and dancing, alone or in combination.[40] Clottes and Lewis-Williams imagine any of these visionary modalities could have been used by Paleolithic shamans. But another surefire way to induce visionary experiences is simple sensory deprivation in the silence and pitch black of a cave. It's one of the easiest, drug-free hacks of human neurobiology, in fact. In total darkness, vivid hallucinations—visual, auditory, and so on—arise quite readily, along with out-of-body experiences, mystical experiences, and sometimes terrifying visions. Caves have been used for this purpose in a wide range of cultures, including often in the context of initiation rituals, where a young initiate is left alone in a cave to have a meaningful or guiding vision.

Combining sleep and dreaming with the complete darkness and silence of a cave or windowless sanctuary—dream incubation—is a particularly potent combination and is also part of shamanic toolkits all over the world. Ben-Gurion University historian Yulia Ustinova, who applies a neurotheological approach to Greek mystical literature and archaeology, shows that in that culture caves were privileged spaces for having specifically prophetic visions and dreams, by giving access to the underworld where the dead dwell.[41] It was believed that the dead, being unencumbered by bodies, had clearer access to the future and thus their spirits could communicate the future to visitors. This is the counterintuitive association between subterraneity and futurity that I hinted at earlier.

In the early 1980s, anthropologist Michael Harner had a supernormal experience that powerfully validated the practice of dream incubation in caves. Attempting a "cave power quest" as described in ethnographies of the Paviotso (Paiute) people of Nevada, he descended alone into a cave in Virginia's Shenandoah Valley and bedded down alone for the night, in the pitch dark. It was scary, as one might imagine. He awoke in the middle of the night after feeling what he thought was a wing of a large bird brush his cheek. He then had a purely auditory experience that he was in the middle of a stampede—hoofbeats and snorting. "'We are Horse,' the invisible animals said, in a communication like telepathy, but stronger." (It is Milne's storm in the head.) After that cacophony faded, it was followed by another smaller auditory stampede: "'We are Bison,' they said."[42] Harner writes that he "felt indescribable awe and gratitude" at this gift in the cave, which he interpreted as a real spiritual encounter. For what it may be worth, although he was in Virginia, it happened to be specifically an encounter with the two most prevalent animals in European painted caves, horse and bison, in that order. He returned to sleep and had further significant dreams, including an encounter with a seductive woman named "Elieth" whom he later identified as the Judaic mythological being Lilith, who reputedly lived in caves and seduced sleeping men.

Incubation played a central role in healing as well as divination throughout the ancient Mediterranean world. Spas or hospitals called Asklepieions, often connected to caves, were places where the sick came to sleep and have healing dreams under the guidance of priests who could interpret those dreams, and there were hundreds of such centers.[43] Although it is not a mainstream view, it has even been argued that the Labyrinth of Knossos in Crete, home of the legendary Minotaur, was a Minoan temple complex and incubation site, not a palace as its excavator Arthur Evans supposed.[44] Cretans, in fact, were dream specialist in their day—the Cretan shaman Epimedes supposedly acquired the ability to leave his body at will after sleeping in a cave most of his life.[45] And the bull, as part of the Minoan/Cretan "brand," had widely known associations to incubation. A Ptolemaic period tablet in Egypt shows a Minoan bull standing behind an altar, with the inscription: "I interpret dreams, for I am entrusted to do so by the god, with good fortune. It is a Cretan who interprets."[46]

Paleoanthropologists may wave professorially gnarled fingers at you, but you'd be forgiven for imagining some symbolic continuity between the mysterious bison-men of Paleolithic caves and Crete's famous Minotaur—some ages-old, pan-European symbolism related to dreams and the dreamworld. It has long been suggested that Paleolithic caves may have been incubation sites.[47] Inaccessible and dangerous, they were certainly not art galleries—invalidating another early theory of cave art that the images were just "art for art's sake."[48] Evidence shows Chauvet was visited by small numbers of people, once in a blue moon. Caves like Chauvet or Lascaux would have been the perfect place to go—or more scarily, be dropped off by a teacher with the only torch—to have dangerous and transformative dreams. That 10-year-old might have brought the wolf along out of caution as much as friendship—there could have been bears in there, incubating and having their own fierce bear-shaman visions.

"That's the guy who was with us, Davey"

The fluidity and permeability indexed by Clottes and Lewis-Williams as central features of the worldview of Paleolithic shamans relate to the solidity of matter, and to the nature of time and change, the universal solvent of that solidity. Fascinated by how the drapery-like undulations of Chauvet Cave's walls produce an illusion of movement when the light source itself moves (as the painters' torches would have), Herzog in his film called the paintings "proto-cinema." Some of the animals are shown with extra legs, suggesting movement in a different way. But that illusion of movement, naturally fascinating to a filmmaker, is predicated on the prior condition of stasis. As William Faulkner put it in a 1956 *Paris Review* interview, "The aim of every artist is to arrest motion, which is life, by artificial means and hold it fixed so that a hundred years later, when a stranger looks at it, it moves again."[49] A hundred or, you know, 37,000. A cinema is really just a variety of camera obscura.

This—the capturing of life and mind in motion, as though in amber, so that some cross-section of our 4-D reality can not only be shown to others later (and reanimated by them) but also compared with later experiences—would have been one of the most important components of that cultural Great Leap Forward. Cave art was not the birth of the human imagination or soul. It was the beginnings of *recording*, and that would have constituted a major discovery-slash-invention: *the permanence of ideas in a world of flux.*

Consider: It was a world we can barely imagine now, where storytelling and imagination had *always* been essentially cinematic, in constant motion and evanescent, the way speech and gesture are always in motion—"flowing out like endless rain" as John Lennon put it. Indeed, the way animals—the principle subject of cave art—are always in motion. The only landscape scene depicted in Chauvet Cave is also in motion: a volcano erupting.[50] In such a world, the capturing and recording of an idea, even if only barely or imperfectly as in a paper cup, would have been a watershed. It would have been a major, perplexing and philosophically exciting discovery that the imagination could be frozen like that.

Those tracks in Chauvet Cave show us a wild animal in the process of being domesticated, tamed. The paintings show us the riverlike, firelike, animal-like imagination being tamed, made to obediently stand still, or sit. And painting was the launching pad for many further discoveries—ultimately, of course, that of writing, which was the taming of speech. That taming only took another 30,000 years, but given how long painting took before it—ten times that long—it shows the beginnings of an exponential acceleration leading from the first storytelling and story-miming on the African savannah hundreds of millennia ago to the rise of social media and AI—like the bone-hammer in Stanley Kubrick's *2001: A Space Odyssey* that becomes an orbiting nuclear platform in an eyeblink.

It hardly can be an accident that the earliest philosophies of which we have written record grappled centrally with the dichotomy of motion and stasis. The sixth-century BC Chinese philosopher Lao Tze wrote of the flow of things, or the Tao, for instance. In fifth-century BC Greece, Heraclitus compared the constant flow of Time to a river. He is best remembered for his aphorism that you can't step in the same river twice, although his main metaphor for the constant energy and motion of things was fire. But every philosophical position, when you dig down, contains its opposite. Famously in opposition to Heraclitus and his fire was Parmenides (same period), who argued that change and motion are illusions, that the reality behind the appearances is permanence. Parmenides was a shaman whose insights came from visionary experiences during incubation in caves.[51] His position would later be upheld and "proved" through the thought experiments of his pupil and adopted son Zeno—for instance the arrow that, once shot, has to pass halfway to its target, and then half of the rest of the way, and then half of the rest, and so on, so that it can never get to the end.

Chalk on chalkboards—not too different from pigment on stone—provided modernity with some of the same insights as the dreams of Parmenides or the animals Ice Age shamans saw in altered states and painted on the rock walls of caves. As far as I know, Hermann Minkowski's image of a block-like four-dimensional spacetime came from simply doing the math and not from a visionary state or a dream. But he was sort of the Parmenides of our times, asserting the permanence underlying the manifest impermanence we experience. The past still exists, it's right here. And so, by implication, is the future. It's right behind the wall. Shamans seem to have discovered that 40,000+ years ago, when they first tamed their imaginations with pictures. And everything I am arguing about art and precognition follows from it.

We don't know anything about individual Paleolithic painters' lives, so we cannot guess which of their images might have been based on dreams or visions that proved precognitive of something the artist was going to encounter in real life the next day or in their near future. But here, modern comparisons can illuminate universal human superexperience. A famous Pennsylvania coal mine disaster provides fascinating evidence that the Greeks may have been right about what might be called the "precognogenic" properties of altered states produced by sensory deprivation underground, and even subterranean prophecy's mediation by the dead.

In 1963, two men from the town of Sheppton, Pennsylvania, Dave Fellin (58) and Hank Throne (28), spent fourteen terrifying days trapped more than 300 feet underground after the shaft of the coal mine they were working in collapsed. (A third miner also trapped in another blocked-off passage, Louis Bova, was never found.) After their rescue, Fellin and Throne reported that they had experienced out-of-body experiences as well as profuse visions throughout their ordeal: a mysterious illumination, as well as strange beings, underground cities, a door opening to a marble staircase, and most oddly but also most reassuringly, the constant presence of a man that the Catholic of the pair, Fellin, recognized as the recently deceased Pope John XXIII. Amazingly, his not-very-religious, officially Protestant companion, Throne, saw the guy too but didn't know who he was—and Fellin didn't tell him, not wanting to alarm his companion. Fellin said he mainly experienced the Pope's presence as just out of view, to his right side[52]—a common experience of explorers and mountain climbers in extreme survival situations, known as the "third man factor."[53] The men independently attested that where they perceived the figure was where the borehole finally broke through into their chamber and through which they were extracted.[54]

Here's the thing: That third man made a real appearance after the miners' ordeal. After they were brought up from the mine and rushed to Hazleton General Hospital, near Sheppton, the two grateful men were amazed when the room they were wheeled into had a big smiling picture of Pope John XXIII on the wall, gazing down at them. "That's the guy who was with us Davey," Throne announced, excitedly.[55]

Believers said it was a posthumously performed miracle. The men's story drew renewed interest among Catholics after John XXIII's canonization by Pope Francis in 2013. John had allegedly performed a miraculous healing of an Italian nun as well (the basis of his canonization), so coming down from heaven to comfort trapped miners wasn't out of character for "the Good Pope," as he was called.[56] But having a dramatic vision or a dream that is "confirmed" in some (sometimes mundane) way shortly later is very much how precognition often manifests. The precognitive imagination is a dramatic imagination. In fact, people commonly describe dramatic or interesting precognitive dreams that turn out to be about relatively banal situations of calm following some stressful or scary ordeal.[57]

Parapsychologists call an ESP experience *veridical* if it is confirmed in some way, or accurate. Those miners' visions of the dead pope were (I believe) veridical precognitive visions of the reassuring picture in their hospital room. But most people are not yet in the habit of thinking four-dimensionally about their extraordinary experiences (let alone mundane ones), so potentially precognitive experiences will almost always be disregarded as delusion or mere hallucination (or *folie a deux* as a writer for *Skeptical Inquirer* argued of the Sheppton miners' experiences[58]). If the experience is taken seriously at all, it will be framed as some other, more intuitive supernatural phenomenon. Even a visitation by a dead pontiff is easier to conceive than a CGI-animated spectacle projected backward in time from one's own future, especially if the spectacle is "about" something as mundane as a picture on a wall. Again, it may take real existing technology to provide the needed metaphors to help people understand their impossible experiences, and time-traveling CGI spectacles are no more a part of our world than the iChronophone. Nor are they even, to any great extent, a part of our science fiction. At least, not yet.

Speaking of science fiction, I think it is entirely within the realm of possibility that the more science-fictional aspects of Fellin and Throne's visions, including the strange humanoids, might have been precognitive too. The so-called Shaver Mystery, a series of allegedly true accounts of subterranean "Deros" and other beings by a welder and former art student from Barto, Pennsylvania (about 65 miles from Sheppton) named Richard Sharpe Shaver, had been popular in *Amazing Stories* in the 1940s and remained an active area of Fortean speculation and storytelling at the time of the Sheppton disaster. There is no indication the miners had read those pulps earlier in their lives, although Fellin at least was old enough; but paranormal speculations about their experience definitely exposed them to it afterward. The men became the focus of Fortean interest and were interviewed for an article in *Fate* magazine, for instance, in 1965.[59] Unless their imaginations were producing this stuff from their prior reading, it could have been producing it from stories they would go on to read or be told in their future. We can only speculate here, but that kind of thing—vivid precognitive dreams and visions about later reading experiences—does happen, a lot, as we'll see later.[60]

In fact, many or all of the shamanic techniques of ecstasy that Clottes and Lewis-Williams suppose were used by Ice Age shamans are potentially precognition-inducing. While there is no direct evidence of the use of psychedelic drugs in Paleolithic Europe or anywhere prior to the Neolithic period,[61] plants and fungi with hallucinogenic and/

or dissociative properties are found worldwide,[62] and such compounds have been used ritually for divination and healing—as well as to experience "immortality"[63]—in many societies, so there is no reason why Paleolithic Europeans would be an exception.[64] Mushrooms containing psilocybin are found throughout Europe, for example, just as they are in the Americas. Hallucinogens like psilocybin and DMT interact with serotonin receptors in the brain, both in synapses and within neurons, and they facilitate rapid neuronal rewiring.[65] University of Greenwich parapsychologist David Luke and Utrecht University parapsychologist Dick Bierman have conducted small experiments that suggest plant psychedelics may facilitate precognition;[66] and there is abundant anecdotal evidence supporting this idea. Psychologist Stanley Krippner had a premonition of JFK's assassination while taking psilocybin, for instance.[67] Psychiatrist Stanislav Grof reported that precognitive and other ESP experiences were so common in therapeutic sessions using LSD (chemically similar to psilocybin and DMT) that they stopped seeming remarkable to him.[68]

A similar impression comes from people taking psychedelics in ritual settings, such as in the Amazon, where shamanic use of hallucinogenic plants remains a living tradition. Ayahuasca is a DMT-containing drug mixture believed by Amazonian shamans to bring information about events remote in space and time. Since the first Westerners' descriptions of this hallucinogenic brew a little over a century ago, it has been considered to induce telepathy.[69] That was the catch-all term at the time for psychic phenomena, and the label (and associated assumptions about mind-to-mind contact) stuck. But when people receive a confirmation after their experience of something they had seen during the experience, such as the death of a family member or somebody else known to them, precognition may really be at work. Missionary/anthropologist Kenneth Kensinger reported, for instance, that during his work among the Cashinahua (Huni Kuin) people of southeastern Peru, several participants in an ayahuasca session told him of the death of his grandfather. Two days later, he received the news by radio.[70] Assuming he then told the presumptive telepaths, precognition of that confirmation is the most likely explanation—the grandfather wasn't *their* relative, obviously.

In May, 1960, poet Allen Ginsberg visited the Ucayali River region of eastern Peru to try ayahuasca. His friend William S. Burroughs had been there, done that, several years earlier—they called the drug by another name, *yage*. Ginsberg's most harrowing and spectacular experience was one of several under the guidance of a curandero named Maestro on the outskirts of the city of Pucallpa. In his journals and in a letter to his novelist friend, he described the feeling of death being imminent (common with the drug) as well as feeling like he had turned into a giant serpent (also common)—he wrote to Burroughs that he had been a "Great lost Serpentseraph vomiting in consciousness of the Transfiguration to come ..."[71] In his terrible transfiguration in his most profound session, the vine also dredged up painful memories and thoughts of childhood and his family. Like some especially intense psychoanalytic encounter, it forced him to come to grips specifically with his lifelong rejection of women, which he could now see was linked to his ambivalence toward his mentally ill mother, Naomi Ginsberg. Naomi had died alone in a mental hospital four years before this *yage* experience, and it was anguishing, thinking of his "poor mother [who] died in God knows what state of suffering ..."[72] This experience left him with the powerful feeling that he wanted to contribute to the continuation of the species by having a child with a woman—not a typical Ginsbergian sentiment, and one that didn't last.

The poet ended his letter to Burroughs with a P.S. that mentioned a coincidence the following morning. He had gone into a Pucallpa bookstore to buy a pen to write his letter, and a radio happened to be playing a Jeanette MacDonald and Nelson Eddy duet called "Will You Remember," from the 1937 musical *Maytime*—a song he had listened to over and over as a kid and "used to weep for joy to hear," as he noted in his journal.[73] He almost broke down crying, hearing this duet about a man and woman in love but whom fate keeps permanently apart. It reminded him, he said, of death, not to mention reminding him, powerfully, of his unloved mother and of the women in his life who had loved him whom he had rejected. He quoted a wrenching line from the song: "will you love me ever?"[74] So, I suggest this coincidence was really an iChronophone call from Ginsberg to Ginsberg: The overwhelming memories and emotions conjured by that "nostalgic Nelson Eddy record," that duet remembered from his childhood, informed the poet's *yage* experience the previous night. It would be exactly how precognitive dreams often work, being shaped or sparked by some emotionally salient experience over the next day or two. (Michael Harner had a similar synchronistic/precognitive experience under the influence of ayahuasca the following year, in the same region of Peru, as we'll see later.)

The commonness of such experiences hints that whatever else hallucinogenic plants or fungi may bring in the form of spiritual and psychotherapeutic-like insight, or contact with other worlds, their use in shamanic contexts could open up some precognitive valve, the same way sensory deprivation and dreaming do. It would mean that it is not just indigenous belief systems (code for "superstition") that have led people to use such substances for divination in so many cultures.

Super Colliders

Whether or not Paleolithic painters used psychedelics, they left direct iconographic evidence that they did use caves for dream-vision quests. One of the most famous therianthropes (animal-men) in cave art is the aforementioned bird-headed man, lying prone with an erection next to a disemboweled bison, in the deepest, most inaccessible part of Lascaux cave, called "the Shaft." It is one of the most famous images in Paleolithic art, and despite inevitable finger-wags from paleoanthropologists, it is an interpretation magnet.[75] The intestines of the bison, spilling out, have a suggestively labyrinthine look to them—we can make of that what we will. The Greeks, at least, explicitly likened caves to entrails, and actual animal entrails have been used for divination purposes in many cultures. But the really interesting part of the image (says the Freudian, phallogocentric male author, in a deep narrator voice) is that erection. So-called ithyphallic figures in religious art are typically assumed to have some meaning associated with fertility or with male power, aggression, or desire, or perhaps to symbolize the ill-defined idea of ecstasy or rapture.[76] It has also been common to suppose that, mundanely, the bird-man had simply been killed, gored by the dying bison; violent deaths that sever the spine sometimes produce an erection. But spinal injury rarely produces a bird's head.

One of the discoverers of what we now call REM sleep, French neuroscientist Michel Jouvet, pointed out that this prone transfigured individual is much more likely dreaming than dead. Erections are a distinctive feature (in males) of that most dream-rich stage of sleep.[77] Jouvet finds it puzzling that the direct association between the erection and dream-rich sleep—something certainly known by prehistoric people, as it is known by awakening adolescent and adult males everywhere—was unknown to medical science until the link was described scientifically in 1944.[78] It is still largely unknown to art historians. But I believe it is an additional neurotheological as well as iconographic bridge to understanding the oldest art and its possible super-dimensions. Lascaux's priapic bird-man is strikingly similar to much later iconography that almost certainly did relate to dream incubation and/or the extraordinary experiences achievable on the precipices of sleep.

For instance, recognition of the prevalence and importance of incubation, lucid dreaming, and shamanic out-of-body journeying in ancient Egypt has grown over the past few decades. It has led to a shift in how the famous "funerary texts" have been interpreted. The New Kingdom-period *Book of the Dead* and the much older *Pyramid Texts* (written ca. 2400 BC, the oldest-known spiritual-philosophical text in human history[79]) have traditionally been described as guides for a pharaoh's experience after his literal death, but they may also have been esoteric guides for shamans/priests to experience their divinity and immortality in this life, through out-of-body experiences.[80] It's exactly what Greek shamans like Parmenides or Epimedes were doing, and it appears to be what numerous images of the god Osiris in Egyptian temples depict, including a stunning series of images in a zodiacal chapel in the late Egyptian temple of Hathor at Dendera, made in the first century CE, during the period of Greek rule in Egypt. Comparison alert: The Dendera Osiris images are strikingly similar to Lascaux's bird-man.[81]

In the Dendera image sequence, the "dead" Osiris reclines on a bier with an erection, over which hovers various birds—in the first, it is Isis as a kite (the raptor, not the toy). It used to be assumed that the birds in all three images were Isis, attempting (per the myth) to resurrect her dead brother/consort with a phallus made of clay after she was unable to recover the real one following the god's dismemberment by Set. But the bird in the final image, seemingly issuing from the phallus, is different: a falcon, representing Horus, who is equivalent in the Osirian mysteries to god's *Ba* or soul.[82] The *Ba* was believed in that culture to be able to leave the body not only after death but during trance or dream states. The separability of the soul from the body is a culturally universal idea, and birds symbolize out-of-body travel or flight of the soul in countless spiritual traditions.

Note for the astrally squeamish and/or just scientifically skeptical: Terms like "out of body" describe what ecstatic experiences feel like and how they have generally been interpreted by experiencers. (*Ek-stasy* literally means standing outside.) Before neurobiology could plausibly be invoked as an explanation—essentially, before the last two or three centuries—out-of-body experiences and lucid dreams would have been powerful validations of the existence of a soul that is not tied to the body and thus, implicitly, survives after the death of the body.[83] They would have been central to shamanic experiences of immortality, of "dying before dying." In our day, with the "advantage" of materialist science and our intuitive understanding that the brain can play tricks on us in dreams and altered states, there is obviously a great deal of debate and disagreement about the real nature of such experiences.[84] For experiencers of a materialistic bent, or even those on the fence, out-of-body experiences, however fascinating, do not necessarily provide spiritual reassurance.

Osiris's erections in the Dendera images were systematically effaced, probably by Coptic Christians, and are still not reproduced in many drawings of these images.[85] But the images were likely spiritual instruction and interpretation for priests, perhaps incubating in these spaces. Osiris, beyond simply a deity, symbolized the human who had achieved divinity, or superhumanity.[86] Priests may have imaginatively identified with the "dead" god as part of the induction of their astral journey.[87] This is supported by a physical component shown right in the images: In the first image with Isis, Osiris is visibly masturbating. In fact, the *kite*-form of Isis was a pun, as it was the same word for *hand*—suggesting that the god's death here and elsewhere in Egyptian iconography and myth is not just literal death (as Victorian afterlife-obsessed interpreters assumed) and that his consort is not just a literal consort. The image sequence seems to depict masturbation as a precursor to out-of-body travel or perhaps to what we would now call a lucid dream.[88]

Oral mythological traditions have been shown to convey information, such as historical information about volcano eruptions, robustly over several millennia.[89] A rock- and cave-art tradition—which is what emerged in the Great Leap Forward—could perhaps encode information even more durably, over a longer frame of time, with initiators passing information on the meaning of images to initiates in highly emotion-rich (and thus memory-promoting) rituals. No one knows the limits of such transmission because they have never been tested. (Amazingly, the erupting volcano depicted in Chauvet Cave dates from a period of active volcanism in the immediate vicinity, so might be a record of a real event.) Rather than presume some radical separateness of temporally distant cultural traditions, based on the presumption of some River Lethe-like amnesic cultural Flood (and thus refuse all comparison), it seems a reasonable hypothesis that the incubation traditions of Ancient Greece and Egypt could have been carrying forward long-established shamanic and specifically dreamwork practices originating in the Ice Age, and that this is what some of the oldest art in the world may be showing.[90] And more to my point in this book, we could even be seeing in cave art the emergence of a dream- and vision-recording tradition that may have encoded and transmitted societal and not just individual prophecies backward in time, not just forward. We'll come back to this idea in Part Three.

You only need to drive about four hours northeast of Chauvet Cave, following the Rhone river along the A41, to get to today's biggest laboratory-cave, the world center for high-energy physics research in a northwestern suburb of Geneva, Switzerland. Like the rolling landscape of the Ardèche gorge with its hidden art galleries underfoot, the pleasant suburbs and wooded country lanes show little hint that beneath the ground are enormous subterranean particle accelerators operated by the laboratory of the 23-member-nation European Center for Nuclear Research, or CERN. Its Large Hadron Collider (LHC)—the largest of these looping caverns, with a diameter of 27 kilometers—seems like a monument to the triumph of scientific materialism. In the LHC, physicists have pushed particles to just shy of the speed of light, smashing them together in order to unlock (or blast open) the innermost secrets of matter. In 2012, CERN physicists announced they had finally found the long-anticipated Higgs Boson, the particle long predicted by the Standard Model of particle physics to give matter its mass, its weight, its substance.

Materialism means different things to different people. You can view it neutrally, as I do, as the high-precision language used to describe and predict things that are measurable. It is sometimes naively caricatured, though, as the idea that everything in the universe, including subjective experience and consciousness, must ultimately be reducible to little balls interacting on a big billiards table. Even the scientists and technicians at CERN no longer view matter in that simplistic way—for nearly a century now, physicists have described matter in terms of waves and "wavefunctions." But people who study psychic and paranormal phenomena often hold the billiard-ball picture up as a straw man: How silly to imagine that you or I, conscious and spiritual beings, could be reduced to electrical signals and the jostlings of neurochemicals in a grapefruit-sized piece of meat (actually, mostly fat) inside a skull. Increasingly influential in academic debates about consciousness are panpsychists, who argue that mind or consciousness is central to the constitution of physical reality, more basic than the Higgs Boson and its cousin particles.[91]

I am agnostic on debates about consciousness, what it is, and how it may or may not be produced by the material brain or by causal interactions. I suspect that deep down, these are debates over linguistic choices and habits of description and that different descriptive idioms, the idealist and the materialist, are both necessary and that neither are subsumable to the other.[92] I do however agree with materialism's critics that the reductive, high-precision technical language and praxis of science are not ideally suited to answer all of the deepest mysteries about our universe, especially those having to do with consciousness and time. A few isolated retrocausation experiments notwithstanding, it is precognitive dreams and art that currently provide the most direct evidence for Minkowski's block spacetime, which remains in physics mainly an article of faith based on the tenets of general relativity. It means the dreaming, visionary, and creative human brain, once tamed, is a cosmological tool, potentially as powerful (if not exactly as precise and predictable) a means of probing the solidity versus permeability of the material world, and the nature of causation and change, as any multibillion-dollar (or -euro) scientific instrument. The Paleolithic incubators would have gotten there first, of course.[93] And as Harner wrote in his book *Cave and Cosmos*, they were the first to publish their results, on those cave walls.[94]

Alluding to a famous quote by panpsychist philosopher Henri Bergson ("The universe is a machine for the making of Gods"), filmmaker and scholar of African philosophies Marques Redd calls the Old Kingdom Temple of Unas at Saqqara, the walls of which bear the *Pyramid Texts*, a "mechanism for the creation of Black superhumans."[95] I love this formulation, and I have to think Chauvet, Lascaux, and other Paleolithic caves were similar contraptions. They were colliders for the creation of Paleolithic superhumans. People removed their shoes, went in people, and sometimes came out superpeople. Maybe they flew.

Postscript: When People Turn into Alligators

The subject of Paleolithic art is deeply personal for Werner Herzog. He told an interviewer that his "first intellectual awakening" came at age 12, when he passed by a Munich bookstore window and caught sight of a book cover showing a horse from the wall of Lascaux. At the time, it was the most famous Ice Age painted cave, having been discovered just 15 years earlier. "It shook me to the core," he said. "I felt a deep turmoil in my heart, an indescribable excitement that remains to this day."[96] Art books are expensive. To save enough money to buy this book of Lascaux cave paintings, the young Herzog got a job as a ball boy at a tennis club. He said it took him more than six months to save up enough.[97]

A self-described "rogue filmmaker" and single-minded pursuer of "ecstatic truth,"[98] Herzog is often regarded as a sort of cinematic shaman.[99] He claims his sole ethic is doing whatever it takes to capture "something that is even beyond what one can dream, something beyond our dreams."[100] So when his producer showed him a *New Yorker* article about the remarkable paintings that had been discovered in Chauvet Cave, twice as old as those in Lascaux, it naturally captivated the romantic director.[101] He set his sights on making a film—*the* film—about what were, at the time, the oldest-known pictures anywhere on the planet.

Since Chauvet Cave is strictly off-limits to the public, Herzog had to fight to win the right to make his film from the French government—not an easy task given the French preference to entrust their cultural heritage to French people. Fortunately, the French Minister of Culture whom he petitioned happened to be a huge fan of the Bavarian director. So Herzog was granted permission to enter the cave with a three-person film crew and a 3-D camera for six days of shooting, just four hours each day, in the spring of 2010.[102] The result was one of his most haunting documentaries, *Cave of Forgotten Dreams*, which won wide acclaim following its debut at the Toronto International Film Festival in September of that year.

A fierce opponent of the literalism that governs typical documentary filmmaking—what he calls "the truth of accountants"—Herzog is a trickster who freely fictionalizes when he deems it necessary to convey some inner truth in his subjects. His documentary includes an interview with a local French master-perfumer who describes hunting for hidden caves using his super-acute sense of smell. It was made up, Herzog later admitted, although it was clearly inspired by the real discoverers' story of finding caves by detecting subtle drafts coming from rock walls.[103] One of Herzog's Rogue Film School students alleges that the director also coached one of the Chauvet researchers, radiometric dating specialist (and circus juggler) Julien Monney, to describe having had nightmares about lions after his first visits to the cave, with its famous lion scenes.[104] But *Cave of Forgotten Dreams* cleaved to conventional truth more than most of Herzog's works, since the director felt he bore a significant intellectual and spiritual responsibility with it. He interviews Clottes and other paleoanthropologists, but is also content to just immerse the viewer in the cave and its art in a meditative way, letting the camera linger on the paintings for long stretches without commentary. He tries to capture, to the extent possible in a 90-minute film, the profound experience that universally grips visitors to this and other such sites. He also describes the weird feeling of being watched by the cave painters, similar to what the cave's modern discoverers experienced when they first stood in the dim light amid its 37,000-year-old images of long-extinct Ice Age mammals.

Undoubtedly the strangest, most memorable, and certainly most discussed moment in *Cave of Forgotten Dreams*, though, is its postscript: a bizarre, quintessentially Herzogian monologue voiced over footage filmed at a reptile farm not far from the cave. Water heated by a nearby nuclear reactor on the Rhone river makes the perfect balmy environment to keep tropical crocodilians. A pair of young albino alligators (Herzog calls them crocodiles, mistakenly) paddle gently in their warm radioactive water to a soaring organ and cello composition by Dutch composer and cellist Ernst Reijseger, as the filmmaker muses in his signature Bavarian accent about another direction of deep time, about some far future, when humans are long gone and the distant descendants of these reptiles will wander into Chauvet Cave nearby and see its paintings of lions and horses and other Ice Age fauna with fresh eyes. He asks, "Are we today possibly the crocodiles who look back into an abyss of time when we see the paintings of Chauvet Cave?"[105]

It is strange and discordant, but as with so many of Herzog's offbeat, inspired artistic choices throughout his works, this postscript has a strange way of sticking in memory. Just as the shamans who made the cave's images may have imaginatively transformed into bison and other animals, Herzog's reverie invites viewers to make a kind of shamanic transformation of their own, becoming irradiated mutant crocodilians wandering a strange landscape, descending into an ancient and forbidden underground place, and seeing art wholly anew, unbiased by human consciousness. Viewers who bought tickets for a 3-D art film about cave paintings left the theater thinking about albino crocodiles in the shadow of nuclear cooling towers.

So get this: In June of 2010, a few months after Herzog had shot his documentary, the director was astonished to read a news story that four alligators from the farm where he had filmed had escaped.[106] They were running free in the countryside—an alligator stampede, you might say. Only three of the animals were caught and returned to the facility, one of them after spending a night in a local jail cell. Another is still out there. It might have frozen to death during a French winter—probably did—but no one really knows. The real possibility of these escaped reptiles actually stumbling into art from deep time, seemingly fulfilling his musing in his postscript, delighted the filmmaker.[107] It seems like his postscript was another prophecy.

Shamanic aptitude runs in families. While it didn't explicitly play into his motivation to make his film about Chauvet Cave, Herzog had an interesting family connection to the ancient Greek tradition of dream incubation, via his grandfather Rudolf. Rudolf Herzog was a classics scholar and epigrapher in the late 19th century who turned to archaeology, driven by an obsession with locating an Asklepieion that had been mentioned in a text by the Greek writer Herodas on the island of Kos. Archaeologists had been digging for several years on Kos in search of it, but with no luck. Showing similar traits that his grandson is now known for, Rudolf Herzog was a visionary, and highly intuitive. In what appears very much like a display of what would later be called psychic archaeology, Rudolf went to Kos in 1902 and, without knowing anything about archaeology, stood in a farmer's field and started digging. He uncovered a Roman bath that turned out to be part of the long-sought temple complex.[108] The Asklepieion of Kos is now a major archaeological site and a tourist attraction for the island.

By the time Werner got to know his grandfather, the aging scholar-archaeologist had succumbed to mental illness or dementia ("he went mad," Herzog said[109]), and he died two years before that horse from Lascaux caught young Werner's eye in the bookshop window. But Rudolf's drive and intuition were a lifelong inspiration for the filmmaker, who made his first feature film on Kos and used one of the surviving members of his grandfather's excavating team in his cast. Herzog, like many shamans, honors his ancestors.

6

Life in the Deep C
Virginia Woolf and Cine-Chronicity

> *Yet I am now & then haunted by some semi mystic very*
> *profound life of a woman, which shall all be told on one*
> *occasion; & time shall be utterly obliterated; future shall*
> *somehow blossom out of the past. One incident—say the*
> *fall of a flower—might contain it. My theory being that*
> *the event practically does not exist—nor time either.*
> —Virginia Woolf, *Diary* (1926)

It is an interesting, strange, and even slightly suspicious coincidence that the categories of *artist* and *shaman* emerged virtually simultaneously within the European thought-world, a little less than 500 years ago.[1] The first European explorers' reports of "devilish rites" practiced by nonwestern ritual practitioners appeared right in the middle of the 16th century, including the first descriptions and imagery of Siberian shamans. The latter portrayals were, of course, exoticized and, from a Christian point of view, evidently demonic. The concept of the artist gifted with divinely inspired genius was born at the same time, with Vasari's 1550 compendium of artists' lives. Vasari gave descriptions of his contemporaries, like his friend Michelangelo, that made them sound like melancholy outsiders and eccentrics—a lot like shamans, in other words, except without the explicitly demonic or heathen associations.

Even though they were raised apart, these twins have had abundant play dates while growing up, where they noticed and puzzled at their similar features.[2] Fast forward to the late 20th and early 21st centuries, and it is now a pop culture cliché that artists fulfill the role of technician of ecstasy in the modern world.[3] When Bill Moyers asked Joseph Campbell, "Who are our shamans?" in his popular 1988 PBS series *The Power of Myth*, Campbell replied, "It is the function of the artist to do this. The artist is the one who communicates myth for today."[4] Performing artists like Jim Morrison, Michael Jackson, and David Bowie have been compared to shamans; some, like German performance artist Joseph Beuys, have explicitly called themselves shamans.[5] The prophetic Philip K. Dick's mystical and/or psychotic experience in 1974—his so-called "2-3-74" experience—has been compared to a "shamanic initiation,"[6] as has the abduction experience of horror novelist Whitley Strieber, described in his book *Communion*.[7] When I was researching this book, David Lynch released a hypnotic video he directed for Scottish musician Donovan, an incantatory new song, "I Am the Shaman."[8] Lynch himself is often called a shaman.

The categories of artist and shaman assuredly do not map exactly or neatly onto each other, but creative people who may know little or nothing about shamanism or related magico-religious roles in other cultures very frequently express ideas familiar from that ur-religion when they describe their own process.[9] Dreams, trance, and visionary states that fall on, near, or parallel to David Lewis-Williams' intensified trajectory of consciousness are part of many creative people's toolkits, for example. Franz Kafka sometimes wrote in a visionary state he called clairvoyance.[10] Salvador Dali dozed in a chair holding a spoon, which would loudly fall on a plate when he fell asleep, rousing him so he could paint his hypnagogic hallucinations. J. R. R. Tolkien spent his late nights in an almost shamanic nonordinary reality he called Faërie, from which he transcribed the ancient Elvish mythology that served as the backdrop of his popular fantasy novels.[11] Lynch uses Transcendental Meditation to "fish" for his ideas from an oceanic collective consciousness he calls the unified field. And of course, use and misuse of mind-altering substances of all kinds (if only cigarettes and coffee, which Lynch considers essential ingredients of "the art life"[12]) figure prominently in many artists' biographies.

Like John Lennon when he wrote "Across the Universe," creators very often feel as if they have no ownership of their best ideas, having experienced those ideas as arriving from outside themselves, "downloaded" in our contemporary idiom. As J. F. Martel puts it, "creating a work of art amounts to collaborating with invisible forces that lead the way."[13] In memoirs and interviews, novelists sometimes describe the surprise they feel when their characters come to life as autonomous beings with minds, thoughts, and voices of their own, doing and saying things they did not plan or predict. Kafka's experiences of characters coming to life and surprising him right there under his pen were some of the most rewarding and exciting of his life, for example.[14] In a shamanic idiom—or at least, an anthropology-of-shamans idiom—these characters coming to life might be called spirits.[15]

Relatedly, creative people over the centuries have described their process as helping something new into the world that they intuited was already there, waiting to be revealed. Michelangelo is only the most famous example. In his book *On Writing*, Stephen King compares writing fiction to excavating dinosaur fossils buried in the earth.[16] In the *Exegesis* Dick wrote in the late 1970s, after his mystical experience, he wrote: "My books are forgeries. Nobody wrote them. The goddam typewriter wrote them; it's a magic typewriter. ... they—my books—are already there."[17] It should be obvious why such an intuition is super-significant if inspiration indeed involves precognition of future experiences in a block universe.

In the Renaissance, creative geniuses were thought to be born under the sign of Saturn—that is, melancholic. While aloofness, eccentricity, and psychiatric conditions are by no means universal characteristics of artists (Paul McCartney, for instance, has always seemed weirdly well-adjusted, for an artist), they are prevalent enough in the biographies of creative people that they have remained central to the mainstream conception of art as a kind of socially sanctioned madness. Schizophrenia-spectrum disorders were prevalent in Bowie's family, for instance.[18] In an interview segment director Brett Morgen included in his 2022 documentary *Moonage Daydream*, Bowie said that his artistic practice began as a way of self-treating what he suspected was incipient psychosis, expressing his eccentricity in a socially acceptable way. Becoming a glam rock superstar-shaman was his way of steering clear of the dismal fate that befell his admired older half-brother Terry Burns, who spent his adult life in a mental hospital.[19] Anthropologists have often seen the shaman or ritual worker, too, as a social role solving the "problems" of mental illness, neurodivergence, or gender nonconformity in their culture or community.[20]

The ability to visualize things vividly in the mind's eye, a component of imagination, falls naturally along a spectrum, but it may be developed through shamanic training or practices that nurture a facility with experiencing the presence of spirits or divine beings.[21] For people who psychiatrists might label "schizotypal," the latter experiences just come naturally. Cine-shaman Werner Herzog claims that once, while driving on a German Autobahn, he had to pull his car over to the shoulder so he could open the door and let out a swarm of butterflies that had appeared in his car. He knew they were not really there, but they were fluttering around him all the same, making it impossible to drive safely. (There's Louise Milne's storm-in-the-head animal stampede again.) Although he was in the country, the director also perceived hundreds of people leaning out of old-fashioned Viennese homes to watch him. He told an interviewer that "whole stories developed out of it."[22]

Proneness to intrusive mental images, along with the related facility of dissociating from the body, may also be opened up by traumatic experiences. Trauma or illness in childhood or adolescence are typical doorways to a shamanic career, and they are part of many artists' biographies as well. The Scottish singer Elizabeth Fraser, for instance, endured childhood sexual abuse and later channeled her ethereal songs for the band Cocteau Twins from some unconscious place.[23] Christopher Knowles has called Fraser a "sibyl"—a kind of shaman-prophet—due to the many synchronicities around her music, including several songs on themes of sirens and drowning that seemed to foretell the 1997 drowning death of her ex-lover, singer Jeff Buckley.[24] Kafka frequently conferred with ghostly presences and had a facility with out-of-body experiences, which seems to have arisen at least partly from early-life trauma, too.[25] The Prague writer often channeled information from his future in his writing.[26] And the same is true of Kafka's contemporary in England, Virginia Woolf.

Woolf was another creative genius who, in another time or place, might well have been some kind of shaman. She saw visions and heard voices, and she was prone to episodes of dissociation and derealization—a mystical sense of the unreality of herself and her surroundings. During long periods of remission from her famous "madness," she actively sought and recorded her fleeting experiences of intensified awareness, or what she called "moments of being."[27] Her *Diary* is full of moments where she is stopped short by the unsolidity of things, as though the very earth cannot bear her weight, yet is also somehow block-like, eternal:

> Now is life very solid, or very shifting? I am haunted
> by the two contradictions. This has gone on for ever:
> will last for ever; goes down to the bottom of the
> world—this moment I stand on. Also it is transitory,

flying, diaphanous. I shall pass like a cloud on the waves. Perhaps it may be that we change; one flying after another, so quick so quick, yet we are somehow successive, & continuous—we human beings; & show the light through. But what is the light?[28]

Fortunately for the modern student of literary precognition, Woolf left posterity a dense record of her thoughts and experiences, including reflections on her creative process. When you add to her published novels, *Diary*, letters, and essays a truly massive critical-biographical industry, we have ample documentation of the life and thought of a brilliant creative mind, making her a rich subject for a kind of psychic deconstruction. While nobody to my knowledge has ever called Woolf prophetic in the literal sense I'm using the term, all you have to do is immerse yourself in this material to find strong hints that she was sometimes channeling from her own future.

The exact nature of Woolf's psychiatric condition has been disputed. There was certainly a depressive component to it, and some now think she suffered from what we today call bipolar disorder, which seems to have run in her family.[29] Woolf was institutionalized on a few occasions and attempted suicide two times when she was young, and she ended her life at age 59 by walking into a river, her pockets laden with heavy stones. She described depression vividly throughout her *Diary*, and a suicidal character in her 1925 novel *Mrs. Dalloway* that drew on her own experiences provides a convincing window onto her hallucinations and occasionally grandiose, psychotic thought patterns that are characteristic of states of mania. More on that novel momentarily.

Woolf's depressive, visionary, and dissociative tendencies may have begun with childhood sexual trauma. She was molested at age 6 by her 22-year-old half-brother, Gerald Duckworth. Then, when she was 13, after her mother died, Gerald's brother George moved into her family home to help care for her and her siblings, and he raped both her and her sister, Vanessa. Again, people who experience abuse and other traumas frequently develop a facility with dissociation as a means of coping and escape; and parapsychologists have tied dissociative states to ESP and other psychic phenomena.[30] (A history of trauma is so prevalent in the lives of paranormal experiencers, in fact, that Jeffrey Kripal calls it "the traumatic secret."[31]) Only relatively late in Woolf's life did she draw a connection between the abuse she had experienced and her lifelong mental suffering.

Woolf's path toward being a great writer from being merely an aspiring one involved learning not just to access but to tame her visions, make them come coherently rather than overwhelm her, even if they did not always come predictably.[32] After she had attained that skill, she recorded in her diary blissful experiences where words and images spilled onto the page from somewhere (somewhen?) else, with a complete effortlessness that shocked and delighted her. In the latter half of her career, it was the question of the origins of her ideas that most fascinated her. In an autobiographical essay called "A Sketch of the Past," she described the astonishing fluidity with which she wrote the first draft of her 1927 masterpiece, *To the Lighthouse*:

> Then one day walking around Tavistock Square I made up, as I sometimes make up my books, *To the Lighthouse*; in a great, apparently involuntary, rush. One thing burst into another. Blowing bubbles out of a pipe gives the feeling of the rapid crowd of ideas and scenes which blew out of my mind, so that my lips seemed syllabling of their own accord as I walked. What blew the bubbles? Why then? I have no notion.[33]

In a letter to her lover, the aristocratic novelist and poet Vita Sackville-West, she described the moment her 1928 novel *Orlando* first came to her:

> Yesterday morning I was in despair. I couldn't screw a word from me; and at last dropped my head in my hands: dipped my pen in the ink, and wrote these words, as if automatically, on a clean sheet: Orlando: A Biography. No sooner had I done this than my body was flooded with rapture and my brain with ideas.[34]

In her diary, she recorded that the first chapter of *Orlando* came "extraordinarily unwilled by me … as if it shoved everything aside to come into existence."[35]

Few writers have given more explicit and constant attention to the amazing effortlessness of artistic creation than Woolf did. Unless and until a person reliably experiences the bliss and ease—indeed, necessity—of creating, it may not quite occur to them that creativity is not

---

some kind of hard labor, consciously hammering together pieces of their influences on some cognitive workbench—Edison's famous "99 percent perspiration."[36] Not that there wasn't perspiration, certainly: Woolf labored obsessively and perfectionistically over every word in her drafts, revising and rewriting, often several times, over the span of years, before completing a book. This in fact can make psychic deconstruction somewhat challenging in her case, since the raw original inspiration has most often been sanded over and reshaped completely by the time it reached publication. But fortunately, as part of that critical-biographical Woolf industry, we also have many of the rough drafts to supplement the diaries and everything else.

Woolf's interest in her own creative imagination grew out of her larger interest, her lifelong subject, which was the flow of conscious experience. It was a subject that already had a long and respectable scientific as well as literary pedigree: what the psychologist William James had in his 1890 *Principles of Psychology* called the *stream of consciousness*.[37] In one way or another, many of Woolf's novels strive to characterize what it is like to be a person with such a stream. However, James would not have sanctioned her methods. The psychologist insisted that introspection was not a proper scientific way of investigating consciousness, nor certainly would he have admitted imagination itself as a method—he famously characterized that as being like trying to catch what the dark looks like by turning on the flame really fast.

"I shall never forgive myself for my carelessness"

The characteristic of conscious experience that has always earned it the metaphor of a stream is its continuity, the seamless flow of thoughts one to another, one idea or sensation morphing into the next. But one of the things the 20th century brought with it, along with accelerated pace, was rupture and discontinuity. Hopping on a train or getting in a motorcar, you could almost step through a door and step out the same door into a separate world. No wonder there are so many portals to other worlds—and magic wardrobes—in the writings of early and mid-20th century.[38] Ruptures feel like doors, fleetingly glimpsed, like the transitions between levels or states of awareness or the passage into dream via hypnagogia. And paradoxically, these ruptures have a way of obliterating rather than reinforcing the sense of time's flow. What they really reinforce and amplify is that sense of "meanwhile" that had captivated the Victorians.

Cinema was one of the main technologies that introduced discontinuity into life and into experience. It was just coming into its own as a popular and artistic form when Woolf was writing, and she consciously or unconsciously imported cinematic techniques like cut-aways and flashbacks into her work.[39] Ironically, this most time-bound of the arts (besides music) led people to even more resolutely *spatialize* time, and to think in terms of simultaneities. No novelistic meanwhile can match the persuasive force of a simple cinematic cut-away, with its ability to obliterate any sense of temporal sequence and create a vivid impression of events occurring simultaneously in separate locations. If the Victorians had enjoyed being transported from a biscuit and tea to a far-off war or revolution in their afternoon paper or a novel, for people of the early 20th century, an instantaneous jump from one scene to another in a moving picture created an exciting feeling of simultaneity even more powerfully.

Mrs. Dalloway, about the simultaneous lives of a nostalgic society wife and a mentally ill war veteran in London on a single June afternoon, is the ultimate literary study in meanwhile and is considered the most cinematic of Woolf's novels. The rough concept had been with Woolf since at least 1902, when she was 20. She described in a letter to a friend the idea for a play she would write about "a man and a woman—show them growing up—never meeting—not knowing each other—but all the time you'll feel them coming nearer and nearer."[40] The character that would eventually play the woman in this duo, Clarissa Dalloway, first appeared in Woolf's debut novel, *The Voyage Out*, in 1915, where she and her husband Richard make a brief appearance as upper-class passengers on a trans-Atlantic steamer. Clarissa Dalloway had a real-life model: Kitty Maxse, a high-society friend of Woolf's mother and her sisters whom Woolf respected and liked for her charm, wisdom, and wit, despite her upper-crust conventionality. Maxse had been for Woolf "a foster mother in the ways of the world,"[41] although Woolf had not had contact with her since 1908. But in the spring of 1922, she revisited her fictionalization of Maxse for a short story, "Mrs. Dalloway in Bond Street." The story follows Clarissa Dalloway on an errand buying gloves and planning for a party she is to host that evening—although really the errand is a skeleton upon which to hang the character's stream of consciousness, her inner life of regret, desire, and anticipation. The story ends with a mysterious explosion outside the glove shop, left unexplained.

A kind of possession took place. Clarissa Dalloway's inner life captured Woolf's imagination so much over the summer of 1922, when she was writing her story, that two days after she completed it, on Wednesday, October 4, she began planning to expand it into a novel. She wrote her intention to begin writing a second chapter, called "The Prime Minister," on the following Friday morning. This second chapter was to shift to a lunch club near the glove store, where a psychotic young man who believes he is Christ is contemplating killing both himself and the Prime Minister. It was this suicidal and homicidal individual who was to be the unknown male counterpart who comes "nearer and nearer" to Clarissa Dalloway over the course of the novel, even though the two never would quite meet. Her working title for this new novel was "The Hours."

So get this: Unknown to Woolf, her model for Clarissa Dalloway, Kitty Maxse, fell over the banisters in her home *that very day*, October 4, and died in a hospital two days later, on Friday. Woolf read of this tragedy in the newspaper on Saturday, and two *Diary* entries reveal her complete preoccupation and sadness about this strange occurrence, and her perplexity about the cause: "How did it happen? Some one presumably knows, & in time I shall hear."[42] She likely wondered if Maxse's fall had been a suicide attempt.[43] Although Maxse had recently taken to drinking, an accidental fall over banisters was something forensic experts regarded as unlikely to happen even if a person was intoxicated. [44] Woolf notes that the dying wit Maxse reportedly told her doctor in the hospital: "I shall never forgive myself for my carelessness."[45]

That Woolf's inspiration for a story about her fictional Maxse and a suicidal man came on the same day as Maxse's possible suicide attempt is uncanny enough. But years later, when reflecting on the initial inspiration for what became *Mrs. Dalloway*, the author recalled that her original idea for her novel was in fact to have Clarissa Dalloway commit suicide at the end, not the war veteran to whom she comes "nearer and nearer."[46] If that's an accurate recollection, it makes this coincidence even more astonishing. Frederic Myers or Woolf's American contemporaries Upton and Craig Sinclair would likely have chalked it up to telepathy. Today, many people would naturally gravitate to a different term: synchronicity.

Carl Jung, who coined the term synchronicity, was a contemporary thinker toward whose ideas Woolf came nearer and nearer over the course of her writing career, even though she never came into direct contact with him or (as far as we know) his writings.[47] It was in the

1920s and 1930s, when Woolf was writing her most daring and brilliant works, that Jung had begun thinking about the metaphysical connective tissue of human lives. He first publicly used the term "synchronistic principle" in a 1930 memorial lecture for sinologist Richard Wilhelm, but he did not publish his famous monograph on the subject until a decade after Woolf's death, and there is no evidence the novelist had ever read Jung's earlier writings on the collective unconscious and its archetypes either. But *Mrs. Dalloway* seems like nothing if not a study in, as well as example of, Jung's "acausal connecting principle."[48]

The necessity of the concept of synchronicity arose directly from Jung's personal and clinical experiences that seemed not to fit existing psychological paradigms or the psychoanalytic theories of his former mentor, Freud. They included meaningful coincidences of all kinds: noticing some unlikely convergence of stimuli that seem related to some pressing issue, for instance, or having a thought or dream that is followed shortly by some "confirmation" in a reading experience or a conversation or a physical encounter. In his 1952 monograph, *Synchronicity: An Acausal Connecting Principle*, Jung cited the common experience of dreaming about a person and then getting a letter from them the next day[49]—nowadays, it would be a phone call or email.

At that time, retrocausation had not been described as a physical possibility, and thus precognition as I am using the term seemed to Jung to lack physical plausibility. He wrote that "it would be absurd to suppose that a situation which does not yet exist and will only occur in the future could transmit itself as a phenomenon of energy to a receiver in the present."[50] The only possible answer, he felt, was to think of such occurrences as somehow outside of time and causality altogether. His term was meant to suggest a flattening of the time dimension— "meanwhile" in its purest form.[51] When he was developing his ideas on the subject for his monograph, he was inspired by then-recent thinking about chance and probability in the young field of quantum physics. The fact that meaningful coincidences in his life and in the lives of his patients sometimes seemed linked to archetypes of the collective unconscious also suggested to Jung that they went beyond any mechanistic understanding of ESP as it was then being studied and theorized by the Rhines at their lab in America.

Jung's specimen case of what he considered synchronicity occurred probably around 1920. A highly rationalistic patient he was treating, a young aristocratic Dutchwoman named Maggy Quarles van Ufford, related a dream she had had the night before her session, of somebody giving her a piece of "valuable ... golden" jewelry in the shape of an Egyptian scarab beetle. While he was listening to this dream account, he heard a scratching on the window behind him, and he turned to see that it was a rose-chafer, a common European relative of the scarab or dung beetle. Like a therapeutic shaman, he seized the opportunity by opening the window, cupping the insect in his hand, and presenting it to his patient: "Here's your scarab," he said. He proceeded to tell Maggy about the rebirth symbolism of scarabs. When he recounted this episode in his book *Synchronicity* three decades later, he said that this magical moment "punctured the needed hole" in his patient's rationalism, letting the magic into her life. Maggy became a longtime follower of Jung and even proved influential on his thinking about topics like Eastern religion.[52]

The scarab story is one that has been perennially re-told not only by adherents of Jung but also throughout the wider world of metaphysical and inspirational writing, as a narrative that would reenchant the world made bleak and meaningless by mechanistic materialism. If synchronicity has a logo, it would be the scarab. But as I've argued at length elsewhere, no acausal connecting principle is needed to understand this anecdote—it was a standard precognitive "Dunne dream."[53] Maggy was handed a scarab in her therapist's office, and this experience refluxed a few hours back in time to appear, symbolically elaborated, in a dream. Recent interpretations of quantum mechanics and recent thinking in quantum biology make such an idea much less absurd than it would have seemed to Jung and most other thinkers of his day. What was not known until recently is that Maggy had other precognitive dreams during her time as Jung's patient, as well as what could be called presentimental physical symptoms and fantasies.[54] On one occasion, she reported a dream that matched an anecdote Jung had read in Frederic Myers' *Phantasms of the Living* just before her session, which (prompted by her dream) he then told her about. She also experienced symptoms and fantasies that matched Tantric symbolism of the chakras Jung happened to be reading about in a then-recent book on Kundalini yoga by a Theosophical writer.[55]

The fact that Jung himself played a role in the fulfilment of these dreams, symptoms, and fantasies seems to have contributed to his unseeing of their precognitive nature. So did their apparent circularity. For instance, he only noticed the insect and handed it to Maggy because she had been telling him her dream about being handed a scarab—a loop. Thinking such causal loops paradoxical (they aren't) acts as a mental block for many people when considering precognition, but it is really the most essential-to-understand fact about the whole subject. The way information from the future travels curved paths in the cognitive spacetime of freely willed individuals, keeping history self-consistent, is a direct implication of the essential self-fulfillingness of all prophecy. Without grasping this circularity, precognitive experiences are bound to sometimes appear archetypal, since the metaphors and symbols we use to understand them—based on our prior knowledge and religious beliefs or, in Maggy's case, her therapist's obsession with ancient myths and symbolism—will often fractally be folded into them in some fashion.

As we saw earlier in the book, people understand the impossible through the lens of available technologies. Just as telepathy had been made thinkable by the telegraph and then radio, synchronicity was arguably made thinkable by movies, the most transformative communication medium of the early and mid-20th century. In the decades when Jung was working out his theories about meaningful coincidence, the pioneering Soviet director Sergei Eisenstein was devising and formalizing the rules of film editing that remain central to the language of that art form and that continue to govern TV and video. *Montage*, the concept most associated with Eisenstein, is the motivated juxtaposition of images, splicing different shots together in a way that replaces boring, generally meaningless causal-linear relationships with interesting, meaningful, acausal ones.

An oft-cited example is Charlie Chaplin's 1936 film *Modern Times*, which opens with a brief shot of a herd of sheep, one of them black, followed by a scene of people spilling out of a metropolitan subway on their way to work. The viewer understands that the crowd of people are like sheep, and when we see Chaplin's Tramp a few shots later, we grasp that he is a "black sheep" who doesn't fit in to the crowd. Nowadays, such a juxtaposition would seem comically ham-handed, but today's deft film and video editing essentially operates on the same manipulation of memory and perception. Through discontinuities—cuts—characters and situations are given meaningful framings, providing a larger-than-life narrative or mythic context. These contextual framings can be powerfully persuasive. Eisenstein was quick to recognize the extraordinary potency of movies as propaganda tools.

Eisenstein's oft-quoted definition of montage, from his 1929 essay "A Dialectic Approach to Film Form," could easily stand as a definition of synchronicity, so long as we just replace the word "shots" with "moments" or "experiences": "[M]ontage is an idea that arises from the collision of independent shots [such that] each sequential element is perceived not *next* to the other, but on *top* of the other."[56] There's that meanwhile, a collapse of the time dimension that imbues what would otherwise be something ploddingly mechanistic and causal with interest and significance. The cinema (and later TV and video) trained 20th-century audiences to see themselves and their lives within a moving-picture frame. That included reading the discontinuities and juxtapositions in our lives as sign-bearing acausal connections. Experienced synchronicities do frequently feel exactly as if some larger film or video editor, some Eisenstein in the sky, is injecting meaning into our life via deft splicing together of stimuli that our understanding of mechanistic causation suggests should not be juxtaposed. Again, our reward system is primed to mark such prediction errors with a burst of dopamine.

Jungian depth psychology as a whole could really be called a cinematic worldview: It "cuts away" from the patient to a larger archetypal setting that reframes the individual's small predicament as an instantiation of something timeless and mythic.[57] In stark contrast to Freud, Jung was not that interested in the messy particulars of a patient's childhood and relationships. He related their mundane inner and outer life to big spiritual themes encoded in myth, and this remains one of the enduring appeals of Jungian writing and clinical practice for many people. In early- and mid-century Zurich, Jung's approach made patients' little comedies seem more like epics, and as a byproduct it gave them an education. Especially for his female patients like Maggy, who otherwise were compelled to fill boring social roles, treatment with Jung was really a master class in history, philosophy, and world religions, along with permission to think and express themselves in a much larger way than their prior lives had allowed.

But for experiences like Maggy's with the rose-chafer, precognition is a more powerful explanatory framework than synchronicity. It places the focus back onto the individual experiencer and their biography— their long self—rather than an impersonal world of archetypes. In so doing, such a framing reveals the ingenuity of the individual's unique imagination. Instead of a wriggling insect, in Maggy's dream she was presented with a "valuable ... golden" piece of Egyptian-style jewelry. It is a brilliant symbolic transformation of the real future situation, conveniently both capturing her therapist's lecture on Egyptian symbolism that ensued after giving her the beetle and expressing the enormous value the moment was going to assume in her life. Her dreaming brain already "knew" that value. What Freud called the primary process effortlessly creates such ingenious (and often, witty) condensed images during dreaming.

The flickering fire of the creative imagination behaves the same way during waking, as can be seen, I argue, with Woolf's inspiration on October 4, 1922, for a novel about her fictional Kitty Maxse coming "nearer and nearer" to suicide, just as news of the real thing was coming nearer and nearer to Woolf.

I see *Mrs. Dalloway* as another powerful piece of evidence that inspiration really is—or at least can be—precognition in disguise. Clarissa Dalloway came to possess Woolf's thoughts as a creative problem to explore, first in a short story the previous summer and then further in a novel, because of the strange, sad news about its real-life model's death looming in her near future. In her first *Diary* entry about Maxse's death, Woolf specifically reflects on her own guilt: "I could not have kept up with her; she never tried to see me. Yet yet—these old friends dying without any notice on our part always ... saddens me: makes me feel guilty. I wish I'd met her in the street. My mind has gone back all day to her; in the queer way it does."[58] Again, survivor's guilt is often the motor of dream premonitions, and premonitory literary inspiration should be no different. The suspicion that Maxse's fall had been deliberate would also have been part of the incident's magnetic pull, because Woolf herself had harbored and even acted upon the same urges. But to me, the most salient and uncanny fact about Woolf's inspiration for *Mrs. Dalloway* is the *form* she envisioned her story taking, already before she found out about Maxse's death: a novel exploring the subliminal substance of human connection, the uncanny psychic link between people, even complete strangers from totally different worlds and on different sides of the mental health and mental illness divide. It's another instance of that fractal geometry of prophecy, the fact of her own seeming occult connection to her subject folded into her concept for her book.

The same autumn Woolf began drafting her novel, the British government published a report on the deferred effects of war trauma. It was in this publication that the term "shell shock" first appeared, even though those deferred effects were already widely in evidence in Woolf's London, where young veterans often displayed the kinds of psychological impacts of trauma that Freud had described in *Beyond the Pleasure Principle*. Clarissa Dalloway's "opposite" in the novel Woolf wrote over the next two years came to be called Septimus Smith, a war veteran struggling with what we would now call PTSD and spiraling toward ending his life by jumping from a window. (The idea of him plotting to kill the Prime Minister was abandoned.) There is possibly a concrete temporal inspiration for this character. Two years earlier, a 21-year-old man, probably a war veteran, had killed himself at a rooftop dance party Woolf was attending. The fancily attired young man, whom nobody at the party knew, just lit up a cigarette and stepped off the roof, falling 30 feet to his death. Only Woolf's brother Adrian actually saw it, and summoned help.[59] As odd as the suicide itself, Woolf noted in her *Diary*, was the indifference of the other party guests inconvenienced by the early cancellation of the soiree, forced to find a new place to dance.

Mrs. Dalloway ends as the party guests start arriving at the home of Clarissa and her politician husband. One guest offhandedly mentions that some young, unknown man has just committed suicide, and over the last few pages, Clarissa's thoughts keep returning to this news. At first she is troubled, even slightly angry that in the midst of her party, death has intruded itself. Then she wonders why and how it happened and has a vivid mental vision of the man's fall, in gruesome detail (his body impaling itself on the spikes of a fence). Finally, Clarissa realizes that, precisely by making her reflect on her life and its joys, the stranger's act has done her a service: "But what an extraordinary night! She felt somehow very like him—the young man who had killed himself. She felt glad that he had done it: thrown it away. ... He made her feel the beauty; made her feel the fun."[60]

It would be easy to misread the latter thought as callousness, but it is the clearest literary expression of what I mean by the singular existential message that transmits backward in time across our worldlines: "but I survived." It is a deep peculiarity of the signifying unconscious that the most rewarding state of affairs for a living organism, survival, can only be signified, framed, by death or catastrophe happening nearby or to somebody else.[61] It is the ability to perceive or think about death that makes us feel most alive, destruction as the cause of our *feeling* our being, if not exactly coming into it, as Sabina Spielrein had put it in her essay that gave Freud the idea of the death drive. Although he would have used some German word, Freud would have said no decent person can openly admit to this *jouissance* of survival, even though everyone feels it or manifests it in some neurotic way.

I believe that in Clarissa's shifting thought process about Septimus Smith's suicide, Woolf is giving us a direct, frank window onto her own shifting thoughts about the news of Maxse's possible suicide after she got the news in early autumn 1922. She is admitting that amid all the shock, sadness, and guilt, there was a reward: The old family friend's death "made her feel the beauty; made her feel the fun." It was precisely this *jouissance* that seems to have refluxed back in time, tugging gently at Woolf's psychic sleeve that whole previous summer when she was writing "Mrs. Dalloway in Bond Street"—the story that ends with an ominous explosion outside a glove shop.

Shaman of the Scientific Sublime

For all of Woolf's overt intention of trying to capture some authentic flavor of mental life, there is something fantastic about the thought-stream of people and things in her books that is profoundly strange. Consciousness *isn't* like that. What she creates is something completely new and, at times, alien. J. F. Martel describes *To the Lighthouse*, for example, as being "as otherworldly as any science fiction novel."[62] I had the very same reaction when I read that book for the first time. I've always thought of Woolf as a secret science-fiction writer.

For instance, I'm sure I'm not the only 21st-century reader of Woolf's 1931 novel *The Waves* to imagine the bizarre monologues of the small children at the beginning of that book as observations by aliens having just stepped out of a spaceship that landed on the lawn of some English country house:

> "I see a ring," said Bernard, "hanging above me. It quivers and hangs in a loop of light."
>
> "I see a slab of pale yellow," said Susan, "spreading away until it meets a purple stripe."
>
> "I hear a sound," said Rhoda, "cheep, chirp; cheep chirp; going up and down."
>
> "I see a globe," said Neville, "hanging down in a drop against the enormous flanks of some hill."
>
> "I see a crimson tassel," said Jinny, "twisted with gold threads."
>
> "I hear something stamping," said Louis. "A great beast's foot is chained. It stamps, and stamps, and stamps."
>
> "Look at the spider's web on the corner of the balcony," said Bernard. "It has beads of water on it,

drops of white light."

"The leaves are gathered round the window like pointed ears," said Susan.

"A shadow falls on the path," said Louis, "like an elbow bent."[63]

Or perhaps they are ancient nonhuman beings who have just taken human form, savoring their new bodies and senses (of course, some would say that's what children indeed are). In any case, it's somehow very *Star Trek*-like.

In 2010, an anonymous article on a blog called "Check Your Facts" claimed that Woolf was the secret author of a 1923 pulp novel called *The Clockwork Man*, about a machine-augmented human from 8,000 years in the future who, because of a malfunction in the clockwork embedded in his head, accidentally travels to Edwardian London.[64] In this novel, the time traveler reveals to the locals that his future society is a matriarchal one in which men's aggressive and destructive tendencies have been overcome by technological implants—males live in what we would now call a virtual reality where they get out their aggressions. The novel is real—and really prescient if not actually prophetic of cyberpunk realities a century later[65]—but it's not true (unfortunately) that its author, E. V. Odle, was Woolf's nom de plume. The blog post was a clever hoax, and Odle turned out to be a real guy—in fact, socially connected to the Bloomsbury circle of writers and intellectuals that Virginia and Leonard Woolf are famously associated with, so Virginia certainly knew him. But the hoax was so believable because the sci-fi is everywhere in her work. Woolf's fiction reflected an awareness and understanding of the new sciences making headlines in her day, and she very consciously engaged with it. In fact, there is now practically a whole sub-industry of critical studies of Woolf focused on Einsteinian and quantum-physical motifs in her fiction.[66]

For instance, in Woolf's 1928 fantasy *Orlando*, the eponymous character's immortality is linked to her quickness when skating on ice—slowed aging being an expected effect of moving close to the physical constant C, the speed of light.[67] And *To the Lighthouse* bears obvious similarity in its premise and themes to the thought experiments on which Einstein had based his theory. The Ramsay family desires to approach the lighthouse across the bay—a longstanding wish of its matriarch Mrs. Ramsay—but finds it cannot actually make the journey, similar to the unattainability of C in Einstein's thought. Only after her death do her surviving family members make the trip. Einstein's theory (filtered through Minkowski) had also given legitimacy to the possible coexistence or simultaneity of past, present, and future. At one point, in a "moment of being" during dinner, Mrs. Ramsay reflects on the ruby-like permanence of that instant, that it will always be there, suspended in the block universe:

> Everything seemed possible. Everything seemed right. Just now (but this can not last, she thought, dissociating herself from the moment while they were all talking about boots) just now she had reached security; she hovered like a hawk suspended; like a flag floating in an element of joy which filled every nerve of her body fully and sweetly, not noisily, solemnly rather, for it arose, she thought, looking at them all eating there, from husband and children and friends; all of this rising in this profound stillness … seemed now for no special reason to stay there like smoke, like a fume rising upwards, holding them safe together. Nothing need be said, nothing could be said. There it was all around them. It partook, she felt … of eternity; as she had already felt about something different once before that afternoon; there is a coherence in things, a stability; something she meant, is immune from change, and shines out (she glanced at the window with its ripple of reflected lights) in the face of the flowing, the fleeting, the spectral, like a ruby; so that again tonight she had the feeling she had had once today already, of peace, of rest. Of such moments, she thought, the thing is made that remains forever after. This would remain.[68]

Another reason Woolf's writings have an otherworldly if not exactly science-fictional quality is that the consciousness of her characters is not "all in the head," just a private, interior affair. There is something transpersonal about it (using a term later applied to Jung's archetypal psychology). All throughout her career, Woolf frequently drew attention to the interzone between private subjective (spiritual) awareness and public life. Her fiction explored reality itself as a kind of permeable, mutable imaginal realm, indeed almost like a collective ocean where humans are the fish. Early in *The Voyage Out*, for instance, Clarissa Dalloway experiences a night of "fantastic dreams [that] were not confined to her indeed, but went from one brain to the other."[69] It's not just sci-fi—it's shamanic. Myers is another psychologist Woolf doesn't mention ever reading, but his "subliminal self," the carrier of telepathic signals, would be an apt description of how a shared un-conscious seems to transcend individual characters in her novels and spills over into other characters and even into objects.[70] In *Mrs. Dalloway*, Clarissa feels "odd affinities" with complete strangers and "even trees, or barns."[71] It is Jean Clottes' and David Lewis-Williams' "fluidity and permeability," again.

Aspects of Woolf's outlook and literary vision also merged interestingly with the ideas of the Theosophists, who were then helping import Indian spirituality to Europe and America. Woolf lived in a milieu saturated with Theosophy, but she largely didn't comment on it. Her nearest and dearest—her father, Leslie Stephen, and then her husband, Leonard Woolf—were standard modernist rationalists, agnostics, and skeptics. Leonard readily ridiculed the mystics of the day like Annie Besant, a Theosophist proselytizer and advocate for Indian home rule; Virginia also briefly satirizes Besant's grooming of Theosophy's new messiah Jiddu Krishnamurti in *The Waves*. But poet and critic Julie Kane argues that Woolf was really bending herself to peer pressure and patriarchal intellectual bullying and was privately much more open-minded to Theosophical ideas than she felt safe to let on. Throughout her life, she had experienced exactly the kinds of visionary states and perceptions those writers described: visions, auras, voices, ghostly presences, out-of-body experiences, and so on.[72] Woolf's big stumbling block seems to have been the uncritical and sometimes (to her) ridiculous claims of Theosophical true-believers, for instance about actual contact with the dead. She felt the dead around her and heard them talk; but they weren't really present, weren't really the dead, any more than the butterflies in Werner Herzog's car were really butterflies. "[O]ne must be scientific, above all scientific," Woolf has her mentally ill alter-ego Septimus Smith reflect at one point in *Mrs. Dalloway*, trying to rein in a blissful hallucination.[73] This sensibility made it easy to outwardly go along with the sneering and ridicule of her husband.

Nevertheless, Kane argues that between 1927 and 1931, in the middle of her career, with the successes of *To the Lighthouse* and *Orlando* having elevated her stature to one of the leading modernist writers, Woolf began to feel freer to finally confront the secret mystical reality she had been experiencing and burying[74]—what she described in her *Diary* in late September 1926 as "something mystic, spiritual; the thing that exists when we aren't there."[75] What gave her permission was partly a new friendship with William Butler Yeats, whom she met in late 1930. She found herself transfixed by the Irish poet's ideas about mythology, the soul, dreams, even fairies and magic—and to her liking, "he also is surprisingly sensible"—"No fluff & dreaminess."[76] But just as importantly, Woolf's reading in 1930 provided a new idiom in which to express her spiritual experiences. It was not the purple-hued Theosophical idiom of the occultists and Yeats, but rather the idiom of the most advanced science of her day (and still, ours), the science of the quantum.

From October 24 to 29, 1927, probably the most important meeting ever in the history of physics took place in Brussels, the fifth Solvay Conference, where the greatest scientific minds of the time gathered to discuss and debate the mysterious behavior of matter at the smallest scales in nature. On this occasion, Einstein is reputed to have reiterated what he wrote in a letter to Max Born the previous year, that "God does not play dice with the universe"—a slur on the indeterminacy or intrinsic randomness advanced by his younger colleagues Niels Bohr and Werner Heisenberg. Bohr's position, which came to be called the Copenhagen Interpretation, prevailed within quantum physics for most of the century, but there have always been dissenters, and dissent has increased in recent years. (Again, some of that dissent is the recent view that what looks like randomness or indeterminacy is really evidence of retrocausation—the quantum reframing that, I anticipate, will ultimately prevail and will make sense of phenomena like precognition.)

It was heady and seemingly inaccessible stuff to nonscientists. But in the years following the conference, the implications of what was debated in Brussels gradually trickled into the popular consciousness via the writings and radio talks of popular authors of the time like Arthur Eddington and James Jeans. The non-solidity then being revealed in quantum physics dovetailed in obvious ways with the ideas of the mystics, not to mention the fluidity and permeability of shamans. And Woolf was captivated, because more than anything else, quantum physics supplied a scientific justification for the experiments she had been doing in her writing for well over a decade by that point. She had been performing on the printed page what Impressionism and Pointillism had been doing in painting: dissolving reality and subordinating it to subjectivity, to an act of observation that somehow affected what was observed.

Woolf always portrayed herself as a literary being through and through, filling her *Diary* with mentions of canonical authors of the past and critical readings of contemporary modernist literary figures. Yet this obscured what seems to have been an active, passionate interest in the sciences. In an amusing collection of anecdotes from his stint assisting at the Woolfs' tiny publishing house, The Hogarth Press, while in his teens, artist Richard Kennedy recalled that Virginia "reads the most extraordinary books." At the time of this observation, it was *The Sexual Life of Savages* by the great Polish anthropologist Bronisław Malinowski.[77] But astronomer Jeans was another. Exceptionally for a mere scientific author, Jeans is mentioned several times in Woolf's *Diary*, including twice in late December 1930, shortly after the publication of his popular book *The Mysterious Universe*.[78]

Jeans was the Carl Sagan of his day: A scientist but mainly a science popularizer, and one with a unique literary gift for evoking the universe's grandeur. *The Mysterious Universe*, which was first delivered as a lecture that November at Cambridge, was his *Cosmos*. And while some of the cosmology is now outdated, one could hardly find a more evocative description, even now, of the new quantum theory that had been discussed by Bohr, Heisenberg, Schrödinger, Einstein, etc. at the Brussels gathering. "The future may not be as unalterably determined by the past as we used to think; in part at least it may rest on the knees of whatever gods there be."[79] He goes on:

> For instance, Professor Heisenberg has shewn that the concepts of the modern quantum theory involve what he calls a "principle of indeterminacy." We have long thought of the workings of nature as exemplifying the acme of precision. Our man-made machines are, we know, imperfect and inaccurate, but we have cherished a belief that the innermost workings of the atom would exemplify absolute accuracy and precision. Yet Heisenberg now makes it appear that nature abhors accuracy and precision above all things.[80]

Jeans marvels that the "play" we see in the universe—not play in the sense of child's play, but looseness, as might be seen in an untightened mechanism—reopens doors that Enlightenment science had seemed to shut:

[T]he picture of the universe presented by the new physics contains more room than did the old mechanical picture for life and consciousness to exist within the picture itself, together with the attributes which we commonly associate with them, such as free-will, and the capacity to make the universe in some small way different by our presence.[81]

Jeans is heralding the demise of materialism, at least in its most reductive forms. And the final chapter of his book, with the heading "Into the Deep Waters," doubles down:

To-day there is a wide measure of agreement, which on the physical side of science approaches almost to unanimity, that the stream of knowledge is heading towards a non-mechanical reality; the universe begins to look more like a great thought than like a great machine. Mind no longer appears as an accidental intruder into the realm of matter; we are beginning to suspect that we ought rather to hail it as the creator and governor of the realm of matter—not of course our individual minds, but the mind in which the atoms out of which our individual minds have grown exist as thoughts.[82]

The visionary last chapter of *The Mysterious Universe* was scandalous to some of Jeans' scientist peers, alarmed that he was becoming mystical. But Kane notes that these ideas would have seemed uncannily familiar to Woolf, whose work had been increasingly exploring the intermingling of mind and matter. "Imagine her surprise," Kane writes, "upon reading that scientists were coming around to believing that the act of observation is bound up with the nature of physical reality."[83] Jeans' writing was so fascinating to Woolf, in fact, that it seems to have reached as much as four years back in time to magnetize her precognitive imagination.

On September 30, 1926, Woolf recorded in her diary a vision of a fin rising from the waves, coupled with a memory of a moment of derealization from her childhood. She felt that this visionary chord was the seed for another book, and she intended to follow the fin where it led:

> *Thursday 30 September*
>
> I wished to add some remarks ... on the mystical side of this solitude; how it is not oneself but something in the universe that one's left with. It is this that is frightening & exciting in the midst of my profound gloom, depression, boredom, whatever it is: One sees a fin passing far out. What image can I reach to convey what I mean? ... Life is, soberly & accurately, the oddest affair; has in it the essence of reality. I used to feel this as a child—couldn't step across a puddle once I remember, for thinking, how strange—what am I? &tc. ... I hazard the guess that it may be the impulse behind another book. ... I want to watch & see how the idea at first occurs. I want to trace my own process.[84]

The Waves, which Woolf embarked on after *Orlando* and which, she believed, was the fulfilment of her "fin passing far out" vision, is the first, maybe still the only, quantum novel—a novel of indeterminacies and of things and people that have both a wavy and fixed nature, the way photons and electrons do in quantum physics. According to Bohr and his Copenhagen faction, particles have no definiteness or solidity until they are measured or observed, at which point their "wavefunction" is said to "collapse" to a definite, determinate state.

Kane notes astonishing similarities between *The Waves* and the themes and specific passages from *The Mysterious Universe*, suspecting that she must have consciously or unconsciously borrowed and inserted them in her novel prior to its publication the following year. But the chronology shows that to be impossible: Jeans' book came out when Woolf was rewriting her novel for the third time, but the core imagery and themes, and especially the initial germ-image of the novel, which never made it into later drafts, were conceived and written as much as three years earlier. They may even have originated in the depression in September 1926 that precipitated her vision of a "fin passing far out."

In the week before that vision, Woolf had described a state of deep gloom that came upon her like waves, which "give one a plunge *into deep waters*" (my emphasis).[85] And she was probably thinking of this wavelike state when she wrote the strange vision that opened the first draft of her novel, which she was then calling "The Moths":

> Many mothers, & before them many mothers, &
> again many mothers have groaned, & fallen. Like one
> wave, succeeding another. Wave after wave, endlessly
> sinking & falling as far as the eye can stretch. And all
> these waves have been the prostrate forms of mothers,
> in their nightgowns, with the tumbled sheets around
> them holding them up, with a groan, as they sink back
> into the sea.[86]

She wrote in the margin of this draft a note to herself: "I am telling myself the story of the world from the beginning. I am not concerned with the single life, but with lives together."[87] She discarded the image of wavelike-mothers falling (collapsing) on a beach—perplexingly for critics, given how singular and powerful it is—but was intent that the repetitive sound of waves surging and crashing on the shore should be "heard all through" her novel. And indeed, barely a paragraph goes by without some reference to waves.

In *The Mysterious Universe*, waves are "heard all through" too, and in various contexts, not just the quantum-mechanical. Jeans begins with a striking primordial scene: the image of widely scattered stars in space—so dispersed that they scarcely perturb each other except on rare occasions, such as when (as it was then thought by astronomers, although no longer) another star passed near enough to our sun in its youth that it raised an enormous tidal wave on its surface, shooting spray out into space. The spray congealed to form the planets of the solar system. This image of waves giving birth to the planets segues to the aforementioned meditation on determinism and chance, and the fact that the story of deterministic causation can no longer be told, in the new quantum theory, except in the aggregate: not a single "life," but lives together, so to speak.

Other images in Woolf's discarded drafts seem taken directly from Jeans' not-yet-published book, too. A 1929 draft of *The Waves*, for instance, describes interludes of waves in sunlight and sunbeams in a room. In *The Mysterious Universe*, Jeans describes rays of light, "the straight edges of a sunbeam in a dusty room."[88] And especially familiar when she read it in 1930 would have been the title of Jeans' visionary chapter, "Into the Deep Waters," the very phrase she had used in her diary to describe her mystical/depressed state four years earlier. Also,

Kane suggests that *The Waves*' focus on six characters who seem to revolve around a seventh character (Percival) seems inspired by Jeans's description, early in his book, of the carbon atom: "six electrons revolving around the appropriate central nucleus, like six planets revolving around a central sun …"[89] Although here too, Woolf had already arrived at her characters and their interrelationships, so if Kane is right, it couldn't have been literary influence of the usual sort, in the usual direction. Literary influence sometimes flows backward from powerful reading experiences in a writer's future, though. I suggest that's exactly what we see with *The Waves*. (We'll see several more examples of artistic and literary retro-influence in Part Three.)

Anti-materialist or post-materialist writers, even some prominent physicists, have often seen the new quantum physics that emerged in the late 1920s as validating an Indian or Theosophical spirituality—what Kane sees Woolf as finding in Jeans' writing. But I think there was more to it for Woolf—or really, a less that was more. As open-minded as she may have been, Woolf was no Theosophist. If Jeans' description of the quantum revolution supplied her with a metaphor or model of the fluidity of things and the interpenetration of subjectivity and objectivity, it was also Jeans' gift at writing about immensity that helped Woolf articulate a much less Theosophical and much more austere spirituality, a via negativa that is closer to Zen than it is to Theosophy.

Critics of Enlightenment materialism sometimes claim that science's Copernican revolutions rob the world of its magic and make our lives seem dismally insignificant in the grand scheme. Sociologist Max Weber called it disenchantment. The disenchantment narrative has been argued to be false in several ways. Spirituality and even spirit worlds in the traditional sense are alive and well in the modern technological world, first of all—even among scientists and other academics, if only in private.[90] But also, thanks to science and technology, we live in a world of mind-ripping immensities that offer a new kind of enchantment largely unavailable to people before the late 19th century. For people of a certain sensibility, the scientific sublime is an enchantment that can provoke more than awe; it can catapult one toward real spiritual experience.

For anyone in our age, the legacy of science, and the technologies that give us our knowledge and our previously unattainable perspectives on nature, always enter in as part of our perceptual and conceptual schemas, what we know about what we see.[91] In his writings on the sublime,

Kant remarked on the ability of telescopes and microscopes to bring the very large and very small within the purview of our senses. *Sublime objects* are those whose colossal scale and/or minute complexity radically upset our familiar conceptual categories and frames of reference.[92] The brain as revealed by neuroscience is a sublime object, in this sense. The late-19th century Spanish pathologist Santiago Ramón y Cayal drew and painted astonishingly intricate tree-like neurons that he saw under his microscope, awed that these delicate structures, connected in vast forest-like networks, somehow underlay our conscious experience. The "impossible" materiality of what, from our subjective point of view, is also something ineffable, irreducible, and spiritual inspired Ramón y Cayal, who called neurons "mysterious butterflies of the soul."

Such contradictions and impossibilities are spiritually generative—in the Rinzai Zen tradition, for instance, contemplating paradoxes, koans, can move a person to mystical rapture. Ramón y Cayal's neuroscience rapture is an experience that was unavailable before the invention of the microscope and the knowledge about the micro-world that it made possible.[93]

Human prehistory is another sublime object, revealed by the technology of radiocarbon dating. The specific awe the 12-year-old Werner Herzog felt gazing at a horse from Lascaux was one that was never possible before the advent of modern techniques for assigning dates to very old things. The teenager who, chasing his dog "Robot," stumbled into that cave in 1940 and saw that horse in person only recognized that it was very old.[94] It's another thing entirely to grasp that it was painted, as the author of Herzog's expensive art book informed him, 15,000 or more years in the past.[95] Lascaux's paintings are now estimated at 17,000-18,600 years old—four times farther from us than Stonehenge or Egypt's pyramids, and still only half as old as the art in Chauvet Cave.

And of course, there is the mysterious universe as revealed by telescopes. The history of astronomical imaging is usually written as part of the history of science (optics and astronomy and space exploration), but it really is as much part of art history and, as such, religious history. There is a direct line of descent from the heavenly vistas in Renaissance and Reformation paintings of Jesus's Ascension to the astonishing nebulae and galactic vistas revealed by the Hubble Space Telescope in famous images like "The Pillars of Creation" (part of the Eagle Nebula). As I write this, the newly deployed James Webb Space Telescope is extending our view into deep space by orders of magnitude. But like with those cave paintings or those neurons, you have to know what you are looking at. Dense "starfields" in a high-resolution deep-space image that turn out to be galaxy-fields, tens of billions of years old and tens of billions of light years away, each spec containing hundreds of billions of stars and perhaps a hundred or a thousand times that many worlds, evoke a sublime rapture of deep space that has to be quite different but, for some, no less spiritually nourishing than seeing the dome of the firmament as an array of campfires or souls of the dead. Plenty of people, from the Russian Cosmists (who we will learn more about in the next chapter) to adherents of the new UFO religiosity described by Diana Pasulka in her books have found creative ways of seeing the cosmos revealed by science as "all of the above," a vast universe or multiverse haunted by innumerable intelligences, awaiting our arrival "if we do not destroy ourselves," as Sagan always admonished.

The scientific sublime is an Earth-bound counterpart and precursor of what has famously been called the Overview Effect experienced by astronauts.[96] Certainly, actually visiting space is probably better, easier (the same way consuming some psychedelic is probably more potent and reliable than meditating or bedding down in a dark cave), but the imagination can still get you there. Contemplating the spatial and temporal vastness of the universe affirms the soul in the same stroke that it destroys the ego, and ego destruction, as any mystic will tell you, is a spiritually productive thing. This fact, to me, is the most important counterargument to the disenchantment narrative: Science—sometimes even at its most reductive—provides endless new opportunities to get our egos out of the way and experience transcendence.

Which is a roundabout way of clarifying what I think the famous self-destroyer Woolf found so nourishing in Jeans. Contemplating immensity is another way of playing gone, like Freud's grandson Ernst with his mirror. Jeans inspired his readers and lecture audiences with descriptions of spacetime's incomprehensible immensity at the scales of the interstellar. His lectures and books were full of slides of astronomical photos of nebulae, etc.[97] He was fond of comparing the number of stars in the universe to the number of grains of sand on earth, not unlike the way Sagan peppered his popular talks with enormous numbers, the "billions and billions" that became his trademark (even though it was late-night host Johnny Carson, imitating him, who actually said the phrase). Bernard, Woolf's writer stand-in in *The Waves*, notes experiences of the scientific sublime: "And the light of the stars falling, as it falls now, on my hand after traveling for millions upon millions of years—I could get a cold shock from that for a moment—not more, my imagination is too feeble."[98] In an essay Woolf wrote in 1927, "The Narrow Bridge of Art," she expressed the inadequacy of traditional artistic and literary forms to express this sublimity:

> That the age of the earth is 3,000,000,000 years; that human life lasts but a second ... it is in this atmosphere of doubt and conflict that writers have now to create, and the fine fabric of a lyric is no more fitted to contain this point of view than a rose leaf to envelop the rugged immensity of a rock.[99]

I think Woolf saw her richest creative moments as tied to that imaginative annihilation of self and ego, the Zen effect some people get from cosmology. In the 1930s, Woolf found the same nourishment in the sublime science fiction of Olaf Stapledon. Stapledon sent Woolf a copy of his novel of vast cosmic history, *Star Maker*, and she replied: "it seems to me that you are grasping ideas that I have tried to express, much more fumblingly, in fiction. But you have gone much further and I can't help envying you—as one does those who reach what one has aimed at."[100] SF novelist and Woolf aficionado Kim Stanley Robinson argues that Stapledon's grand cosmic vision prompted Woolf to push her last novel, *Between the Acts*, in a cosmic direction, toward deep time.[101] It ends with a kind of flickering vision of prehistoric humans lurking in the modern landscape, a lot like what the modern spelunkers, and Herzog, experienced when they stood in Chauvet Cave the first time: "The house had lost its shelter. It was night before roads were made, or houses. It was the night that dwellers in caves had watched from some high place among rocks."[102] I can't help but think that in *To the Lighthouse* and *The Waves*, especially, Woolf was already anticipating something of this ego-destroying cosmic vision, packing it into the moments of being her characters like Mrs. Ramsay experienced.

Woolf eventually succeeded in merging with the waves she loved when she filled the pockets of her coat with stones and walked into the River Ouse, near her home, on March 28, 1941. In the note the 59-year-old writer left for her husband, Leonard, she said she was hearing voices and did not think that she would recover from her illness this time. The critic Pierre Bayard, alert for ways in which "tomorrow is written" in literary works, argues that her writings contain premonitions of her final act.[103] Her *Diary* entries, essays, and fiction are indeed full of images of water, waves, and seeking the watery depths. How much of this is truly precognitive of her suicide is forever indeterminate though, like the velocity of an electron when you know a lot about its position, or trying to see what the dark looks like by quickly turning on a lamp. Artists often consciously or unconsciously fulfill their own myths and prophecies; that doesn't necessarily make their prophecies any less authentically precognitive, but it makes it impossible to tease apart the many causal vectors with any confidence.

That said, I do strongly suspect that Woolf's vision in September 1926 of a "fin passing far out" was a precognitive one, and that it was precognitive not just of *The Waves per se* but also, mainly, of how she would eventually end her life. She did not yet know Freud's work very well—the Woolfs' publishing house had only just begun publishing Freud's first English translations—so she would not have thought to free-associate on that brilliant product of her primary process. But visions, like dreams, sometimes speak in puns, and what is a *fin* in the favorite language of her lover Sackville-West but "the end"?

Postscript: "Many miles away ..."

In the late 1600s, an alchemist named Johann Joachim Becher tried to explain combustion by proposing a fire-like substance called *phlogiston* that was contained in combustible materials. This was really just a placeholder for a theory that required a later understanding of oxidation reactions—there's no such thing as phlogiston, in other words. In a 1972 book on coincidence and ESP research, *The Roots of Coincidence*, Arthur Koestler argued that Jung's theory of synchronicity had more than a whiff of phlogiston about it. Although he admired many of Jung's contributions to psychology, he argued that the synchronicity concept was an example of what philosophers sometimes call "misplaced concreteness" and didn't really explain anything. The inherent contradiction in scientifically explaining physical events acausally made Jung's term, he believed, a "non-starter."[104]

It would be an understatement to say that the modern era did not get Koestler's memo. Synchronicity today is more popular, and arguably more culturally relevant, than ever before. It is the subject of countless books and blogs not at all confined to Jungian psychology and metaphysics. The past decade has seen a flood of self-help books with titles like *Connecting with Coincidence* and *Super-Synchronicity* and *The*

Synchronicity Key.[105] "Synchromystics" actively draw connections, however improbable, among historical events, popular culture, archaeology, and occult writings as a means of accessing the collective unconscious or divining the archetypal logic of history.[106] UFO experiencers sometimes consider synchronicities to be messages or interventions from the nonhuman intelligence(s) behind the phenomenon.[107] Synchronicity is now, arguably, a worldview, one that goes well beyond Jung and depth psychology.

There's an interesting irony in this: Koestler's harsh critique of synchronicity in *The Roots of Coincidence* may be at least partly responsible for the popularity Jung's concept now enjoys.[108] The reason is that many readers in the 1970s first encountered the idea of synchronicity via Koestler's book. In fact, it was that book, not Jung's writings on the subject, that actually inspired The Police's mega-hit "Synchronicity II" (and other songs on that theme) on that band's final album in 1983. Although band frontman Sting is depicted on some versions of the album cover studiously reading the distinctively minimalist Bollingen Press paperback of Jung's *Synchronicity*, the rocker-reader was actually a Koestler fan, not a Jung fan.[109] Koestler's *The Roots of Coincidence* may therefore go down in history as one of the more culturally decisive instances of the "Streisand Effect," inadvertently giving energy to a meme you are trying to discredit.

"Synchronicity II" is worth mentioning because it is strikingly like Woolf's *Mrs. Dalloway*, both structurally and in its theme of violent mental breakdown coming nearer and nearer to its main character. A repressed, downtrodden man endures various humiliations at home and then at work, then returns home. "Many miles away," a long-slumbering monster rises from the water of a "dark Scottish loch" (Ness, one presumes) and casts his shadow on the door of a nearby cottage. The juxtaposition implies something terrible is about to happen, simultaneously, at both homes … or perhaps they are the same home. Sting doesn't even need to sing "meanwhile," because to us it is understood. A premodern listener, before the world of the 19th century novel or 20th century cinema and TV, might not have grasped this, imagining the events as unfolding in sequence rather than being mapped onto each other.

I agree with Koestler's misgivings about synchronicity as an explanatory framework for meaningful coincidences, but Jung's mid-century writings on synchronicity did an important service: They made it permissible, at least in clinical contexts, to talk about experiences that truly defy Enlightenment understandings of causality. Framing unlikely anecdotes in terms of archetypes and individuation allows them to be expressed in a culturally "safe" fashion, since the writer is generally not making any claims of ESP or any similarly paranormal phenomenon that would trigger the skeptics. Had Jung not written his book *Synchronicity*—and arguably, had Sting not been photographed reading it on the cover of *Rolling Stone*'s 1983 Album of the Year, thanks to Koestler's *The Roots of Coincidence*—we might today have fewer such stories. Moreover, synchronicity is a concept that, when understood in light of more recent thinking about precognition, could prove to be central in a future theory of religion and culture more generally—we'll circle back to this at the end of the book.

Arise O Prophet! Work My Will
Andrei Tarkovsky in the Fourth Bunker

*Art is born and takes hold wherever there is a timeless
and insatiable longing for the spiritual, for the ideal
… in an artistic creation the personality does not assert
itself, it serves another, higher, and communal idea. The
artist is always the servant, and is perpetually trying
to pay for the gift that has been given to him as if by a
miracle.*
—Andrei Tarkovsky, *Sculpting in Time* (1985)

*I am convinced that Time is reversible. At any rate it
does not go in a straight line.*
—Andrei Tarkovsky, Diary entry (February 8, 1976)

Despite the obvious parallels, academics resist sweeping generaliza-
tions and comparisons like artists=shamans. For Richmond University visual culture scholar and practicing shaman Robert J. Wallis,
the conceptual entanglement of art and shamanism over the centuries
is a problem to be critiqued. It is, he argues, a "constructed, discursive"
move, a spurious invocation of some perceived elective affinity between
two categories of human that have been portrayed, he thinks too sim-
plistically, to have melancholy, madness, and linkages to supernatural
forces in common. The equation of artists and shamans obliterates cultural differences and ignores local framings, and it romanticizes artists
as "individuals who are somehow, perhaps via such vague terms as 'genius' or 'neurosis,' uniquely connected to a special or dangerous realm
of inspiration."[1]

Wallis describes that romanticizing like it's a bad thing, but I get it. Neither *shaman* nor *artist* are well-defined and they do blur greatly around the edges. There is a long unfortunate history of using the image of the superstitious, demonic, or mentally ill shaman to invalidate the thought-world of other cultures and thereby abet the colonialist project. Within a century of the first explorers' reports of Siberian shamans, for example, Siberia had been annexed by Russia for its natural resources like fur, and many of its cultures were obliterated in the process—parallel to the fate of indigenous peoples in the Americas at the same time.[2] Today, shamanism and its techniques of ecstasy have themselves been appropriated and commodified, turned into tourist attractions.[3] But I suspect that academics' retreat into critique has as much to do with that whiff of the supernatural that clings to lay conceptions of shamanism, that "special or dangerous realm of inspiration." Similar refusals and retreats are the norm in scholarly biographies and art and literary criticism too, almost like there's a force-field around the question of inspiration and super-experience more generally.[4]

Again, the common theme of art and religion for as long as we can look back in human time is our "impossible" dual nature as human and superhuman, what Jeffrey Kripal glosses as "the human as two."[5] Science and scholarship since the Enlightenment have largely refused to acknowledge that super-twin when it has tiptoed barefoot into our home and demanded to be taken seriously as something beyond science fiction or superstition. Kripal describes an academic "immunological response"—"ignore the super, downplay it whenever it appears, erase it if you can, and, if you must talk or write about it, reduce it to something social, moral, and political."[6] If it's inspired and inspiring, it must be a problem, something socially constructed.

When you hold this in mind and squint at history, the co-birth of artists and shamans nearly 500 years ago begins to look like more than just a funny coincidence. If I didn't know better, I might almost think that the concept of the artist—and with it, the languages of aesthetics and criticism launched by Vasari's *Lives of the Most Eminent Painters, Sculptors, and Architects*—emerged as an early manifestation of an immunological response against the threatening supernormal dimensions of creativity that what passed for anthropology in that age was beginning to illuminate.

I don't know better, actually.

One way of looking at "the arts" since the Renaissance is as a kind of cultural preserve, a safe haven for "our" superpeople, but one that exacts a price, a buy-in to mainstream Christian norms and, later,

Enlightenment framings of human possibility: *You're alright, we accept your quirks, and we won't burn you at the stake for being witches, as long as you don't go claiming that your superpowers are real.* The more contemporary, post-witch-burning version of this formulation might be, … *we won't put you in an asylum.*

The fate of the shaman in the scientific imagination has abetted the masking of those "dangerous realms." Half a millennium after shamans entered the European thought-world, we are long past literally demonizing them—their special powers have been totally drained. Thus, to say artists are like shamans is hardly radical or dangerous anymore, just a pop-culture cliché, because shamans are largely seen as some kind of fluffy New Age appropriation or a quaint relic of primitive belief systems. To say instead that artists are shamans *and* that shamans (and thus artists) manifest actual superabilities, superpowers—that's a claim to provoke eye-rolls and *X-Files* music for many.[7] But I hope you are starting to be persuaded that there is an authentic super dimension, a supernature, to what artists are doing when they create. Creativity, as we saw with Virginia Woolf, often involves altered states of being, intensified possibilities of consciousness, and people in those intensified altered states make real magic, performing impossible feats, including recording future upheavals in their lives that should be totally unknowable by any currently accepted understanding of causality.

Coolly gracing international film festivals in tinted glasses and sleek suits, Andrei Tarkovsky hardly looked the part, but the Russian director struck many people, both fans and people who knew him well, as a modern shaman.[8] According to Layla Alexander-Garrett, a translator, photographer, and writer who became close to Tarkovsky in the mid-1980s and chronicled the making of his final film, *The Sacrifice*, the director had all his life been obsessed with decoding chance occurrences, signs, coincidences, and dreams.[9] He had a habit of losing precious film scripts or his wallet, and always they would be returned to him, or through some twist of fate he would find them again.[10] She writes that "at critical moments in his life some kind of mysterious inner voice strangely guides him"[11]—that voice that saved his life in Siberia, for instance.

In a 1992 book on the overlaps between shamanism and modern art, *Dreaming with Open Eyes*, Michael Tucker singles out Tarkovsky as a "person of extraordinary shamanic sensitivity," based on the many shamanic motifs and images that appear in his films. Tucker didn't mention it—and perhaps he did not know it—but among those who take seriously the possible super-dimensions of creativity, Tarkovsky was already notorious for seemingly having precognized the worst-ever nuclear accident, Chernobyl, in his 1979 masterpiece, *Stalker*. In fact, *Stalker* is part of a larger precognitive pattern in the filmmaker's life, and the layers of prophecy in that film alone are astonishing.

Most of the action of *Stalker* unfolds in the Zone, a silent landscape of overgrown ruins created by an unspecified disaster years before, where spacetime itself is uncertain and only shaman-like rangers, stalkers, can guide trespassers through. At the heart of this ruined realm is a room where, it is said, one's deepest wish will be granted. This is why two men, a famous writer (played by Anatoly Solonitsyn) and a prominent scientist (Nikolai Grinko), have paid dearly to have the Stalker (Alexander Kaidanovsky) lead them to this magical destination. It is not that the Stalker knows the way—because the way is never the same as it was last time—but because he knows the indications, and knows how to test the reality there, to guide his companions safely.

Like the Grail Kingdom from the Arthurian romances and Richard Wagner's opera *Parsifal*, the Zone is an enchanted but desolate place, where time itself seems to slow down in the vicinity of the traumatic yet life-giving miracle at its center.[12] Filmed partly in the toxic environs of an abandoned Estonian hydroelectric facility downstream from a chemical plant spewing polluted waste, Tarkovsky's setting could serve as the prototype for practically every post-apocalyptic landscape in cinema or fiction, before or since. It is the dead marshes that surround Mordor, for instance, in Peter Jackson's adaptation of J. R. R. Tolkien's *The Two Towers*. With armored Elvish corpses lying just under the water, Jackson's landscape was clearly modeled on the marsh over which one of Tarkovsky's tracking shots slowly inches, toward the Stalker's sleeping hand. Just under the water are objects from various times, partly exposed in the mud: a metal tray, a syringe, coins, a religious icon, a gun, a spring, a fish, a bathroom tile, a calendar.

Once the trio penetrate the building at the heart of the Zone, impossibly filled with something like snow drifts, they find just an empty, dirty room with decaying plaster and water covering the floor—a nothing. They bicker and fight and hesitate to go in. The Stalker himself won't even consider going in. He reveals that his predecessor and mentor, a legendary master-stalker named Porcupine, went in, and came out to find himself a rich man. He hung himself after that, because he had gone in seeking to bring his dead brother back to life—his brother, whom he had led to his death in the Zone. The room knew better than Porcupine did his own heart's true desire, and it was not pretty or noble.

Whether the danger of the wish-granting room is that your deepest wish won't be what you believe or expect it to be, or whether it is that you won't be able to articulate it with the exactness demanded by the letter-fixated tricksters of folklore, is left ambiguous. Either way, the story of Porcupine scares the writer and the scientist, and the climax is an anticlimax. The writer turns on their guide and accuses him of toying with them. The scientist pulls out a small nuclear device he had smuggled in his backpack to destroy the room and the superstition it represents. But both men realize the pathetic absurdity of their gestures, and they back down from their threats. The journey to reach the room seems to have somehow been the point. It is enough to come to the threshold and not walk through.

At the end, on their return to civilization, when we see how the Stalker lives in a poor dwelling, with a crippled, mutant daughter, we understand exactly his fear: that somehow his obvious wish to cure his daughter or provide better for his family may not be his deepest. It is thus better to remain in the dark about our deepest desires lest we end up rich but self-hating, like Porcupine did.

Again, the first of *Stalker's* prophecies is well-known: On April 26, 1986, seven years after the film was released, an explosion and fire in the fourth energy block of Chernobyl nuclear reactor outside Pripyat, Soviet Ukraine, released enormous amounts of radioactive contaminants that left the environs of Pripyat uninhabitable for centuries to come. Many of the workers struggling to contain the fire died immediately or over the following weeks and months from radiation sickness, and cancers and birth defects are still common in the region. The World Health Organization estimated that the total death toll attributable to the disaster will ultimately be over 4,000.

Today, Chernobyl's ruined Reactor 4 sits at the center of an "exclusion zone," 30 kilometers in radius, from which nearly 120,000 people had to be evacuated, and which was thereafter guarded by armed soldiers, just like the Zone in *Stalker*. Photos of the abandoned Soviet-era housing blocks of Pripyat, overgrown with weeds and overrun with animals, also look just like settings from Tarkovsky's movie.[13] Real-life youth "stalkers," emulating the film, stealthily guide paying clients into the irradiated, mutant-haunted region.[14] (Just as I completed this book, researchers at Princeton reported that wolves in the Chernobyl exclusion zone are actually thriving, due to mutations that protect them against the cancerous effects of radiation.[15]) A popular video game called *S.T.A.L.K.E.R.: Shadow of Chernobyl* even mashed up Tarkovsky's spiritual sci-fi meditation with the real wilderness the reactor created. It has spawned three sequels as of this writing.

Tarkovsky had adapted his story from the brilliant but less spiritual 1971 novel *Roadside Picnic* by Boris and Arkady Strugatsky. In the novel, the Zone was created by an extraterrestrial force or visitation, and Stalkers lead scientists into the Zone to retrieve artifacts discarded or left behind by the aliens, like trash after a picnic (hence the title). But to better focus on the spiritual dimension, Tarkovsky made the cause of the Zone in his film more ambiguous, implying that it may have been something like a nuclear disaster. The only mention of its cause is, uncannily, "a breakdown in the fourth bunker."

But the Chernobyl prophecy only scratches the surface. *Stalker* embodies other premonitions that are much more personal to the director, and it is an understatement to say that those would not make a good video game.

The 47-year-old Tarkovsky experienced many difficult setbacks while making his film, including having to re-shoot nearly the whole movie when a Moscow film lab improperly developed the new Kodak film stock that had been used, making a year's worth of footage unusable. A deteriorating relationship with his Director of Photography also resulted in Tarkovsky hiring a new cinematographer, as well as firing many of his crew. Although initially despondent, the ever-determined Tarkovsky pleaded and negotiated with the Soviet film boards to reshoot his picture. He and his remaining crew and actors returned to the horribly polluted locations in Estonia, where the outdoor scenes had been shot, so they could reconstruct the poorly developed footage.[16]

The first of the tragedies was the death of Solonitsyn ("The Writer") from a rare and aggressive lung cancer in 1982, at the young age of 47, just two years after *Stalker* was released. The loss of Tarkovsky's friend and favorite actor, whom he had discovered (casting him in the title role of his 1966 film *Andrei Rublev*) and who was supposed to star in his next two films, was devastating to the director.[17] But Solonitsyn's death took on a new, even darker meaning in December 1985, four months before the Chernobyl disaster, when Tarkovsky himself, then only 53, was also diagnosed with a rare, incurable lung cancer. It perplexed the doctors because he was not a smoker, having given up cigarettes over a decade earlier.[18] Lung cancer would also later (in 1998) claim the life of Tarkovsky's wife Larisa, who had served as his Assistant Director on *Stalker*.

This cluster of deaths led the film's sound designer, Vladimir Sharun, to assert, very plausibly, that the polluted landscape where they had filmed *Stalker* (twice) in 1978 had caused these fatal cancers.[19] Sharun noted that the pollution was visible in the water and that even during filming some of the crew suffered skin reactions. Whether or not Sharun is right—another rumor later circulated that the KGB had "cancered" Tarkovsky because of his announced defection from the USSR in 1984 and alleged anti-Soviet themes in his films[20]—the director would undoubtedly have noticed the coincidence of his own and his friend Solonitsyn's rare lung cancers and possibly would have drawn the same connection his sound designer later made.

After his diagnosis in late 1985, the increasingly depressed (and busy) Tarkovsky wrote very little in his journals, so we are forced to speculate. But if he did draw such a connection, then he would have seen that he bore responsibility for killing both himself and his friend through his artistic obsession of completing *Stalker*, including going back to the highly toxic location to re-shoot his film after the disaster with the film stock. If this is the case, then it would make the tragic lesson of Porcupine that forms *Stalker*'s centerpiece even more prophetic than the Zone itself (or its "fourth bunker"): Like Porcupine, Tarkovsky would be to blame for the death of someone he loved as a result of having led him through a toxic landscape on a Quixotic—or indeed, Ahab-like—personal quest for artistic glory. Impossibly, the film he was so driven to make contained a prophecy of his mistake.[21]

I argued in *Time Loops* that people sometimes neurotically—or artistically—"work through" traumas that haven't happened yet. I believe this is exactly what happened with Tarkovsky: *Stalker* was inspired by a future trauma that his inspiration (and obsession) directly caused. It is a time loop caught in amber.

In late December, 1978, right in the midst of trying to complete the film, the director wrote of a premonition weighing on him, of a downfall that was somehow tied ironically to his creative frenzy: "For some time now I have had the feeling, which is becoming more and more acute, of being on the brink of a period of tragic trials, of foundering hopes. And this is at a moment when I am possessed as never before by the urge to create."[22]

Sharun notes that that tracking shot across the shallow water seems to contain its own part of the prophecy: "we can see submerged in water a card torn from a calendar with the date 28 December. This day was the last day of Tarkovsky's life, he died on 29 December 1986."[23]

Time Turned Inside Out

Tarkovsky was fond of quoting his favorite poet, Pushkin, on the fact that an artist could not help being a prophet, much as he may resist that calling. Pushkin's 1826 poem, "The Prophet," describes a six-winged seraph killing, dismembering, and resurrecting the poet, giving him the prophetic gift:

> And with his sword he cleft my chest
> And ripped my quaking heart out whole,
> And in my sundered breast he pressed
> A blazing shard of living coal.
> There in the desert I lay dead
> Until the voice from heaven said:
> *"Arise O Prophet! Work My will ..."* [24]

When I read this, I cannot help thinking of Philip K. Dick, who joked in a letter to a pen pal during a hospital stay that the doctors were about to remove his vital organs and replace them with old radio parts.[25] It's how shamans are called to their vocation in dreams: dismembered and reassembled. Tarkovsky, fascinated with shamanism and an avid reader of Carlos Castaneda—he had planned to make a film of Castaneda's popular Don Juan books—was certainly aware of this.[26]

Tarkovsky was interested in all aspects of mysticism and the paranormal. He consulted spiritual healers. He studied the works of Theosophists like Rudolf Steiner and books on Indian philosophy and Buddhism. He insisted on the reality of extraterrestrial visitation. In August 1975, Larisa, their five-year-old son Andriushka, and some guests witnessed a brightly lit, mushroom-shaped UFO near the Tarkovskys' home in Myasnoe, in the Russian province of Ryazan.[27] It enveloped them with light and then vanished—his son could talk of nothing else the whole next week. And unsurprisingly, given his propensity to be guided by a life-saving inner voice, the director was interested in psychic phenomena and parapsychological research. At the very end of *Stalker*, the Stalker's mutant daughter telekinetically moves some glasses across the surface of a table. This scene was based on real research by Soviet parapsychologists with a woman named Ninel Kulagina, who was filmed moving small objects on a table apparently through the power of her mind, although debunkers claimed that the films used some kind of trickery.[28] Tarkovsky was a friend of parapsychologist Eduard Naumov, who had made some of the films of Kulagina and had even been imprisoned for two years because of his suspicious contacts with Western parapsychology researchers.[29] The director filmed the *Stalker* telekinesis scene with Naumov's help—but using hidden fishing line in this case, not mind power.[30]

It is perfectly natural that the most mystical of Russian filmmakers gravitated to making science-fiction films. Spirituality and scientific speculation are a natural pairing in that country, in a way that they have not been for Westerners. The Cosmist school of 19th-century philosopher Nikolai Fedorov and his intellectual descendants melded a nationalist Eastern Orthodox mysticism with materialist futurist ideas for which "out there" is putting it mildly. Fedorov believed that our human mandate and destiny was to fulfill New Testament prophecy through what we would now call biotechnology, by bringing about the physical resurrection of all past humans using "knowledge and control over all atoms and molecules of the world."[31] He was writing on this theme more than a century before the first cloned sheep, Dolly. Parapsychological, ufological, and what we would now call New Age ideas were and are part of this fertile current in Russian thought.

One of the leading Cosmist thinkers of the first decades of the 20th century, whose writings were particularly influential on Tarkovsky, was Pavel Florensky, sometimes called the "Russian Leonardo."[32] Florensky was a polymath theologian, art historian, and mathematician who was executed by Stalin's secret police in 1937 for concealing the location of an Eastern Orthodox saint's relics (his head, specifically, which the police had orders to destroy). Florensky thought that the medieval worldview was closer to the truth than the science of the modern world, at least until Einstein. In addition to an innovative contribution on the "reverse perspective" used in Russian icons, which inspired Tarkovsky when making his film about icon-painter Andrei Rublev, Florensky also wrote about the imaginary geometry of time-reversed objects as predicted by Einstein's theory of relativity. Applying imaginary geometry to Dante's *Divine Comedy*, he showed that the narrator and his guide Virgil traverse something like a Moebius strip or a Klein bottle, topological exotica in which continuous travel in a single direction leads you to the same point where you started, but on its opposite surface. The geometry of such objects is, he argued, the geometry of the kingdom of God.[33]

In his last theological work, his 1922 book *Iconostasis*, Florensky applies a similar analysis to dreams, arguing that they are proof that time flows in both directions. He specifically cites dreams whose causal logic leads inexorably and seamlessly to some startling stimulus (such as a loud noise) at the end that wakes the dreamer. J. W. Dunne also wrote of such dreams in *An Experiment with Time*, and they may really be the most common but overlooked form of precognitive dream— overlooked, because they always invite the easy rationalistic explanation that the dream-plot has been concocted by the sense-making brain only after the fact, upon waking. Such explanations, which Freud also invoked, preserve us against cognitive dissonance but appear flimsy when considered in light of the compelling evidence for other, longer-range precognitive dreams—like Freud's own dream of Irma's Injection.

Dream time, Florensky writes, is "*turned inside-out*" like the imaginary geometries and topologies he explored in his mathematical-theological explorations.[34] He also argues that dreams' "spiritual structure" expresses and embodies the two-way mediating nature of religious icons. The iconostasis is the icon-laden screen in Eastern Orthodox churches, separating the nave of the church from the Holy of Holies. In its mediatory role as barrier but also bridge or access point, the iconostasis is considered theologically equivalent to Christ. Florensky saw dreams, with their inside-out time, as reflecting the same spiritually mediatory role.[35] I can't help but find in Florensky's *Iconostasis* also an irresistible way of "rereading" the permeable cave wall as described by Jean Clottes and David Lewis-Williams: a two-dimensional plane mediating the mundane and sacred that, in special states of consciousness along an intensified trajectory, was traversed obliquely, like venturing along a hypersurface of a Moebius or a Klein bottle. Art as passage to the impossible interior, art as abduction. The interior is really the exterior, transfigured.[36]

The structure of the dream in Florensky's *Iconostasis* is essentially the structure of *Stalker*. The narrative about a miserable man not going into the room that might fulfill his wishes actually presents the contents of the room he does not (seemingly) go in. In this respect, the film is like a permutation of another philosophical sci-fi classic, a 1959 Robert Sheckley short story originally published in *Playboy* as "The World of Heart's Desire" but frequently anthologized as "The Store of the Worlds." In it, an old man in a run-down shack on the edge of town peddles a drug that will take users to a dimension where their deepest wishes are fulfilled. The main character, Mr. Wayne, hesitates upon first visiting the old man, and he leaves saying he will consider the offer. Later he resolves to go back and take it, yet he continually hesitates, continually procrastinates, because the mundane demands of his work and tedious family routine make him too busy. Eventually he wakes up in the old man's shack, in a dismal post-apocalyptic "real world," and pays the old man everything he owns—just some scraps—satisfied that indeed the drug (which he did in fact take on that first visit) did as promised: The banal tedious reality of an ordinary life was actually what he wished for.[37]

Science writer James Gleick, in a book on time travel and the common sci-fi trope of changing the past, writes that "regret is the time traveler's energy bar."[38] The same could be said of precognitive artists trapped by dark fates. I believe we ought to read their most darkly prophetic works not from the standpoint of when they were made, but from the standpoint of the artist later when they confront their mortality, reflecting on their artistic and career choices that led them to that point. It is hindsight regrets or mixed feelings that may be found to be reflected already in their work, perhaps even supplying its initial inspiration. I suggest *Stalker* should be seen not as an expression of a hopeful 47-year-old artist-mystic in 1978-1979, when he made the film, but as an expression of a gravely ill 54-year-old artist-mystic in 1986, when he belatedly realized his single-minded artistic obsession to make that film had claimed the life of a friend and was fast claiming his own, and wishing to undo that past mistake. We should see the pain- and guilt-wracked face of Kaidanovsky's Stalker as Tarkovsky's own pain- and guilt-wracked face, from that belated vantage point.

In hindsight, the overwhelming setbacks Tarkovsky experienced would likely have seemed to the superstitious director like warnings unheeded. But I think that also, like Freud's dream—and here is where Freud's own theory retains its special relevance—the film was specifically a guilt-absolving fantasy, a *wish*, about his own as well as his friend's *survival*, from that belated vantage point. We should see the Stalker's refusal to enter the room as Tarkovsky's own wish not to have made the mistake of leading his friend and himself to their deaths. The characters in the film survive their journey and return to the world wiser and humbled. Who wouldn't wish for that impossible do-over, in his awful circumstances? Indeed, *Stalker* makes me wonder: How often are our thoughts and ideas and creative epiphanies really premonitions of some later hindsight wish, repairing some mistake we are *right now* in the process of making, but distorted as in some funhouse mirror and thus unrecognizable?

Incredibly, Tarkovsky's final film, *The Sacrifice*, entirely written and shot before his cancer diagnosis and largely conceived even before Solonitsyn's, is about the desperation of an artist facing tragedy to repair his fatal mistakes and bring about an alternative history via some personal sacrificial ritual. How, unless Tarkovsky had indeed been dismembered and coal-implanted by Pushkin's seraph, could he have known?

The Sacrifice began as a vague concept in 1980 called *The Witch*.[39] It centered on a man given only a year to live because of a terminal illness (of course), who then seeks the help of a woman reputed to have magical powers. Solonitsyn was to play this character. Tarkovsky's journals give hints of how the story evolved over subsequent years. In a 1983 version, the protagonist—a philosopher, specifically—was to have been diagnosed with cancer, then being instructed by an old friend to have sexual relations with a poor local dressmaker whose powers, he says, can cure him.[40] The final, filmed version of the story changes the existential threat to nuclear Armageddon.[41]

In the film, Erland Josephson plays Alexander, a depressed retired actor living with his hectoring wife and young son in a spacious house in rural Sweden, where his adult daughter and his family doctor (who may be having an affair with the daughter) have come to celebrate his birthday. Otto, the local postman (Allan Edwall), visits the house to give Alexander a rather excessive present—a precious antique map (he explains that "all gifts require a sacrifice"). Otto turns out to be a mystic and a collector of uncanny paranormal occurrences—very much like the early-20th-century American cataloguer of impossible events, Charles Fort.[42] Otto tells the story of one of his many cases: a widow who had had her portrait taken with her son before the latter went off to war and was killed at the front. Decades later, he says, she went to a photographer in another town to have her portrait taken, and the photograph contained a ghostly image of her son in his military uniform, still age 18, standing beside her. Beyond merely cataloging such incidents, Otto claims he actually goes to great lengths to verify them with supporting evidence.

While Otto is visiting, a TV alert somberly announces that war has broken out; citizens are urged to stay calm, but the mood is gloomy. Alexander's family is able to hear military jets or missiles flying overhead. In solitary terror and desperation, Alexander prays: He will give up speech and even give up his family and his house to end the war.

Otto then privately confides in him that there is one chance to save everything—save the world. Alexander must go to the home of his own servant, Maria—who is actually (Otto says) a witch—and sleep with her. Alexander hesitates, but then gets on his bicycle, rides to her house, and bares his soul to her—a kind of confession about his failings as an artist and as a son. They then sleep together (levitating off Maria's bed). Alexander returns home, falls asleep, and then wakes to find that there is no nuclear war—things are normal, no one is panicked. Was it all a dream? We don't know. But keeping his promise, Alexander falls silent, methodically sets fire to his home while his family is out for a walk, and finally, running around the burning house like an ecstatic (and silent) madman, is taken off by an ambulance, presumably to a mental hospital.

We are led to believe that through his acts, Alexander has not "ended the war" but rather prevented it from ever happening. If only he remembers it, we can ask if he really is a madman or if he really changed the future through a strange ritual recommended by his Fortean friend. There is no way to know what is "really real," whether any of it was a dream, and whether his sacrifice (giving up speech and his house and family) is actually a significant history-altering pact with the silent universe … or whether it is just a psychotic break. Tarkovsky himself bemoaned the fact that some viewers would inevitably adopt the latter interpretation.[43] He was a believer in real magic, and he saw the world-altering effects of Alexander's prayer, and of his sleeping with the witch Maria, as real.[44]

American viewers of *The Sacrifice* will recognize its narrative conceit as a more somber, Slavic/Scandinavian permutation of Frank Capra's 1946 holiday favorite, *It's a Wonderful Life*, where an angel provides suicidal George Bailey (James Stewart) a tour of a profoundly dark counterfactual world without him in it, where Mr. Potter's greed has prevailed and made a Waste Land of the once-pleasant Bedford Falls (now sleazy Pottersville). In light of this terrifying vision, Bailey's reality, with its many challenges, setbacks, and small joys suddenly seems worth living—he made a positive difference. (Richard Kelly's excellent 2001 science-fiction film *Donnie Darko* obeys the same logic.) While ordinary life for Alexander had seemed difficult in various ways—his wife doesn't understand him and his family and friends are tedious in the extreme (and so is he)—the alternative is far worse, and his brief glimpse of that alternative, a nightmare of panicked people running through the streets, reveals ordinary banal life as something miraculous.

The dead tree Alexander and his son had watered ritualistically and hopelessly at the start of the movie is seen to flower in the final scene. The Grail Kingdom has come to life, even in the absence of the Grail King.

Tarkovsky finished shooting the film just prior to his cancer diagnosis. Famously, the camera jammed during the most crucial scene of the film, a single long take of Alexander's house burning to the ground. The house had to be rebuilt so the six-minute scene could be re-shot. It was only the worst of several bad omens the director experienced during the making of this film, including also an ominous owl encounter.[45] Tarkovsky edited the film during his final year in France but was not well enough to attend its premiere at the Cannes Film Festival in May 1986, where it won the Grand Prix and other prizes. Andriushka, then 15, collected the awards in his father's place.

The Sacrifice contains dialogue that is haunting rather in the way the widow's son in Otto's story haunted her photograph. For example, the physician offers a cigar to Otto, who refuses: "I was in a morgue once, and saw the insides of a corpse. He'd been a lifelong smoker. I saw his lungs inside. I haven't smoked since." In the original script, but not the final version of the film, the curious doctor asks what the cause of death had been. "A terrible thing," Otto says. "Better not to think about it any more."[46]

From Nothing

Cy Twombly, Time Machines,
and Creation ex Nihilo

In order to do anything creative, we must be
unhistorical. Creation begins today, it has no history and
no cause, creation is always creation from nothing.
—C. G. Jung, *Visions Seminar* (1933)

The painting makes me want to run naked!
—Anonymous visitor to the Menil Collection,
Houston (1990s)

Have you ever strolled through an art gallery and felt like the paintings were like hunters' trophies, creatures killed and stuffed and mounted, their magic power taken away by being ripped from their natural habitat and hung up, out of reach, on a wall in a kind of warehouse? Have you imagined that those objects could do more damage, work real wonders, if let out into the world—or if the real world was let in to them? A big difference between, say, the art in Paleolithic caves and the art in the Smithsonian or the Museum of Modern Art or any other modern art gallery is that freedom to do and to be magic.

The study of artistic response and magical or spiritual beliefs about art is its own fascinating topic, far too large to be considered in this book.[1] But people who are privileged to enter painted caves report overwhelming emotions. Jean Clottes told writer Gregory Curtis that after new researchers are permitted their first visit to Chauvet Cave, it is expected that they will not be able to get much work done the next few days—they are immobilized by what they have experienced. The power is palpable.[2] When "our" art or literature provokes more than a safe "aesthetic" reaction, for instance some hard-to-control response in the body, the result may be concern and efforts at control. Pornography is only the most obvious example. The rise of the novel in the 18th century is another: This new literary form provoked cultural authorities to worry at the emotional excitement that mass-printed stories were producing—imaginations were running rampant, about all kinds of things.[3] Then of course there are the comics, that subversive 20th-century vehicle for the super (but also violence and sexuality) that aroused similar fears and even legislative measures in the 1950s.[4] And of course there have been innumerable examples in the history of religions where iconism, picturing the divine—or beliefs about the relationship between pictures and the divine—has been policed by religious authorities or been the focus of sometimes violent sectarian conflict. People can become very passionate about pictures.

The category of artist, originally bequeathed us by Vasari, and with it the set of social and economic practices that surround art in the modern world, including the industries of publishing, academic criticism, galleries and auction houses, and so on, constitute a collective conceptual sink for this kind of passion, for ecstasy and the impossible.[5] The discourses and institutions of the arts neutralize, or at least contain, that power and magic. Again, they go along with that immunological response that blinds us to our superhumanity.

The slight but significant differences between art art and shamanic art prove the rule. An imposition of boundedness in space and time on the former is one difference. One of the definitions of art that I learned in a college aesthetics course—I don't know who said it originally—was the presence of a frame. Even a sculpture has a footprint and a kind of "personal space"—often a base or stand and perhaps a fence or ropes around it—that demarcate it from its mundane surroundings. In contrast, some petroglyphs are meant to be interacted with, physically. The Nkisi N'kondi figures that inspired Michael Richards are power-containing objects whose power is liberated by the "user" pounding nails into them. A book or movie has a definite beginning and an end, another, temporal kind of frame. A myth, on the other hand, may not be clearly demarcated but part of a beginningless and endless cycle.

Art art is also bounded temporally in another, more fundamental way: We say of a work of art that it is finished, and that it becomes a work at that point, not a sketch or something left unfinished or, least of all, left for the audience to complete. Seeing how vigorously many people have protested the right of filmmakers like George Lucas to change their own works afterward shows how entrenched this view is—and we now call such after-the-fact directorial changes "cuts" to distinguish them as separate, well-defined works. In contrast, cave and rock art is typically retouched and sometimes embellished by different hands, in perpetuity, over generations or centuries—even millennia. Julian Monney, the scientist describing the fake lion dream in *Cave of Forgotten Dreams*, also describes a (not-fake) Australian Aboriginal rock artist carefully retouching a piece of very old rock art, explaining that it was not really him moving his hand.[6]

Even when artists like Michelangelo have explored the liminal-seeming aesthetic of the unfinished, it would be unthinkable—and illegal—to try and finish their works for them. Yet, the most powerful art and writing invites fantasies of transgressing those boundaries: writing or drawing or singing ourselves into the work, working ourselves into the story or contributing to it.

Whenever I visit my favorite art gallery, the Philadelphia Museum of Art, I'm gripped by the wish that I could stay overnight, incubate, in the cave- or sanctuary-like room containing Cy Twombly's *Fifty Days at Iliam*, a 10-panel 1978 series inspired by Alexander Pope's translation of Homer's epic about the Trojan War, *The Iliad*. (It's right down the hall from the room containing Marcel Duchamp's masterworks, including *Nude Descending a Staircase, No. 2*.) Without any windows, and without any other visitors, and with just a single candle or a camping headlamp to illuminate the darkness, it would be the perfect space for incubation, and the dreams would probably be powerful—my *Ba* would surely fly free of my body. But such a thing is unheard of, impossible, within the contemporary understandings of art. And even if I were somehow allowed my fantasy, I surely wouldn't have the audacity, once my *Ba* returned, to get up and add my own contribution to Twombly's images, with paints or a pencil of my own. It would be vandalism, a violation, to embellish or make some change to what is complete, finished.

Artistic creation as a never-finished process, with all its hesitation and uncertainty, false starts and erasures, seems to have been a lifelong fascination for Twombly, a painter and occasional sculptor from Virginia who lived most of his life in Italy. He is best known for large white or gray canvases with colorful abstract or semi-figurative images and scribbled and partially erased writing, mostly relating to the Classical literature and mythological themes that obsessed him. Some of his works, such as his giant 1970 *Treatise on the Veil*, evoke the aesthetic of lessons or figures on a chalkboard that have been repeatedly overwritten.

Even though many of Twombly's canvases are dominated by handwriting, they are the closest things to cave painting in modern art that I know—much closer than anything by Picasso. In fact, on a furlough from his army service as a cryptographer in 1955, Twombly checked into a motel room along a Georgia highway, drew all the blinds to shut out the light, and taught himself to paint in the pitch dark—starting with simple shapes and working up to more complex forms like faces of people he knew. Many of his works from across his career look like cave art, but from an alternate prehistory where writing was invented before pictures.

After his move to Italy in the late 1950s, the young Twombly's work was dominated by light mythological themes, such as the Birth of Venus and Leda and the Swan. He painted numerous versions of the latter myth in the first years of the 1960s, for example. But over the course of 1962 and 1963, Twombly's themes took a different direction: He began creating works related to the theme of ancient and historical assassinations, including that of the deposed Roman general Pompey (*Death of Pompey*, 1962), Julius Caesar (*Ides of March*, 1962), and Giliano de Medici, the assassinated brother of Lorenzo de Medici (*Death of Giliano de Medici*, in several versions between 1962 and 1963), among others.[7] Critics have puzzled over this dark turn in Twombly's career.[8] When the world rocked with shock and grief after the assassination of the beloved American president John F. Kennedy in Dallas on November 22, 1963, it may have seemed to the painter that he had sniffed some kind of archetype in the air. Did he think he had prophesied the assassination, which people all over the world (if not in the U.S.) naturally assumed had been a political act or coup?

JFK's assassination made such an impact on Twombly that, over the course of a couple weeks in December, he proceeded to paint what is often considered his first major work, a series of nine large canvases on the subject of another ancient political assassination, that of the Roman emperor Commodus, in a plot instigated by his mistress. This series was arguably prophetic too, but in a different way from his previous works. For one thing, like Woolf's *Mrs. Dalloway* and Tarkovsky's films, *Nine Discourses on Commodus* is another perfect example of the principle that we should look to the future biography of the artist, not just to big world events, for the most interesting examples of the precognitive imagination at work.

Commodus was one of the most colorful and despised of Roman Emperors. A young megalomaniac and a tyrant, he was the opposite of his stoic dad, the venerable philosopher-Emperor Marcus Aurelius. Casting himself as a living Hercules, Commodus had his own likeness placed on statues of that god. To the disgust of Coliseum audiences, he staged bloody spectacles in which he killed scores of exotic animals with arrows and "defeated" hapless (undoubtedly drugged) slaves in single combat. He was a god in his own eyes, but he was also quietly ridiculed by the Roman political elite as an upstart and a joke. On one occasion, after decapitating an ostrich in the arena, Commodus went over to the senators' theater box with the bird's severed head in one hand and brandished his sword at them with the other, as though to say "You're next." According to the historian Cassius Dio, the senators chewed on laurel leaves to keep from laughing. After his mistress, Marcia, discovered her name on a list of people he planned to execute, she arranged for his killing. Failing to poison him in his food, she and some co-conspirators sent the Emperor's own wrestling partner, a man with the impossibly perfect name Narcissus, to strangle Commodus in his bath.[9]

Which all weirdly resembles the unexpected outcome of Twombly's frenzied inspiration to examine the life and death of Commodus in his art.

The painter was proud of his series, showing intensifying splashes of color (yellow and red) on large grey canvasses with graphite grids and writing visible underneath, like sequential frames in an unfolding violent tragedy subjected to a kind of forensic analysis. *Nine Discourses* may have been consciously influenced by the sequential Zapruder film frames, showing Kennedy's motorcade in Dallas and his assassination, which were published in *Life* magazine just a week after the tragedy.[10] Twombly was fascinated by language and writing, and his title may also have reflected the influence of Michel Foucault's then-recent writings on madness and prisons. When Twombly shipped the large panels to his friend and gallery owner Leo Castelli in New York, he expected his reentry into the New York art scene would be celebrated after his years of quietly pursuing his own intellectual and artistic vision in Italy. He didn't make the trip to Manhattan for the show in March 1964 but sent along with the paintings an ancient bust of Commodus that he had purchased and that had given him inspiration when making the paintings. It was displayed at the entrance to the exhibit.

The result was not at all what Twombly hoped and expected. Instead of making a splash, the exhibition was viciously panned by critic after critic. The worst review, in the May-June issue of *Arts Magazine*, was a single paragraph in the "In the Galleries" section by abstract sculptor Donald Judd, which begins:

> Twombly has not shown for some time, and this adds
> to this fiasco. In each of these paintings there are a
> couple of swirls of red paint mixed with a little yellow
> and white and placed high on a medium-gray surface.
> There are a few drips and spatters and an occasional
> pencil line. There isn't anything to the paintings.

Judd then commented that none of the panels were as good as an
older piece by Twombly that had been used to advertise the exhibition,
in which he at least "had something in mind."[11]

What motivated Judd's and other critics' derision? The enlarging
splotches of red and yellow unfolding across the paintings, looking very
much like a time-lapse of a spray of blood and gore from a gunshot,
may have hit too close to home for an art world and a nation still processing (or denying) that its king's head had been blown off in public in
an almost Roman-seeming bit of political sacrificial theater. The European, historical theme (really apparent only in the series' slightly preten-
tious title and the bust) also was at odds with the then-current taste for
pop art and minimalism. And adding to the difficulty, the Gallery hung
the paintings out of their intended order.[12]

In hindsight, the smug damning reviews are readily dismissed.
Twombly's *Commodus* series is now seen as bookending one of the most
important bodies of abstract art of the latter half of the century. Although not regarded as among Twombly's best works, the series even
assumed a kind of cult status because it was so infrequently exhibited
to the public. (Since no museum at the time was interested, the artist
eventually sold the series to a private collector. It is now displayed at the
Guggenheim Bilbao.[13]) But at the time, the critical derision came as a
huge blow to the 36-year-old Twombly, and it was a significant setback
in his early career.

The theme of delusional megalomania followed by nemesis at the
hands of Narcissus, the salient features of the life and death of Commodus, exactly encapsulated how Twombly himself would reflect on
this debacle. Inflated with feelings of confidence on the eve of the show,
the harsh and dismissive response left him feeling like the New York art
world had, instead of welcoming his re-arrival and seeing him as a new
art hero (or Hercules), simply laughed him off as a naïve and preten-
tious joke. The bust he sent was glaringly out of step with the times, a

miscalculated gesture uncannily reminiscent of Commodus's threat to the senators with the ostrich head. Twombly's choice of subject for this series, then, like his previous assassination-themed works, seems very much like a premonition, this time not of some history-altering public event but of a private emotional and career "fiasco." The kicker is that, similar to Tarkovsky's *Stalker*, the work that caused the fiasco was also, I am suggesting, caused *by* the fiasco, in a loop. Without the fiasco, there would have been no work, just like without the work, there would have been no fiasco.

The debacle prompted Twombly to seek inspiration elsewhere than in Rome, where he had been living. In the spring of 1964, while drawing in his tower studio in a Greek castle owned by his aristocratic in-laws (his wife Tatiana Franchetti was a baroness), he watched astonished as a piece of cloud broke off the main cloud and drifted down through one window of the studio and out the other side. This miracle, which was witnessed by his lifelong assistant/lover Nicola del Roscio, inspired various new drawings and paintings.[14] Sounds like a sign. Sounds shamanic.

"Right here in this room!"

In the October 1955 issue of *Galaxy Science Fiction* there appeared a wonderful story by William Tenn called "The Discovery of Morniel Mathaway." An art historian from the 25th century named Glescu, recipient of his time's equivalent of the Nobel Prize, is granted the unique and costly privilege of traveling back in time to visit the atelier of a mid-20th-century Greenwich Village painter named Morniel Mathaway, to study how the artist (the greatest ever, by late-25th-century standards) created his works. Glescu's acclaimed books had been studies of Mathaway's paintings. But what Glescu finds, to his surprise and dismay, is that Mathaway is a talentless fraud, as well as a trickster and thief. Instead of painting masterpieces, he simply cheats people. At the end, he even steals poor Glescu's time machine. Trapped in the past, the bewildered art historian has no choice but to assume the identity of the famous "painter"—they wear the same size clothes, fortunately, so he can look the part by dressing from Mathaway's closet. He proceeds to paint the paintings he remembered from his books. Thus, he himself is the master he had studied.[15]

Physicist and quantum-computing pioneer David Deutsch described something similar to Tenn's scenario in a 1991 paper, applying the idea to mathematics instead of modern art:

> A time traveler goes into the past and reveals the proof of an important theorem to the mathematician who had later been recognized as the first to prove it. The mathematician goes on to publish the proof, which is then read by the time traveler before setting out.[16]

Physicists treat information and its conservation with a kind of holy reverence, so Deutsch was perturbed by his own thought experiment: "Who thought of the proof?" Where in this causal loop did the solution to the theorem originate? What was the source of this new knowledge in the universe? Just as there is no scene in Tenn's story where Glescu "came up with" his idea for any of his masterpieces—he just copied them from memory—there is no scene in Deutsch's thought experiment where the mathematician stayed up all night doing calculations, not even some eureka moment where his rational brain hit upon a solution to the problem after some period of unconscious incubation. In both cases, some new information in the universe—an art masterpiece or a solution to a mathematical problem—comes into being ... wait for it ... *ex nihilo*. It's the very thing that happens at the beginning of the biblical book of Genesis.

This kind of scenario, sometimes called the "bootstrap paradox," has always been a favorite of more discerning and interesting time-travel storytellers, such as Tenn. Unlike the familiar changing-the-past plots, where a time traveler causes or threatens to cause some disastrous change in the historical timeline and must undo it, there's really nothing paradoxical about bootstrap scenarios, so the term "bootstrap *paradox*" is a misnomer—it is really what is known in logic as a tautology. Tautologies bother logicians and careful thinkers because it is always unfair to support a premise by its antecedents, but there is nothing in physics that says the laws of the universe must be fair, or that they must obey the rules of logic or debate club. In physics, a causal loop is called a "closed-timelike curve" or "closed-timelike line."

If the last half-century of physics has taught us anything, it is that physical reality does not play by the tedious rules that would prevent creation from nothing. For instance, some of the old conservation laws ("matter cannot be created or destroyed," etc.) are increasingly thought to hold for delimited, well-defined physical systems, not the universe as a whole.[17] New things constantly arise from nothing, without anyone doing a lick of work. Empty space, if you zoom way in, is really a seething "quantum foam" where layabout particle-antiparticle pairs arise out of emptiness, uncaused and undeserving, and crash together again with a great release of unworked-for energy (the so-called quantum fluctuations of the vacuum). The physicist Richard Feynman proposed that those pairs may really be the same particle, traveling forward and then backward in time, in little closed loops. And as Feynman's colleague John Wheeler argued in the late 1980s, matter is just information by another name. So if matter can be created from nothing, it is not much of a stretch to say that knowledge can be too. It just … bugs us.

Paul Nahin notes in his book *Time Machines* that the underlying anxiety about bootstrap scenarios arises from something like the Protestant work ethic: "the creation of knowledge demands hard work!"[18] In neither Tenn's story nor Deutsch's thought experiment was there any of Edison's famous perspiration. In both cases, the knowledge was just given to the individual. And the implication is that, if the artist just copied the paintings from his book, and if the mathematician just "got" his proof without sweating over it, then neither are really deserving of all their recognition. The mathematician should give back his Nobel. And more fundamentally, causality as we understand it—the mechanistic causality of the Enlightenment—is not deserving either.

Since there is nothing actually self-preventing about a causal loop, Deutsch renamed bootstrap scenarios "pathology," not paradox, because they simply violate Karl Popper's dictum that "knowledge comes into existence only by evolutionary, rational processes."[19] But in fact, such loops would be the rule in a self-consistent universe that includes time travelers, or time-traveling information.

At the risk of scandalizing my stern, hard-working, penny-pinching Dutch ancestors bent over their ledgers in some bank-like Calvinist afterlife, Thomas Edison's quip about the predominance of perspiration in genius is a total distraction, even an ideological one. There is no reason the Protestant ethic, or the labor theory of value, or really any kind of socially sanctioned perspiration needs to underlie the creation of new ideas. To really understand creativity, we must move beyond the craft and industry metaphors, such as Stephen King's boys in the basement, and embrace the more ouroboric picture painted by modern physics. Just as the vacuum produces particles and energy out of the void, for free, real creation produces new knowledge, new ideas, out of nothing. Karl Popper, bless his heart, was simply wrong.

Two strange episodes in Twombly's later life demonstrate this principle, I believe, nearly as well as Tenn's fictional Morniel Mathaway. They are incredible time loops, this time involving inappropriate or audacious audience responses to his paintings and the artist's prophetic pre-sponses to those responses. They were dialogues with his eccentric, passionate fans, impossibly across decades of time.

Consider, first, Twombly's 1977 triptych *Three Dialogues: Phaedrus*, based on Plato's dialogue by that name. The Platonic dialogue starts with a speech by the Athenian Lysias on the greater virtue of prudence over passion that Socrates' friend Phaedrus recites secondhand for him; it is followed by a speech by Socrates on more or less the same theme; and lastly, Socrates reflects on the fault of his own and Lysias's discourses and offers a corrective where he upholds the virtues of passion and divine madness over a more restrained and calculated approach to love. A discourse, a response, and lastly a kind of erasure. Twombly's first panel shows a diagonal red form on white, looking a bit like a giant wound or a red lipstick trace; the middle panel is a solid field of white; the third, smaller panel looks like some text that has been blotted out and feels like a kind of correction and afterthought to the previous two panels.

In July 2007, *Three Dialogues: Phaedrus* was on exhibit in an Avignon museum, and a Cambodian-French artist, Rindy Sam, kissed the blank white center panel—spontaneously, she claimed—leaving a red lipstick trace. She was arrested and tried in a French court for vandalizing a work of art. In a statement before her trial, the defendant claimed that her kiss "was an artistic act provoked by the power of art":

> I take responsibility for my act. This white canvas inspired me. I am told it is forbidden to do such things, but it was totally spontaneous. I just gave a kiss. It was a gesture of love; when I kissed it, I did not think it out carefully, I just thought the artist would understand.[20]

The plaintiffs called it "rape" instead. Their lawyer said, "I do not share [Ms. Sam's] vision of love. For me love requires the consent of both sides." Twombly was not amused by Sam's act either. At the time of the trial's verdict several months after the kiss, restorers had been unable to completely remove the lipstick from the white canvas, having tried 30 different chemicals.[21] Red, it turns out, is the most indelible lipstick color. Sam was found guilty and made to pay a 1,000-euro fine to the owner, a 500-euro fine to the gallery, and a symbolic 1-euro fine to Twombly himself.

Did Sam know the classical reference being made in Twombly's work? Was it prophetic of the artist that his passion-provoking work was his interpretation of a set of Platonic dialogues on the theme of passion versus restraint and attempting to define what love is? It is hard not to see Twombly's triptych, with its initial diagonal "kiss" (or wound), inviting blank white central panel, and final erasure, as a premonition of his work being "completed" by a viewer provoked to mad passion by the power of art and then laboriously and imperfectly cleansed of this inappropriate, transgressive stain—all culminating in a trial in which the plaintiffs and defendant debated the ethics of love and sexuality. Loopy, right?

Sam's accusers granted that she might not have understood what she had done wrong, but it is possible her act was not as spontaneous as she claimed in court. If she "thought the artist would understand," it may be because of a similarly transgressive response sometime in the 1990s, by another young Frenchwoman, to one of Twombly's greatest works, his huge *Untitled (Say Goodbye, Catullus, to the Shores of Asia Minor)*, when she visited Houston's Menil Collection, where it is on permanent display. A security guard, Guillermo Leguizamon, strolled into the big, otherwise empty room and found the young woman in a kind of reverie, dancing in front of the painting, not a stitch on. After composing himself, Leguizamon approached her and said, "I can admire your beauty, madam, but if you don't put on your clothes, you'll be more famous than Cy Twombly himself." She obediently put her clothes back on, but as she was leaving, she wrote in the guest book, "The painting makes me want to run naked!"[22]

Unlike the later business with his *Phaedrus* triptych, Twombly *loved* that *Say Goodbye, Catullus* had had such an effect on a viewer. Interviewed by *New York Times* writer Ralph Blumenthal in front of the same painting while on a visit to Houston in 2005, the usually shy and soft-spoken painter eagerly recounted the story:

> "Right here in this room!" Mr. Twombly affirmed. He was delighted, he said. "Wouldn't you be? That's pretty good. No one can top that one. Come on. How many people?"

Unless Sam's act in Avignon was genuinely spontaneous, as she claimed, this *New York Times* story is how she might have gotten her idea to kiss *Phaedrus*—perhaps she was hoping for a similar reaction from the artist. (And thus her act, like the "debate" in Plato's dialogue, also seems as though it cannot quite make up its mind between spontaneity and premeditation.)

Here's the thing: Did that unnamed Frenchwoman in Houston know, let alone grasp the coincidence, that despite the unrelated, Catullus-inspired title the artist ultimately gave his massive painting (his largest work), it is really "about" (abstractly, of course) the myth of Orpheus and Eurydice? Orpheus's beautiful music inspires Eurydice to dance in a grove with nymphs. Her beauty captures the eye of a god, Aristaeus; running to flee his lust, she's bitten and killed by a viper, and Orpheus then descends to the underworld to get her back. Long story. Even if the young woman somehow gleaned the artist's mythological inspiration from the collection's wall text and knew the myth, Eurydice's attire is not specified in textual retellings, nor is there anything literally figurative in Twombly's painting itself that would suggest it. The artist, however, surely knew the iconographic tradition: that in many paintings and most sculptures and friezes, the dancing, dying, or dead Eurydice is naked or barely clothed. Her dance in the grove to Orpheus's beautiful music is a nude dance. Her run is a naked run.

Again, powerful art makes people want to transgress (or at least, with *Say Goodbye, Catullus*, weep—some form of overwhelm with that painting is commonly reported[23]). And in these cases, as with *Nine Discourses*, I suggest that the later unpredictable response—or Twombly's own reaction to it (delight, in the Houston case)—was part of his initial inspiration. The works caused their response, which caused the works. I'm quite serious: In time-loops world, it makes perfect sense that an anonymous Frenchwoman, and Leguizamon's story about her, nude-dancing in the painter's future, may have been the source of his inspiration back in 1972 to do a huge, danceable-to painting about Orpheus and Eurydice (he didn't complete it until 1994). It makes perfect sense that a premonition of his work being passionately kissed (a kiss that would be only incompletely erased) was the inspiration for a triptych about Plato's *Phaedrus* in 1977. Precognitive dreams sometimes span decades of a person's life, and precognitive inspiration should be no different.

I find it amusing that the snarky postmodern pulp writer Tenn, thinking he was just lampooning the pretentions of American artists in

Twombly's era of Abstract Expressionism, might have actually provided the real—albeit "impossible"—answer to the question motivating this book: Where do new ideas come from? The answer is that ideas really can—and perhaps ultimately, always do?—arise from nothing, from the donut-hole at the heart of a time loop that extends between the artist's precognitive inspiration, that drowsy vision on the pillow perhaps, and their looking back upon their finished work later.[24]

There was no point in Twombly's life, I suggest, when he (or his calculating-assembling brain) "came up with" *Nine Discourses on Commodus* or *Three Dialogues: Phaedrus* or *Untitled (Say Goodbye, Catullus, to the Shores of Asia Minor)*. Somehow, through a miraculous (perhaps quantum-computational) trick that we cannot yet fully explain, the painter just fast-forwarded to these concepts. They were effortless symbolic elaborations of tremors refluxing back from his future, and his paintings then caused the situations that created those tremors. If we wanted hard evidence for the biblical idea that real things, meaningful things, and (in the case of *Say Goodbye, Catullus*) *big* things can arise from nothing, all we have to do is look at those paintings.

But really, we can look at many of the works I have been examining, for the same evidence. Would the young Werner Herzog have been inspired by the story of Lope de Aguirre and written a film script about him had it not been for his own terrifying brush with fate, and news stories about Juliane Koepcke's impossible survival in the Amazon, lying in wait? Would Virginia Woolf have become inspired to think about and examine the life- and death-musings of Clarissa Dalloway without Kitty Maxse's strange seeming-suicide coming down the pike? Would Andrei Tarkovsky have felt moved to adapt the Strugatsky brothers' *Roadside Picnic* in the late 1970s without his personal tragedies looming nearly a decade ahead? I think the answer, in each case, is no. These are all, I suggest, works that essentially were created from nothing. This is the miracle of art, and the reason that we are really superhumans, indeed gods, when we create. "The aesthetic" as a category is really a whitewash and a smokescreen hiding this divine magic.

Art is artifact, is relic, a memory of talismans and idols, and galleries a dim memory of caves that shot superhuman souls into the Paleolithic night. I'm a big fan of humanity—don't get me wrong—but the discourses of the human perpetually neutralize, obfuscate, or deny our superhumanity, cut it down to humanity. We didn't just get to superhumanity before humanity, it is humanity that has often tried to kill (or at least disempower and deny) the superhuman. *Homo kryptonite.* The effect, the hypnotic trance we are all in, especially if we are the product of higher education, is that when we talk about art's roots in supernormal experience or magic, few imagine we are talking about real magic. Guess again. Maybe what distinguishes artistic geniuses from the rest of us is just that they, on some level, get it.

In *House of Priam*, one of the name-list panels in Twombly's *Fifty Days at Iliam* series that makes me want to sleep in the best possible way, CASSANDRA, repeatedly overwritten and erased, is the central focus, dwarfing the other names of the members of her house. It has provoked scholarly head-scratches, because unlike the other characters in the list, the Trojan prophetess is barely mentioned in his source text, Homer's *Iliad*.[25] Why would Twombly do that? Art historians don't get it: Twombly *knew*. He understood the life and pains of a prophet in a disbelieving or unready world.[26]

The Unborn

Zen enlightenment experiences frequently involve a direct perception of the miraculous from-nothing-ness of things. Probably the best example is the experience of one Japanese teacher from the 17th Century, Bankei, who saw in a moment of Satori that the resolution to everything, the answer to everything, was in what he called the Unborn.[27] He had this realization after wearing himself down through years of strenuous sitting-meditation and ascetic practice in a small hut. He caught tuberculosis as a result, and the enlightenment came when he spit up a gob of black phlegm on the wall. Both his doubts and his disease went away after that.

Bankei went on to preach his message to students in temples and monasteries around Japan, some of whom secretly wrote down what he said for posterity. These talks are a bit repetitive, since he really only preached a single message: It was common, he always stressed, to describe Buddha Mind as unborn and undying—with the emphasis always on that last, non-perishing aspect. That is, it was common in Zen and other schools to talk about permanence, which again has been the deep teaching of many gurus around the world, such as Parmenides. But what Bankei saw directly, and tried to get his pupils to see directly, was that the real crux was in the first term, "unborn"—that is, uncreated, unoriginating. It goes without saying, he said, that something unborn does not die—you don't need to waste time focusing on the not-dying if you can really "get" that non-origination, the non-beginningness, of

Buddha Mind.

What Bankei meant by the Unborn is partly what we would nowadays call the unconscious, both in its Freudian and in its neuroscience sense: that which guides us effortlessly, without conscious or deliberate thought. The Zen teacher used the example of walking down a crowded street. Nobody thinks about where they are going, but nobody collides. That effortless choreography is the Unborn in action. And he called it Unborn because the mind that does such a dance, that unconscious, comes from nowhere, has no origin—it simply is.

Bankei is effectively saying that the body's tacit knowing of how to step to avoid jostling with others in a crowd—or any other physical skill we don't think about—is the same as that mathematical proof in Deutsch's thought experiment, received by the mathematician from his Nobel-Prize-winning older self. Nowhere in the spacetime of your mind did you "figure out" where to walk or how to act so skillfully. There is no shriveled little homunculus inside your head manning the controls. And contrary to what neuroscientists assume today with their "predictive processing model,"[28] the computation going on in the brain might not actually be calculating probabilities and generating predictions, as we assume must be the case. Computation is probably the wrong word entirely for what the brain really does—another metaphor for the unknown, rooted in contemporary technologies but destined for the waste bin of obsolete ideas. Even the word "cognition" might be misleading—invoking as it does the "cogs" of a machine turning. Brain activity might really be the constant buzz of receiving information refluxing from its own future—a future that its own actions will have created. Thought itself might be more like the fast-forward button on a CD or tape player, skipping forward to some "right answer," cheating by looking at the answers at the back of the book, and then back-justifying its rightness with some culturally sanctioned story of hard mental labor.

The Unborn is a tough idea to swallow—try it. We—or at least our conscious egos—desperately want things to have a rational origin, an identifiable cause in the past. But I think we should listen to what Bankei is saying, precisely because it is devastating for our most cherished worldviews. There's no explanation, at least not one that simply traces a thought or behavior back to some beginning, whether it be colliding particles or mythic demiurges pulling new animal species from holes in the ground. Bankei is yanking away from his students—and now, thanks to his diligent students who recorded his talks, from his modern readers—any security in some just-so story that would tie off the origins of anything in some neat bow. In case you were unaware, in a Zen context, that "yanking away" is a good thing—it is a forcing of fundamental issues that, in the prepared mind, leads to the kind of enlightenment experience that Bankei had after spitting up a globule of black phlegm on the wall. Creation ex nihilo and the block universe that allows it to occur are koans, riddles intending to awaken you to something truly amazing about reality and our own superhuman nature. Creativity, I am arguing, is literally the Unborn in action. So, I bet, is thinking—in any form.

It offends our sensibilities because of capitalism and its big guilt trip, that we aren't working hard enough for what we have. But the tesseract brain is not a Protestant. Other traditions have not been so hung up on effort. Oddly enough, despite our stereotype of Asian traditions emphasizing years of arduous study and painful practice, even the Zen teachers weren't hung up on effort. Bankei hated and regretted that he'd wasted so much time, and caused himself so many needless health problems like tuberculosis, on his path to enlightenment. He wanted to spare his students that effort, fast-forward them to the blissful realization that there's no originating work done anywhere in the universe, no laborious manufacture.

No perspiration. No sweat.

PART THREE

ALIENATED MAJESTY

There is no God and no Devil, but there is indeed a psychic system close to us, a gigantic entity, a Pacific ocean of the spirit of which we are nothing but evaporating droplets. We should explore it, name it, measure it.
—Jacques Vallee, *Forbidden Science 3, On the Trail of Hidden Truths* (2016)

9

Culture in Reverse
Future-Plagiarism and the Anxiety of Precognitive Influence

The kernel, the soul—let us go further and say the substance, the bulk, the actual and valuable material of all human utterances—is plagiarism. For substantially all ideas are second-hand, consciously and unconsciously drawn from a million outside sources ...
—Mark Twain, Letter to Helen Keller (1903)

The more you look at creativity from the standpoint of time loops, the more it appears problematic to lay claim even to our best, most novel-seeming ideas. They may have come from nowhere, with no originating labor. Or—and this is the possibility we now turn to—they may come from other creators we have yet to encounter or interact with, who themselves may have gotten them from nowhere or perhaps from others, in turn. Even if Mark Twain got his psychic modality of influence wrong in his *Harper's* essay on mental telegraphy, mistaking precognition for something like telepathy, he problematized the cultural implications of all this rightly. What are those cogs in cognition really doing? Could it be that much of what we call thinking is really just fast-forwarding to encounters with other people's thoughts? Are we really just fish in a river of ideas that flows around and past us, from others and from our future?

To begin exploring the larger, cultural implications of the precognitive imagination, we should start with the New England essayist and mystic Ralph Waldo Emerson, who provided an innocent-seeming concept that holds huge import for any paranormal understanding of the flow of ideas from person to person and across historical time. It comes from his 1841 essay "Self-Reliance." He wasn't thinking about precognition, but warning about the failure of most people to notice and follow their inner light or spark. "A man should learn to detect and watch that gleam of light which flashes across his mind from within, more than the lustre of the firmament of bards and sages. Yet he dismisses without notice his thought, because it is his." In other words, most of us don't pay attention to our own unique genius, simply because it is our own—belonging to little old me, some dumb schlub. And here's the important part: The result of this self-denial, Emerson says, is a particularly disappointing reading experience that is all-too-familiar if you have any kind of thwarted or self-inhibited aspiration to express yourself originally. "In every work of genius," he writes, "we recognize our own rejected thoughts; they come back to us with a certain alienated majesty." We are, when that happens, "forced to take with shame our own opinion from another."[1]

There's a lot to unpack in that powerful term *alienated majesty*. Encounters with genius may make ordinary people feel small and awed—it's part of our appreciation of great ideas, great literature, and great art. But for creators who have ambitions to express thoughts that feel to them utterly original and unprecedented, such encounters can sometimes radiate with an unbearable and even uncanny power.

The dread that geniuses feel at being scooped by other geniuses is the kernel from which the literary scholar and critic Harold Bloom spun a whole gnostic-Freudian literary hermeneutic in the 1970s: Forget that the book we are reading may have been written years or centuries before we were even born, because the unconscious has no sense of time. What Bloom called "strong poets"—although it could apply to thinkers or creators in any medium—feel deeply threatened by the works that resonate most strongly with what they themselves would like to say and wish they had said first. Those works thus radiate with fascinating/horrifying sublimity, that alienated majesty, that must be resisted at all costs.

Competitiveness arising from a desperate refusal of the writer's own belatedness is the energy of literary creation, Bloom argued—he called it the anxiety of influence.[2] The need to be original also distorts the writer's reading of those predecessors. For Bloom, the tracing of hidden influences is no longer the point when studying the strongest poets; the main thing is discerning in their work the signs of their avoidance of their most obvious and important influences, their "swerves" to avoid copying or feeling as though they have copied, the subtle traces of their fear at Emerson's experience of finding their own best ideas already expressed by another. Bloom applied this to the world of poetry and created what he called a "map of misreading"—a start toward a kind of literary genealogy of influence and its anxious defenses from literary fathers to their sons (Bloom's canon is mostly men) down through the centuries.[3]

What does the possibility of precognition do to Bloom's theory of influence-anxiety and creative revisionism? What if those inspired gleams of light flashing across our minds are not just *coincidentally like* something we will read later, perhaps by some famous canonical writer? What if "our own" best thoughts actually issue from those later, powerful reading experiences through a retrocausal process? That is, what if our most original-seeming ideas are often or always premonitions? And by extension, what if powerful reading experiences are powerful in part precisely because of the sense of familiarity or déjà vu that we bring to them, having precognized them?

All in the Family

The question of retrograde literary influence seems to have been anticipated by members of a French Surrealist-Futurist group founded in 1960 called the Workshop of Potential Literature, *Ouvroir de Littérature Potentielle*, or "Oulipo." They were creators of literary games and provocations designed to challenge traditional academic modes of reading and to explore the creative powers of artificial constraints. Their members would write poems using a single letter, for instance, or take an existing poem and substitute all its nouns with the noun seven words away from it in the dictionary (the N+7 method). Among their innovations was the idea of "plagiarism by anticipation" (*le plagiat par anticipation*)—a term coined by one of Oulipo's co-founders, mathematician Francois Le Lionnais. It meant intellectual property theft in reverse, "anticipating—and, from a certain perspective, stealing—the subjects, styles, and even the precise words of writers not yet born."[4]

Oulipo didn't do much with this causally outrageous premise, but it was taken and greatly elaborated four decades later by another French critic-provocateur, Pierre Bayard, in a 2009 book borrowing (or really originating?) the Oulipean term, *Le Plagiat par anticipation*. There, Bayard argues, among other things, that Sophocles actually borrowed the plot of *Oedipus the King* from Freud's *The Interpretation of Dreams* and not the other way around, that in one anomalous "drip" painting the Renaissance painter Fra Angelico plagiarized from Jackson Pollock, and that Franz Kafka had love affairs with the spirits of women writers from his own future.[5]

Like the games of the Oulipeans who were his touchstones, Bayard's future-plagiarism hermeneutic obeys strictures—constraints. One sure indicator that an earlier work has plagiarized from a later one, he says, is that the presumptive future-plagiarist works in a lower class or form of literature and borrows from a higher one. Sophocles' *Oedipus the King*, for instance, was not some high literary work as we now treat it, but a popular entertainment—specifically, a whodunnit (i.e., who brought ruin on Thebes?). Another Bayardian stricture is that presumptively borrowed elements may not be well developed or may even be dissonant within an earlier work. The fact that the detective, Oedipus, discovers that he himself is the killer, living in ignorance of his own guilt, is a totally modern device, something not seen in European literature until the era of Poe, and thus truly, jarringly out of place in late-fifth-century BC Greece. Ergo, Sophocles must have got the idea of Oedipus from Freud, not vice versa.

Bayard's provocations are aimed at livening up literary criticism, reintroducing play and joy. His goal with his book was liberating students of literature from rigid rules of interpretation and argument, showing them that the reader is really the original one in the literary equation, not the writer. He is not that interested in finding plausible physical or psychological mechanisms of backward influence. And in the end, even critics who have applied Bayard's model to literary criticism do so more as an interesting game or exercise to reveal previously unseen dimensions of a piece of literature, rather than in any seriousness. The philosopher Slavoj Žižek cites Bayard's anachronistic interpretation-games as illustrations of Jorge Luis Borges' idea that great artists (Kafka in Borges' case) "create their predecessors" by shining new light upon their influences and causing us to see literary tradition in a new way—what could be called an analytic of hindsight bias.[6] Žižek is quick to distance himself from any notion that retrograde literary influence might be literally true—in that case, "we would have to embrace the New Age topic of synchronicity and mystical communion between spirits from different epochs."[7] And Eric Naiman, in an Afterword to a collection of essays applying the concept of anticipatory plagiarism to Russian literature, concedes that "it is difficult for a scholar to maintain the pretense of taking this idea sufficiently seriously all the way through to the end of an article, let alone a book. Doing so may give the impression that we are doing an influence study in drag, with the travestying of chronology merely serving to affirm linear time's inescapability."[8] His Afterword is tellingly titled "But Seriously Folks ..."

Well, you know, *hold my beer*. Writers' experiences are often reading experiences, and reading experiences are, for a writer, sometimes overpoweringly emotional experiences—both threatening and exciting for all the reasons that interested Bloom—making them especially precognition-worthy. If writers and artists are precognitive, if they are affected by experiences in their future, then it follows that influence *must* often happen in reverse. And lo and behold, this is indeed what comes through startlingly clearly when artists' and writers' works are examined with an eye to possible precognition. Influence—or plagiarism if you want to call it that (although it is never and, by definition, *could* never be intentional)—does go backwards. Alienated majesty is the energy that fuels it. But Bayard is wrong, I believe, in thinking that it is always lesser artists, or artists working in lower strata or marginalized genres, who borrow precognitively from the higher. If anything, the opposite tends to be the case. We already saw that the quintessentially literary Virginia Woolf mucked about precognitively in—and seemingly borrowed ideas and images from—the unliterary science popularizers of her time like James Jeans.

Mind you, the kind of proximal, within-lifetime sort of memory-in-reverse anticipatory influence I suggest may have been operative with Woolf and Jeans is not the kind of influence Bayard is suggesting in *Le Plagiat par anticipation*. Sophocles, in Bayard's most amusing example, did not live long enough to actually physically read Freud, obviously. But the famously neurotic Kafka, with his notorious father issues and also an intense ambivalence about psychoanalysis, did almost certainly read some Freud and definitely consumed Freud's ideas in psychoanalytic lectures in a Prague salon he frequented, in newspaper and magazine articles by Freud's disciples, and in books and articles by other Freudian psychoanalysts.[9] Moreover, Kafka seems to have written those threatening psychoanalytic reading experiences into his earlier fiction, on multiple occasions.

The centerpiece of Kafka's novel *The Trial*, for instance, is a parable told to accused man Josef K. by a priest in a cathedral, about a "man from the country" coming before the Door in the Law. The open door is guarded by a doorkeeper, who despite all the man's pleading and cajoling and paying of bribes, claims he cannot admit him "at this time." The man waits his whole life, and then when he is about to die, he asks the doorkeeper, "Why, if this is the Door in the Law, has nobody else come seeking entry?" The doorkeeper says, "Because this door was meant only for you. I will now shut it." A light shines from beyond the door as it closes and the man from the country breathes his last breath. It is one of the most famous things Kafka wrote. Although *The Trial* was only published after his death in 1924, he published this parable as a stand-alone story, "Before the Law," in the 1915 New Year's issue of a Jewish magazine, *Selbstwehr.*

The Law in this parable and in *The Trial* as a whole is sometimes interpreted in terms of the role of the Torah in Judaism. But being in perpetual guilt, held at arm's reach by a Law that is nevertheless intended only for you, is, as numerous writers and biographers have noted, also *exactly* the essence of the Freudian.[10] Later the same year that Kafka published his parable, Freud published his now-classic article "Repression," which contains the following metaphor for an undesirable idea that, like a former guest that proved undesirable, must be prevented from ever entering one's home again: "I must set a permanent guard over the door which I have forbidden this guest to enter, since he would otherwise burst it open."[11] It sounds as if Kafka might have been precognitively reading Freud when he was writing *The Trial*—or plagiarizing him by anticipation—since chronology makes ordinary linear influence unlikely. Unfortunately, despite frequent mention of Freud in his diary and letters, we don't have direct evidence of which texts by Freud Kafka read or when he read them, so there is no way to know for sure if and when he ever read "Repression" or saw it quoted by some other writer. We are forced to make of this particular coincidence what we will.

But consider another small story called "The Cares of a Family Man" that Kafka penned around the same time he was writing *The Trial* (between 1914 and 1917) and published in his 1919 collection *A Country Doctor.* Just a few pages long, it is a father's musings about a "creature" that he has observed inhabiting his home, taking the form of a wooden star-shaped spool of thread. It is called Odradek, and the narrator begins with speculations about the derivation of this name. It is a Slavic-sounding word but one that has no immediate and obvious meaning in Czech (spoken in Kafka's Prague and which Kafka spoke well), although in fact it can carry several interesting connotations, including something discarded, something disorderly, or something dejected or discouraged.[12] *Od-* is a Czech prefix meaning "from" or "out of," and *odrady* is discouragement.

Odradek resembles the typically Kafkan protagonist—something discarded, discouraged, and rejected. But the narrator's musings on this trash-like object-being center on an anxiety that it actually is more permanent than he is. The story concludes:

> I ask myself, to no purpose, what is likely to happen to him? Can he possibly die? Anything that dies has had some kind of aim in life, some kind of activity, which has worn out; but that does not apply to Odradek. Am I to suppose, then, that he will always be rolling down stairs, with ends of thread trailing after him, right before the feet of my children, and my children's children? He does no harm to anyone that one can see; but the idea that he is likely to survive me I find almost painful.[13]

Meanwhile Odradek lies there quietly on the floor, discarded yet somehow eternal.

"The Cares of a Family Man" seems very much like it was inspired by Freud's grandson Ernst's fort-da game with the spool in *Beyond the Pleasure Principle*, about the often -painful compulsion to repeat that drives the traumatized. *Odradek* even sounds like "fort-da" (or "ooooh-aaah"). But such an influence is temporally impossible: "Cares of a Family Man" was published a year before Freud's book. This coincidence of images and names is rather too close to be coincidental, I suggest. It looks very much like a case of retrograde literary influence from a reading experience in Kafka's future—Bayard's plagiarism by anticipation. As with "Repression," we have no proof Kafka read *Beyond the Pleasure Principle*, either when it was published or any time before his death in 1924. However, he was very interested in Freud at this point in his life—anxiously so. And since the book specifically concerned war neuroses and trauma, it is the one title out of all of Freud's works that would have been especially interesting to him, both personally and professionally in his day job as a lawyer for an institute that handled claims related to various workplace traumas and injuries.

I need to stress: The fort-da game isn't just some trivial detail picked at random from *Beyond the Pleasure Principle*. It is the most remembered and most-cited scene in the book, the only thing (besides the term "death drive") that most readers take away from it, and the nucleus of Freud's theory of the repetition-compulsions that come to perplexingly dominate the behavior of the traumatized. It is also the seed from which grew a whole psychoanalytic subfield of developmental work on children's play and the earliest emergence of symbolic thinking—the work of D. W. Winnicott and others. Kafka was precognizing effectively the primal scene of the psychoanalysis of creativity. And the advanced-players' version Ernst engaged in with a mirror is one that would have resonated especially strongly with the Prague writer, who fantasized in myriad ways, both in his fiction and in his diaries, about disappearing. Kafka, like little Ernst, liked to play gone.

Kafka would especially have understood firsthand the link between playing gone and trauma: As a child, he endured major psychological traumas from his stern and domineering father. In an early, unfinished novel fragment called "Wedding Preparations in the Country," he even described the ambivalent protagonist dissociating from his physical body to avoid having to attend his own wedding, "as he always did as a child in matters that were dangerous"[14]—clear evidence that the author knew from personal experience the relationship between dissociative states and trauma. Such states opened him to mystical experiences he called clairvoyance—a term he got from then-famous occultist Rudolf Steiner, whose lectures he attended in Prague. He eventually learned, like Woolf, to channel these visionary experiences into his fiction.[15]

Kafka would have named Goethe as his most towering, to-be-defended-against literary father figure, but arguably it was Freud and psychoanalysis that was really his greatest and most urgent source of influence-anxiety. His fiction was trespassing on the exact domain—Oedipal anxiety and neurosis—that Freud's new science was busily mapping. It thus makes perfect sense that Kafka would have jostled with Freud and his ideas precognitively. It is toward situations that instill the most anxiety and ambivalence that the precognitive unconscious seems to orient itself—part of that prophetic sublime discussed in Chapter 4. We are drawn toward the orbit or vicinity of our worst threats, things we survive but at a price. Kafka's manifest dislike of Freud's overly clinical approach to the mind masked his real fear of being scooped in his literary explorations of the father-dominated unconscious mind. Appropriately enough for a neurotic writer who didn't realize he was a precog, his attempts at evasion of this towering cultural influence seemingly drove him headlong into some of his feared influencer's most arresting images.[16] It's that Oedipal logic of fate, again.

There is nothing more Oedipal than a time-travel story. In one way or another, many such narratives in science fiction circle around, if not directly confront, what Freud regarded as the core fantasy lurking in the unconscious since childhood, the imagined scene of one's own conception.[17] A man traveling back in time may fall in love with or protect someone mother-like, or replace someone father-like, or both. James Cameron's *The Terminator* is an example: A soldier, Kyle Reese (Michael Biehn) travels back from a postapocalyptic future to protect Sarah Connor (Linda Hamilton), the mother of future resistance leader John Connor, from a robot assassin (the Terminator, Arnold Schwarzenegger). In the process, Kyle and Sarah fall in love, and he becomes his own leader's father.[18] In keeping with the fractal geometry of artistic prophecy, time-travel stories often convey ideas and motifs backward in the cultural timeline, via the precognitive mechanism we are contemplating.

Octavia Butler was a writer of literary speculative fiction who is today being recognized as a prophet of the culture wars, ecological collapse, and societal fragmentation of the 21st century. Fascinated with New Thought and the possibility of developing ESP abilities, telepathy featured prominently in her works.[19] She is sometimes thought to have foretold various societal developments in her novels, including the AIDS epidemic in her 1984 novel *Clay's Ark*, about a parasitic alien microorganism brought to Earth from a space mission. And much has been written about her two dystopian Parable novels, her 1993 *Parable of the Sower* and its 1998 sequel, *Parable of the Talents*. The latter, penned a decade and a half before Donald Trump started using the phrase "Make America Great Again" in preparation for his presidential bid, describes a religious zealot using that slogan in a 2032 campaign.[20] Like Woolf and Kafka, Butler also seems to have channeled the works of other artists from her future—including, oddly enough, Cameron's *Terminator* franchise. It is another example of a literary writer precognitively borrowing ideas from future works of lower status, contra the presumption of Bayard.

The 1979 novel sometimes regarded as Butler's masterpiece, and the one most often assigned to students as an American classic (versus low-status SF), is *Kindred*.[21] In that novel, a 20th-century Black writer named Dana is repeatedly "summoned" back to a Maryland slave-owning plantation by Rufus Weylin, the son of the plantation owner, who turns out to be her multiple-great-grandfather. Dana had known that she was descended from a Rufus Weylin but hadn't previously known he was white. Over the course of repeated unwilled visits to the past, she must ensure that her multiple-great-grandmother Alice, Rufus's slave, bears the daughter, Hagar, that she knows will be her ancestor. It requires enduring Rufus's mistreatment and cruelty toward his slaves, at least until Hagar is born and safely out of his hands.

Butler cited as her conscious inspiration for *Kindred* a fellow member of a Black student union in college who harbored anger at earlier generations of Black Americans who had, he thought, failed to fight against their oppression with enough resolve or vigor. Thinking of all the compromises and accommodations her own mother had had to make just to see that Butler had a stable home and an education, the student's thinking struck her as naïve.[22] Consequently, Butler wanted to examine the legacy of Black oppression through the lens of a time traveler who finds she must make difficult choices in the past, not only to survive but to ensure her own existence in the first place—that is, preventing the grandfather paradox that would occur if she somehow got in the way of Alice bearing Rufus's child. In effect, Dana becomes part of her own backstory, and in doing so, she has to endure and accommodate to the injustices around her, including the abuse of Alice by Rufus, which leads to Alice's eventual suicide after Hagar is born.

With her novel, Butler subverts the Oedipal fantasy present in so much, usually white-male-written SF that past history might be changed for the better. The lesson comes through—it is the theme of much of Butler's work, in fact—that survival requires difficult accommodations and arrangements. Simplistic, "black and white" thinking will not work. Resistance or rash action could, in an impossible situation like a Maryland plantation, get you beaten or killed or permanently separated from your family. Inspired by *Kindred*, writer and activist Rasheedah Phillips offers a great term for the causal circularity that really rules a time-travel universe: "Black Grandmother Paradox."[23]

Here's where the precognitive influence comes in. Butler felt it was important—necessary to the story—that Dana not return to the future whole, unscathed by her adventures in the past. So at the end of the novel, after Dana knows that Hagar is alive and safely away from the plantation, she stabs Rufus during an attempted rape. As she is pulled back to the future the final time, the dying Rufus grasps her arm and will not loosen his grip. Her arm becomes effectively caught in time. Dana survives her return journey to 1976, but minus an arm.

Butler was no literary snob. She loved comic books, *Star Trek*, and the trashy sci-fi of her childhood, even though she always knew she could do it better. (It was when viewing the terrible *Devil Girl from Mars* on TV when she was 12 that she realized she wanted to be a writer, since it would be so easy for her to tell a better story than that 1954 B-movie.) Five years after *Kindred* was published, Butler would have seen and surely enjoyed Cameron's hit movie about a robot assassin from the future traveling back in time to kill the mother of a future rebel leader. In the final conflict between Sarah Connor and the robotic Terminator, the torso of the robot claws its way after the heroine in a big hydraulic press, reaching out and nearly grabbing her before she is able to push a button to finally crush and destroy it. Its arm is the only thing visibly unscathed, and we lastly see that arm being carried away by employees of Cyberdyne Systems, the company responsible for building the murderous AI defense system Skynet that (we know) will eventually start a nuclear war and build Terminators to finish the job of eradicating humanity. In the 1991 sequel, *Terminator 2: Judgment Day*, the arm turns out to be one of two pieces of future technology, along with a piece of the robot's CPU, that enable engineers at Cyberdyne to build Skynet. In other words, Skynet bootstraps itself into existence, through its failed act of sending a robot killer back in time to change the past.

So, in the *Terminator* films, as in *Kindred*, a time-traveler—indeed a time-traveling killer—ends up leaving one of its arms in the past during a final conflict. Here's the detail that provides the needed tracer, or smoking gun, that the influence went in the backward direction, from *The Terminator* to *Kindred*, and not vice versa: Cameron's original treatment and his eventual script for *The Terminator* do not mention an arm. Cyberdyne workmen recover from the hydraulic press just a small "piece of the crushed Terminator … [a] micro-computer chassis."[24] But it was natural, in filming the scene, that the machine's arm that reached out to grasp Sarah became the main visible surviving fragment. Which means that its role as a MacGuffin for the sequel would only have emerged when the script for that sequel was being developed. There is no indication that Cameron had read or been influenced by *Kindred* when conceiving and writing his films. So, unless we are going to chalk this up to coincidence—two time-travel stories in which the killer leaves their arm in the past during a final conflict—then there had to be influence, and available evidence points to the influence running in temporal retrograde. In seeking a way to gravely if not fatally wound her time-traveling Dana, Butler reached several years into her future to grasp a fascinating plot twist in a thrilling SF movie franchise. Butler, like many ingenious writers and artists, was a time traveler.

Note that, like little Ernst's spool, the Terminator's arm is an object that ends before it begins, that is destroyed in order to come into being. As I said earlier, such objects are weirdly magnetic to the precognitive imagination of artists and writers (and dreamers).

Besides the popularity and pop-culture influence of the *Terminator* franchise, there is another reason we can be safely sure Butler saw, and more importantly, *thought about*, Cameron's films. Her good friend and mentor, Harlan Ellison—himself a writer of some classic time-travel stories for television, and famously litigious—had been plagiarized, in the usual way, by Cameron. In its premise about soldiers from the future chasing each other into the past, and even in their opening scenes of future battlefields with lasers cutting across the sky, *The Terminator* clearly copied one of Ellison's *Outer Limits* episodes from 1964, called "Soldier," and Cameron even admitted being influenced by that TV series when writing *The Terminator*. Ellison sought compensation from the film studio, and ended up being credited in the home video version of *The Terminator*. Butler surely knew about Cameron's copying of her friend's story and might have seen the movie for that reason alone.[25]

Miracle Working

While ordinary plagiarism can be deliberate, it often happens by accident. For instance, in 1976, a U.S. district court judge in New York found that ex-Beatle George Harrison had infringed the copyright of a Ronnie Mack song, "He's So Fine"—recorded in 1963 by The Chiffons—with his 1970 hit "My Sweet Lord." Harrison denied consciously having the Chiffons' recording in mind when writing his song, but he admitted he had heard it. Nobody, though, even that judge, thought his copying was intentional. In his written opinion and order, Judge Richard Owens, an opera composer in his spare time, wrote sympathetically:

> I conclude that the composer, in seeking musical materials to clothe his thoughts, was working with various possibilities. As he tried this possibility and that, there came to the surface of his mind a particular combination that pleased him as being one he felt would be appealing to a prospective listener; in other words, that this combination of sounds would work. Why? Because his subconscious knew it already had worked in a song his conscious mind did not remember. Having arrived at this pleasing combination of sounds, the recording was made … and the song became an enormous success. Did Harrison deliberately use the music of "He's So Fine"?

I do not believe he did so deliberately. Nevertheless, it is clear that "My Sweet Lord" is the very same song as "He's So Fine" with different words, and Harrison had access to "He's So Fine." This is, under the law, infringement of copyright, and is no less so even though subconsciously accomplished.[26]

Sometimes, though, such cases are perplexing, because the presumed plagiarist has no recollection of having encountered the allegedly copied work. If a precognitive mechanism is operative in the creative life—if some of our best ideas come from other creators we encounter in our future—then it must call into question our assumptions about more mundane examples of apparent plagiarism in which the allegedly copied work preexists the copy. How often might it be the case that presumed plagiarists are precognitively channeling already-existing works they have not yet encountered?

In the autumn of 1891, when she was 11 years old, the deafblind future author and activist Hellen Keller wrote a story called "The Frost King," about a polar frost giant and his wayward fairy servants. King Frost, living in the far North, sends his fairy servants on a mission to deliver some jars of rubies and gold to Santa Claus, to distribute to the world's children. On the way, they become tired of their errand and hide the jars in the trees so they can play. The sun comes out and melts the jars, so the contents spill out over the trees. The angry King Frost comes and finds the frightened fairies, but since the trees are so beautiful and bring such happiness to the children, he forgives them for their error.

Keller wrote the story as a birthday gift for Michael Anagnos, the Director of the Perkins Institute in Boston (now the Perkins School for the Blind), and it was printed in the school's alumni journal and then reprinted in the newspaper of the West Virginia Institution for the Education of the Deaf and Dumb and Blind. But a reader of the latter publication discovered that Keller's fairytale was nearly the same as a story by Margaret T. Canby that had been published before Keller was even born, called "The Frost Fairies." The stories are substantially the same, with even several verbatim phrasings, and they end identically, with the narrator asking in the final sentence if they can think of any better reason for the glorious colors of the leaves in Autumn.[27]

A tribunal for an 11-year-old girl sounds rather draconian, but that's what resulted. Keller was accused of deceptively pawning off a plagiarism as her own composition. After a terrifying inquisition, Perkins staff found the mortified girl guilty of thieving Canby's story.[28] It was a humiliating, traumatizing incident. She much later wrote in her autobiography:

> The two stories were so much alike in thought and language that it was evident Miss Canby's story had been read to me, and that mine was—a plagiarism. It was difficult to make me understand this; but when I did understand I was astonished and grieved. No child ever drank deeper of the cup of bitterness than I did. I had disgraced myself; I had brought suspicion upon those I loved best.[29]

Keller and her teacher, "miracle worker" Annie Sullivan, left the Perkins Institute after this verdict. Besides being traumatic, the experience was also bewildering for both of the women. Keller assumed that Sullivan must have read "The Frost Fairies" to her as a child, via touch signs, and that it stuck in her memory unconsciously. But Sullivan could not recall reading the story to Keller, nor could Keller recall having it read to her:

> I racked my brain until I was weary to recall anything about the frost that I had read before I wrote "The Frost King"; but I could remember nothing, except the common reference to Jack Frost, and a poem for children, "The Freaks of the Frost," and I knew I had not used that in my composition.[30]

Conducting her own investigation, Sullivan found that a Brewster, Massachusetts, woman with whom she and Keller had stayed in the summer of 1888, a Mrs. Sophia C. Hopkins, believed she had had a copy of Canby's book of stories and thought she might have read from it to Keller while relieving Sullivan. But Hopkins didn't remember the story, and she couldn't even produce a copy of the book.[31]

Ten years after Keller's humiliating tribunal, in 1901, a French psychologist named Theodore Flournoy coined the term *cryptomnesia* to describe the stealthy way information encountered over the course of life can insinuate itself into an individual's memory without their conscious recollection of ever having seen or encountered that information. Psychologists now consider it a type of source-monitoring error—that is, a failure to correctly identify how we know something we know, or why we think something we think. It has become a handy explanation for the kind of plagiarism Keller was accused of. One assumes that, like George Harrison, she didn't consciously intend to steal another artist's work, just that her creative imagination produced a memory that she misrecognized as her own original idea.

Flournoy himself was less interested in plagiarism among artists than he was in providing a plausible, non-paranormal explanation for veridical information provided by honest-seeming mediums of his day. His case study of cryptomnesia was a well-known Swiss medium who went by the name Hélène Smith, who claimed to be in psychic contact with the inhabitants of Mars and even spoke Martian. When analyzed by linguists, Martian turned out to have the same grammar as Smith's native French. More importantly, details she provided of the Red Planet corresponded to books that Flournoy argued she could have read earlier in life, including then-popular speculations on Martian civilization by an author named Camille Flammarion. Smith wasn't consciously lying or deceiving, in other words—she honestly thought that the information coming to her in her trances was from minds on Mars—but what flowed from her entranced lips was, Flournoy confidently proclaimed, merely the products of her own prior reading, inhabitants of her memory.

Carl Jung was an expert on this source-monitoring error and the ways it commonly manifested both in mediumship and in creativity. As a young man, he had become interested in Spiritualism though the mediumship of his cousin Hélène "Helly" Preiswerk, whose trances became the subject of his 1901 doctoral dissertation. In her altered states, Helly produced interesting, veridical (arguably, precognitive) material. For example, during one séance in 1895, the 13-year-old girl channeled the personality of her racist dead grandfather, who asked her family to pray for her aunt Bertha, who (he said, via Helly, in a deep voice) had "given birth to a little n—r";[32] Bertha had emigrated to Brazil two years before, and no one in the family yet knew that she had married a local mestizo man and had indeed, at the time of this séance, just given birth to a mixed-race boy. The family received a letter from Bertha a few weeks later informing them of this scandalous fact.[33] Jung was disappointed to discover, however, that some of the contents and themes of Helly's mediumship came from things she was reading, including as a matter of fact those same books by Flammarion that may have in-formed Smith. Mars was a popular subject for mediums in the 1890s. And another personality called "Ivenes" that Helly channeled in her trances produced utterances that appeared to duplicate the contents of a book on Spiritualism that Jung himself had given her.

Jung later serendipitously discovered a striking instance of plagia-rism by cryptomnesia in Friedrich Nietzsche's late, inspired work *Thus Spake Zarathustra*. In Chapter XL, the philosopher wrote:

> Now about the time that Zarathustra sojourned on the Happy Isles, it happened that a ship anchored at the isle on which the smoking mountain stands, and the crew went ashore to shoot rabbits. About the noon-tide hour, however, when the captain and his men were together again, they suddenly saw a man coming toward them through the air, and a voice said distinctly: 'It is time! It is highest time!' But when the figure drew close to them, flying past quickly like a shadow in the direction of the volcano, they recognized with the greatest dismay that it was Zarathustra . . . 'Behold,' said the old helmsman, 'Zarathustra goes down to hell!'[34]

Jung remembered having read exactly such a vision in an old book by Justinus Kerner called *Blätter aus Prevorst*:

> The four captains and a merchant, Mr. Bell, went ashore on the island of Mount Stromboli to shoot rabbits. At three o'clock they mustered the crew to go aboard, when, to their inexpressible astonishment, they saw two men flying rapidly toward them through the air. One was dressed in black, the other in grey. They came past them very closely, in greatest haste, and to their utmost dismay descended into the crater of the terrible volcano, Mount Stromboli. They recognized the pair as acquaintances from London.[35]

Jung wrote to the philosopher's sister, Elisabeth Förster-Nietzsche, and learned from her that she and Friedrich had read Kerner's book together as children. He was sure that Nietzsche did not deliberately plagiarize but simply, in a condition of emerging mental illness and grandiosity, mis-took a childhood memory of this text as his own idea. In *Man and His Symbols*, Jung describes how easily writers may fall victim to such errors:

> An author may be writing steadily to a preconceived plan, working out an argument or developing the line of a story, when he suddenly runs off at a tangent. Perhaps a fresh idea has occurred to him, or a different image, or a whole new sub-plot. If you ask him what prompted the digression, he will not be able to tell you. He may not even have noticed the change, though he has now produced material that is entirely fresh and apparently unknown to him before. Yet it can sometimes be shown convincingly that what he has written bears a striking similarity to the work of another author—a work that he believes he has never seen.[36]

Note here that "producing material that is entirely fresh and apparently unknown to one before" is a strikingly clear description of both inspiration and precognition too. And in some cases where cryptomnesia is presumed operative, there may be no actual evidence that the individual had previously read the article or book, as Jung did happen to be able to verify in the case of Nietzsche. For Flournoy, it was simply sufficient that sources on Mars existed (such as Flammarion's popular books); he supposed that Ms. Smith had probably encountered these sources and simply forgotten reading them. He had no actual evidence of this, though.[37] In the absence of a memory—anybody's memory—of the individual having actually read the source in question, cryptomnesia can only ever be a supposition. But here's the thing: Once accused of reproducing previously published material, the individual surely *does* read the work in question … and feels quite acutely Emerson's alienated majesty. So it raises the question: How often might presumed plagiarism really be precognition, unrecognized? How often are creative writers really essentially acting as mediums, unknowingly channeling their *future* reading of already-existing sources?

Children are notoriously bad at source monitoring, making it easy to believe or assume that Keller had indeed been read "The Frost Fairies" when very young and consciously forgotten the fact.[38] It is certainly possible. But her work's close duplication of Canby's text somewhat strains belief as cryptomnesia, given that presumably several years separated her exposure to the latter story from when she wrote her own. Keller's fairytale *exactly* matches Canby's story, point for point. Nietzsche's anecdote, by comparison, captures the gist of Kerner's narrative—hunting rabbits on a volcanic island and seeing some familiar figure or figures fly into a volcano—but there are differences too. Contrary to the Freudian presumption that we retain intact memories of all our experiences and only seemingly forget things through a process of repression, it is now known that memories of the past (autobiographical memory) are largely ad-hoc imaginative constructions, created on the fly from building-block-like schemas. Remembered factual material (semantic memory) is far from perfect too, as anybody cramming for a final exam can attest.

Reading Keller's and Canby's stories side by side gives the impression that Canby's story really had been consciously copied—which seems highly implausible—or at the very least, that it was just freshly read and studied, perhaps even in a state of emotional excitement, the kind of situation that enhances encoding of new experiences or to-be-remembered material. If we just reverse the usual temporal sequence, it definitely *was* freshly read and studied, shortly in her future. It was read to her in the context of that humiliating investigation and tribunal. Cryptomnesia explanations, while plausible-sounding and surely applicable in many instances (such as the Nietzsche case), are in some subset of cases like Keller's no less far-fetched than a simple Dunnean precognitive mechanism.[39] (There is an argument that production of veridical information in mediumistic contexts might often operate on such a mechanism: not channeling a dead person but mentally fast-forwarding to something the medium will learn in their future about that dead person, perhaps from the client or sitter—i.e., precognition in disguise.[40])

Canby herself, the supposed-to-be-aggrieved author of "The Frost Fairies," forgave and supported Keller. Like many people, she felt it was a travesty to accuse such a young girl of plagiarism. She was mainly flattered, not to mention astonished that Keller could have remembered her story in such detail presumably several years after it had been read to her, and thus took it as a "wonderful feat of memory" and testament to Keller's extraordinary mental powers.[41] Indeed. If precognition was really operative here, it is possible that Keller's choice of theme reflected—or perhaps, pre-flected—Canby's generous reaction: King Frost in both stories is initially angry that his riches are so carelessly taken and disposed of by his wayward fairy servants, but he ends by forgiving them—similar to how Keller might have imagined Canby's response to her accidental misappropriation of the older woman's story.

Keller thereafter never wrote another word of fiction, so chastened was she by her awful experience. It was to restore her trust in herself that Sullivan encouraged her former pupil to write her autobiography, *The Story of My Life*. Consequently, we have no further literary evidence to subject to psychic deconstruction. But was Keller indeed a medium, of sorts, precognizing her future reading of Canby's story in the context of her plagiarism case? There is no smoking gun, here, but we cannot just dismiss such possibilities because they seem causally verboten. Consider: As reading experiences go, which is more memorable—just encountering a new, exciting idea, or encountering a new, exciting idea having already had that idea oneself? Being confronted with some putative "original source" in a stressful tribunal, or in a psychical investigation of one's mediumistic claims, or in a letter from another author remarking (whether angrily or admiringly) at the similarity of one's work to theirs, would count as highly premonition-worthy circumstances. These are exactly the kinds of equivocal, indeed sublime (in the sense of ego-destroying) experiences that magnetize the precognitive imagination.

The impossible lurks everywhere—hidden inside ordinary quirks of psychology, camouflaged in common anomalies of memory and prevalent pitfalls of creativity. It lurks in the simple act of reading. If precognition is real, our inability to source-monitor our own future makes mediumistic channeling from already-existing but not-yet-read cultural sources an inevitability. This has major implications for how we think about apparent creative borrowing. At least some cases where second-rate or "derivative" artists are held to be unoriginal because they have seemingly copied a better or better-known one could really be cases of precognitive influence, plagiarism by anticipation.

It was Twain's humane sensitivity to such possibilities, and to the reality that our best and most original thoughts might *never* be our own, that led him to console his friend Keller in a supportive 1903 letter:

> Oh, dear me, how unspeakably funny and owlishly idiotic and grotesque was that 'plagiarism' farce! As if there was much of anything in any human utterance, oral or written, except plagiarism! The kernel, the soul—let us go further and say the substance, the

bulk, the actual and valuable material of all human utterances—is plagiarism. For substantially all ideas are second-hand, consciously and unconsciously drawn from a million outside sources, and daily used by the garnerer with a pride and satisfaction born of the superstition that he originated them; whereas there is not a rag of originality about them anywhere except the little discoloration they get from his mental and moral calibre and his temperament, and which is revealed in characteristics of phrasing. ... [N]inety-nine parts of all things that proceed from the intellect are plagiarisms, pure and simple; and the lesson ought to make us modest. But nothing can do that.[42]

Postscript: "I never saw a more striking coincidence"

In 2015, a pair of enormous L-shaped laser interferometers, 3,000 kilometers apart, detected a cosmic tremor from the collision of two black holes in a distant galaxy 1.3 billion miles away, the same number of years ago, somewhere in the southern sky. It was the first proof of Einstein's prediction that such a collision of massive objects could produce ripples in the fabric of the universe. Spacetime had actually squeezed like jello from this ancient collision.

Supermassive creative and scientific geniuses sometimes collide too, and the ripples they produce in cultural spacetime are proportional to their efforts to avoid the collision or extricate themselves from their entanglement. As I write this, in the third decade of the 21st century, the fabric of science is still wriggling, jello-like, from the devastating "chance" collision of two giants of Victorian biology, more than a century and a half ago, on opposite ends of the Earth.

The coincidental co-discovery of natural selection in the first few months of the year 1858 by Charles Darwin in England and Alfred Russel Wallace in Southeast Asia has long been a head-scratcher for biographers and science historians. In his *Harper's* article, Twain listed it among examples of what he imagined could have been products of mental telegraphy—either Darwin or Wallace broadcasting their thoughts via mesmeric currents to the other. Many of the details of the Darwin-Wallace affair are indeed suggestive of something fishy—whether superhuman fishy or just human fishy remains an open question. There are strong hints of both.[43]

What we know is this: By 1858, Darwin had been laboring for decades on the problem of how new species emerge from old ones. He had catalogued abundant evidence on his travels over two decades earlier aboard the HMS *Beagle*—the finches of the Galapagos, etc.— and after that devoted himself to the study of domesticated animals and their variations. He later claimed to have converged on the idea of natural selection, at least in its general outlines, already in the late 1830s but didn't feel much hurry to publish. His wealth and social position enabled him to work on his intellectual pursuit in leisure, with the collegial engagement and support of numerous colleagues—the best and brightest of the Victorian sciences. There seemed to him little doubt that, once he had his ducks in a row and published his book, the glory for such a monumental scientific breakthrough would fall to him. This, despite warnings by his friend, geologist Charles Lyell, that he should hurry, lest he be scooped by some other scientist.

Among those Darwin corresponded with over evolutionary questions was a younger Welsh explorer, Wallace. Wallace came from a more modest background and had limited formal education, but he was gripped by the same question that had obsessed Darwin: What accounts for the variation in species between different habitats? How do species change or new species arise? Unlike Darwin, his efforts to solve the problem came from extensive study of animals and plants in their native environments all over the planet, not in domestication. He traveled the globe, from the Amazon to the islands of Southeast Asia, then called the Malay Archipelago, to collect zoological specimens. And he was every bit as brilliant as Darwin. His research spanned various fields including biogeography, zoology, and anthropology. Unlike the upperclass Darwin, Wallace was also a socialist, and a Spiritualist.

Wallace said that, one day in February 1858, when laid up with malaria on the volcanic island of Ternate (now part of Indonesia), the answer to evolution came to him in a stroke of insight: that the motor of evolution was a process Thomas Malthus had already described in the context of human populations, of the weak being out-reproduced by the strong.[44] He quickly drafted an article containing his inspiration, "On the Tendency of Varieties to Depart Indefinitely from the Original Type," and sent it to Darwin in England, whom he thought would approve. When Darwin received his letter and article in June, he felt probably the most devastating alienated majesty in the history of alienated majesty. He quickly wrote an anguished letter to Lyell:

> Your words have come true with a vengeance—that I
> would be forestalled. ... I never saw a more striking
> coincidence, if Wallace had my m.s. sketch written
> out in 1842 he could not have made a better short
> abstract! Even his terms now stand as Heads of my
> Chapters.[45]

Whenever we see that word coincidence, of course, we should be
on the alert for possible precognition, plagiarism, or both. Darwin
claims to have roughed out his theory 16 years earlier (1842) in a never-
published paper and a later draft that he showed to only one person,
his friend Joseph Dalton Hooker, with instructions to publish only if
he died before he could complete his long-awaited book. But there's
no proof of when he wrote these drafts. And despite numerous letters
available to shed oblique light on the affair, the crucial one—Wallace's
June 1858 letter to Darwin accompanying his article—has gone missing. This prevents us from examining the postmarks, since the exact
date Darwin received the letter would say much about his honor or dis-
honor. (For what it's worth, this was the same month, over in America,
that Samuel Clemens lost his brother Henry in a steamboat disaster
after dreaming of it.) There is some reason to believe, based on the
known arrivals of mail boats, that Darwin could have received Wallace's
letter as much as two weeks before he said he did, giving him time to
draft his own claimed original version of the theory based on it. Nor
do we have the initial letters that Darwin and his friend Hooker wrote
back to Wallace in July 1858 informing him of the news that his article
had been read along with a paper of Darwin's at a July 1 meeting of the
Linnean Society, the meeting that historians have often considered the
birth of the theory of evolution by natural selection.

Without any consideration of possible precognition on either Darwin's or Wallace's part, critics of the Darwin industry have naturally
gravitated to suspicions of plagiarism or, at least, of a systematic skewing of scientific prestige in Darwin's favor. Wallace was off on a remote
Indonesian island and lacked the social and scientific connections Darwin had. There was no way for Wallace to "cheat," and there were many
ways Darwin could have. Darwin was even forced to acknowledge the
uncanniness of the coincidence in that letter to Lyell. So, some critics
say, Darwin's hindsight claims to have already arrived at his theory are
dubious, that Wallace may really deserve credit for being the first to
hit on the complete solution—that species depart from other species

through a process of groups out-competing other groups.

But the possibility of precognitive influence has to be considered, and there are strong hints that it could indeed have been at play. That Wallace said his idea came to him when laid up with a malarial fever is the biggest one. Lacking firsthand experience with malaria and the astounding dreams its fevers can produce, most historians and biographers depict Wallace reclining in some hut with nothing to do, and using his down time to focus his mind, as though all he had were a flu. Wallace himself, in his own much later reflection, downplayed the irrational delirium of a fever dream, no doubt fearing to tarnish the world's impression of him as a careful and rational thinker with his brilliant problem-solving faculties intact.[46] But the reality of malarial fevers is significantly more dramatic: Excruciating headaches are punctuated by intense chills and very high temperature spikes wherein obsessive and strange semi-dreams go on and on for hours, seemingly. They are debilitating and hardly conducive to calm theorizing or rational deduction. But they are, like other altered states, conducive to paranormal invention "from nowhere." I know firsthand, having had malaria, and even having had an arguably precognitive experience in one of my deliriums, which I will describe in the Afterword.

I think it is very possible—albeit, yes, forever unprovable—that in his fever dream, Wallace was precognizing Darwin's confirmatory letter to him in response to his own letter, or even his competitor's *On the Origin of Species* published the following year. Those would have been monumental reading experiences, indeed precognition-worthy. The exactness with which, as Darwin admitted, Wallace's phrasings matched his own chapter headings, etc., suggests such a precognitive influence.

But the really interesting question is: If Wallace was precognizing Darwin, could Darwin have been precognizing Wallace, in turn?

The general picture Darwin painted and that his followers have painted certainly *could* be right: He worked ploddingly from the evidence, hammering together his theory over decades following his *Beagle* voyage, and converging on the theory's outlines already in the late 1830s or early 1840s—like Wallace later, also influenced by Malthus—and then patiently, unhurriedly assembling evidence that would substantiate the theory sufficiently and fill out the details for a book he knew would be a bombshell. Then he got Wallace's article, which contained a more concise and clear formulation, along with (helpfully) a better grasp of the mechanisms of species divergence to go along with his own crucial insight of natural selection.

Maybe.

But I think we should not forget the alienated majesty factor. We know, because Darwin hints as much, that Wallace's letter was probably the most awful moment in Darwin's scientific and creative life. It glowed with the radiance of his own unpublished thoughts. And it is precisely that radioactive glow, deeply carcinogenic to the ego, that radiates backward in time in a creative genius's tesseract brain. I thus cannot believe—I genuinely cannot—that Darwin wasn't at least dimly precognizing Wallace's letter and article when he formed and assembled his theory. How much of the pieces may have come to him in dreams, we will never know—most scientific geniuses in the shadow of the Enlightenment have not liked to talk about any role the irrational, and dreams, may play in their process—but precognition bends and shapes even conscious creative noodling, as I believe we can see with Paul McCartney and the song "Get Back."

The most sublime implication of ideas arising through loops between creative minds is that they are, like some of those Cy Twombly paintings, literally from nowhere. Consider: *If* Wallace got his idea from Darwin, who got his idea from Wallace, then neither of these men "did the work" of solving the most famously vexing problem in the history of biological science. It would be a historical irony of even greater magnitude than the role of prophecy-evading Oedipus in Sigmund Freud's prophecy-denialist theory of the unconscious: that the very theory of natural selection, so often seen as the nail in the Creationist coffin, arose in a scandalously *biblical* manner, *ex nihilo*.

Unfortunately, at this historical distance and with so many puzzle pieces missing, we are reduced to speculation about this particular case. But I do suspect such situations could be far more common than anybody has yet noticed, and could help account for the many, many cases of parallel artistic creation and scientific discovery that are head-scratchers for culture historians and that invite offhanded attributions to the occult workings of a collective unconscious—the subject we are about to turn to.

There's a further confounding factor in the Darwin-Wallace affair, though. Nearly three decades before Darwin's and Wallace's papers were presented side-by-side at the Linnean Society, a little-known Scottish forester named Patrick Matthew published a book called *Naval Timber and Arboriculture* that contained, wait for it, the theory of evolution by natural selection. Although less detailed than Darwin's or Wallace's work, and less supported by evidence, it has been acknowledged by a growing number of intellectual historians that neither Darwin nor Wallace really deserve credit for being the first to hit on the idea. The fact that you, dear reader, are only now hearing about this is itself its own interesting narrative and its own mini-study of the distorting effects of hindsight when academic traditions loyal to a founder, Darwinians in this case, manage successfully to uphold a traditional narrative of discovery and glory. Counternarratives get silenced.

When Matthew read *On the Origin of Species* upon its publication, he wrote to Darwin asserting his own originality in hitting upon the theory. Darwin replied, acknowledging that Matthew had clearly got there first but claiming he had not been aware of Matthew's book until just then. This is possibly true: Matthew had never written further on his insight, and it only appears in an appendix to his 1831 book on a rather niche subject, forestry in the service of shipbuilding. However, a forensic criminologist and part-time literary detective named Mike Sutton has provided ample evidence supporting the claim that both Darwin and Wallace could well have been exposed indirectly to Matthew's ideas via contemporaries who had read his book, even if they had not read his book themselves.[47] Sutton pulls no punches: Darwin's glory for discovering evolution by natural selection is founded on fraud and coverup. He doesn't really address the possibility that Darwin and/or Wallace may have seen Matthew's argument at some point but consciously forgot it. And of course, he doesn't mention the to-me-more-plausible idea that Darwin and Wallace had not read Matthew's book beforehand but read it afterward and maybe precognized that reading experience the same way, and for the same reasons, that Keller might have precognized Canby's "The Frost Fairies" during her tribunal. We know for certain that Darwin *did* read Matthew *after* being confronted by that author—if nothing else, it would have been another alienated-majesty moment. Similarities of phrasing—such as the fact that Matthew used the incredibly similar phrase "natural theory of selection" (versus Darwin's "theory of natural selection") point, for Sutton, to plagiarism. To me, they could just as easily point to precognition.[48]

Of course, these speculations can turn us in spirals. There is also the possibility that Matthew, back in 1831, was precognizing Darwin. There is really no telling. The bottom line, and the main takeaway, is that precognition needs to be considered a confounding factor in many debates about originality, plagiarism, and influence. Rubbing my temples and squinting, I foresee that future Superhumanities departments will make a central place for time loops and alienated majesty. There are no doubt some fascinating dissertations to be written in the para-psychohistory of science, once the stigma against precognition recedes.

Whatever else it teaches us, the Darwin-Wallace affair stands as a lesson against procrastination: If you've got an idea, hurry and publish it, lest you encounter "your" idea in the writing of another. Indeed, that anxiety, that natural hurry not to be scooped by rivals, may be more than the competitive drive toward innovation in culture and science, the motor of scientific and technological advancement. Because of the ironic way the anxiety of influence actually *attracts* ideas from the future, it may also be one of the most important drivers of prophecy—the retrograde flow of ideas and information from the future into the past in a society.

Aliens and Archetypes
From the Collective Unconscious to the Unified Field

You can go into the future. It's not easy, and you can't do it when you want to, but it can happen.
—David Lynch, *Room to Dream* (2018)

I paint from reality, I put several things and ideas together and perhaps, when I have finished, it could show the future …
—H. R. Giger, Interview (1979)

When trying to explain the kinds of artistic, literary, and scientific coincidences I have been exploring, people will often invoke Carl Jung's theory of the collective unconscious. Colloquially, people may use that term to mean a common cultural reservoir of ideas, a zeitgeist, thoughts in the air, housed in no one head but available to all heads. When we talk about the collective unconscious in this loose way, there is the sense that if we drilled down, we might find ordinary social mechanisms underpinning it—i.e., just "culture" in the anthropological sense of the term: art, religion, folklore, technology, lifeways, myth, and so on. Ideas may be shared in cryptic but still mundane ways, leading to the illusion of some psychic connection. Jung, however meant something much more specific: a phylogenetically ancient repository of instincts and symbols, a common psychological inheritance transcending the individual mind-brain and going beyond the particular material symbols of the individual's culture.

Jung's theory drew on several antecedents. Most obviously there was the Platonic world of Ideas. Jungian psychology is sometimes seen as a

20th-century reframing of Platonic idealism, as filtered through Neo-platonic philosophers of the 3rd and 4th centuries who influenced some of Jung's favorite 19th-century writers.[1] In Platonic thinking, archetypal patterns or forms imprint themselves on human development and on human affairs. A 19th-century biological twist on this idea, the evolutionary ideas of German zoologist Ernst Haeckel, also shaped Jung's thinking. Haeckel's "biogenic law," captured in the phrase "ontogeny recapitulates phylogeny," held that the development of an organism reflects the phases of its earlier evolution, somehow retained—mammalian embryos looking like fish or tadpoles, for instance. Jung's theory transposed Haeckel's controversial (and now, mostly discredited) law from the body's development to that of the psyche.[2]

The idea of a transpersonal archive of culture and memory was also part of the zeitgeist when Jung was writing, thanks to Victorian occultism and Theosophy. Theosophy's founder, Helena Petrovna Blavatsky, had written of an "akasa" (from the Sanskrit word *Ākāśa*), a luminous information-bearing field similar in some ways to the aether held by physicists at the time to be responsible for the transmission of light waves. Subsequent Theosophical writers like Charles Leadbeater fleshed out the later-popular notion of an "Akashic record," a kind of cosmic memory bank bearing a permanent record of human events that an enlightened person can consult at will.[3] In his 1888 book *Esoteric Buddhism*, A. P. Sinnett claimed that the Akashic record was an ancient Buddhist idea.[4] In fact, like so many folkloric and metaphysical ideas popularly thought to be ancient and foreign, it was purely a Victorian invention, owing much more to then-current social and technological innovations—in this case, the massive expansion of print archives and photography in the latter third of the 19th century. Both of these developments gave Victorians a new sense of their lives as *information* and, along with it, a notion of the permanence of that information—a sense that that information could be imprinted on a recording surface and stored.[5] Psychical researcher Frederic Myers' ideas about the personality's survival of bodily death were also shaped by these developments; in the opening paragraph of his 1893 autobiographical essay, "Fragments of Inner Life," he wrote, "I hold that all things thought and felt, as well as all things done, are somehow photographed imperishably upon the Universe …"[6] Jung took these 19th-century occultist and scientific currents and repackaged them in more up-to-date psychological terms.

Sigmund Freud, who prioritized the individual's unique early life experiences in the formation of the psyche and its complexes, found the idea of an ancient, transpersonal, universal unconscious mystical and baseless. It was Jung's insistence on it that precipitated their break in 1913, despite Jung having previously been heir-apparent to the psychoanalytic movement. But Jung felt he needed the concept to explain patients' dreams and fantasies that quite often contained ancient mythological motifs and symbols that, he asserted, they couldn't possibly have encountered in the course of their education or their reading. Maggy Quarles' scarab dream would be an example—in his 1952 *Synchronicity* monograph, Jung parenthetically remarked that Maggy "did not happen to know" the rebirth symbolism of Egyptian scarabs before he explained it to her in his consulting room.[7] But psychiatry historian Richard Noll has shown that Jung's many claims of this nature were often strained, based mainly on gender and class presumptions about who reads (or knows) what.[8] Noll argues, in fact, that Jung's signature theory had its roots, ironically, in the very phenomenon of cryptomnesia that the psychologist seems to have understood so keenly, because much of his presumptively archetypal material could in fact be found in then-popular books.[9]

The smoking gun evidence Jung frequently cited for the reality of a collective unconscious was a hallucination reported by a schizophrenic patient named Emile Schwyzer at Zurich's famous Burghölzli mental hospital, of the sun with a swaying, wind-producing phallus. It corresponded to a Mithraic mythological motif Jung was familiar with, and throughout his career he claimed that no sources were available prior to when this story was collected, probably in 1909, that might have suggested this image to the patient. But Noll discovered that the solar phallus was readily found in several then-recent sources, including a 1907 book by Theosophical writer G. R. S. Mead. In the early years of the century, the Theosophical Publishing Society had saturated Europe and America with Theosophy-inflected translations and commentaries of ancient sacred texts from the Far East and Near East, ranging from ancient Egyptian religion to Buddhism, Hinduism, and Yoga. Many of Jung's patients were well-read spiritual seekers, the very audience for this kind of material. So were many Burghölzli patients—some were neo-Pagans (the original "Bohemians") who had been committed to the institution by their bourgeois families alarmed at their drug use, sexual promiscuity, or other socially unconventional behavior and values.[10]

Hellenistic mystery cults were especially hot stuff in Jung's milieu. In the early 19-teens, Jung developed a meditative technique he called active imagination as an avenue to exploring his own unconscious. In that state, directed fantasies (the "active" part) intermingle with autonomously arising dreamlike or hypnagogic scenes. In one of his early descents into his unconscious in December 1913, Jung experienced a ritual apotheosis as Aion, a Mithraic lion-headed deity.[11] Blavatsky had written about similar visionary initiations under the guidance of ancient teachers. Jung's initiation closely followed a ritual described in a book Jung had on his own bookshelf: a two-volume study of Mithraic texts, iconography, and archaeology by Franz Cumont that had been published in 1900. Christianity-inflected interpretations of Mithraic initiations in that book that corresponded with Jung's experience were subsequently discredited by later research, though. This provided Noll with a tracer—his own smoking gun—showing that Jung's visions were not of some authentic cult practice buried in his ancestral memory but came from his reading of Cumont.[12]

For Noll, the bottom line is that Jung believed he had discovered an eternal wellspring of common feeling, thought, and symbolism connecting all people, when in fact he had really discovered the reach of the Theosophical Publishing Society and the shared interests and obsessions of western civilization's discontents at a certain specific historical/cultural moment. Incidentally, a similar criticism has long been leveled at Freud too: that the overwhelming prevalence of Oedipal motifs in patients' dreams and fantasies was at least partly a product of suggestion, patients reading Freudian psychoanalytic literature, and their efforts, unconsciously, to please their therapist.

But the possibility of misrecognized precognition—and in some cases, its demonstrable likelihood—redeems Jung and Freud somewhat from the charge that their core theories rested solely on cryptomnesia and clinical echo-chambers. Some of what critics like Noll have naturally assumed was patients producing in their dreams material from prior reading may really have been precognitive/presentimental orientation toward the reward of learning something exciting in their near future, whether from a book or from their doctor, directly.

This is certainly what was operative with Maggy and her scarab dream, for instance. It must be said, Jung's claim that his patient didn't know anything about the symbolism of scarabs before she had her dream is somewhat dubious: The solar symbolism of scarabs was fairly widely known, appearing for instance in Theosophical writings, and the beetles' rebirth symbolism may have been, too. Scarab jewelry had been popular since the Egyptian Revival of the late 19th century; the French

---

jewelry designer Lalique, for instance, was famous for his Egyptian-style scarabs. As a woman from a wealthy aristocratic family in Holland, Maggy likely knew the language of jewelry, whatever she knew or didn't know about ancient Egyptian religion. Still, even if she had some prior idea what scarabs meant, she couldn't possibly have known that someone was going to hand her a live beetle and deliver a lecture on Egyptian religious symbolism the day after she dreamed of being given a piece of golden scarab jewelry.[13] And Maggy may have been just the tip of the iceberg among Jung's patients, as other clinical anecdotes in his work can be read in similar Dunnean-precognitive terms.[14]

Without a theory of dream precognition, or a sensitivity to how such dreams may be self-fulfilling—the part that feels paradoxical, even though it isn't—it was quite natural for Jung and his followers to misrecognize these confirmatory moments as evidence of an objective collective unconscious. And there's no telling how often such misrecognition occurs. Even that Burghölzli patient, Schwyzer, need not have read about solar wind-producing phalluses if, in his near future, he was going to tell that vision to an authority who could perhaps validate it and explain its archetypal meaning to him. And even if Jung had Cumont's book on his bookshelf, we needn't assume he had read about that Mithraic initiation ritual yet. Like ordinary dreams, the scenes that arise in Jungian active imagination sometimes contain biographical material from the individual's future.[15] It is possible that he could have been divining the not-yet-read contents of his own library in his soul-spelunking—a kind of spontaneous version of what Craig Sinclair was intentionally doing with the unopened books on her husband Upton's bookshelf.

Jung's descents into his unconscious were recognizably precognitive in some instances. His first series of visions in October 1913, for instance—of Europe awash in blood and corpses, among other terrifying imagery—seemed in hindsight to be premonitions of World War I, a realization that provided reassuring validation of the legitimacy of his active-imaginal practice.[16] Jung was an avid reader and bibliophile, and there is evidence that his insights and inspirations on other occasions preceded some confirmation in a new book, suggesting precognitive influence as their source. For example, one contemporary author with whom Jung felt close resonance was the Prague novelist (transplanted from Austria), Gustav Meyrink. Jung had been working on his "Red Book" (*Liber Novus*)—his illuminated-manuscript record of his visionary experiences—for a few years already when Meyrink wrote his most esoteric novel, *The White Dominican*, published in 1921. It describes a "Cinnabar-red book" that contains the secrets of eternal life, and Jung told an American colleague who was translating his manuscript for possible publication that Meyrink's novel used some of the same symbolism that he himself had encountered in some of his initial active-imagination experiments.[17] It raises the possibility that in Jung's altered states he was (among many other things) precognizing Meyrink's novel.

In the following decade, Jung dreamed about finding a hitherto-unknown wing or annex of his house that was full of wonderful books, mostly from the 16th and 17th centuries: "Large, fat folio volumes, bound in pigskin, stood along the walls. Among them were a number of books embellished with copper engravings of a strange character, and illustrations containing curious symbols such as I had never seen before. … It was a collection of medieval incunabula and sixteenth-century prints."[18] He adds that before he had this dream, he had placed an order with a bookseller for a Latin alchemical text that he thought might have a needed reference. "Several weeks after my dream a parcel arrived containing a parchment volume of the sixteenth century with many most fascinating symbolic pictures. They instantly reminded me of my dream library."[19] Alchemical books became an obsession and fascination for Jung in the subsequent years, and he eventually acquired a library of 16th- and 17th-century texts quite similar to what he had seen in his dream. He had interpreted this "unknown wing of the house" in his dream as an undiscovered, unexplored aspect of his own personality already awaiting him that he later moved into or inhabited, "something that belonged to me but of which I was not yet conscious."[20]

Like Freud's unconscious, Jung interpreted not-yet-conscious aspects of the self as a buried, hidden, or submerged "meanwhile"—something already existing but waiting to be dug up, excavated. But his description also works quite well if it simply describes discoveries and experiences awaiting us in our own future: Our future life does indeed "belong to us" in a way that we are not yet aware of; and it is indeed already there, albeit in a different form than Jung imagined. It's the yet-untraversed segment of our long, serpent-seraph self, snaking through the block universe.[21]

Why the Long Face?

Jung usually described (and even visually diagrammed) his universal, transpersonal unconscious as a subterranean stratum, like the shared core of the earth, a depth where our individuality intersects with the collective. But in a 1946 essay on "The Psychology of the Transference," Jung used a different metaphor, one that Virginia Woolf would have resonated strongly with—the individual as a wave on a collective ocean:

> Although this [non-individual] psyche is innate in every individual, it can neither be modified nor possessed by him personally. It is the same in the individual as in the crowd and ultimately in everybody. It is the precondition of each individual psyche, just as the sea is the carrier of the individual wave.[22]

David Lynch, who describes "catching the big fish" from a larger ocean of (un)consciousness he calls the "unified field," would also agree with this image.[23] One of the most visionary American film directors, Lynch is another of those modern shamans who gets his ideas in non-ordinary reality, via a kind of meditative semi-trance he calls daydreaming—similar if not identical to Jung's active imagination. The filmmaker described his method to Charlie Rose:

> I dream but I don't go by nighttime dreams. Nighttime dreams are there sometimes—some good ones—but it's daydreams that I love: sinking down, sitting comfortably in a chair where you might be controlling some of the thoughts and directing yourself here or there, but at a certain point, the dream takes over and you enter in a place where things are unraveling before you without your intervention. And many things can present themselves that way, and sometimes ideas that you fall in love with.[24]

Again, active imagination and its variants may be highly precognogenic. As may have happened with Jung and Meyrink, fiercely original creative people fishing for new ideas with such methods—or simply plumbing the depths of their unconscious for purposes of individuation—may accidentally catch not-yet-expressed ideas of their contemporaries on their hooks and reel them in. This is exactly what I believe happened with Lynch's surreal 1977 directorial debut, *Eraserhead*.

Eraserhead is a relentlessly dismal film—so impossibly dismal and dark that the only possible response is laughter. It opens with an image of a grotesque, ghostly spermatozoon snaking from the mouth of the main character, a hapless schlub named Henry Spencer (played by Jack Nance). A deformed man, seemingly in space and called (in Lynch's script) "The Man in the Planet," pulls a few levers and the spermatozoon shoots out and splashes into a watery void. It is implicitly (or symbolically) the origin of a mutant or alien baby that Henry's girlfriend Mary (Charlotte Stewart) has given birth to. Henry lives in a depressing industrial district, in a rented room decorated with little plants growing from piles of dirt. The film focuses on Henry's ambivalent care for this limbless, sick being, which Lynch and his crew affectionately called "Spike." It may or may not be a human child, and Henry may or may not be the father. The rumor was that Spike was made from a fetal calf, or possibly a dead rabbit, animated through some internal mechanism, but Lynch refuses to divulge his secret.

Kafka's *The Metamorphosis* was a major inspiration for *Eraserhead*, and as with so many of that Prague writer's stories, much of Lynch's body of work could be classified as science fiction, yet there is a way in which it actively resists all explanatory rubrics and classifications, and that genre designation is seldom applied to him. The sci-fi elements—scenes in outer space, for instance—are presented as possibly jokes, or dreams, or stage sets. Because what he "really means" cannot be pinned down, genre reductions don't stick.

In interviews, Lynch has called *Eraserhead* his most spiritual work—claiming that the story was born from opening the Bible to a page that had an answer he was seeking:

> The way it happened was I had these feelings, but I didn't know what it really was about for me. So I get out the Bible and start reading, and I'm reading along, reading along, and I come to this sentence and say, 'That's exactly it.'[25]

Of course, Lynch refuses to reveal what Bible passage it was.

Lynch made the film that resulted from this biblical inspiration slowly, on a shoestring budget, over the first two thirds of the 1970s, while studying at the American Film Institute in Los Angeles. It was not a hit when it came out, but it quickly acquired a cult following from midnight showings, and it immediately marked Lynch as one of the most original filmmakers of his generation. Stanley Kubrick later cited it as one of his favorite films, and made the cast and crew of *The Shining* watch it before making his 1980 adaptation of the Stephen King novel.

Eraserhead is many things—a "dream" about the anxieties of fatherhood, most obviously. Lynch was a young father during the years he made the film—his daughter, Jennifer Lynch, was three when he started his project. But the paternity in the film is also figurative, prophetic, and impossible: Two years after *Eraserhead* shocked and disturbed art house audiences with its story about a man burdened with caring for a mutant or alien long-faced baby, a much larger audience of moviegoers was shocked and revolted by the most audacious birth in cinema history, the larval Xenomorph bursting out the chest of Kane (John Hurt) in Ridley Scott's *Alien*. Scott's film is about a seven-person crew of astronauts awakened from hypersleep to investigate a distress signal on a remote moon. They find a derelict alien ship with a giant fossilized pilot and a hold full of alien eggs, one of which "hatches" and covers Kane's face with a hand-like organism that plants a seed inside his chest. The larval alien (or "chestburster" as it is called in *Alien* lore) that rises over Kane's corpse on the USS *Nostromo*'s lunch table is essentially an eviler, bloodier version of both the spermatozoon at the start of *Eraserhead* and the mutant/alien baby Spike: All these creatures are limbless and have elongated heads, although the chestburster, unlike Spike, lacks eyes. The elongated eyeless head is the most distinctive feature of the adult Xenomorph as well, which proceeds to decimate the *Nostromo*'s crew.

Lynch was distressed enough by the similarities between the creatures in *Alien* and those in his movie that it caused an unfortunate, awkward rift between him and Swiss painter H. R. Giger, who had designed the creatures and alien environments in *Alien*. According to Giger, Lynch thought that he and director Scott had copied *Eraserhead* when they designed and filmed the chestburster scene.[26] The painter only found out about Lynch's concern years later, after reaching out to the director, via mutual friends, to ask about collaborating with him on Lynch's third feature film, *Dune*, since he was such an admirer of the director's work. Lynch never replied to the painter directly.[27]

Giger stated in interviews that the plagiarism Lynch suspected simply wasn't possible, and indeed scrutiny of the chronology bears him out. Ridley Scott never saw *Eraserhead* during *Alien*'s production. The director asked that Giger's design for the chestburster resemble a 1954 painting by Irish painter Francis Bacon called *Crucifixion*; the design was additionally determined by Giger's own designs for the adult eyeless Xenomorph, which itself was based on two of his own H. P. Lovecraft-inspired paintings (*Necronom IV* and *Necronom V*) that preceded

Eraserhead by several years. Also, Dan O'Bannon's original screenplay "Star Beast" was completed in 1975, and the scene in that script reads as follows—essentially identical (even in its description of the creature) to what was eventually filmed, except for the filmmakers having changed the name of the hapless crewmember "Broussard" to Kane:

```
Broussard's face is screwed up into
a mask of agony, and he is trembling
violently from head to foot.

              BROUSSARD
         (incoherent shriek)
     OhmygooaaAAAHHHHH!!!

A RED SMEAR OF BLOOD BLOSSOMS ON THE
CHEST OF BROUSSARD'S TUNIC.

THEIR   EYES   ARE   ALL   RIVETTED   TO
BROUSSARD'S CHEST AS THE FABRIC OF HIS
TUNIC IS RIPPED OPEN, AND A HORRIBLE
NASTY LITTLE HEAD THE SIZE OF A MAN'S
FIST PUSHES OUT.

   Everybody SCREAMS and leaps back
   from the table.  The cat spits and
   bolts.

   The disgusting little head lunges,
   comes  spurting  out  of  Broussard's
   chest  trailing  a  thick,  wormlike
   tail—splattering  fluids  and  blood—
   lands  in  the  middle  of  the  dishes
   and food on the table—and scurries
   away while the men are stampeding
   for safe ground.

   When  they  finally  regain  control
   of   themselves,   it   has   escaped.
   Broussard lies slumped in his chair,
   a  huge  hole  in  his  chest,  spouting
   blood. The dishes are scattered and
   the food is covered with blood and
   slime.[28]
```

The "horrible nasty little head the size of a man's fist ... trailing a thick, wormlike tail" sounds similar to Spike and exactly like the extraterrestrial spermatozoon that issues from Henry's mouth at the start of *Eraserhead*, as well as numerous similar creatures that are stomped to death by a chipmunk-cheeked "Lady in the Radiator" during one of Henry's reveries late in the film. But again, the "Star Beast" script preceded *Eraserhead* by two years.

Even though ordinary borrowing or influence really is impossible here, in either direction, it would be understandable for Lynch to have been perplexed at the closeness of these star larvae and to have felt something like Emerson's alienated majesty when watching *Alien* in a theater in 1979. In the unconscious, there is no sense of time and causality and logic. Lynch might have doubted not just Giger's and Ridley Scott's originality but also—and perhaps mainly—his own. Apart from the physical similarity of Lynch's creatures and the larval Xenomorph, there is also a metamorphosis in a vision: Henry dreams of his own head flying off and being replaced by a large version of Spike's, rising from the neck of his shirt. It is like being reborn as Spike—as well as like the rapid metamorphosis of *Alien*'s chestburster into the adult, long-headed Xenomorph. At the end, Henry rips open Spike's swaddles and stabs the screaming creature, which although utterly vulnerable, seemingly cannot be destroyed. In *Alien*, too, the Xenomorph seems indestructible until Sigourney Weaver's Lieutenant Ripley blasts it into space at the end of the film.

This is the thing about creativity: Precisely because ideas from nowhere do not feel like ours, we are perpetually uncertain of their true parentage. When some other artist's work comes to seem uncomfortably close to their own vision, it puts the artist dedicated to midwifing this original, alien stuff—or catching and mounting the big fish from the unified field—on the horns of an unresolvable dilemma: to accept and embrace, or to distrust and reject. *Eraserhead*, I argue, is essentially a premonition, in movie form, of Lynch's "alien" future thought: a disturbing, annoying realization that a trespass had occurred in some direction, thus a reminder of the worst thing in the world for a serious artist—to have been unoriginal. Lynch would have doubted his own parentage as well his baby's viability, and that doubt is expressed right there *in* that baby. Spike is a self-doubting infant with a possibly *Alien* parent, another impossible—and, one might add, "unborn"—object. And we can plug Lynch himself into the space marked by his movie's ambivalent maybe-papa, Henry, saddled with a mutant and helpless creation he's not sure is his own and is not sure he can possibly love. The situation, caring for a mewling, crying, and sickly alien child becomes unbearable, and his final efforts to destroy it result in his becoming it.

And here's the thing: How is it that an artist might attempt to deal with a disavowed work, or a sketch they are unhappy with, other than by blotting it out? Lynch's title, *Eraserhead*, comes from the subsequent part of the aforementioned dream-hallucination of Henry, that his head, having been dislodged from his body now inhabited by Spike, ends up in a puddle in front of some dilapidated warehouse; it is retrieved by a boy who sells it to a factory that makes erasers. His head is used as the raw material for erasers. Thus, in that same unconscious time-muddle, Lynch's "head" is trying to erase his creation ex-post-facto.

"I saw it. I saw the future."

The specific life context in which Lynch would have first seen *Alien*, in the months leading up to the fraught production of his second feature film, *The Elephant Man*, may be highly relevant to the anxieties that I believe his debut feature was foreshadowing, anxieties over his abilities as a maker of big-budget, commercial films.

The Elephant Man tells the mostly true story of Joseph Carey Merrick, called "John Merrick" in the film, a man in Victorian London born with terrible cranial, facial, and body deformities. Although told in a "realistic" fashion—Lynch did not write the original draft of the script—it begins with a very Lynchian hallucinatory vision of the mother being injured by a circus elephant during her pregnancy. There was a popular theory in the Victorian era that birthmarks and deformities reflected experiences and injuries suffered by the mother.

In his 2018 memoir *Room to Dream* (co-written with Kristine McKenna), Lynch describes the pre-production of *The Elephant Man* as his dark-night-of-the-soul experience as a filmmaker, from which only the continuing support and generosity of producer Mel Brooks kept him psychologically afloat.[29] The film's English cast, especially the prickly Anthony Hopkins (who plays Merrick's doctor, Frederick Treves), did not trust the young American director's ability. And most frustratingly, prosthetics Lynch had devised for the actor playing Merrick to wear were not working. In fact, it was around this crisis that Lynch experienced a rare vision that felt to him precognitive. He writes,

> [O]ne day I was walking through the dining room and suddenly had a déjà vu. Usually a déjà vu feels like, "Oh, this has happened before," but as I entered the

déjà vu it got slippery and it went into the future! I saw it and I said to myself, "The Elephant Man makeup is going to fail." Because I saw it. I saw the future.[30]

The makeup ended up failing, just as he had foreseen. We can make of that what we will—a skeptic would certainly chalk it up to self-fulfilling prophecy. But what is important here is how traumatic this failure was for Lynch: He went through a depressed, even dissociative period that he compared to America's "four dark days" in 1963 after JFK had been assassinated:

> When I was awake I couldn't stand being awake, and when I was asleep it was solid nightmares. I thought it would be better to kill myself, because I could hardly stand to be in my body. It was something so powerful that I thought, How can anyone stand to be in a body with this torment.[31]

Brooks, fortunately, came to the rescue. Another artist was hired to handle the makeup and allow Lynch to focus on his main task, directing the movie. The end result was a resounding success. *The Elephant Man* was the second-highest-grossing film of 1982, after *The Empire Strikes Back*.

We typically prophesy shocks and upheavals when we will have survived a close encounter with them, but also, especially, when we feel bound to them somehow. This may be partly what makes them traumatic: our boundness, and thus our struggle to extricate ourselves from the thing that is too close for comfort. It may, in extreme cases, be simply the fact that we have prophesied an event that binds us to it, perhaps through confusion that we may have somehow *caused* the event—as in the case of traumatized people who dream regularly of disaster reports they read in the media, a kind of precognitive neurotic symptom. Well, Lynch was bound to *Alien*, and *Alien* to Lynch, because his uncomfortable relationship with that film did not end in 1979. Guess who is inside all those prosthetics and makeup playing John Merrick in *The Elephant Man*? John Hurt, the very actor who had "given birth" to the alien baby in *Alien*.

When Giger learned that an adaptation of Frank Herbert's classic sci-fi novel *Dune* was to be Lynch's next project after *Elephant Man*, the painter reached out to Lynch via mutual friends, and it was then that he learned of Lynch's belief that the *Alien* creators had plagiarized his work. Lynch conveyed via those friends that despite his admiration for Giger's paintings, he did not want his third major motion picture to be associated with *Alien*. There was no such hope, though: Alejandro Jodorowsky's original effort to make *Dune* in 1974-5 had given the world Giger and *Alien* in the first place. Giger had been "discovered" by Jodorowski, and Jodorowski's special effects person, Dan O'Bannon, went on to write *Alien* and introduced Giger's work to Ridley Scott. Consequently, *Dune*, regarded as Lynch's only failure, would perpetually be compared, very unfavorably, to the Jodorowsky *Dune*-that-wasn't, and fans of Herbert's book would look at *Alien* as a suggestion for how great that *Dune* might have been had it had a different director and creative team.[32]

So, effectively, *Alien* would have been an uncomfortably close presence for Lynch for a significant chunk of his early career. I suggest that Lynch's *long face* over this sequence of career crises and regrets, all connected in various ways to *Alien*, is bundled into the premonitory content in *Eraserhead*. That overwhelmingly dismal film foretold Lynch's difficult second decade as a director and its haunting by Scott's blockbuster.

I promised there was more to the story of Lynch and Giger and their intertwining creative careers, though. There is striking evidence that the precognitive influence between these two creative visionaries went in both directions, not just one, and that this is what I like to call a PSC, a precognitive-synchronistic clusterfuck. Giger's Oscar-winning work for *Alien* contains what I believe is a clear tracer of *Lynch's* influence on *him*, also in temporal retrograde.

Giger was not a contributor to the story or script of *Alien*, but to an unusual or even unique degree for a big-budget feature film, his artistic vision contributed to elevating what could have been just a blockbuster SF/horror thrill ride to what has been acknowledged by film scholar Stephen Mulhall as an authentic and enduring work of philosophy.[33] The film and its sequels are commonly cited cultural touchstones for feminist theorists, transhumanists, and Lacanians, among others, and it is partly thanks to Giger. Elsewhere I argue that Giger's work in that film encodes a warning about the "fall" of consciousness into technology, akin to ancient Gnostic theologies of the fall of spirit into matter.[34] But Giger's visual/sculptural horrors also seem to embody or encode what I believe were the visionary painter's own future ambivalent thoughts and realizations having to do directly with Lynch, a director with such a similar vision to his own, and Lynch's rejection of his overtures to collaborate.

When Giger saw *Eraserhead* on a trip to New York in 1977, he was stunned by the film and realized that Lynch was a fellow-traveler in the same darkly surreal districts he had been exploring in his paintings. But what is especially stunning in light of Lynch's later work is not the similarity of Giger's chestburster to Lynch's Spike, but Giger's utterly original vision for what came to be known as the "Space Jockey," the ancient fossilized star pilot in the derelict alien ship carrying the Xenomorph eggs. The giant figure, with a roughly humanoid upper body but fused to its cockpit seat in a reclining position, and with an *elephantine head*—a kind of trunk extending down the front of its torso—is a very literal "elephant man." This alien, merged with its seat, has a hole in its chest from having birthed a Xenomorph aeons earlier. The posture of the Space Jockey is similar to the seated position that Merrick was forced to sleep in, lest his head deformities suffocate him. (*The Elephant Man* ends with Merrick's suicide, lying flat to sleep instead of sitting propped up on pillows.) And this creature's face looks uncannily like the cloth-shrouded face of Hurt's Merrick when he went out in public and as he appears in the film's posters.

Although it had been *Eraserhead* that first caught the attention of Giger, it was *The Elephant Man* that confirmed the Swiss painter's love for the American director. Giger saw clearly the similarity between his own monochrome "biomechanoid" aesthetic and the industrial-wasteland imaginal of Lynch. Unlike Lynch, however, Giger seems to have felt less threat than simple admiration—again, it was this film that led him to reach out to Lynch about the possibility of collaborating, only to learn of Lynch's plagiarism concerns.

Giger would have been well aware that John Hurt was the common denominator in *The Elephant Man* and *Alien*. His Space Jockey thus seems almost like a condensed dream-image about this cluster of situations and people that entangled him with Lynch. His designs for Scott's blockbuster embody a kind of premonitory realization about Lynch as the original "birther" of the larval alien, given material form in a gigantic scene-stealing set-sculpture. Like all dream images, products of the primary process, this set sculpture is an object that condenses multiple associations into a singular, sublime thing: an elephant head; a recline in a couch or chair (what object is more associated with the role of a film director than their chair?); a long, movie-camera-like object that the being is staring into; and in a time-reversal of the usual trajectory of a killing shot, something has flown *out* of its heart instead of penetrating it. Again, from Giger's side, there was less anxiety and more simple regret about his rejected overture to collaborate with his most admired director. And this, I suspect, may account for why Giger's premonitory impossible object is less hideous and more sublime, lonely, even strangely hopeful—"elegiac," as one writer describes it.[35]

The nexus *Eraserhead-Alien-The Elephant Man* was the result of a creative vortex, two deep-diving genius visual artists brought into too-close proximity via a clusterfuck of precognition fueled on Lynch's side by terrible influence-anxiety and on Giger's side by longing and rejection. In his novel *Cat's Cradle*, Kurt Vonnegut described a group of people bound by synchronicity a Karass. He meant something warm and congenial by this—a kind of secret family bound by a common fate. The PSC I'm trying to describe is something more fraught, more ambivalent, the situation of creative contemporaries bound by common themes and concerns, but who find themselves awkwardly encountering their own ideas in each other's work and others' ideas in their own, despite their best efforts to avoid such a troubling or annoying situation. If I'm right in my earlier speculations, Darwin and Wallace might fit this description; elsewhere I describe a similar relationship between the Romantic poet/critic Samuel Taylor Coleridge and *Frankenstein* author Mary Shelley.[36] PSCs seem to me like astronauts bound to each other by a tether in deep space, circling, coming together and crashing, then flying apart, only to be yanked back together. They can't escape each other, try as they might. They become the victims of intertwining time loops, a kind of time knot.

In early 2002, in the chatroom of Lynch's website, davidlynch.com, a fan asked the director what he thought of Giger; Lynch replied, "One night I went to the place where Giger gets his ideas."[37] I can guess it was a subterranean place. Many of Giger's most astonishing scenes appear set in dimly-lit biomechanical chasms or canyons deep under some far-future, post-apocalyptic Earth.[38] However the director imagined it, I have little doubt this encounter in the unified field confirmed for him (if there was any real doubt to begin with) that the parallels between *Eraserhead* and *Alien* indeed arose from something more paranormal or spiritual than mere plagiarism. Another Lynch and *Alien* fan, Dominic Kulcsar, who compiled background material on the misunderstanding between Lynch and Giger on his blog *Alien Explorations*, remarked "It was a strange situation to have arisen. But that's the collective consciousness for you …"[39]

"Suppose it comes and envelopes your face while you are quietly asleep"

The deep strangeness of culture when social actors are superhumans, precogs, and dreamers is nowhere better illustrated, I believe, than in an uncanny premonition of *Alien* by, of all people, the French psycho-analyst Jacques Lacan, in a seminar that he gave at the École Normale Supérieure in Paris a decade and a half before that film came out. It is one of the oddest and most improbable examples of Bayardian future-influence (or plagiarism) that I know of—but its seeming impossibil-ity points to the last major theme we will be exploring in this book, the possible backward transmission of ideas in a society, across larger swathes of time than the individual lifespan.

First, some background: For Lacan, as for other thinkers in the French structuralist tradition, aspects of culture like myth and lan-guage came close to being a kind of collective unconscious, albeit of a less metaphysical or Platonic nature than Jung's construct.[40] Lacan re-worked Freud's core ideas around the insights of the early-20th-century Swiss linguist Ferdinand de Saussure, who argued that signifiers (words, symbols) derive their meaning from their place in chains or webs of other signifiers and are only arbitrarily connected to their referents. Lacan called this the Symbolic order, considering it loosely connected to the fantasy constructs of the more visual imagination (the Imagi-nary) and totally disconnected from the bedrock of reality, including the body and its drives (the Real). The personal unconscious is ruled, if not absolutely determined, by the structures of language, and his ana-lytic method was to reconstruct the chains of signifiers that are the fur-rows that channel a patient's desires.

Although he was far more Freudian than Jungian, Lacan was not a materialist. During a 1975 visit to MIT, he scandalized Noam Chomsky and other luminaries by repudiating neuroscience: "We think we think with our brains; personally, I think with my feet. That's the only way I really come into contact with anything solid."[41] Although Chomsky called him an "amusing and perfectly self-conscious charlatan,"[42] the psychoanalyst was being true to his philosophy in his MIT comment, not merely being provocative. Outside the bounds of the Symbolic, it is impossible to call the brain or even the external world "physical," because even that would be a symbolic designation. In fact, in his prin-cipled agnosticism about the materiality of mind, Lacan's thinking is strikingly similar to some interpretations of Zen Buddhism.[43]

Central to Lacan's theory is that, prior to acquiring language, the human being is like an undifferentiated protoplasm, a thing of pure libido or life-instinct; once the child enters the Symbolic order, this libido splits off and becomes a kind of separate, parasitic "organ" from which the person is forever alienated. Which brings us to his seeming *Alien* premonition: In his May 1964 seminar, "From Love to the Libido," the psychoanalyst symbolized this parasite-like nature of the libido through the figure of an impossible-hypothetical organism he called the "lamella" that flies out of an egg, attaches itself to a person's face, and cannot be cut off:

> Whenever the membranes of the egg in which the foetus emerges on its way to becoming a new-born are broken, imagine for a moment that something flies off, and that one can do it with an egg as easily as with a man, namely the *hommelette*, or the lamella.
>
> The lamella is something extra-flat, which moves like the amoeba. It is just a little more complicated. But it goes everywhere. And … it survives any division, and scissiparous intervention. And it can run around.
>
> Well! This is not very reassuring. But suppose it comes and envelopes your face while you are quietly asleep …
>
> I can't see how we would not join battle with a being capable of these properties. But it would not be a very convenient battle. This … organ, whose characteristic is not to exist, but which is nevertheless an organ … is the libido.
>
> It is the libido, qua pure life instinct, that is to say, immortal life, irrepressible life, life that has need of no organ, simplified, indestructible life.[44]

"Lamella" is a play on the words omelette and *homelette* ("manlet" or small man). Since his version of the unconscious consists of chains of word associations, Lacan's seminars were full of such puns.[45] But what any viewer of *Alien* will note is that this creature is an unbelievably exact template for the "face-hugger" in Scott's film.[46] When astronaut Kane (Hurt) cautiously approaches an egg in the hold of the Space Jockey's ship, it opens and a hand-like organism leaps onto his helmet, melts through the glass with acid, and fastens itself to his face. It then resists efforts of his crewmates to remove it from his face with a laser scalpel (surviving "scissiparous intervention" as Lacan put it), while it plants the seed of the chest-bursting Xenomorph in the astronaut's unconscious body. The crew then "join battle" with this superbeing. Like the lamella, the various stages of the Xenomorph's complex life-cycle seem like nothing more or less than "irrepressible ... indestructible life."[47]

Given what we have already seen in these last two chapters, you might expect me to confidently proclaim that the French psychoanalyst eventually saw *Alien* and was precognizing it here. Such a claim would be too far-fetched. Lacan was 78 and already failing in 1979, when *Alien* was released. He gave his final seminar, with difficulty, in 1980, and he died in 1981. Despite how sci-fi Lacan's description of the lamella seems—indeed, much of his work puts a slightly science-fictional spin on Freud's core ideas—he was not a science-fiction fan, so I have a hard time imagining that the elderly intellectual saw Ridley Scott's blockbuster when the French version appeared in Paris cinemas in September 1979. And while Lacan's description of the lamella was published in English translation in 1978 in his book *The Four Fundamental Concepts of Psychoanalysis*, it is just as hard for me to imagine any of *Alien*'s creators, least of all Dan O'Bannon, who described the face-hugger in his 1975 "Star Beast" script, being drawn to difficult French psychoanalytic theory, such that they could have been influenced by Lacan (either in the usual way or precognitively) when making their film.

But there is another (im)possibility to consider. Even though Lacan says his little story is a "myth"—he was explicitly trying to out-do Aristophanes' fable of the primordial dual-bodied human that Zeus sundered, as related in Plato's *Symposium*—the psychoanalyst is clearly describing a dream, probably a nightmare. A flat, amoeba-like thing flying from an egg and attaching itself to a sleeping person's face is a creature from the unconscious—but whose? It doesn't need to be the collective unconscious as Jung formulated it, nor Lynch's unified field. There could be an actual person who had this nightmare.[48]

Like Jung, and like Freud, Lacan spent his days receiving patients and listening to their dreams. Lacan left very little information about his patients—he wrote no case studies, etc., as Freud had, so mostly all we can do is speculate and surmise. But might Lacan have heard from one of his younger patients a nightmare of being smothered by a terrifying face-hugging creature? Might he have been so struck by the image that it found its way into his own thinking and writing as a figure for the irrepressible, immortal life-instinct? Then, as now, few took seriously the idea that dreams could literally be precognitive—it certainly wasn't on Lacan's radar, any more than it had been on Freud's—so nobody involved would have suspected that such a nightmare could have been premonitory of a terrifying scene in a popular American movie the patient might have gone on to see some years later. Striking or scary movie images are common targets of precognitive dreams, though, and *Alien* surely found its way into many people's unconscious that way.[49] For instance, in his book *Dreamer*, CG artist and precognitive dreamworker Andrew Paquette records a dream that foreshadowed the chestburster scene and other disturbing images from *Alien*, the night before his first viewing of the movie.[50]

We can go one step farther in our speculation here. Weirdly, one of the rare fragments of information about what psychoanalytic sessions with Lacan were like comes from a patient named Suzanne Hommel, whom Lacan treated in 1974. When Hommel was interviewed for a 2011 film commemorating the 30th anniversary of Lacan's death, she described a fascinating and life-changing moment from her therapy, in which she told her doctor a nightmare she had had of the Gestapo rounding up Jews in her neighborhood. She had been a child during the war and was clearly still haunted by those memories as an adult. Instead of finding archetypal meaning in this nightmare, as Jung might have done, or asking the patient to free-associate on its images, as Freud would have, Lacan rose, went to her, and like a shaman, stroked her face tenderly. She immediately understood this as a *geste à peau*—a transmutation of the word "Gestapo" into "gesture to the skin." It cured Hommel of her terror and remained a powerful moment in her life when she recalled it after nearly four decades. She said she could still feel Lacan's hand on her cheek.[51]

Going and touching a patient's face, however tenderly, would violate professional boundaries today—indeed much of what went on in the psychoanalytic clinics of Freud and Jung too would now be considered highly inappropriate. But it provides a striking window into Lacan's method. And it is strangely coincidental that this patient, *Hommel*, would fit right into that chain of word-associations around lamella—omelette, *hommelette*, and so on. Could *this patient*, nightmare-prone Suzanne Hommel—she would probably have been in her mid or late 30s when she was treated—have had a nightmare that was really a premonition of a scene in *Alien* a few years later? If so, did her dream enter Lacan's own precognitive unconscious to emerge in one of his own dreams or a bit of waking inspiration sometime in the spring of 1964, when he was formulating his ideas about the libido for that seminar?[52]

All we can do is treat this as an interesting thought experiment—we'll never know. But whether or not it occurred exactly as I imagine it might have, such a person-to-person transmission of powerful imagery back through time, via dreams, must at least sometimes occur in dream-sharing contexts like psychoanalytic communities and, as we will see later, in shamanic traditions. That face-hugger, conceived by O'Bannon and brought to irrepressible life by *Alien*'s creative team, is perhaps another of those impossible objects that especially like to fly backward through culture—like the alien larva going back to burst out of the imaginal daydreamworld of Lynch when he conceived *Eraserhead* in the early 1970s, or like little Ernst's spool retrofluxing to emerge under Kafka's pen (probably first his dreams) as Odradek, or like James Cameron's Terminator-arm being seized by Octavia Butler's precognitive imagination to become Dana's arm in *Kindred*. Over longer time-ranges, such retrograde transmission could be a hugely important vector of prophecy, ideas and images from the future being sent into the past of a society.

Whether we call it the collective unconscious or the unified field—or perhaps invoke some (slightly) older term like the Akashic records—our increasingly information-rich world invites some metaphysical mirror, a metaphorical wellspring of ideas and images that transcends us in space and time. About a decade after Jung first developed his ideas about the collective unconscious, the Russian Cosmist geochemist Vladimir Vernadsky and the French Jesuit theologian Teilhard de Chardin popularized the idea of a "noösphere," a superordinate "layer" of mind or reason over the biosphere and atmosphere, representing the highest or most advanced stage of human evolution.[53] It was somewhat like Jung's collective unconscious, but imagined as a future development rather than a psychic vestige of our ancestral past; and instead of being the core of the spherical world, it was an outer layer, metaphorically above rather than below.

Perhaps capitalizing on the intrinsic appeal of something like a noösphere, today's Silicon Valley entrepreneurs have leveraged the term "cloud"—a tech slang term from the early internet era—to encourage users to imagine the web's myriad servers as a nebulous and magical information field hovering, perhaps protectively, over our heads. We all know, though, that when you zoom in, the cloud evaporates, replaced by data centers and communications networks of unbelievable and growing complexity—real interactions among real people and real machines, unfolding in real (albeit inconceivably rapid) time. I argue that the same is true of the collective unconscious. It is a handy term, convenient shorthand for what, when you zoom in, is an unbelievably complex web of actual human beings' meaningful real-world encounters with each other and with the material stuff of their culture (books, movies, websites, etc.). The fact that those actual human beings are really superhuman superbeings (who mostly don't know it) and that they orient toward these meaningful encounters precognitively not only adds to the complexity and strangeness of this human info-cloud, it makes culture itself a paranormal, indeed impossibly alive (or alive-seeming) phenomenon.

The paranormal aliveness of culture is an idea that has been explored throughout Jeffrey Kripal's work; and some of the tech innovators and entrepreneurs interviewed in Diana Pasulka's *Encounters* imagine that future AI may be the realization of the noösphere, a true nonhuman intelligence already communicating with experiencers of the UFO phenomenon.[54] As we will see in the next chapter, earlier adumbrations of an intelligent informational entity autonomously meddling in human affairs can be found in the writings of one of the internet's pioneers, astronomer and ufologist Jacques Vallée, as well as in the novels and letters of Philip K. Dick, with his famous vast, active, living intelligence system, "VALIS." The irony is that their theories, too, may have arisen partly from the same trickster-like loops of consciousness and culture that gave rise to Jung's theory of the collective unconscious.

VALIS-PM
Philip K. Dick, Jacques Vallée, and Control Systems

When this irreversible learning is achieved, the UFO phenomenon may go away entirely. Or it may assume some suitable representation on a human scale. The angels may land downtown.
—Jacques Vallee, *The Invisible College* (1975)

I asked Zebra once what its name was. It had no name, in the sense that we have names (e.g., Bob, Pete, Tom, etc.). So I asked what it was. It responded in its beautiful bell-like voice,
"We are the Elohim."
—Philip K. Dick, Letter to Ira Einhorn (February 10, 1978)

In Steven Spielberg's 1977 blockbuster *Close Encounters of the Third Kind*, an electrical lineman in suburban Indiana named Roy Neary (Richard Dreyfus) sees and is sunburned by a UFO on a rural road at night. Thereafter, he becomes obsessed with mental images of a tall, strangely scored rock formation that he attempts to realize in sculpture—first in various "sketches," in shaving cream and fork-scored mashed potatoes, and then ultimately in a massive pile of dirt over chicken wire hauled into his family's living room from their yard. During his frenzied work, he happens to look over at the TV during a story about a (government-hoaxed) chemical spill at Devil's Tower,

Wyoming. He sees immediately that this distinctive formation in the middle of nowhere is what he has been obsessed with, and knows he has to go to that site, defying the roadblocks, and meet his destiny—a massive UFO landing.

It can sometimes be instructive to interpret science-fiction stories by temporarily removing the sci-fi elements, imagining the film without those. When you squint in this way at *Close Encounters*, it is clearly as much about art and the creative process as it is about alien visitation. Roy's arc in the film is exactly like the process of creating any artwork like a painting or a film or a novel: a sudden, unexpected, and even otherworldly inspiration and an overpowering need to explore or work through it as a creative problem, sometimes even at the expense of family and personal relationships. Inspiration famously never lets you go until you stand back, dirt all over your clothes and hair tousled, and, like God at the end of Creation, finally see the thing you've made as good. And if you are paying attention, you might then happen to look up and see a TV broadcast, or nowadays an item on social media, that matches what you created, leading you to wonder about synchronicity and to imagine a higher guiding hand in all of it.

Viewers of Spielberg's film naturally interpret Roy's creative obsession with Devil's Tower as a telepathic thought-implantation from the UFO he saw. That is probably what the director intended us to think—many real UFO witnesses experience what they interpret as telepathically transmitted thoughts and downloads. But note that it makes just as much sense to interpret Roy's tower-obsession as his own innate, usually ignored precognition, a possibly intrinsic part of his creative imagination that is awakened, not instilled or implanted, by his encounter. Crises and turning points of all kinds, not only paranormal ones, are liable to jostle loose the restraining bolt that has been inhibiting our creativity and precognitive capacities, leading to those synchronicity storms and other impossibly uncanny experiences. Indeed, yet another non-sci-fi way of reading *Close Encounters* is as a depiction of the Jungian midlife crisis and its psychic/psychological transformations as well as familial disruptions.[1]

When I think about Roy in *Close Encounters*, precognizing a news story with a pile of dirt and chicken wire in his living room, and with an estranged family who cannot comprehend him, I can't help thinking of Philip K. Dick. The same kind of uncanny engagement with popular culture, the literally alien-ated majesty of seeing in the media something he had just written about—not to mention the various upheavals, confusions, and pains that precognitive inspiration may cause in an artist's life—were all-too-familiar features of Dick's biography.[2]

No doubt as a function of his precognitive attunement, Dick was arguably the most brilliant pulp SF writer ever. Fortunately for the researcher, Dick was also a tour guide—if sometimes unreliable—to his own precognitive imagination. His habit of sharing his experiences in letters enables us to correlate the precognition in his creative output with the precognition in his dreams to a much greater degree than we can with most writers or artists. He was baffled, sometimes delighted, when his dreams and visions came true or when scenes from his stories played out in his life, and he was always eager to share these experiences with friends and associates. But some of the most stunning fruits of Dick's precognitive imagination escaped even his own notice. For example, the initial inspiration for what is often considered to be his masterpiece, his 1981 novel *VALIS*, was, I argue, a striking case of precognitive literary influence, Bayardian plagiarism by anticipation.

It began with the extended mystical experience or psychotic break (depending on your point of view) that Dick experienced in late winter and spring of 1974, which he called his "2-3-74" experience. After the delivery of a pain reliever to his house following a dental procedure, the writer began seeing visions and receiving downloads of information from somewhere or somewhen else. A feminine "AI voice" spoke to him in his hypnagogic states. At night, he also saw vast numbers of abstract artworks in a range of styles—what he interpreted as the contents of a Russian art museum—making him suspect he was the target of a Soviet ESP experiment. He also saw galley proofs of not-yet-written books and what he thought was information about the future printed on the back of a baby's cereal box, as well as other brilliant/surreal imagery. As the experience gradually waned over the next few months, he became increasingly depressed and paranoid and wrote furiously his ever-morphing theories of what had occurred in notes and letters to friends that were eventually published after his death as his *Exegesis*.

Whatever else it was, "2-3-74" seemed like the perfect premise for a novel, and already in June of that year, Dick started writing one. Thinking of it initially as a sequel to his 1960s alternate-history novel *The Man in the High Castle*, what Dick wrote during the remainder of 1974 was the first iteration of what eventually became *VALIS*. We are fortunate to have his first complete version, which he sent to his editor in 1976 and was published posthumously in 1985 as *Radio Free Albemuth*. It is relatively straightforward for a Dick novel and presents in the clearest form many aspects of his experience as he also told it in letters from the period. It also shows specifically how he opted to interpret those experiences literarily—that is, for purposes of telling a good sci-fi story—which is somewhat different from what he came to suspect really happened.

The novel focuses on Nicholas Brady, a record-store clerk in Berkeley and friend of the "Phil Dick" writer-narrator (the novel switches to Nicholas as the narrator midway through). Brady describes the nightly information downloads, as well as vivid previews of situations that he would then live through, such as a vision in 1971 of what he thought was a Mexican neighborhood that later turned out to be the LA suburb of Fullerton. This, like the downloads, was a real experience of Dick's—Fullerton is the city in Orange County where the writer ended up living from 1972 to 1976 (i.e., his vision was seemingly precognitive).[3] In the novel, Nicholas determines that the hypnagogic imagery he has been experiencing every night are transmissions from an extraterrestrial teaching satellite lurking since ancient times in our solar system, sent from the star system Albemuth (Fomalhaut). The satellite's transmissions are activating the higher consciousness of select people on Earth to resist the forces of an evil U.S. president, Ferris F. Fremont (numerologically 666, the Antichrist), who hails originally from Orange County—clearly and obviously Richard Nixon, thinly veiled. Dick in real life hated and feared Nixon, believing him responsible for the assassinations of the 1960s that preceded Nixon's rise to power. In the novel, Fremont's forces send a missile to destroy the satellite, and they hunt down and kill those who have been awakened by it, including eventually Nicholas.

Among Nicholas's (and the author's) experiences are "dreams of a peculiar repetitive nature, in which large open books were held up before his eyes, with printing like that of old Bibles."

> In each dream he either read or tried to read the printing, with meager results—at least to his conscious mind. There was no telling how much he absorbed unconsciously and repressed or forgot on awakening: probably a great deal. I had the impression, from what he said, that he was shown enough writing in his dreams to have taken the equivalent of a crash course—in what, neither he nor I could tell.[4]

When Nicholas describes the source of these mind-transmissions, he calls it "Valisystem-A"—Dick's original title for the novel—and then just "Valis," explaining that this term is short for "Vast Active Living Intelligence System."[5] This term may have come to Dick between June 28 and 29, 1974. On the 28th, he sent a long letter to a Canadian academic friend and fan, Peter Fitting, describing his experiences and his new novel idea in great detail but without mentioning the title. (It is the same letter where he described humanity being "talked to" by a future that is more coherent, animated, and purposeful than the present.) The next day, June 29, he wrote a shorter letter to his new pen pal, Claudia Bush, a student at a Midwestern university who had contacted him because she was writing a paper about his work; in this letter, he described the novel and gave his title and explanation of the acronym. I suspect that "Valis" or "Valisystem" came to Dick first, perhaps on the night of the 28th, and that his unpacking of this word, "Vast Active Living Intelligence System" is what linguists call a back-formation. In his letter to Fitting, he described many strange words coming to him in his hypnagogic states, including names like "Sadasa Ulna" that became characters in his novel. "Valis" may have been one of these words, and if so, it would have invited or demanded some kind of linguistic exegesis.[6]

In 1974, the same year Dick had his experience and wrote this first iteration of his novel, San Francisco computer scientist and astronomer Jacques *Vallée* wrote a book about the intersections of ESP research and UFOs called *The Invisible College*. With chapters related to his work with UFO witnesses in America and France, psychic research involving famous psychic and UFO contactee Uri Geller, and the ufological dimensions of religious visions such as Marian apparitions, it is a strange and fascinating book. It explores the linkages throughout history of psychic phenomena, nonhuman/alien visitation, and the roots of religion. Vallée specifically argues that encounters such as the appearance of the Virgin Mary at Fatima in 1917 and similar events that fill the larger literature on UFO-like encounters represent a "control system." This system interacts with our mythologies and spiritual beliefs via exceptional individuals who, he notes, frequently experience enhanced psychic ability and mystical as well as telepathic-like experiences during, preceding, or in the aftermath of their otherworldly encounters. Some, he describes, report mechanical voices telepathically being beamed into their heads.

In the book, Vallée cites a notable conversation with the French writer/editor/provocateur Jacques Bergier, best-known to American readers of occultism and the paranormal as coauthor of the early-1960s bestseller *The Morning of the Magicians*:

> In 1973, Jacques Bergier proposed to me an amusing explanation for the existence of these books which seem to emanate from a cosmic source and, like the Bible, have come to us through automatic writing or some other form of psychic revelation. There exists, he postulates, a civilization in our galaxy which is broadcasting at regular intervals some cosmic education program, much in the same manner as the French National Radio is every day broadcasting selected lectures in philosophy and history from the Sorbonne. Just as the French are beaming these broadcasts to Africa and other remote places, we could well visualize an advanced civilization broadcasting very advanced concepts on psychic wavelengths, to be picked up by gifted prophets on earth and millions of other retarded planets![7]

This idea of Bergier's is the *exact* premise of Dick's literary spin on his "2-3-74" experience, as found in *Radio Free Albemuth* and, later, *VALIS*. Indeed, the entire premise of Vallée's book, of a nonhuman control system, seems like it could have "inspired" Dick—it is a *Vallée control system*, uncannily similar to "Valisystem." But chronologically, an ordinary influence is impossible: *The Invisible College* was not published until 1975, a year after Dick came up with the word "Valis" and wrote the first iteration of his story. Vallée and Dick did not know each other and never met, although the ufologist read some of the novelist's letters to a mutual friend in 1978, as we will see shortly. I confirmed with Tessa Dick, Phil's wife from 1973 until 1977, that he did indeed read some of Vallée's books during a period of intense ufological interest in 1977. Tessa could not recall which books her husband read, but *The Invisible College* was the most recent at that point.

I suggest that Dick was precognizing *The Invisible College* as part of his "2-3-74" awakening-slash-breakdown, "downloading" that future reading experience among the other images and mumbling voices filling his liminal hypnagogic world during those months. Supporting this interpretation is the fact that "Valis" looks specifically like a French word, which an English reader (without the all-caps and the explanation "Vast Active Living Intelligence System") might naturally presume was pronounced the way "Vallee" looks (va-LEE); the accent over the first *e* (making it va-LAY) doesn't appear on the covers of most of the ufologist's English books. Dick might have heard "Vallee" in one of his hypnagogic states and naturally assumed it was spelled "Valis."

"Valis" *is* "Vallee," I believe. It was a name and a nexus of associated ideas transmitted from Dick's own future, from a reading experience about three years hence, and thus another case of literary influence that, like the planet Mercury, sometimes goes in retrograde—even though the ultimate iteration of Dick's premise was only ever published some years after *The Invisible College*, the book I believe he was precognizing.

Although Dick never explicitly drew a connection to Vallée, he was uniquely open to such a precognitive interpretation of his experiences. Several years earlier, an article by Soviet parapsychologist Nicolai Kozyrev had suggested to him that time was an energy, which could reverse its flow under special circumstances. He believed in fact that he had specifically precognized that article when writing his 1969 novel *Ubik*, about a spray-can product with time-retarding properties.[8] The novel also links the product Ubik to the degradation of the atmosphere, a couple years before the impact of aerosols from spray cans on the ozone layer became a focus of environmental awareness and activism.[9] And in those first descriptions of "2-3-74" in letters to Fitting and Bush in late June 1974, Dick framed his experiences as retrograde transmissions from the future via tachyons, which he read about in an article on coincidence by Arthur Koestler in the new (July 1974) issue of *Harper's*:

> In some laboratories an active search is going on for hypothetical 'tachyons'—particles of cosmic origin which are supposed to fly faster than light and consequently, according to orthodox Relativity Theory, in a reversed time direction. They would thus carry information from the future into our present, as light and X-rays from distant galaxies carry information from the remote past of the universe into our now and here. In the light of these developments, we can no longer exclude on a priori grounds the theoretical possibility of precognitive phenomena ...[10]

Such backward-in-time tachyonic broadcasts made the most sense of the images, text, and mumblings Dick had received nightly for three months beginning in March of that year, especially since some of them did seem precognitive. In his June 28, 1974, letter to Fitting, Dick described how these physical speculations opened the door to a kind of teleology that in the past could only have been articulated in religious terms:

> Without the tachyon theory I would lack any kind of scientific formulation, and would have to declare that "God has shown me the sacred tablets in which the future is written" and so forth, as did our forefathers, back on the deserts of Israel under the sky as they tended their sleeping flocks. Koestler also points out that according to modern theory the universe is moving from chaos to form; therefore tachyon bombardment would contain information which expressed a greater degree of Gestalt than similar information about the present; it would, to us at this time continuum, seem more living, more animated by a conscious spirit, thus giving rise to the idea of God. This would definitely give rise to the idea of purpose, in particular purpose lying in the future.[11]

It is possible that Dick's UFO interest in 1977 was sparked by seeing *Close Encounters*, which was released in mid-November of that year and itself had been significantly inspired by Vallée's research. The Frenchman was the model for Spielberg's fictional ufologist "Lacombe" played by Francois Truffaut. The movie made a big impression on Dick, who mentioned it in letters late that year in connection to his own evolving theories of extraterrestrial intelligence. And one of Dick's dreams from three years earlier, in December 1974, which he related in another one of his many letters to Bush, seems to have strikingly precognized that exciting movie experience and various associations to it in his future.[12] In the dream, The Nitty Gritty *Dirt* Band introduce him to a world of childlike "shy and gentle creatures," who show him a piece of futuristic technology. He attempts to take a cake that has been scored around its edges as though by a fork, which he believes is some kind of relief map. One of the creatures in a position of authority forbids him eating the cake, telling him that it belongs to "Mrs. Fields."

On awakening, he associated this person with famous UFO abductee "Betty Fields"; in fact, he was misremembering the name—it is Betty *Hill*, wife of Barney Hill. A "dirt" revelation, child or childlike alien beings, a piece of fork-scored food that's really a map and that belongs to a UFO witness/abductee—it's a strikingly precognitive dream about Spielberg's blockbuster, I believe. (The cake was possibly precognitive in another way: Mrs. Fields was a brand of soft cookies and brownies that opened its first store in 1977 in Palo Alto and quickly became a popular and widely advertised nationwide franchise—thus from the same time period as *Close Encounters*.[13])

Interestingly, in Dick's dream, the "shy and gentle creatures" were really ourselves in the future—thus a built-in time gimmick. At the end of his letter to Bush, and after offering various joke explanations for his experiences (including that he was the "reincarnation" of Jefferson Starship lead singer Grace Slick, still very much alive), he writes:

> Claudia, let me lay this theory on you, seriously. These are not space travelers, they are time travelers, from the future; they are here to tinker with our present, to make small but vital adjustments in order to direct it toward a specific outcome.[14]

Although Dick tried many different interpretations of "2-3-74" over the subsequent months and years, he often returned to the idea that he was receiving messages from the future or even that he was being haunted by a long, perhaps immortal version of himself that extended through time, including both the distant Roman past (where he was a secret Gnostic Christian) and perhaps the far future. His evolving understanding took him ultimately in a theological direction—he didn't really think there was an extraterrestrial probe in orbit awakening a psychic elect to the crimes of Nixon. But the latter, dark Gnostic premise had color and drama—it made for legitimately terrific (if not terrifically legitimate) science fiction. So that was the direction his creative imagination took him for the first version of his novel. In *VALIS*, he incorporated the plot of *Radio Free Albemuth* in the form of a film-within-the story, representing just one of the main character Horselover Fat's multiple interpretations of his strange experiences.

THE LORD IS AN EXTRATERRESTRIAL

Culture is a *vast artistic-literary influence sea, precognitively mediated* (VALIS-PM—the nighttime formulation). It is almost as if, the more that geniuses try to find their own unique truth, the more they discover their own future ambivalent encounters with each other and accidentally wind up borrowing (plagiarizing, in Bayard's terms) from each other in their futures. As we saw with David Lynch and H. R. Giger, sometimes precognitive influence is bidirectional, intensifying the convergence or resonance of ideas between creators. Could Vallée have been precognizing Dick and *VALIS* when he wrote *The Invisible College*, the same way that Dick was precognizing Vallée? It is not impossible.

Like Dick, Vallée was (and is) extremely aware of the operation of precognition in his own life and work, and his journals published as *Forbidden Science* record numerous precognitive dreams and even instances of waking precognitive inspiration. In the third volume, *On the Trail of Hidden Truths*, for instance, he records an episode virtually identical to Craig Sinclair's BLACK MAGICIANS experience. During a long wait to board a plane in Sydney at the end of a business trip to Australia in August 1980, he found himself toying with an idea for a novel about terrorists taking over an oil drilling platform. The movie that he then watched during his flight was a thriller starring Roger Moore called *ffolkes* … about terrorists taking over a North Sea oil rig.[15] Being friends with the CIA-funded ESP researchers and psychics at Stanford Research Institute like Hal Puthoff and Ingo Swann, whose work led to the famous Star Gate remote viewing program, he understood then-current thinking about psychic abilities and was early to point out the inherent difficulty of distinguishing clairvoyance from precognition.[16] Yet some of his synchronistic experiences seemed, to him, to defy any explanation involving existing ideas of space and time.

In the second volume of *Forbidden Science*, subtitled *California Hermetica*, the ufologist records a walk he took one day in October 1973 with Puthoff. Vallée was telling his companion he thought the UFO problem and parapsychology were connected and that they were both more than just scientific questions but were also hermetic quests or initiations, "an enigma like that of the Sphinx" … at which point, the two men turned a corner and found themselves face to face with a pair of sphinxes behind a chain-link fence. Vallée writes with amusement that his companion "must have thought I had known about the statues all along and had maneuvered him to the spot deliberately."[17]

Vallée came to regard such experiences as what he called "intersigns," levers in that control system shaping human history and culture.

Another intersign in the winter of 1975-1976—although really, I argue, a time loop—was a turning point in the ufologist's thinking about the nature of psychic and paranormal phenomena. Returning to Paris from a trip to Barcelona in December 1975, Vallée was dragging a suitcase through a corridor of the Paris metro when his eye was drawn to a piece of graffiti scrawled in black pen on a poster:

THE LORD IS AN EXTRATERRESTRIAL WHO
HAS RETURNED IN A FLYING SAUCER.
Order of Melchizedek,
Rue Jules Valles Paris XI[18]

The very next day, the ufologist tracked down the headquarters of the Order of Melchizedek in a working-class district, on a street with a name close to his own, and received the standard guru's greeting to a stranger, "You have come at the appointed time."[19] He spoke with champagne-drinking but otherwise impoverished members of the sect, who believed themselves to be in contact with extraterrestrials trying to elevate our civilization from barbarism. On his return home to America, he discovered that there was a branch of the group in San Francisco. He attended their gatherings to learn more about UFO beliefs as a kind of modern cult.

The incredible intersign occurred just two months after his initial encounter with the Melchizedek group, when he was in Los Angeles and hailed a cab from his hotel on Sunset Boulevard to get to a radio station for an interview on la Cienega Boulevard. When he looked at the receipt the next day, to submit his expenses for the trip, he saw that the erratically driving "buxom blonde" cab driver who had picked him up had signed her name … Melchizedek.[20] Checking the LA phone directory, he found only one person with that surname. The odds against that one person driving the cab he happened to hail on an LA street, in the midst of a research obsession with a UFO cult called the Order of Melchizedek, are impossible to calculate but must be astronomical.

Much like Carl Jung decades earlier, Vallée concluded that a new theory of information and causation may need to be built to account for such astonishing coincidences. A Newtonian causal understanding of events is not up to the task; if, on the other hand, we imagine the universe as organized as a kind of vast database of information, where our concerns and obsessions become search terms, we may (he suggested) inadvertently summon or attract events associatively related to them.

It was in the 1970s that physicists were beginning to rethink matter as information and causation as a kind of information-processing, or computation. At the end of the decade that followed, physicist John Wheeler coined the phrase "It from Bit," to express the idea that the universe can be thought of as a big computer. (The science of quantum computing emerged from this paradigm.) But Vallée, who melded his understanding of computer networks and databases with a love of medieval and Renaissance natural philosophy, pointed out that the organization of information in a computer memory closely resembles the premodern view of the universe governed by correspondences. The Renaissance alchemist Paracelsus wrote that all things bear some "signature" of their associative links to other objects in God's creation.

In the 1979 book Vallée wrote based partly on his Melchizedek research, *Messengers of Deception*, he suggested that space and time as we understand them are arbitrary cultural constructs and that a new physics of information could adopt the hermetic idea that the world may really be organized as a vast system of meaningful correspondences in which (shifting to a computer-science idiom) "keywords" could function as search terms and evoke a particular response:

> If there is no time dimension as we usually assume there is, we may be traversing events by *association*. Modern computers retrieve information associatively. You "evoke" the desired records by using keywords, *words of power*: you request the intersection of "microwave" and "headache," and you find twenty articles you never suspected existed. Perhaps I had unconsciously posted such a request on some psychic bulletin board with the keyword "Melchizedek." If we live in the associative universe of the software scientist rather than the sequential universe of the spacetime physicist, then miracles are no longer irrational events.[21]

In other words, researching Melchizedek was (in Vallée's view) like entering that name in a cosmic Google search; a nearby cab driver by that name was the top hit.

The Paracelsian cosmos ruled by signs and signatures is not too different from the personal unconscious as mapped in Freudian and especially Lacanian psychoanalysis. Lacan was famous for saying the unconscious is "structured like a language," its objects deriving their meaning from their connections to other objects, the chains or webs of associations in which they are embedded. The associative structure of the psyche is not really controversial, even for those dubious of psychoanalysis. Psychologists who study memory know that information is stored and accessed in the human brain associatively. In searching our memories for information, we do precisely what Vallée described: We "traverse events by association," and those associations operate exactly the way Freud described in his work on dreams: Associations are irrational, governed by root metaphors that are often highly concrete (even superstitiously simple-minded), and operate by puns and various literary devices and tropes—precisely the logic of surrealism, myth, and folklore. And they are situated in distinct spatial environments that are often familiar or related to the environments of our early life and formative years. One of the most compelling recent theories of dreaming is that it is the nightly experience of new long-term memory associations or junctions being created in the brain—essentially the "art of memory" practiced by Renaissance mages like Ramon Llull and Giordano Bruno, but operating automatically while we sleep.[22] The psyche is essentially hermetic in structure, even if the Real (per the Lacanian logic) evades the grasp of the Symbolic.

I suggest that the associative laws that govern memory and imagination can account for intersigns like Melchizedek, the same way they account for other synchronistic experiences. We only have to grant that the imagination is a precognitive imagination and that memories are sometimes from our future. Again, synchronicity is what it feels like when we precognitively orient toward rewards and interesting turning points, even objectively random coincidences, without being aware that it is our future self pulling the strings. As I hinted earlier, I even wonder whether *all* our thoughts and (what we imagine to be) intentions might really be premonitions of salient experiences, encounters, and discoveries ahead in our lives. Even our obsessions and neuroses are frequently premonitory, as I argued in *Time Loops*. To have a mind, I propose, is really to be a medium.

If so, it would have been the ufologist's precognitive unconscious—or, Bankei's Unborn—that nudged him toward the metaphor of the riddle of the sphinx at the same time he and Puthoff were about to come face to face with real sphinxes on their walk. And according to this logic, the radiant, impossible name Melchizedek on that cab receipt in the landscape of Vallée's future could have skewed the ufologist's attention toward noticing that name scrawled on the wall of Paris metro months earlier, taking it as potentially significant, and then studying the group that it represented. It was the cab receipt that would have retro-caused his prior interest in Melchizedek the cult even though it was that prior interest that made him notice the receipt and find the whole thing incredible. Another loop.

Our natural causal bias acts as a force field against such retrocausal interpretations, though. We will gravitate to some more causally intuitive framing, such as that the ufologist's interest in Melchizedek the cult "summoned" the LA cab driver from some universal server, the same way Jung imagined that a conversation about scarabs during a particular therapy session summoned a rose-chafer beetle to his office window. Such a framing is abetted by the seeming mismatch between the magnitude of Melchizedek as a consequential international UFO group and a mere "random" LA cab driver with that surname showing up shortly *after* he had begun his research. The latter encounter has less weight and objective importance in this daisy chain of events, so we have a hard time imagining it as in any way causal, even retrocausal. It's as wrong-feeling as the entropy-violating logic of a film running backwards—a shattered mug drawing together on the ground and flying up, intact, to the edge of a table. In the purely physical world, it is the broken mug that has more entropy and less utility—indeed it has become trash—but in the subjective landscape of one's morning, those shards may be far more impactful or salient, especially if it happened to be your favorite mug.

The father of modern information theory, Bell Telephone Laboratories mathematician Claude Shannon, equated the amount of entropy in a system with the amount of information it contains. However, he also recognized that in order to work with and use information scientifically and technologically, one had to divorce it from the strictly psychological problem of meaning, or the value an individual user assigns to a piece (or bit) of information.[23] But in a universe that includes time-traveling tesseract brains, meaning—that is, subjective mattering or salience—is what we can no longer leave out of our causal stories. Of all the various points in Vallée's life when he intersected with the word "Melchizedek," it was his discovery of the name on his cab receipt that was the *most* salient and impactful, precisely because it was so impossible. It was a major prediction error. So I suggest that the ufologist's research into Melchizedek was effectively a premonitory "symptom" of that later discovery of the cab receipt, even though he only noticed the receipt (and it only mattered) because of his research.

Which brings us back to Vallée's connection to Dick. I suggest—although here, it would be less easy to "prove"—that the ufologist's discovery of his own surname, alienated in the writings of a clearly visionary but off-kilter science-fiction writer, might have had a similar retro-effect on his thinking that the discovery of that buxom blonde cabbie's surname on that receipt did.

In his journals, Vallée frequently remarks on the similarity of *VALIS* to his own thinking, and even counts Dick's writings as among the literary works he most treasures. In 1988, he wrote that Dick "touched the ultimate problem": that there is no God or Devil, but "a psychic system close to us, a gigantic entity, a Pacific ocean of the spirit" in which humans are but droplets.[24] Even though the ufologist and the novelist never met, it may be significant that Vallée got a preview of *VALIS* three years before it was published. In the winter of 1977-78, an associate of his, the environmental activist and connector Ira Einhorn, published "A Disturbing Communique" in the counterculture journal *The CoEvolution Quarterly* about alleged Soviet psychotronic research—attempts to use microwaves and other broadcast technologies in mind control.[25] Dick read this article and wrote several long letters to Einhorn about his "2-3-74" experience and his own supposition that he might have been the target of exactly such an experiment. Probably assuming the ufologist would find them interesting, Einhorn then shared copies of these letters with Vallée. In the second of the letters, Dick specifically named the ET entity he was in contact with "V.A.L.I.S." (as well as "Zebra" because of its ability to camouflage itself).[26] He wrote that he thought his ability to see and interact with this entity was enhanced or potentiated by the Soviet transmissions. It was on the basis of these letters that Vallée saw the close link between his own thinking and that of Dick but also drew the conclusion that Dick's insights came with mental illness and some deep trauma.[27]

At the end of Dick's first letter, dated February 9, 1978, he specifically requested that Einhorn keep what he wrote, or at least his identity, confidential—a request that Einhorn clearly ignored. This was by no means the most serious ethical lapse in Einhorn's life. Exactly at the time Dick was corresponding with him, through the year of 1978,

Einhorn's former girlfriend Holly Maddux was slowly decomposing in a trunk in a closet of Einhorn's Philadelphia apartment. She had gone missing the previous September. Police found her body in March 1979 (neighbors had been complaining for months of a strange smell), and this led to Einhorn's arrest and then flight to Europe, where he lived for many years under an assumed name and no longer had contact with Dick or Vallée. Einhorn eventually was extradited to the United States, convicted of Maddux's murder, and spent the rest of his life in prison. Vallée's journals contain several reflections on Einhorn and the tragedy that befell Maddux.

Psychological scientists know that we are drawn to pay attention to our name (or variants) when we see it. And we have a special relationship to our surname, in particular. It is what Lacan called "the Name of the Father," the central signifier that puts the young human in the realm of the Symbolic order, alienated from their parasite-like split-off libido or life-instinct (that lamella). In *Time Loops*, I "went there" in reflecting psychoanalytically on Dick's relationship to his own unique surname (I'm a phallogocentric male author, remember) … but what about Vallée? The Order of Melchizedek had its headquarters on Rue Jules *Valles*, for instance—did that help draw the ufologist's attention in that metro station? And more importantly, did the word "V.A.L.I.S." radiate or glow when the ufologist first encountered it in the letters Einhorn gave him in 1978, in conjunction with ideas strikingly close to what he had argued in *The Invisible College*?

There is no smoking gun, in this case, but given the circumstances, it is surely a possibility. Again, anxiously original artists and writers (and scientists, in the case of Vallée) are drawn to each other precognitively—it is the anxiety of influence that draws them, like a gravitational pull. Despite struggling to avoid each other, they collide. It reminds me of the way billiard balls shot backward in time at their younger selves always drive them *toward* the wormhole, not away from it—one of the ironic effects of time loops. I imagine that when Vallée first encountered Dick's beliefs about a nonhuman psychic system in those letters, it would have been like being drawn to a child he did not know he had fathered. Little did he suspect that he himself had provided the name for Dick's control system. And while it was certainly his own father, not Dick's imagination, that gave the ufologist *his* surname, it is not impossible that Dick's ideas in those letters could have precognitively magnetized his thinking when he wrote *The Invisible College* back in 1974.[28] I specifically wonder whether the weird and perhaps uncomfortable circumstance of having read those letters against the sender's explicit wishes, thanks to the mediation of a man who turned out to be a murderer, might have added to their ultimate salience. Those letters might have been brightly radioactive in the landscape of Vallée's long self—forbidden knowledge, if not exactly forbidden science.

In their evocative metaphors of intelligent electricity and giant psychic entities just out of view, controlling our lives and interactions, Californians Dick and Vallée were both reaching toward an understanding of the same thing Jung was trying to understand decades earlier in Zurich: the stunning effects produced when we engage with culture and other cultural actors precognitively, with only a dim understanding—or for most people, no understanding—that we ourselves (our long selves) are the agents of these uncanny, impossible convergences. Our own precognition makes culture itself a kind of vast, active, living intelligence system (or vast artistic-literary influence sea). And as I tentatively proposed in the case of the theory of natural selection, *if* the precognitive influence between Dick and Vallée did indeed go both ways, then it is conceivable that *nobody* "came up with" the idea of a nonhuman/psychic control system: It may have simply arisen from a loop between two creative lives—that is, from nothing and nobody.

The Information Singularity[29]

Early in *Radio Free Albemuth*, Nicholas explains to the Phil Dick narrator an experience of seeing himself standing by the bed gazing down at him protectively, theorizing that it must have been his older self, visiting him across time. This was based on an experience Dick actually had in the 1950s—waking up and seeing a figure standing over his bed. When he reflected on this experience decades later, he surmised that that very hindsight reflection on this episode was possibly a real transtemporal visitation by his present self to his younger self. Remembering his past was, at least in that case, actually projecting himself *into* his past, astrally. (Since writing my book on precognitive dreams, *Precognitive Dreamwork and the Long Self*, I have received emails from several people reporting similar experiences.)

In the novel, the narrator raises the following doubt: "Had it been a future self he would not have recognized it, since it would have been altered from the features he saw in the mirror. No one could ever recognize his own future self."[30] That last sentence should be double- or triple-underscored, in bold, and goes back to the laws governing time travel that we explored earlier in the book: There's no such thing as clear, video-quality precognition. Premonitions of the future are always oblique and incomplete. You cannot recognize them for what they are except (sometimes) in hindsight. It is not really because of our aging facial features, nor some paranormal force that would distort things. It is that in the world built from time loops there is simply no backstory to a non-misrecognized visitation across time. It can't happen, simply because it didn't. (If you're shopping for a good Zen koan, that last sentence is quite effective.)

Because of our ever-evasive Br'er Rabbit-like free will, we would act to prevent any foreseen future by creating a different one—again, even if the foreseen future is generally positive. We humans are incorrigible that way. And since our efforts to create a better future are always part of the backstory of the actual future, the future is always transfigured when we perceive it in the present. It appears or is interpreted under some kind of symbolic aspect. It is common for dreams and visionary states to personify abstractions or use objects to stand for people. Even our thoughts are transfigured—again, our premonitions get interpreted and experienced as expectations, wishes, or just random musings. We sometimes experience precognition as decisions that feel freely willed—an argument made by parapsychologist Edwin May, who took over the ESP research connected with the Star Gate program after Puthoff's departure in the 1980s.[31] It is why a precog's life, in hindsight, so often seems governed by some bewildering trickster. And of course, as we've seen repeatedly, creative intentions and decisions can often be premonitory too.

In the mid-1980s, Vallée's theory that the UFO phenomenon involves a kind of equivalence of energy and information drove him toward a truly inspired project: to build on his mountain land at Spring Hill, near San Francisco, a combination library and observatory, what he called an "information singularity." His idea was that by concentrating esoteric knowledge and by being a site for meditation and reading, this singularity would actually coax the phenomenon out of hiding, into the open, so he could observe it with the aid of his telescope. So, like Jung six decades earlier at his Bollingen retreat on the shore of Lake Zurich, Vallée built a tower, filled it with his substantial library of esoteric books, and decorated it with stained-glass windows showing figures that were central to his personal mythology: Bishop Agobard welcoming a visitor from Magonia (the legendary land beyond the clouds), an imp modeled on one at Chartres Cathedral, a knight bearing the

Holy Grail, Isis holding the Book of the World, the 12th-century German polymath and mystic Hildegard of Bingen, and the Old Testament prophet Melchizedek, after whom the Order of Melchizedek had been named. Each scene appeared under the sign of the rose (*sub rosa*, meaning secret or esoteric and also signaling the ufologist's lifelong interest in the Rosicrucian order).

In his journals, Vallée records much enjoyable time and study at his Spring Hill retreat in the late 1980s and early 1990s. But this information singularity did not have the permanence of Jung's Bollingen tower, nor did it exert the gravitational attraction toward nonhuman intelligences (or control systems) that Devil's Tower exerted in Spielberg's *Close Encounters*. By the mid-1990s, the local encroachment of illegal marijuana growers in the area had made the location less safe and appealing to spend time at; and the ufologist had observed no obvious UFO-related phenomena there. So he moved the books and stained glass, first to another weekend home in Point Reyes, then a few years later back to San Francisco.[32] "They" did not take the bait.

Or did they?

I first heard of, and became fascinated by, Vallée's library of hermetic texts in the books that first drew me to Jeffrey Kripal's work more than a decade ago, *Authors of the Impossible* and *Mutants and Mystics*.[33] In his research for those books, Kripal had visited Vallée, and being a bibliophile, he took particular interest in Vallée's library. By this time, the books and the windows had been installed back in San Francisco, where the volumes exceeded the carrying capacity of the ufologist's bookcases. Kripal writes:

> I had spent time in other writers' libraries and found this an especially direct pathway to their authorial souls. These are symbolic spaces whose details are all significant: which books are there (or not there); how they are organized; what sort of art sits alongside which books; and so on. The Vallee Collection, which spills out into rooms and hallways, did not disappoint.[34]

As a modest library-assembler myself, I know from personal experience that it is the secret wish of bibliophiles to have their libraries be interesting to others. Freudians, move along, but size matters. We collect books for ourselves, but deep down we are imagining our book collection being perused and admired by guests and friends and strangers.

Vallée naturally wanted someone—or some *thing*—to take an interest in his library. He envisioned summoning a UFO, or perhaps some ufological message, some synchronicity, to manifest, like the alchemists of old. I picture Rembrandt's famous etching of Faust in his study, marveling at a luminous symbol-wheel that has appeared mid-air. Well, in the future, someone did finally visit his library, and wrote at great length about it.

In *Mutants and Mystics*, Kripal writes that among the books in Vallée's collection that the two bibliophiles discussed was a collection of illustrated autobiographical narratives called *Opus* by Pre-Raphaelite-influenced comics artist Barry Windsor-Smith. Windsor-Smith described some stunning precognitive visions while he was working on *Conan the Barbarian* comics for Marvel in the early 1970s, as well as a trans-temporal visitation to his child self, strikingly similar to what Dick experienced and described in *Radio Free Albemuth*.[35] (In a second *Opus* volume, the artist also described a sighting of a giant UFO in 1966 that resembled the mothership in *Close Encounters*.) And in a long chapter on the ufologist in *Authors of the Impossible*, Kripal summarizes Vallée's writings and his thoughts on the nature of the UFO phenomenon, including the idea that it represents a control system that may be reaching across time. Like Dick—and who knows, perhaps even partly because of Dick—Vallée grasped that whatever it is that is intervening and shaping human history via our beliefs is doing so from a position in our own future, a future that is smarter than the present. As Kripal describes,

> the psychic technology Vallee imagines depends on the manipulation of time as well as space ... a future technology projected, somehow, back into our present. Such a hypothesis ... implies that these need not be space aliens from another planet. They may well be human beings from another time, from the future. They may be us. The future technology of folklore that Vallee is imagining here, in other words, is a technology that we may be using on ourselves to manipulate our own past, to control, as it were, our belief systems and mythologies that lie well below the present political system or cultural fad of the day.[36]

By the time they met in person, Kripal had already sent advance avatars into the ufologist's library, in the form of his books on mysticism and religious experience, his own symbol-radiating orb hovering in the air. Kripal notes that when Vallée first read his books, he was impressed by the constant appearance of the word "hermeneutics"—an academic term that was not yet part of Vallée's lexicon but that resonated strongly with him. Vallée's entire work on UFOs takes a hermeneutic approach—closely related to his own explicitly *hermetic* approach, as both words are rooted in the messenger, diplomat, and translator role of the Greek god Hermes.

I consider it more than a funny coincidence that Vallée should have devoted such attention to his library-tower in the late 1980s, imagining that it might attract some manifestation, some "they" (or "we") that may be reaching from the future into their/our past, and then two decades later would entertain amid those books and art a scholar of religion who found in that library the key to his hermetic quest, writing about it, at length, in not just one but two books. Few bibliophiles are so fortunate—as Cy Twombly said of the Frenchwoman who disrobed in front of his painting in Houston, "That's pretty good. No one can top that one." Was Rice University historian of religions Jeffrey Kripal the "UFO" Vallée had been waiting for?

Kripal's visits proved hugely significant for the ufologist. During a later meeting with Kripal in Berkeley in 2014, Vallée, then in his 70s, expressed concern about the ultimate fate of his research archives, his voluminous files from decades of work as a UFO researcher. This wish to create a safe home for his files to be studied by others after his death led ultimately to the creation of the Archives of the Impossible at Rice University, beginning with the donation of Vallée's archive in 2018. The Rice archive quickly grew to include other archives related to the study of UFOs and ESP research, such as those of the CIA-funded remote viewing program at Stanford Research Institute in the 1970s and 1980s and the thousands of letters received by horror novelist Whitley Strieber after the publication of his 1987 book *Communion*.

I'll just say it: I think Vallée's intention to create a library/observatory/tower to attract the phenomenon was really a premonition of Kripal's arrival and involvement in his life two decades later. Like all premonitory hopes or wishes, the effect he imagined/hoped to produce with this information singularity was transfigured in and by his imagination. It acted like a trickster. Only after he thought he had failed and dismantled his information singularity did the UFO show up, in human disguise, and take a special interest in his volumes spilling out into the hallways in his San Francisco home—what was present, what was missing, how they were arranged, and so on. That Vallée had thought of his Spring Hill project as an "information singularity" is, to me, the clearest support (there can never be proof) for this thesis. The Archives of the Impossible is a real information singularity, and indeed, in his opening address for the Archives, with Vallée in attendance, Kripal explicitly compared the ufologist's initial donation to a "black hole" whose gravitational pull drew in those other important contributions.[37] A singularity is another term for black hole. Yet Kripal was not thinking of Vallée's information singularity when he used this metaphor—he intended his metaphor only to signify the "gravitas" of the ufologist's gift.[38]

I certainly wouldn't suggest that UFOs are nothing more than symbolically disguised religion professors in our future, or that there is nothing more to the paranormal than our own yet-unlived biography. But I think that that biography, one's serpent-seraph long self, is a big unacknowledged (and as-yet, mostly unstudied) part of it. Our future shows up, symbolically transformed, in our nightly dreams and waking synchronicities (or intersigns). And if you are a creator of any kind, it shows up, transformed, in your creative inspirations and intentions— including the building of alchemical-ufological towers. If I had to offer my own control-system theory, it would be precisely this: It is Bankei's Unborn, the time-looping, bootstrapping nature of creation constantly operating in our lives, drawing in meaning and meaningful encounters like a gravitational singularity. But since the one thing the imagination cannot imagine is *nothing*—one of Freud's greatest insights[39]—it supplies some metaphoric *something* as a screen or placeholder for the ex-nihilo nature of creation. It might be horses or bison pressing out the walls of a cave, it might be a fin rising from the water in a vision, it might be a ghost, it might be a UFO or even just the *idea* of UFOs. VALIS is nothing if not protean, and exactly as Dick and Vallée grasped, it has a funny way of disappearing right when you think you've torn off the mask.

Note the similarity in what I'm suggesting about symbolic transformation/transfiguration of our future lives to traditional theological understandings of prophecy: how the divine itself can only be seen indirectly or obliquely, perceived only by being misperceived, and how the truth can only be shown through a kind of fiction or "trick," as Kripal puts it.[40] The divine is like our future, trying to talk to us in our more vulnerable and permeable moments, but forced to use a kind of blurry pantomime, a game of charades. Art and even "science" (at least in its older, hermetic sense, the sense that especially interests Vallée) are vessels of prophecy, veils hiding (keeping things *sub rosa*) at the same time that they reveal.

Tradition and Tesseract
Culture, Synchronicity, and Prophecy

*A child cried. Rightly far away a horn sounded. All
taken together meant the birth of a new religion.*
—Virginia Woolf, *Mrs. Dalloway* (1925)

Social scientists in the long shadow of Darwin and Wallace have often puzzled over the imaginative dimensions of myth and religion,
as well as the emergence of art 50,000-40,000 years ago. Myopically
focused on the practical matters of adaptation to a harsh natural world
and to individual and group fitness, they have sometimes bent their
imaginations to try and grasp how belief in gods and superpeople (that
don't exist) and miracles (that don't occur) and the creation of beautiful
objects and images (that serve no obvious practical purpose) could have
contributed, and could still contribute, to the survival of individuals,
groups, and the species.

Evolutionary and sociobiological explanations for art and religion
range from uninspiring and boring to slightly ridiculous. Boringly, religion will often be reduced to its role in creating group identity and
cohesion. This view, associated with the French sociologist Émile Durkheim in his 1912 book *The Elementary Forms of Religious Life*, makes
sense as long as you remove the science fiction parts from the human
movie, as I did with *Close Encounters*. (That's the standard move in the
sociology and anthropology of religion.) Aesthetic response, by the
same token, will be explained as an accidental side effect or byproduct
of our practical, tool-making imagination. That's Steven Pinker's argument.[1] Art is also sometimes explained as a kind of peacocking, a sexual
strategy enhancing the artist's attractiveness to mates—except, ahem,
for when it actually makes them less attractive. That kind of thing.

My favorite truism (being sarcastic here) is that religion and art help people "make sense" of their world. Since the brain craves answers to mysteries like "where did the first people come from" and so on, storytelling supplies needed answers, even if our myths are complete fictions.

I don't know. Surely attending a worship service once a week provides some sense-making and that social cohesion and "collective effervescence" central to Durkheim's thinking. But the work of Diana Pasulka and Jeffrey Kripal demonstrates that the extraordinary experiences that lie at the heart of religious traditions only leave experiencers more confused, not less. Like the best art, the most profound experiences of the sacred or the paranormal traumatize or at least trouble, taking experiencers outside the already-known and the rational, unsettling and destabilizing their prior beliefs.[2] Paranormal phenomena that create and punctuate religious traditions serve as much a deconstructive function as a (classically) constructive one—they act as enzymes breaking down outworn worldviews, providing what Harvard UFO abduction researcher John Mack called "ontological shock." They change societies and social structures through this shock, not just reinforce them.

In the middle of the last century, the French anthropologist Claude Lévi-Strauss elevated myth by calling it the "science of the concrete," as though science is the telos, and humans throughout their long history have been striving toward the discovery of the scientific method. He argued that mythological motifs are like phonemes in a language that help us cognitively manipulate nature and, in the process, innovate.[3] There's certainly much truth there. But what if the contribution of myth to innovation, indeed the contribution of all nonliteral modalities of knowing and expression, is also to facilitate the backward-transmission of impossible knowledge from the future—that is, knowledge that can *only* be fast-forwarded to, not assembled through any kind of systematic cognitive or cultural labor? If precognition and the time loops it produces are anywhere near as central to human life as I believe they may be, then this offers a new, even "functional" way of seeing these most impractical of human activities.

In this final chapter, I will briefly sketch how I see precognition—again, generally misperceived or misrecognized—operating as a factor in culture. It is a two-part model. First, precognition powerfully entrains individuals to religious traditions via experienced synchronicities. When some new belief system is able to provide a framing for an impossible or impossible-seeming experience, it may lead to a conversion to the new worldview. Second, religious traditions, being multigenerational, act as channels or carriers of information refluxing back from the collective, not just individual, future. The artistic recording of impossible experiences mediates this retro-transmission.

Conversion—The Force of Traditions

As Arthur Koestler argued in *The Roots of Coincidence*, there's really no such thing as synchronicity, if by that word we mean some structuring principle in the universe that by itself explains impossible convergences of events. Synchronicity is a phenomenological-descriptive term, denoting the experienced significance of events in juxtaposition, the meaningful montage of our lives. Retrocausation, virtually unthinkable when Jung was writing, is the physical principle that explains synchronicity, particularly as it is recruited and "scaled up" in the 4-D tesseract brain.[4] Our long selves—not some impersonal acausal connecting principle—are the makers of that montage.

Again, quite often, a synchronicity may involve a dream or a vision or spontaneous train of thought—"I was just thinking about X and then saw X." But precognition also works as a coincidence-detector and homing device, drawing us to be in the presence of, and then to notice, various kinds of convergences and similitudes. Even random or arbitrary coincidences are highly rewarding for the association-loving brain. They are what structure our memories and our long selves, just as they structure a language. So the thinking feet (as Jacques Lacan might have put it) direct our steps toward coincidences, which we then take as "intersigns"—like Jacques Vallée's sphinx-inflected walk with Hal Puthoff in 1973.

Religious traditions may foster the kinds of visionary experiences such as dreams that are liable to be precognitive, building buy-in to the belief system by producing synchronicities and being poised to integrate those experiences into a metaphysical worldview. In her book *Encounters*, Pasulka describes synchronicity as "often the engine of spiritual and religious belief"[5] by seeming to confirm an individual's beliefs or the validity of a new belief system into which they are being initiated. For instance, she tells a story related to her by an archaeologist working in Australia: A young native initiate reported a lucid dream of flying into a cave with petroglyphs on the walls and encountering a painted sorcerer imparting secret knowledge to him. The next day, the initiate actually was led into a cave and met the man from his dream ... and that elder taught the young man the technique of inducing lucid dreams.[6] (Again, the fractal geometry of prophecy—and here, even the substance of the elder's teaching seemed to flow backward in time.) These initiatory confirmations are the kind of scene that I imagine played out innumerable times with innumerable barefoot youngsters during the long millennia when glaciers covered much of the planet.

Today we mostly encounter religious ideas via churches and books, not caves. But synchronicity still underlies the impact of those encounters, via that alienated majesty described by Emerson. It contributes specifically to the authority and reality of a religious tradition—for instance, seeing a religious picture that feels weirdly familiar because you saw something like it a couple nights ago in dream, or opening the Bible "randomly" to a passage that articulates some feeling or some thought you were just having on your drive home from work. It will seldom if ever occur to us that the later experience may really have retro-caused the prior dream or thought. I suggest our tesseract brains may constantly be feeding us ideas from our future, which we construe as the aimless meanders of that Virginia Woolfian stream of consciousness. Again, religions recruit and amplify this natural process.

The techniques of ecstasy used in shamanic traditions may be highly precognogenic, for example. We saw earlier that a common denominator of psychedelic experiences in ritual settings is synchronistic-seeming confirmations afterward of something seen or encountered during the altered state. Allen Ginsberg's 1960 *yage* experience may have been shaped by his emotional response to an old song playing in a bookstore the next morning. Anthropologist Michael Harner's first ayahuasca experience a year later, during anthropological fieldwork among the Conibo Indians in the same region of Peru, has much in common with Ginsberg's experience. As Harner describes in his 1980 book *The Way of the Shaman*, his awe-inspiring and terrifying vision began with a "carnival of demons" and, presiding over them, "a gigantic, grinning, crocodilian head from whose cavernous jaws gushed a torrential flood of water"[7] that drowned the landscape, leaving only sea and sky remaining. Many other images and scenes followed, including dragon-like creatures that had come to earth from outer space after an ancient cosmic battle, as well as benevolent bird-headed people in ships. The next day, Harner wrote down and tape-recorded his profound and frightening experience in as much detail as possible; he especially struggled to call to mind an esoteric secret, specifically what felt like a "revelation," about the dragons' "innate dominion of living matter" and their role in the evolution of life on earth.[8]

The anthropologist felt like he had escaped with some piece of forbidden knowledge, and he needed to share his story with someone. There was an evangelical missionary couple not far away on the river—they were, he said, "a cut above the average evangelists sent from the United States: hospitable, humorous, and compassionate."[9] So, although he was an atheist, he strapped his outboard motor on a dugout canoe and went to tell these Christians of his experience. When Harner described the huge reptile vomiting a flood of water, the woman and her husband exchanged a surprised look. They picked up a Bible, opened to the Book of Revelation (12:15), and read to their guest: "And the serpent cast out of his mouth water as a flood…"[10] This was especially weird, given that he had specifically felt like his vision was a "revelation." And when Harner went on to describe the dragon-like beings fleeing to earth after a cosmic war, it got even weirder. The stunned missionaries read further from the same biblical book:

> And there was a war in heaven. Michael and his angels
> fought against the dragon; and the dragon fought and
> his angels. And prevailed not; neither was their place
> found any more in heaven. And the great dragon was
> cast out, that old serpent, called the Devil, and Satan,
> which deceiveth the whole world: he was cast out into
> the earth, and his angels with him.[11]

That the "drink of the witch doctors" had revealed to Harner some of the same cosmic history revealed to the evangelist John during his exile on the island of Patmos 1,900 years earlier was as mind-blowing to the missionaries as it was to the 32-year-old atheist anthropologist. Had Harner received confirmation of an ancient cosmic truth under the influence of the drug? Or, had he received a dramatic hologram-transmission from his next-day self, as I suggest happened with Ginsberg?[12]

Kripal calls precognition one of the "special effects" of the religious imagination. The metaphor is quite apt, because special effects in a film give verisimilitude to a story. Without an understanding or even an inkling of their own precognitive capacities, it would be natural for any initiate in a dream-vision quest or participant in an ayahuasca session to draw from their synchronicities the inference of an objective spiritual or perhaps archetypal dimension. Unlike writers and artists in a modern world, for whom originality is paramount, ordinary people seeking external validation and meaning may find confirmation experiences arising from unrecognized precognition to be profoundly spiritually reassuring. In other cases, such experiences may destabilize and deconstruct the individual's prior belief system and usher in a new one. In that case, the experience may result in a conversion to the new worldview.

When Harner brought details of his impossibly Bible-infused ayahuasca visions to his village's master shaman, he described the dragons he had seen (as "bats," the closest word he knew in their language) and how they had told him they were the real masters of the world, but he didn't say anything about them being from outer space. The shaman replied, "Oh, they're always saying that. But they are only the Masters of Outer Darkness."[13] It was this confirmation that converted the anthropologist, setting him on the path to learning everything he could, not about the Bible, but about shamanism as a technique of ecstasy and healing.[14] He devoted his career to learning about, practicing, and teaching basic shamanic methods and what he took to be a real, objective spiritual geography (upper and lower spirit worlds, etc.) to Western, urban students.

Similar processes would have been operative in the ancient world, perhaps even at the roots of Christianity. In a rather stunning detective project involving evidence from archaeobotany and archaeochemistry as well as classical writings and iconography, Brian Muraresku has restored legitimacy to an old theory from the 1970s that the mystery cults of Greece involved the consumption of psychedelic brews and that such brews were central to early Christian ritual too—the "psychedelic Eucharist" theory. In Greece at least, experiencers of the Eleusinian mysteries regarded it as the best and most important experience of their lives, strikingly similar to how some participants in LSD and psilocybin experiments today describe their experiences. The early Christian mass may have been similarly life-transforming. If Muraresku is right about its psychedelic component, and if researchers like David Luke are right about the precognogenic properties of psychedelics, then the ritual likely also produced the kinds of synchronicities that would have powerfully reinforced converts' belief in the objective rightness, not just efficacy, of their new Christian religion.

Without the benefit of powerful tools like the ancient Greek *kykeon* brew, mainstream churches in the modern world may not be very helpful in inducing these kinds of extraordinary experiences, nor are they all that effective at framing such experiences for people when they are accidental or spontaneous. The unreligious Sheppton, Pennsylvania, miner

Hank Throne did not convert to Catholicism after discovering that it was the "Good Pope" accompanying him and Dave Fellin in their subterranean tomb, for instance. But he did become more spiritual after his terrifying but miraculous ordeal, and he went on to found his own nondenominational Christian church in his town.[15] Over the past century, paranormal experiencers have been driven increasingly toward what are now called "spiritual but not religious" worldviews—it's now the fastest-growing religion in the U.S., according to surveys.[16] Carl Jung's movement in Switzerland provides vivid examples of this process. When Jung "confirmed" Maggy Quarles' scarab dream by handing her a wriggling rose-chafer, for instance, it provoked a kind of conversion experience—it opened her to the miraculous. Maggy went from being an overly rational, inaccessible person on Jung's couch to becoming an integral part of his group (critics have sometimes called it a cult[17]), contributing to his thinking about various topics in ways that have only recently been revealed by researchers.[18] (Jung also fell in love with her—a story I tell elsewhere.[19])

The same pattern, a synchronicity centered on some mythological motif, leading to an intensified interest in Jung and belief in an objective archetypal reality, is also found throughout more recent Jungian writings. In his book *Trauma and the Soul*, for instance, analyst Donald Kalsched reports a patient who brought him a dream about a hooded child on a beach and a dolphin leaping in the waves; Kalsched shortly thereafter read exactly that image in one of Jung's books, and he excitedly told the patient about it. "That a contemporary patient, a businessman and stockbroker that was completely unaware of these ancient symbolic parallels, should dream of a recovered hooded child in connection with leaping dolphins is about as dramatic an example of what Jung meant by the archaic and typical (archetypal) components of the deep unconscious as could ever be imagined."[20] More likely, the patient was precognizing being told by his excited therapist about this image from a book by Jung—his dream prompted the therapist's divulgence, which in turn retro-caused the dream, in a loop. It was undoubtedly an incredibly validating, perhaps even life-changing moment for the patient, as the scarab incident had been for Maggy.

Like Roy Neary in *Close Encounters*, it is not uncommon for people to be awakened to their innate precognitive ability during or following a UFO experience. In *Encounters*, Pasulka describes a UFO experiencer named Len, whose dreams of situations and people that he subsequently encountered converted him from his former atheism to a spiritual-but-not-religious outlook.[21] Many of the scientists and engineers Pasulka interviewed experienced frequent precognitive dreams and synchronicities, in many cases validating a belief in higher or non-human intelligence playing a direct role in human affairs.[22] Dreams, synchronicities, and ascetic/meditative "protocols" reinforce the newly coalescing belief system around the UFO phenomenon similarly to how ayahuasca experiences reinforce the ontologies of Amazonian shamans.

The bottom line: It may partly be our innate and at this point largely unrecognized precognitive abilities that make us spiritual if not religious. We believe, like we live, in loops, even if we inevitably use other idioms and other cosmologies to understand the dreamtime landscape of our long selves.

The same principle would apply to artistic response and fandom. Much if not most of the art people encounter in daily life, until the past few centuries, has been religious—again, art and religion are the twin strands of culture's double helix through most of its history. But today, most images and texts that people in the developed world interact with come from the worlds of secular mass media, including entertainment and news media. Precognizing things read in the news or seen in movies builds a powerful attachment to those media. It gives alienated majesty to any novel or movie or song and elevates the charisma of the author or the artist or the performer.

Shaman-performers like David Bowie have perfectly understood the religious or cult-like qualities of modern fandom, even if they have not necessarily grasped the precognitive mechanisms behind their audiences' bond to them. They create spectacles that are vivid and strange enough to be as precognition-worthy as a UFO encounter or an encounter with a saint or guru or healer. How many fans of rock stars have dreams about them before seeing them in concert or on TV? I sometimes wonder how many Londoners in January 1969 had strange dreams of a rock band playing up above, out of sight, in the sky, only to have such an unlikely dream-situation confirmed a few days later—the Beatles' January 30, 1969, rooftop concert, as shown in *Get Back*.

I'll cite a real personal example, here: One evening in late August, 2014, in a hypnagogic vision while meditating in bed (my own protocol, to use Pasulka's idiom), I was directly addressed and briefly tutored by one of my idols, David Lynch, on the necessity of meditating in front of corpses. It was an idea I vaguely associated with esoteric or Tantric Buddhism, and it was startling to hear the director's distinctive

Midwest voice in my head extolling such an obscure and exotic practice. The experience just lasted a few seconds, and I was simultaneously shown a few unusual paintings that the director had made: One was of a strange figure in a vast muddy field. At that time, I was only slightly aware that the director was a painter and I hadn't seen any of his paintings. Two days after this brief vision, on Sunday morning, I opened the Arts section of *The New York Times* to a multi-page feature about an upcoming exhibition of Lynch's paintings in Philadelphia. The painting behind him in the photograph atop the article was the muddy picture I'd seen during meditation, and the long article included the detail that he was allowed to study the cadavers in the Philadelphia morgue after hours, when he was an art student in that city in the late 1960s.[23] I've since become as much a fan of Lynch's paintings as of his movies and TV projects, if such a thing is possible.

I've had enough similar experiences involving books and films that I cannot attach metaphysical or occult meaningfulness to them. I don't think I was in touch with the traveling spirit of David Lynch (if only!). If it happens to me with an article about an artist in *The New York Times*, it happens to everyone, around any media, and around any kind of celebrity or charismatic figure. The potency and prevalence of such experiences as mechanisms of cultural engagement and entrainment remain unexplored. We can only guess at how important they may be.

The same is true, it must be added, of the possible role of precognition in advertising, social movements, and political ideologies. Ideologies are belief systems, and individual buy-in to them might rest on similar synchronistic experiences to those at the heart of religious conversions. As Sergei Eisenstein understood all too well, those cinematic cut-aways that give meaning to our lives are always motivated. We don't typically choose them, we are readily manipulated by them, and they can be fictitious or false. Charismatic political leaders mobilize their followers in some of the same ways gurus do, and the same ways performers and artists engage and inspire their audiences. Advertising works on similar principles.[24] A more fully fledged science of precognition will need to emerge, working in tandem with that Superhumanities Kripal calls for, to even begin to study the role the precognitive imagination plays in all these domains of social life and behavior.

Prophecy—A Hidden Function of Traditions

So, why do we have these precognitive capacities, if we cannot see the future clearly and almost always misrecognize prophecy as something else? As they say in science, more research needed. But we can surely hazard some guesses that what every now and then makes us feel like the butt of some trickster's jokes—and even occasionally leads us astray or opens us to manipulation—is on some deeper level, or most of the time, beneficial. Any faculty that has arisen and been maintained can be reasonably presumed to contribute to a species' fitness. And the fact that precognition so often keys in on future situations where we have survived or withstood either a real existential peril or a challenge to our security or ego points strongly toward some Darwinian solution. Precognition undoubtedly has something to do with survival.

My working hypothesis is that precognition is just the occasionally visible portion of a very basic orientation toward any organism's persistence in the block universe, very generally (that is, very imperfectly) carrying the organism around, rather than headlong into, catastrophes. If I were a betting person, I'd put a lot of money on the idea that such an orientation is and was operative on even the simplest forms of life. Even single-celled organisms without nervous systems as we understand them are intelligently behaving, and like neurons, they contain structures, including microtubules, that appear to be quantum information processors.[25] Retrocausation-harnessing organic molecules, precursors of microtubules, may be what enabled the emergence of life out of inert matter in the first place.[26] Nervous systems scaled it up and orchestrated it.[27] And cultures, civilizations, would be emergent information processors built from intelligently behaving, precognitive social animals like ourselves.

I am generally not a believer in Nostradamuses or Bayardian plagiarism from futures beyond the individual's embodied life. Whatever the material or immaterial nature of consciousness per se, I am comfortable tying the informational constituents of the self, including our memories (and "premories"), to the physical—and mortal—body and brain. Again, I think it is our physical body, with its quadrillions of material (which just means measurable and thus information-carrying) particles, that connects us to the future and is thus the locus of our supernature. It means that we only *directly* precognize things we will learn during our lifetimes. Cases of artists who seemingly prophesied events after their death are relatively rare. Edgar Allen Poe's fictional Richard Parker, cannibalized by his fellow shipwreck survivors, is one notable outlier: The real *Mignonette* tragedy, with its cannibalized cabin boy Richard Parker, occurred 46 years after Poe's novel *The Narrative of Arthur Gordon Pym of Nantucket* was published and 35 years after the author's death. On the other hand, the then-commonness of the name Richard Parker, the then-frequency of maritime cannibalism, the long time-lag, and the fact that so many other details don't align, put this case in a gray area for me.[28] (Arthur Koestler, who published this story in *The Sunday Times* in 1974 as the most striking of many coincidences submitted to him by readers, would certainly disagree.[29])

But even if we have physical sell-by dates, we are not islands. We communicate, we talk, we share, we are embedded in societies that transcend us. Cultural traditions are composed of precognitive individuals whose careers and lifespans are staggered in time: parents and children, teachers and pupils, initiators and initiates. It may be a cliché, but it's true that teachers learn from their students and that parents learn from (and in the old Sam Levenson joke, catch insanity from) their kids. Healers also learn from their patients, as I suggest happened with Jacques Lacan and some younger patient who may have had a precognitive dream of *Alien*. The ability of elders to learn from the next generation could be more important a factor in our persistence as a species than we remotely suspect. Cultural traditions may act as conduits of information retro-flowing from farther points in the future than a few years or decades hence.

The possibility that precognition could operate not only individually but on a collective level, over long timespans, forces us to consider that it might fulfill a kind of social steering function for civilizations, and that cultural systems themselves, especially art and religion, are its vectors.[30]

In Arthur C. Clarke's 1953 novel *Childhood's End*, advanced alien beings called Overlords arrive over Earth in huge ships to husband humanity toward its next evolutionary leap, becoming a species capable of fully participating with other galactic civilizations as part of a single Overmind. The telepathic human children in the novel who assume this birthright represent the next stage of our development, already adumbrated in mostly latent psychic ability. The uncanny familiarity of the Overlords, when they finally reveal their physical form after 50 years over Earth's capital cities, is a symptom of that latent ability: When they show themselves, they look just like devils from Christian art, having leathery wings and horns. There is speculation about a "racial memory" of encounters with this species in our evolutionary past, but the Overlords explain that those devils in our art traditions were more likely a long cultural premonition of the beings who would bring about our species' "end" (although really a transition). Prophecy misrecognized as archetype, in other words.

When Clarke wrote *Childhood's End*, he was undoubtedly think-ing of real, fateful first-contact events in human history that had re-portedly been foretold in prophecies. The most famous is the arrival of the renegade conquistador Hernan Cortés in the Aztec capital of Tenochtitlan in the year 1520, supposedly fulfilling Aztec prophecies about the calamitous return of their god Quetzalcoatl. By somewhat remote (52-1) odds, that year was a "1-Reed" year, the traditional year of Quetzalcoatl's birth and death and the year he was expected to return and challenge the local rulers. Historians have disputed the astrologers' prophecies, some assuming this had to be European mythmaking and/or psychological warfare, the Spaniard's shrewdness at fitting himself into the myths of the people he was conquering. The last thing a seri-ous postcolonial social scientist is likely to take seriously is the bad-TV premise that the Aztecs really did prophesy the collapse of their civi-lization in the form of a bizarrely Quetzalcoatl-like white conqueror. But in a reconsideration of the evidence and what he calls the "irony of empire," Harvard anthropologist and religion scholar David Carras-co argues that the fragile political reality of early-16th-century Mexico actually anticipated bad 1960s TV. There really were prophecies—the Aztec elite did see Cortés as Quetzalcoatl—and (yes) Cortés used those prophecies, and the political instability of the Aztec Empire at that his-torical moment, to his advantage.[31] The Spaniards were less benevolent, unfortunately, than Clarke's Overlords or the childlike aliens that pour out of the mothership at the end of *Close Encounters*.

The countless dreams and artworks foretelling the *Titanic* disaster and 9/11 show clearly that people do routinely prophesy big turning points in their culture, just as they prophesy turning points in their per-sonal lives. And crucially, if there is a cultural tradition that encourages dreams and visions and inspiration, then in theory at least, prophecy should transmit backwards across generations: not only a sacred river but a sacred Amazon, flowing into the past.

Any post-Renaissance art tradition, where creators driven by the anxiety of influence precognitively scoop each other, is one potential conduit of information retro-flow. Precisely insofar as they avoid copy-ing their predecessors, artists may end up channeling the ideas of those who come (slightly) after them, in a kind of daisy chain, back through history. For instance, earlier writers or artists in the 1960s or 1970s might have precognized Dana's mutilation in the dramatic final conflict in *Kindred*, the way Butler had precognized the final conflict in *The Terminator*. There may have been writers earlier in the 20th century or late in the previous one who precognized Kafka's Odradek or his Door in the Law.[32] I certainly wonder how far back in pop culture Jacques Vallée's control system might have percolated as a fictional or mythic motif, via Philip K. Dick and whoever was precognizing Dick, and whoever was precognizing them, and so on back through the decades. On my blog, I speculated that SF writer Max Simon Ehrlich might have been one of them: His Gnostic-themed 1967 *Star Trek* teleplay, "The Apple," was about a civilization ruled by a planetary control system/ god named *Vaal*.[33] Grant-funded graduate students in some future Superhumanities department might have the resources, time, and person-power (perhaps augmented with AI tools) to create a more robust 4-D diagram of artistic-literary influence, a detailed map of precognitive (mis)reading. Now, here, I can at best suggest and speculate.

But art and literary traditions placing a premium on inspiration are probably a relatively new thing in the human story. It is even easier to see how such a retro-transmission mechanism would work in the context of an initiatory cult placing a premium on precognogenic altered states like dream incubation or the consumption of psychedelics.

In the Amazon, mestizo shamans-in-training repeatedly consume ayahuasca (and/or other drugs, depending on the tradition) under the guidance of a teacher.[34] The teacher listens and provides interpretation and guidance, setting expectations for the initiate and also comparing the initiate's experience with their own. In all this, the pupil may be precognizing the interpretation of the teacher, the way (I suggest) Harner was precognizing the village elder's "But they are only the Masters of the Outer Dark." But the teacher is likely learning something from these encounters too. The teacher may remember seeing some of the same material in their own visions earlier in life, having precognized these divulgences by their students. As may occur in any dream-sharing community or in a therapeutic community like Jung's in Zurich, a sort of resonance may occur, in which everyone's dreams and visions start to resemble those of the other participants—leading all parties to interpret and understand this activity as the mapping of an objective spiritual or archetypal realm.[35] Through this process, information from the future would be transmitted, initiate to initiator, pupil to teacher, across generations, back through time. It would make cultural evolution far more Lamarckian than most anthropologists nowadays would like to acknowledge, having a genuinely teleological component to it.

As hinted at by those Aztec prophecies, one place we might look for evidence of such backward cultural transmission would be the historical and anthropological literature surrounding cultural contact. There are other cases that hint at a culture's prior "preparation" for their first contact with Europeans. Famously, when Captain James Cook arrived in Kealakekua Bay on Hawaii Island in 1779, the locals took him for the god Lono because of another surfeit of coincidences. Cook's arrival coincided with the Makahiki harvest festival in honor of the god. His clockwise circumnavigation of the island prior to making landfall resembled the clockwise processions of the festival. And his ship, HMS *Resolution*, even physically resembled artifacts associated with the festival. So, the Hawaiians filled canoes with gifts and brought their "god" ashore to honor him. All was well until Cook departed a month later but had to return shortly afterward to repair a broken mast on the *Resolution*. On his return—which was after the Makahiki festival had ended—hostilities broke out and Cook and some of his crew were killed. It no longer fit the myth.

It is another case of history prefiguring bad 1960s TV—and greatly offending postcolonial anthropologists. Sri-Lankan anthropologist Gananath Obeyesekere, for example, argued that the Cook story was the product of European mythmaking, not Hawaiian.[36] But as with the Aztecs and their Spanish Quetzalcoatl, the debunkers of this historical/anthropological curiosity have ended up being debunked.[37] In a devastating book-length rebuttal to Obeyesekere, University of Chicago anthropologist Marshall Sahlins provided abundant compelling evidence that the Hawaiians really took Cook to be their Lono.[38] Is it another case where local tradition had subtly, over years or decades or centuries, been inflected by a monumental future arrival of "aliens"? Were the coincidences not really coincidences? We can only speculate, but at least it makes for a fun—and I don't think frivolous—thought experiment.

Another famous, controversial head scratcher is the alleged knowledge of Sirius B—the invisible (to the naked eye) white dwarf companion of Sirius A—by people of the Dogon culture of Mali, in West Africa. French anthropologist Marcel Griaule was an amateur astronomer, and when he led an expedition to Mali in 1933, he was surprised to learn from a blind Dogon elder named Ogotommeli that the binary nature of the Sirius star system was somehow known in his tradition—seemingly, impossibly. It had been discovered by European astronomers in the 19th century. This anomaly led author Robert K. G. Temple in the mid-1970s to argue that humans had been in contact with visitors from the neighborhood of Sirius in the remote past—it remains a pillar of the "ancient aliens" hypothesis. Temple's influential 1976 book *The Sirius Mystery* is likely the reason Phil Dick changed the origin star of his ET teaching satellite from Fomalhaut/Albemuth to Sirius in the final version of his novel, *VALIS*.[39] Debunkers have argued that earlier contact with French astronomers may have given the Dogon information about Sirius, or that their prior knowledge about the Sirius system was exaggerated by Griaule. I am not in a position to weigh the evidence; but another, never-broached possibility is that the pre-contact Dogon learned about Sirius B from none other than Griaule, in their future. Could Ogotommeli have somehow passed information gleaned from his interactions with Griaule to his own teacher, earlier in life—and so on, back through generations—so that it was already awaiting Griaule's arrival as part of established cosmological lore among his people? Again, we can only speculate, but this kind of process should be expected if precognition plays any role in cultural traditions.

Besides writing and oral transmission person-to-person, cultural information and values can be encoded silently in all varieties of material-cultural practice such as pottery, jewelry, tool-making, and so on. Inspiration can enter in subtly even in a craft tradition, so innovation from the future could theoretically be transmitted materially in that tradition and may well have been for the vast majority of humanity's long prehistory—a certain technique of knapping flint, a certain curl on the lip of a pot, and so on. Teachers and masters of craft traditions would have learned a certain amount from their students this way, although retrograde information flow would have been a trickle. Wedding a figurative visual-art tradition like what emerged in the Great Leap Forward to religious initiation, tied to visions, would have greatly opened the informational spigot from the future, beginning that cultural acceleration that led to writing and now to AI and quantum computers and whatever is next. Pictures, like stories, can readily be precognized in dreams and other altered states. Paleolithic caves could have been the first superconductors of prophecy, besides being supercolliders of religious experience.

Bottom line: If precognition is real, then traditions must be tesseracts. The human cable, composed of billions of interweaving, twisting strands, should be a conductor of information in both directions in time. Just as an artistic practice embeds the individual creator in a story of their own future survival of some transition or upheaval—that "but

I survived" signal that is often present in a precognitive dream or inspiration—traditions ought to do the same for a society. But backward-in-time transmission of information through any channel, especially the hybrid classical-quantum computer system of a culture, will hardly have video-quality clarity or fidelity. Beyond just the normal "lossiness" or degradation of information as it is transmitted in any medium, in any direction, cultural knowledge flowing in temporal retrograde would also be subject to symbolic distortions for all the Einsteinian-Freudian reasons we have explored. Information from the future will be granular, oblique, symbolic, greatly reduced in resolution. One imagines that it might look precisely archetypal.

Again, an individual's dream symbolism condenses somewhat equivocal future thoughts and experiences in a way that draws them subtly toward the future where they have those thoughts and experiences. So-called archetypal symbols may arise in a similar way on a collective level. Archetypes of the collective unconscious may represent the informational motor of future-fulfilment, the long-body of prophecy, not something contained in a phylogenetically ancient reservoir of symbolic motifs as Jung thought. They emerge again and again, with such majesty, in visions and dreams—and find their way into our art—because they represent our hitherto-uncharacterized precognitive engagement with culture, in some cases bearing subtle warnings about close if not fatal encounters ahead in our individual as well as collective timelines. As the Aztec prophecies show us, prophecies can be, and maybe always necessarily are, equivocal.

In his *Dune* novels, Frank Herbert imagined a far-future, galaxy-spanning feudal humanity secretly shepherded by superhuman matriarchs, whose breeding program results in a human, Paul Atreides, who has fully developed precognitive powers, or "prescience." Paul passes on his prescience to his son, Leto II, who as God-Emperor takes over the breeding program and assumes the role of cosmic steward. In the fourth novel in the series, *God Emperor of Dune*, Leto II is thousands of years into his reign, living as a hybrid cross between human and a sandworm (long story), and he sees that humanity is doomed to extinction through its aggression and weakness. Through tyrannical and harsh policies, he sees himself as being a "predator" in the ecological sense, challenging the species and thereby increasing its evolutionary fitness. Whatever doesn't kill humanity, as Nietzsche might say, makes it stronger.

It's a despicable, fascist philosophy for a leader, of course. Herbert seduces the reader to sympathize somewhat with his therianthropic antihero, though: The God-Emperor sincerely has humanity's long-term survival as his authentic motive, even if his methods are cruel. We are led to be believe that he (and he alone) can actually see the myriad forking paths of future history, mostly all leading to disaster or oblivion. At the end of the novel, the worm-god is assassinated by a woman, Siona, a product of his own breeding program who is able to evade his prescience—this being precisely the outcome he had hoped to achieve through his multimillennia-long, predatory reign.

Herbert's fictional premise in his series is that prescience reveals what are commonly called "possible futures" in the ESP literature: actual future outcomes that may or may not happen. Such an idea is ultimately paradoxical—if a foreseen outcome never happens (i.e., because it was prevented or averted) then where would the precognitive vision come from? (Again, I believe that invoking multiple timelines and "many worlds" is a cop-out—but that's another long argument for another long book.[40]) But Herbert's tying of prophecy to the question of survival—and specifically that knife-edge between survival and extinction—reflected, I believe, a keen intuition about how it would, and does, really operate in our individual and collective lives. It operates as a kind of homing mechanism oriented toward the persistence but not easy contentment of our serpent- or wormlike long selves in the block universe.

If we substitute Herbert's morally dubious man-worm Leto II with the Darwinian realities that underlie precognition, the notion that prophecy might act as a kind of trickster-predator in our lives and guide us roughly toward, rather than away from, existential challenges is, I suspect, close to right: Owing to the inherently differential or oppositional nature of signification, there would be no "but I survived" signal were we to be bent away from traumas and challenges altogether—again, that would be paradoxical. Consequently, fate's magnetic lines of force carry us toward experiences that challenge our security or our egos as a price of surviving graver existential calamities looming nearby. Generally speaking (there are exceptions), we follow a presentimental homing beacon of near-misses, of being grazed by disaster but not colliding full-on, survival but at a cost.[41]

Material nature is Nietzschean in that it is harsh, as Darwinian biology has long stressed, but it is also super. It contains a kind of transcendence or transcendence-potential within it—a potential that (I strongly suspect) led, billions of years ago, to the emergence of life, and later to intelligence, and only much more recently to the prophetic superconductivity of human culture. The price of our superhumanity, however, seems to be that we are a traumatized species. No half-human, half-worm God Emperor is needed to inflict this trauma, although in history, many such figures have tried. Through our most ancient superpower, we entrain ourselves to traumas on an individual level, and because of the archetypal river of prophecy that our traditions carry, we entrain ourselves to traumas on a collective level—that is, a path that threads precariously between a primrose untroubled Eden and one that leads headway to destruction or oblivion.

I imagine this is how the time loops that are the secret substance of our lives function as a cultural homeostat or regulator—indeed, a control system—pushing/pulling us toward a middle path between Heaven and Hell by operating on the very subtle preverbal level of myth and image and symbol. It is a homing beacon from the future. That future is one where we and our descendants have survived, but at some cost. We already survived in our future, and hints of that flowed far back into our past—possibly (I like to imagine) back to the very beginning.

Staying for the No Credits

I'm not a big believer in originality. I think Mark Twain was right. As a writer, I would admittedly love to be credited with novel ideas about precognition and time loops, but intellectually I know that my ideas, like anybody else's, come largely from other people, including other writers I haven't read yet. I suspect if you could somehow use tracer dye to study the currents of thought that flow through our minds, you might find that most of them, most of anybody's original-seeming ideas, flow from social interactions and cultural experiences in our shared futures. And the same way the mighty Amazon ultimately originates in myriad negligible trickles on glaciers high in the Andes, if you traced big cultural ideas to their ultimate sources, you might find that they all have their beginnings in funny little unwilled, unnoticed loops in real, mostly anonymous people's lived lives. They would seem trivial or trash, like a random name on a cab receipt.

In *Changed in a Flash*, the book Kripal co-wrote with lightning-struck precog Elizabeth Krohn, he notes that the spontaneity and effortlessness of 3-D cinematic-like mystical and near-death visions hides that they have been co-created by countless real experiencers of visions and supernatural wonders over the centuries and millennia—those perpetual loops of consciousness and culture that inform or mediate people's extraordinary experiences. But he notes that unlike a movie, where you can see the names of everyone who contributed to it when the credits roll at the end, there are no credits rolling at the end of typical religious experiences. If there were, religion historians would want to stay for them, gaining some insight into the real human experiences that, over time, gave shape and form to the collective religious imagination, the paranormal "super story" in which we are all embedded.

Kripal then tells how he shared his "credits rolling" metaphor with Colombian anthropologist Luis Eduardo Luna, who has written about the iconographic traditions of Amazonian shamans.[42] Luna laughed and described how he had posed *exactly* the same question—"Who is behind this?"—during a couple of 3-D cinematic ayahuasca experiences of his own. Luna said he had been rewarded in one case with a vision of little aliens holding up a movie screen, and in another case with credits rolling after his experience was over.[43]

Was it just a coincidence that Kripal and Luna had the same question about visionary religious traditions and used—or in Luna's case, directly experienced—the same image/metaphor of movie credits? Most people would chalk it up to that and give it no more thought. Or, had Luna precognized Kripal's highly singular metaphor of the religious imagination during experiences with what, from the literature (I have no firsthand experience), sounds like an irrepressibly precognogenic substance? And, could Kripal in turn have gotten his credits metaphor, also precognitively, from Luna's vivid description of his all-too-perfect experiences? There's no way to prove it, but I suspect this was another PSC—the most exquisite and perfect kind of PSC, where an idea arises not only from nowhere, but also literally from nothing. I suspect there was no point in the life of either Kripal or Luna where one of their brains "did the work" of coming up with that movie-credits metaphor. They each got it from the other, in a loop.

In fact, that's exactly what I take to be the point of Mother Ayahuasca's jokes in response to Luna's questions about the genius(es) behind the ever-evolving religious imagination: *Nobody* can be credited. Ideas, images, even brilliantly acute metaphors, always arise ultimately from nowhere, nothing, and nobody, from time loops between human lives and within a single life.

Nobody did the work. Nobody perspired. So, no credits.

Afterword

Living Creatures, Flying Blenders, and Long Selves

"This is your last chance. After this, there is no turning back. You take the blue pill—the story ends, you wake up in your bed and believe whatever you want to believe. You take the red pill—you stay in Wonderland and I show you how deep the rabbit hole goes."
—Lily Wachovski & Lana Wachovski, *The Matrix*
(1999)

You must change your life.
—Rainer Maria Rilke, "Archaic Torso of Apollo"
(1908)

On the wall in my study is a large diagram of a flying saucer, drawn by an unnamed amateur artist, surrounded by passages from the Book of Ezekiel hand-penned in block letters. Arrows made with a pen and ruler connect those passages to different parts of THE LIVING CREATURE, as the vehicle is labeled. Early in my career, I worked as an assistant editor for a now-defunct magazine about biblical literature and art, and I rescued this drawing from a stack of rejected unsolicited submissions. It was a high-quality magazine, with beautiful images and invited articles by academic religion scholars and art historians, but we also received many submissions from non-academics—independent researchers, "outsiders"—expressing unique, sometimes fascinating, sometimes obsessive perspectives on all things related to the world of the Bible. Some of the submissions bore the signs of severe mental disorder. Nobody on our tiny staff had time to read all the contributions people sent, many of which were hand-written and hand-illustrated. The article this image was meant to illustrate was missing—probably it had been thrown out—so it is an orphan. I had it framed and have cherished it ever since as a piece of found folk art.

I'm not an expert on the Bible or biblical prophecy—my stint at that magazine did not last long enough. But like many children of the 1970s, having grown up with the paperbacks of Erich von Däniken and the wonderful Leonard Nimoy-hosted series *In Search Of …*, I knew all about Ezekiel as an early UFO experiencer. What they now call "the phenomenon" long predates the late 1940s, when flying saucers first entered the popular imagination, so I don't assume whoever penned the illustration on my wall was in the mentally disordered category of un-solicited submissions—although obsessive, absolutely, given the dense halo of handwritten captioning around the Living Creature. Many eminently healthy people, such as Jacques Vallée, have entertained the idea that Ezekiel, like countless lesser-known experiencers over the mil-lennia, encountered something otherworldly, and that such encounters have been calculated to change or evolve our cultures, our beliefs, our biology, or possibly all three.

My research on precognition over the past decade tangents ufol-ogy in certain ways, but I'm not a ufologist—I have no idea what the prophet in sixth century B.C.E. Babylon encountered. Yet when I think about artists and writers in their inspired moments, I think a lot about poor bewildered Ezekiel: I picture him clutching his robe with one hand against the blowing dust, shielding his eyes from the blazing light with the other, as those famous wheels within wheels turned, multi-animal-headed people zooming around, with a booming voice thunder-ing at him about the wickedness of his people. I wonder if his wife later applied cream to his face to mask his inexplicable sunburn, like Roy Neary's wife Ronnie (Teri Garr) in *Close Encounters*.

The awe of many writers and artists throughout history when they first encounter their muse, their sacred river, their daimon—there seem to be almost as many words for "it" as there are creators—is similar to the awe experienced by Ezekiel. They sense that they are in the presence of something not of this world, something impossible. Sometimes it leaves them with tears of joy. They usually lack the words to articulate it. So, in the lucky event that they gain enough recognition for their inspired work that the public takes an interest in their creative process, they are seldom if ever able to give a satisfying response to the question we started with, "Where do you get your ideas?" It would be like asking

Ezekiel where the Living Creature came from. It came from nowhere.

Having accompanied me on this journey, I hope you are persuaded that culture—high and low and everything in-between—consists of vessels of the super, time-defying backward transmissions from our personal and collective futures. Creators channel and manifest the impossible. It means there's a core impossibility buried in the most inspired works that affects us, even if we are not consciously aware of why or how. Like an irradiated UFO landing site, a film like *Stalker* or *Eraserhead*, a novel like *Mrs. Dalloway* or *VALIS*, or a painted bison on a Paleolithic cave wall still glow with the energy of an encounter with the impossible. We are scarred, changed, perhaps evolved a little by that radiation. Yet because we lack the eyes to see it and largely the imagination to imagine it, we pass over this mutation, imagining ourselves moved and mutated only within permissible parameters of movement and mutation. That is, only slightly, only vaguely. So, let's expand our imagination and open our eyes … but, put on sunglasses.

This is the part where I come clean that my interest in the from-nowhere precognitive imagination is much more than academic. I too have had awe-inspiring encounters with my creative daimon, a daimon who in a few cases turned out to be a time traveler. In fact, my inspiration for this book, if I could pinpoint a single one, was a time loop that had a diameter of more than 20 years and involved a late-night instance of my own creative frenzy. It even centered on UFOs, even if it didn't involve a close encounter as spectacular and harrowing as Ezekiel's.

It began in 1998, when I read Whitley Strieber's *Communion* for the first time. I was then living in Atlanta, Georgia, writing my PhD dissertation in anthropology but always looking for more interesting diversions. I'm not sure what drew me to pick up Strieber's book in a used bookstore near the Emory University campus. Probably, like many people, I was drawn by the haunting alien face on the cover. I was curious. At that point, I had little knowledge of the UFO topic besides those 1970s paperbacks and movies like *Close Encounters*. As a scientifically trained person, I had developed a knee-jerk disbelief about most paranormal claims, although I had no firm beliefs against aliens or extraterrestrials. I was open-minded on that, but skeptical. Like many readers, I was pulled inexorably into Strieber's account—it was scary to be sure. But I didn't know what to think of his story of being abducted and medically examined by terrifying alien-looking "visitors." I didn't completely believe that this wasn't just a case of sleep paralysis, a phenomenon I had experienced many times and that is easily mis-interpreted as a kind of paranormal assault or abduction. My main thought about Strieber's book, in fact, was its comic possibilities, and I felt moved one evening to write a parody.

In an inspired writing session at my computer that took me late into the night and next morning, the words flowing out like rain, I banged out several pages of dialogue between a distressed UFO contactee and a hypnotherapist slowly recovering the man's suppressed memory of an awe-inspiring encounter ... with a flying blender. The beauty and perfection of the appliance, once his memory came back, amounted to a spiritual revelation for my character. It surely wouldn't hold up, now—my hard drive is filled with never-finished attempts at fiction—but at the time, I was proud of these pages of (I thought) pretty hilarious dialogue that had come effortlessly from God-knows-where.

In 1998, when I channeled this from-nowhere (and destined-for-nothing) idea, I had no idea that a little over a decade later, I would have my first UFO sighting—directly over the Philadelphia Museum of Art, as a matter of fact—and then would spend my free time over the next decade writing blog posts, articles, and books about paranormal subjects including not only UFOs but also, mainly, psychic phenomena. I certainly had no idea that, through this writing, I would get to know a man named Jeff Kripal and be invited by him to a symposium on UFOs at the Esalen retreat in Big Sur, California. The "Beyond the Spinning" symposium in January 2019 was a significant and humbling experience for me, being included among the elite of ufology, including authors like Vallée, who by then I had come to greatly admire. By this point, my knowledge of the UFO subject and of experiences like that of Strieber was far greater than in 1998, of course—I don't know what happened to the author of *Communion* any more than I know what happened to Ezekiel, but I know that mere sleep paralysis doesn't cut it as an explaining-away. Imagine my utter shock, though, when in a Wednesday morning talk, UFO historian Greg Bishop gave a Powerpoint presentation on the surreality of UFO encounters that concluded with the observation that they can manifest as virtually anything. A UFO could even be ... a flying blender. Because he was sitting in the chair directly behind me, Strieber, the very author whose book I had been parodying one night over two decades earlier, would not have been able to see my jaw drop as a memory of that old literary attempt came flooding back. Vallée, sitting to my right, could have.

The odds against this convergence of people, images, and ideas in my life, two decades after my few hours of nocturnal inspiration, are astronomical. It was a feeling of awe at the impossible. And funnily enough, it was exactly *an immobilizing sense of awe* sparked by his sudden recovered memory of a flying blender that my character had felt in my story. In other words, that story, in its premise as well as in its details, fractally mirrored a real situation in which I found myself two decades after I was inspired to write it.

By this point, I was no stranger to precognitive experiences, mainly dreams. I had just published my first book about the topic—it was the reason for my invitation to the Esalen event. But whenever they occur—that is, whenever you realize that some past dream or vision or bit of creative writing had been precognitive of some experience you are living through *right now*—you may almost be immobilized by the realization that you really are a long self in a block universe. Again, I've had plenty of other writers and creative people—real artists, not to mention many, many dreamers—describe to me similarly jaw-dropping experiences. It is especially astonishing when the dream or vision or story occurred so many years earlier, in a completely different phase of one's life and completely different physical or geographical locale. I had been a very different person in 1998 than I was in 2019.

Jeff had already asked me to give a short presentation to the larger Esalen community on some aspect of my work that evening (Wednesday), so I spent that afternoon preparing a Powerpoint presentation— "Where Do Ideas Come From?"—that was the initial seed of the book you now hold in your hands.

Another experience at the end of that week had been foreshadowed in a dream that was also, like my blender story, nearly two decades old at that point. I still had a detailed, dated record in my electronic journal, although I hadn't turned it into a story. In the dream, I had been in a restaurant on a cliff with a wall of big windows overlooking a sea where stylized fish-like dolphins played, and I was stunned to see the sky over the sea opening up, like a rip or tear in space—a kind of vertical spindle-shaped door or wormhole to some other reality, from which I expected a UFO to emerge. The portal had a kind of fractal quality around its rim, like the recursive electric paisley of a Mandelbrot set. On the last morning of the symposium, I and a couple other participants were having breakfast with Vallée in the Esalen dining room, which has a wall of windows facing a cliff overlooking the Pacific. All week I had watched dolphins play in the water below. Vallée was telling me about an artist friend of his and turned his smartphone toward me, showing me one of this artist's drawings—of the sky opening up, a spindle-shaped sky portal, over a group of people on a beach. It was almost exactly what I had seen in my dream from 19 years earlier, a time before I knew who Jacques Vallée was and before there were smartphones. Again, words can't express the awe one feels at these moments of dreams coming true and time loops resolving.

Esalen is a kind of sacred site for the spiritual-but-not-religious and a setting where impossible or magical experiences and encounters are famously common. Some guests that week, not part of our group, reportedly saw a UFO over Esalen's famous cliffside baths. And the day before Greg's talk on weirdness like flying blenders, Vallée had given a presentation on synchronicity, which sparked an animated discussion about the simulation hypothesis, a theory that has lately gained ground among the Silicon Valley tech elite, Vallée's professional milieu as a venture capitalist. The simulation hypothesis proposes that we live in a virtual world created by some higher intelligence, very much like the premise of the *Matrix* movies.[1] I don't subscribe to this hypothesis, but almost as if to prove me wrong, just minutes after we adjourned for lunch, several members of our group, including some of Jeff's graduate students, were astonished to encounter actor Laurence Fishburne while walking to the Esalen cafeteria. Fishburne played Morpheus, Neo's (Keanu Reaves) mentor in the *Matrix* trilogy—the one who famously offers Neo the choice of taking a red pill (go deeper down the rabbit hole) or a blue pill (the story ends). None of us had known that he was on the grounds. Amazingly, there had been lots of jokes just minutes earlier about red and blue pills being taken alone or in combination.

Like a sea we swim in, precognition is so pervasive, I believe, that we ordinarily don't even see it. Besides dreams and creative projects, it skews our daily perceptions and our thoughts. It even bends the subject of conversations—which is what I think happened with our group discussion about the *Matrix* just before encountering Morpheus himself. (I find that far more plausible than the idea that we somehow "summoned" Fishburne from some cosmic synchronicity server.) Special settings like Esalen may foster paying more attention to these kinds of things, but mostly, nobody pays attention—and for most of my life, I didn't. It is only these experiences of precognition over the past several years, like my dreams and that blender story, that have forced me to reconsider similarly amazing creative experiences earlier in my life, which I'd previously swept under my mental rug because they made no rational sense at the time.

For instance, I'll never forget the "inspired" collage I made in 1992, out of construction paper, as a gift for my then-wife, who was about to leave to do ethnographic fieldwork in a remote village in Papua New Guinea. We were both graduate students. The collage depicted two frogs in a jungle discovering a mysteriously discarded set of women's underthings. I have no idea where this idea came from. A few months later, after I arrived for a stay in her rainforest abode, we attended a meeting in the village headman's house one night where among the pressing matters being discussed was the recent discovery of a brassiere in the forest—a problematic and troubling discovery for the men. They didn't know what the discarded garment portended, or what woman could have left it. As the mysterious underthing in the forest was pondered by firelight, my wife and I just exchanged WTF looks, remembering that collage I had made.

Some months later, after I returned to my childhood home in Morrison, Colorado, to prepare to begin my own dissertation research, it happened again. Having neglected to take my antimalarial drugs for the requisite two weeks following exposure to tropical mosquitos, I fell ill with malaria. I was overcome with chills and my temperature rose to more than 105 degrees Fahrenheit in the space of an hour. As Alfred Russel Wallace knew, a malarial fever is no joke: Intense shaking, chills, and sweats lead to a miserable headache and delirium. The fevers strangely occur on alternating days, a day of relative reprieve (just the pounding headache) in-between. In one of my long sweaty deliriums under a pile of comforters, a movie played out in my head, which although maddening on one level (as deliriums are) was also brilliant and funny. I later jotted notes on it with the vague intention to write it as a screenplay (not that I, a 25-year-old social scientist-in-training, really knew anything about writing screenplays, but whatever). My cinedelirium was a cheerful musical about Adolf Hitler, the absurd comedic premise being that he had somehow been misunderstood by history and wasn't really such a bad guy after all.

That evening, after my fever broke, I excitedly told my feverdream-movie to my father, who said, "They made that movie in the 1960s. It's *The Producers*." I had never heard of the film, but like Craig Sinclair upon cracking open the novel *Patricia* that had been sent to her husband, excitement at "my" wonderful idea deflated, hearing my father describe the old comedy starring Zero Mostel and Gene Wilder. These were the days of VHS rental chains, so not long after my fevers lessened, probably the following week, I rented *The Producers* and was stunned to see something close to the spectacle I'd remembered from my delirium—although of course, considerably better. At this point, I don't think precognition was even part of my vocabulary. I must, I assumed—or perhaps, my psychologist dad explained—have heard a synopsis of Mel Brooks' now-classic 1967 movie at some point and just consciously forgotten it.

Needless to say, now I no longer think this was cryptomnesia, let alone mere coincidence. In fact, I even wonder if my precognitive imagination during an altered state in 1993 had specifically drawn me toward a movie called *The Producers* as a comment on my divulgence, fully three decades later, of that very anecdote in a book on precognition and creativity that culminates with Jeff Kripal's observation that there are no credits for the religious—and I would add, artistic—imagination. *Producers* are the first people named when the credits roll at the beginning or end of a film. The same kind of ultra-witty long-term loops are discovered in precognitive dreamwork, so why not with inspiration too? Although believe me, in my case, there was a lot of perspiration along with the inspiration—and perhaps that, too, was part of my precognitive unconscious's joke: I didn't get to take any credit, but I did get to sweat.

Other dreams and stories I had written or made fragmentary notes on in the 1990s also turned out to connect to my precognition research roughly two decades later and big events in my life connected to it, including precious personal encounters and connections I have made because of my writing. There are too many to mention. At the time, those products of my primary process turned my interests naturally toward Carl Jung and occultism because they seemed archetypal and alchemical somehow. Gradually, and partly because of my own UFO sighting, that Jungian-hermetic interest veered toward paranormal research. So, those dreams and stories were essentially like billiard balls shot back in time through wormholes at my younger self, deflecting me (thanks to my necessary misunderstanding, at the time) toward the future I lived. A big loop, or knot of loops, predicated entirely on the *im*possibility of seeing clearly the future doing its nightly semaphore in my dreams and its daily semaphore in my writing.

It is true for you, as well. You have an already-existing long self, extending some indeterminate amount of years or decades into the future. Unpredictable experiences in that expanse of time are quietly and subtly influencing you now. And your thoughts and experiences in the present, in your now-unfolding life, influenced your past, even bent the path you took in life to get to where you are. It is thus a valuable exercise to unsweep previously swept impossible experiences, excavate the weird and uncanny meanders of your creative life. If you are an artist or writer, look at your old works and reflect on how they may have foreshadowed what came later. Even if you don't consider yourself a creator but still have unfinished creative projects in some box from school, or on an old hard drive, dig them out, brace yourself, and look again at them. You might be amazed at what you find.

From Now, Here

The biggest surprise of pursuing this whole business of precognition over the past decade has been discovering that it is not really about expanded human potential in the sense of developing some *new* superpower or some future ability people are evolving toward, like the younger generation of telepaths in *Childhood's End*. Nor is it something that only some rare elite possess. That's not how I understand super-humanity. Rather, experiencing precognition, whether in meditation, dreams, or creative endeavors, invariably brings you face to face with the super-ness and sublimity of your biography, no matter how mundane it may seem on the surface. It gives inspiringly weird new meaning to the seemingly random twisting paths your life may have taken, and reminds you that there is a yet-unlived future ahead.

Our 4-D nature is on the one hand obvious, but it's also as forgettable as a dream. The slippery elusiveness of time reminds me of Palmolive dishwashing soap, in TV ads from my childhood: "You're soaking in it!" We're soaking in time-the-dimension without being able to perceive that dimension directly—and somehow, everything in our experience conspires to occlude the fourth dimension from our thinking. It has always been here, underlying the basic effects and forces of our experience, including our synchronicities; but again and again, we turn time into space, which at best mystifies and at worse forces us to deny those phenomena. Precognitive experiences, when faithfully recorded in a journal, help undo this great forgetting of our long self, and it is why I consider precognitive dreamwork and lifework and artwork a "gnosis," a reawakening to something super and impossible (but real) about our humanity.

People often read about precognition and other psychic phenomena in search of metaphysical solace, about the continuity of consciousness beyond death, and so on. I know that some of my readers come to my books expecting such affirmation, but it is something my vision of the long self and the block universe cannot readily provide. If the physical body is the information cable linking us to our future, as I believe evidence and current physical theory suggest to be the case, then precognition cannot enlighten us about what happens to consciousness, or the soul, after death. I wish it could, especially in light of heartbreaking current events that feel almost like a campaign to normalize death and destruction and the cutting-short of long selves.

9/11 was the first overwhelmingly traumatic news event of my life, and the second is the ethnic cleansing of Palestinians in Gaza. It is hardly the first, let alone the biggest, genocide in history, but it is the first to be captured by smartphones and shared, hour by hour, on social media; and it has made completing this book in the winter of 2023-24 inordinately difficult. The subject of the precognitive imagination feels *really* trivial when compared to the grief of Palestinian fathers and mothers holding their murdered children, doctors forced to perform amputations and other life-saving surgeries without anesthetic in Gaza's bombed-out hospitals, and unarmed, starving teenagers blown apart by drones. People of conscience in the United States must watch helplessly as our leaders support the atrocity and even supply the bombs.

Among the more than 30,000 long selves cut short as of this writing was that of professor and poet Refaat Alareer, whose last poem, "If I Must Die," foretold "a child, somewhere in Gaza … awaiting his dad who left in a blaze— / and bid no one farewell / not even to his flesh …"[2] Alareer, a vocal critic of Palestine's occupation, was killed along with his brother, sister, and their children in an airstrike on December 7, 2023. Was it a premonition? "If I Must Die" is another of those artworks marooned in the quantum no-man's-land of uncertainty, as far as literal prophecy is concerned: That the 44-year-old father of six would leave in a blaze (with no opportunity to bid farewell even to his children) was fairly predictable in the fourth week of the unrelenting Israeli military offensive, when he wrote the poem and pinned it to the top of his Twitter feed.[3]

To be sure, there are many in Israel, as around the globe, who are sickened by what is happening. I imagine that somewhere in that country right now, as I write this, there is an Ezekiel, or many Ezekiels, who are being thundered at by blazing, multi-headed LIVING CREATUREs about the wickedness of their leaders and military. Perhaps in the future, when this is all over (and the world has moved on to some other horror), an Israeli Jacques Vallée will collect and write about those close encounters and their psychic sequelae.

Jeff often stresses in his work that there is nothing intrinsically moral or ethical about the paranormal and the sacred. People who have paranormal experiences can be bad people. He's the historian of these things, and I'm sure that in the larger sweep of long superhumanity, he's right. But many who see UFOs, for instance, realize then and there that their lives are bigger and more serious than they had previously imagined. Their imagination quickly enlarges, and they often feel called upon to be better and do better.[4] Indeed, the anomalous lights I saw over the art museum had the same message for me that a radiant antique sculpted torso of the god Apollo had for the Austrian poet Rainer Maria Rilke in one of his most beloved poems: "You must change your life."[5]

Experiencing precognition in dreams and creativity has a similar effect, making you want to change your life. Seeing firsthand the reality that you are a long self in a block universe reinforces the value both of your own and of all the other long selves whose biographies interweave with yours, to make up the tapestry of our civilization. In my last book, written in the shadow of American atrocities at home, I wrote of a "long self revolution," awakening to the vastness of our lives as a way of awakening to the vastness and value of each other's—"a revolution of imagination and care, of empathy and anti-cruelty."[6] So if there is a moral or ethical implication of my argument, it is this: You must change your life in *this* life, not wait for the next one.

But while there's not exactly metaphysical solace, there is a kind of hope in this dreamwork and life-work and art-work, even if the hope comes with a challenge. It is not unlike the hope and challenge that Nietzsche offered with his vision of the Eternal Return: The philosopher thought that all of this would play over and over, like an album on endless repeat, until the end of time. It's also like the hope and challenge that Frederic Myers' expressed with his belief "that all things thought and felt, as well as all things done, are somehow photographed imperishably upon the Universe."[7] These are 19th-century, pre-Einsteinian, pre-Minkowskian ways of describing the Parmenidean universe of permanence. The block universe *is*, in a way, a kind of afterlife. So it is a universe we should all try to be better in, because it is all recorded—every act of wickedness, and every act of care and compassion. Like those bisons and horses on the walls of Chauvet Cave, our lives are painted on the walls of spacetime permanently, pictures to be revisited, movies to be replayed, as long as there are time travelers, or time-traveling con-sciousnesses, to hit the rewind button.

Introduction

[1] Stephen King, *Bag of Bones* (New York: Scribner, 2018), 176; see also Stephen King, *On Writing* (New York: Scribner, 2010).

[2] Armand D'Angour, *The Greeks and the New* (Cambridge, UK: Cambridge University Press, 2011).

[3] See Eric Wargo, *Where Was It Before the Dream?* (forthcoming).

[4] Jonah Lehrer, *Imagine* (Boston, MA: Houghton Mifflin Harcourt, 2012), 251.

[5] Mihaly Csikszentmihalyi, *Creativity* (New York: Harper Perennial Modern Classics, 2013).

[6] Maria Popova, "Networked Knowledge and Combinatorial Creativity," *The Marginalian*, August 1, 2011, https://www.themarginalian.org/2011/08/01/networked-knowledge-combinatorial-creativity/.

[7] Nick Chater, *The Mind Is Flat* (New York: Penguin, 2018); Arthur Koestler, *The Act of Creation* (London: Picador, 1964).

[8] Oliver Sacks, *The River of Consciousness* (New York: Vintage Books, 2017).

[9] Martin Gardner, *The Wreck of the Titanic Foretold?* (Amherst, NY: Prometheus Books, 1998). I discuss this case in detail in Eric Wargo, *Time Loops* (Charlottesville, VA: Anomalist Books, 2018).

[10] Steven Marcus, "Norman Mailer: An Interview," in *Conversations with Norman Mailer*, ed. J. Michael Lennon (Jackson, MS: University Press of Mississippi, 1988).

[11] "Bhopal Disaster," Wikipedia, accessed on November 6, 2023, https://en.wikipedia.org/wiki/Bhopal_disaster.

[12] Don Delillo, *White Noise* (New York: Penguin, 1998).

[13] Pierre Bayard, *Le Titanic fera naufrage* (Paris: Les Éditions de Minuit, 2016); Boris Kachka, "What Michel Houellebecq Represented to the Charlie Hebdo Shooters," *Vulture*, January 7, 2015, https://www.vulture.com/2015/01/michel-houellebecqs-role-in-the-paris-shooting.html.

[14] "Michel Houellebecq: 'Am I Islamophobic? Probably, Yes,'" *The Guardian*, September 6, 2015, https://www.theguardian.com/books/2015/sep/06/

michel-houellebecq-submission-am-i-islamophobic-probably-yes.

[15] Randal C. Archibold, "A Prolific Father of Haitian Letters, Busier than Ever," *The New York Times*, April 29, 2011, https://www.nytimes.com/2011/04/30/world/americas/30haiti.html.

[16] "2010 Haiti Earthquake," Wikipedia, accessed on November 6, 2023, https://en.wikipedia.org/wiki/2010_Haiti_earthquake.

[17] Archibold, "A Prolific Father"; "In Chaos of Post-Earthquake Haiti, Artists Create Poetry amid Rubble," *PBS News Hour*, January 26, 2011, https://www.pbs.org/newshour/show/in-chaos-of-post-earthquake-haiti-artists-create-poetry-amid-rubble.

[18] Ivette Romero, "Theater: Frankétienne's Premonitory Play, 'Melovivi,'" *Repeating Islands*, March 10, 2010, https://repeatingislands.com/2010/03/10/theater-franketienne.

[19] There is also Stephen King's 1978 *The Stand*, sometimes considered his magnum opus, which could be seen as prophesying the cultural context of the COVID-19 pandemic. After a virus—also a leaked bioweapon—decimates the country, survivors find themselves polarized into two warring factions that are strikingly reminiscent of the impossibly fraught political-social-racial landscape that emerged during the Trump administration: a violent, fascist faction led by the malevolent trickster Randall Flagg in Las Vegas versus a more liberal, civic-minded faction intent to peacefully rebuild society. The latter group converge on Boulder, Colorado under the leadership of an elderly Black woman they had seen in their dreams, Mother Abigail.

[20] Bayard, *Le Titanic fera naufrage*.

[21] "Paris in the Twentieth Century," Wikipedia, accessed on November 6, 2023, https://en.wikipedia.org/wiki/Paris_in_the_Twentieth_Century.

[22] Somewhat uncannily, a solution for recharging the crippled capsule's battery may have come to NASA engineer Art Campos from the film version of *Marooned*, which he coincidentally saw on the very evening he got the call about the real crisis unfolding in space. See Nancy Atkinson, "13 Things That Saved Apollo 13, Part 11: A Hollywood Movie," *Universe Today*, April 27, 2010, https://www.universetoday.com/63721/13-things-that-saved-apollo-13-part-11-a-hollywood-movie/.

[23] Kim Stanley Robinson, a hard-SF writer not given to paranormal woo, has been startled by some of his impossibly accurate prophecies. In his 2005 novel about climate change, *Forty Signs of Rain*, he gave the name Sandy to a superstorm that floods Washington, DC. Seven years later, the most devastating and costly hurricane ever to affect the Eastern Seaboard of the U.S. happened to have that very name. After leveling parts of Jamaica, the real-life Sandy went up the coast, causing considerable damage in DC suburbs, then flooding New York City and causing destruction as far north

as Canada. Robinson called it "a coincidence, but quite a coincidence" (Kim Stanley Robinson, *Green Earth* [New York: Del Rey Books, 2015], xiii). Because of the severe destruction and high number of deaths caused by this superstorm, the World Meteorological Association, which names Atlantic hurricanes according to a strict protocol (no, they didn't name it Sandy after Robinson's novel), forever retired the name Sandy, to be replaced by Sara in future rosters ("Tropical Cyclone Names," NOAA, accessed on November 6, 2023, https://www.nhc.noaa.gov/aboutnames.shtml#atl).

[24] Anthony Peake, *A Life of Philip K. Dick* (London: Arcturus, 2013); Wargo, *Time Loops.*

[25] D. Scott Apel, *Philip K. Dick—The Dream Connection* (Middletown, DE: Atomic Drop Press, 2014).

[26] Peake, *A Life of Philip K. Dick.*

[27] Wargo, *Time Loops.* Unfortunately, Robertson died just a few years after the *Titanic* disaster, possibly as a result of a medication he was taking to help him stop drinking. He was not able to capitalize on his reputation as a prophet.

[28] Bayard likens literary prophecy to a seismograph in *Titanic fera naufrage.*

[29] Wieland Schmied, *Friedrich* (New York: Harry N. Abrams, Inc., 1995).

[30] "Victor Brauner," Wikipedia, accessed on May 3, 2023, https://en.wikipedia.org/wiki/Victor_Brauner.

[31] Kevin Burwick, "Christopher Guest Reveals Real-Life Inspiration behind Spinal Tap," *Movieweb*, June 15, 2017, https://movieweb.com/spinal-tap-movie-true-inspiration-christopher-guest/; "Life Imitates Comedy: Spinal Tap Uncannily Anticipated Black Sabbath's Very Own Stonehenge Debacle," *DangerousMinds*, November 19, 2013, https://dangerousminds.net/comments/life_imitates_comedy_spinal_tap_uncannily_anticipated_black_sabbaths; "Spinal Tap: The Origins of Stonehenge," *Spinal Tap Fan*, accessed on September 22, 2023, http://www.spinaltapfan.com/articles/stonehenge.html.

[32] "Spinal Tap."

[33] Philip Oltermann, "'At First I Thought, This Is Crazy': The Real-Life Plan to Use Novels to Predict the Next War," *The Guardian*, June 26, 2021, https://www.theguardian.com/lifeandstyle/2021/jun/26/project-cassandra-plan-to-use-novels-to-predict-next-war.

[34] Peter Schwenger, *Fantasm and Fiction* (Stanford, CA: Stanford University Press, 1999).

[35] Shaun Kitchener, "Charlie Brooker Compares Black Mirror to THAT David Cameron Pig Rumour," *Express*, December 30, 2015, https://www.express.co.uk/showbiz/tv-radio/630455/Charlie-Brooker-Black-Mirror-David-Cameron-pig-2015-Wipe. Brooker also Tweeted: "Just to clear it up: nope, I'd never heard anything about Cameron and a pig when

coming up with that story. So this weirds me out" ("https://Twitter.com/Charltonbrooker/Status/645738652442734592?Lang=En," X (Formerly Twitter), accessed on September 22, 2023.)

36 Wargo, *Time Loops*.

37 Jeffrey J. Kripal, *The Superhumanities* (Chicago, IL: The University of Chicago Press, 2022), 78.

38 Etzel Cardeña, Ana E Iribas, and Sophie Reijman, "Art and Psi," *Journal of Parapsychology* 76 (2022): 3-25.

39 Zora Neale Hurston, *Dust Tracks on the Road* (New York: Amistad, 2006); see also Kripal, *The Superhumanities*.

40 Wargo, *Time Loops*.

41 J. F. Martel, *Reclaiming Art in the Age of Artifice* (Berkeley, CA: North Atlantic Books, 2015), 14.

42 Alan Lightman, *A Sense of the Mysterious* (New York: Vintage Books, 2005).

43 Also, as was vividly revealed in the era of "Me Too," overvaluing a person's genius acts as a shield against accusations of abuse or other misbehavior. Brilliant men's contributions to society have often been regarded as too important to worry about their faults or the people they may have hurt or wronged. See Amanda Hess, "How the Myth of the Artistic Genius Excuses the Abuse of Women," *The New York Times*, November 10, 2017, https://www.nytimes.com/2017/11/10/arts/sexual-harassment-art-hollywood.html.

CHAPTER 1: Sculptor of the Impossible

1 Moukhtar Kocache, "The Artist Residency Program in the Twin Towers" (presented as part of the February 28, 2002 International Foundation for Art Research symposium, September 11th: Art Loss, Damage, and Repercussions), accessed on January 22, 2024, https://www.ifar.org/nineeleven/911_residency1.htm.

2 Tara Bahrampour, "Losing a Studio, but Not a Calling," *The New York Times*, September 30, 2001, https://www.nytimes.com/2001/09/30/nyregion/reverberations-losing-a-studio-but-not-a-calling.html; Holland Cotter, "The Studios Were Lost, but the Artists Get Their Day," *The New York Times*, December 3, 2001, https://www.nytimes.com/2001/12/03/arts/art-review-the-studios-were-lost-but-the-artists-get-their-day.html.

3 One of the residents in the 1999-2000 winter cycle, Martina Gecelli, photographed the many dilapidated, abandoned offices. Another, Susan Kelly, made a pilgrimage all the way from the lobby to the 91st floor of Tower One via the stairs, for a performance piece called *The Land of the Far Beyond*.

Emily Jacir bought something from each of the numerous stores in the World Trade Center and documented these purchases, for a piece exploring global trade called *My America (I am Still Here)*. See Kocache, "The Artist Residency Program."

[4] Carola Dertnig, *... but buildings can't talk* (Vienna: Triton Verlag, 2002), 20.

[5] Ibid., 14.

[6] Cotter, "The Studios."

[7] C. Carr, "The Witnessing Eye," *Village Voice*, June 4, 2002, https://www.villagevoice.com/the-witnessing-eye/.

[8] Josmar Lopes, "Lost Navigator: Michael Richards—A Story of Redemption through Art," *Josmar Lopes*, September 12, 2015, https://josmarlopes.wordpress.com/2015/09/12/lost-navigator-michael-richards-a-story-of-redemption-through-art/.

[9] Rinker Buck, "Artists: Victims Now Shed Light on Tragedy," *Hartford Courant*, March 12, 2002, https://www.courant.com/news/connecticut/hc-xpm-2002-03-12-0203120187-story.html.

[10] Sheryl Nonnenberg, "Stanford Presents 'Michael Richards: Winged,'" *The Almanac*, February 14, 2019, https://www.almanacnews.com/news/2019/02/14/stanford-presents-michael-richards-winged; Ade Omotosho, "Travails and Contrails: Michael Richards at MoCA North Miami," *Art in America*, September 27, 2021, https://www.artnews.com/art-in-america/aia-reviews/michael-richards-museum-contemporary-art-north-miami-1234604967/.

[11] Sharon Pendana, "Sept. 11: Remembering 3 Lives Lost," *The Root*, September 2, 2011, https://www.theroot.com/sept-11-remembering-3-lives-lost-1790865634.

[12] Quoted in Josmar Lopes, "Michael Richards' 'Winged' Takes Flight: A Voice Once Silenced Cries Out Anew (Part 2)," *Josmar Lopes*, January 29, 2017, https://josmarlopes.wordpress.com/2017/01/29/michael-richards-winged-takes-flight-a-voice-once-silenced-cries-out-anew-part-two/.

[13] Lopes, "Lost Navigator."

[14] Nonnenberg, "Stanford Presents."

[15] Ibid.

[16] Cotter, "The Studios." If it is not the same piece, this may have been similar to a 2000 sculpture also lost in his WTC studio, called *Every Nigga Is a Star*, in which "a metallic, uniformed man straddles a comet like a bull rider, poised to careen through the cosmos" (Omotosho, "Travails and Contrails").

[17] Lopes, "Michael Richards' 'Winged'." An unnamed colleague quoted

in *The Independent* reported that Richards' last two unfinished sculptures "were bronze versions of himself pierced by airplanes and accompanied by meteors and flames" (Adrian Dannat, "Obituaries: Michael Richards," *The Independent*, April 15, 2014, https://www.independent.co.uk/news/ obituaries/michael-richards-9260645.html).

[18] Pendana, "Sept. 11."

[19] I am riffing on Jeffrey Kripal's term "author of the impossible." See Jeffrey J. Kripal, *Authors of the Impossible* (Chicago, IL: The University of Chicago Press, 2010).

[20] Ian Stevenson, "A Review and Analysis of Paranormal Experiences Connected with the Sinking of the *Titanic*," in *The Doomed Unsinkable Ship*, ed. W. H. Tantum (Riverside, Connecticut: 7 C's Press, 1974).

[21] Terry Keefe, *Premonitions of the Titanic Disaster* (Kibworth Beauchamp, UK: Matador, 2021).

[22] Graham Green, *A Sort of Life* (New York: Simon and Schuster, 1971).

[23] John Valentini, *Imagining 9/11*, PDFCoffee, 2011, accessed on January 17, 2024, https://pdfcoffee.com/imagining-9-11-pdf-free.html.

[24] Ibid., 3.

[25] Ibid., 18.

[26] Jim Woodring, "Here's a strange one," Facebook, May 19, 2018, https://m.facebook.com/jimwoodringcartoonist/photos/heres-a-strange-one-i-drew-this-on-september-10-2001-and-immediately-sent-a-file/10160393479735634/.

[27] Alec Recinos, "A Détourned Office Space," *Rhizome*, June 23, 2017, https://rhizome.org/editorial/2017/jun/23/airworld/.

[28] Gardner, *The Wreck of the Titanic Foretold?*

[29] "Skeptics: Did Edgar Allan Poe Predict a Shipwreck?," StackExchange, accessed on January 17, 2024, https://skeptics.stackexchange.com/ questions/27480/did-edgar-allan-poe-predict-a-shipwreck.

[30] Specifics of the fictional episode also differ from the real later tragedy—the men in the real lifeboat did not draw lots but killed the sick cabin boy as he slept, for instance.

[31] "The Man Who Paints the Future" (*Extraordinary People*, Season 1, Episode 1, Channel 5, 2003), YouTube, accessed on January 22, 2024, https://www. youtube.com/watch?v=gQP13EQ0dJo. The detail of the coincidental date of Mandell's dream, September 11, 1996, is important: Significant upheavals in dreamers' own lives or in the news are very often dreamed about exactly a year or multiple years earlier, on the same date—what I call "calendrical resonance." See Eric Wargo, *Precognitive Dreamwork and the Long Self*

(Rochester, VT: Inner Traditions, 2021).

32 Yulia Ustinova, *Caves and the Ancient Greek Mind* (Oxford, UK: Oxford University Press, 2009).

33 Peter Struck, *Divination and Human Nature* (Princeton, NJ: Princeton University Press, 2016).

34 Ustinova, *Caves.*

35 P. Ben Dixon, David J. Starling, Andrew N. Jordan, and John C. Howell, "Ultrasensitive Beam Deflection Measurement via Interferometric Weak Value Amplification," *Physical Review Letters* 102 (2009): 173601-1-4.

36 Yakir Aharonov and Jeff Tollaksen, "New Insights on Time-Symmetry in Quantum Mechanics," *arXiv* (2007): arXiv:0706.1232v1; Huw Price, "Does Time-Symmetry Imply Retrocausality? How the Quantum World Says 'Maybe'?" *Studies in History and Philosophy of Science Part B: Studies in History and Philosophy of Modern Physics* 43(2) (2012): 75-83; Huw Price and Ken Wharton, "A Live Alternative to Quantum Spooks," *arXiv* (2015): 1510.06712v2; Huw Price and Ken Wharton "Taming the Quantum Spooks," *Aeon*, September 14, 2016, https://aeon.co/essays/can-retrocausality-solve-the-puzzle-of-action-at-a-distance.

37 "God does not play dice with the universe" (Einstein quote), Wiktionary, accessed on February 4, 2024, https://en.wiktionary.org/wiki/God_does_not_play_dice_with_the_universe.

38 Giulia Rubino et al., "Experimental Verification of an Indefinite Causal Order," *Science Advances* 3(3) (March 24, 2017), https://www.science.org/doi/10.1126/sciadv.1602589.

39 William Gibson, *The Peripheral* (New York: Berkley, 2014). One of Gibson's premises is that his characters, once they communicate across time, live in different, parallel timelines called "stubs." For reasons I have explored elsewhere, I disagree with this common SF conceit: Time travel, informational or physical, is perfectly consistent with a single historical timeline, and in fact raises the dramatic stakes for any time travel premise. Writer Ted Chiang has explored this in some of his short stories, including the story on which the movie *Arrival* was based (see Wargo, *Precognitive Dreamwork*, for a discussion of Chiang's work).

40 See Wargo, *Time Loops.*

41 Johnjoe McFadden and Jim Al-Khalili, *Life on the Edge* (New York: Crown Publishers, 2014).

42 Christian M. Kerskens and David L. Pérez, "Experimental Indications of Non-Classical Brain Functions," *Journal of Physics Communications* 6(10) (2022): 105001, https://doi.org/10.1088/2399-6528/ac94be.

43 Charles Honorton and Diane C. Ferrari, "Future Telling": A Meta-Analysis

of Forced-Choice Precognition Experiments, 1935–1987," *Journal of Parapsychology* 53 (1989): 281-308.

[44] Brenda J. Dunne and Robert G. Jahn, "Information and Uncertainty in Remote Perception Research," *Journal of Scientific Exploration* 17 (2003): 207-41.

[45] Julia Mossbridge, Patrizio Tressoldi, and Jessica Utts, "Predictive Physiological Anticipation Preceding Seemingly Unpredictable Stimuli: A Meta-Analysis," *Frontiers in Psychology* 3(390) (2012): 1-18. That the robust evidence cannot be accounted for by some statistical fluke or manipulation has been shown by Jessica Utts, a former president of the American Statistical Association. See Jessica M. Utts, "An Assessment of the Evidence for Psychic Functioning," *Journal of Parapsychology*, 59 (1995): 289-320.

[46] Fernando Alvarez, "An Experiment on Precognition with Planarian Worms," *Journal of Scientific Exploration* 30 (2016): 217-26; Rupert Sheldrake, *Dogs That Know When Their Owners Are Coming Home and Other Unexplained Powers of Animals* (New York: Three Rivers Press, 2011).

[47] Daryl Bem, "Feeling the Future: Experimental Evidence for Anomalous Retroactive Influences on Cognition and Affect," *Journal of Personality and Social Psychology* 100 (2011): 407-25.

[48] Daryl Bem, Patrizio E. Tressoldi, Thomas Rabeyron, and Michael Duggan, "Feeling the Future: A Meta-Analysis of 90 Experiments on the Anomalous Anticipation of Random Future Events" [version 2; referees: 2 approved], *F1000Research,* 4 (2016): 1188.

[49] The Precognition subreddit (r/precognition) is one place online where many people share their precognitive experiences.

[50] Wargo, *Precognitive Dreamwork*.

[51] James C. Carpenter, "First Sight: A Way of Thinking about the Mind, and a Theory of Psi," in *Extrasensory Perception Vol. 2*, ed. E. C. May & S. B. Marwaha (Santa Barbara, CA: Praeger, 2015).

[52] Joseph McMoneagle, *The Stargate Chronicles* (Charlottesville, VA: Hampton Roads, 2002).

[53] Wargo, *Precognitive Dreamwork*.

[54] Alan Moore, *Jerusalem* (London: Knockabout, 2016).

[55] Douglas Clark, "Quoting Einstein: Einstein and Michele Besso," *Quoting Einstein*, June 27, 2013. http://quotingeinstein.blogspot.com/2013/06/einstein-and-michele-besso.html.

[56] Kripal, *Authors of the Impossible*; Dinesh Sharma, "Why STEAM Needs the Humanities to Understand Science," *Psychology Today*, December 29, 2021, https://www.psychologytoday.com/us/blog/leaders-in-the-making/202112/why-steam-needs-the-humanities-understand-science.

⁵⁷ Ayad Akhtar, *Homeland Elegies* (New York: Little Brown, 2020).

⁵⁸ "'Homeland Elegies' Novelist Reflects on Homesickness and the Immigrant Experience," *NPR*, September 14, 2020, https://www.npr.org/2020/09/14/912667645/homeland-elegies-novelist-reflects-on-homesickness-and-the-immigrant-experience.

⁵⁹ Alexandra Schwartz, "An American Writer for an Age of Division," *The New Yorker*, September 21, 2020, https://www.newyorker.com/magazine/2020/09/21/an-american-writer-for-an-age-of-division.

⁶⁰ "Dani Shapiro on Her New Novel 'Signal Fires,'" *NPR*, October 22, 2022, https://www.npr.org/2022/10/22/1130725579/dani-shapiro-on-her-new-novel-signal-fires.

CHAPTER 2: Steampunk Connection

¹ Mark Twain, "Mental Telegraphy: A Manuscript with a History" (orig. published in *Harper's*, December, 1891), *Robert A. Heinlein*, accessed on January 22, 2024, https://www.nitrosyncretic.com/rah/telepath.html.

² Ibid.

³ Ibid.

⁴ Ibid.

⁵ Ibid.

⁶ Ibid.

⁷ Elizabeth Greenfield Krohn and Jeffrey Kripal, *Changed in a Flash* (Berkeley, CA: North Atlantic Books, 2018).

⁸ Jeffrey Kripal, *Comparing Religions* (Chichester, UK: Wiley, 2014).

⁹ Roger Luckhurst, *The Invention of Telepathy* (Oxford, UK: Oxford University Press, 2002).

¹⁰ Elizabeth Lloyd Mayer, *Extraordinary Knowing* (New York: Bantam, 2008).

¹¹ Richard Rose, *Living Magic* (New York: Rand McNally, 1956).

¹² Kripal, *Comparing Religions*.

¹³ Ron Powers, *Mark Twain* (New York: Free Press, 2005); Mark Twain, *The Autobiography of Mark Twain Volume 1* (Berkeley, CA: The University of California Press, 2010).

¹⁴ Powers, *Mark Twain*; Twain, *The Autobiography*.

¹⁵ Upton Sinclair, *Mental Radio* (Charlottesville, VA: Hampton Roads, 2001).

¹⁶ In an article on the Sinclair experiments for the Boston Society for

Psychical Research, the society's research officer, Dr. Walter Franklin Prince, compared Craig's "resolute inquiry" to the famous *Cogito* of Descartes: "She is satisfied with 'I am,' not because 'I think,' but because 'I am conscious of thinking'; but she does not readily grant the '*I* think.' She wants to know, 'Am *I* doing all the thinking I am conscious of?'" (quoted in Sinclair, *Mental Radio*, 138).

[17] Mary Craig Sinclair, *Southern Belle* (Jackson, MI: University Press of Mississippi, 1999), 265.

[18] Sinclair, *Mental Radio*, 195.

[19] Ibid., 195-6.

[20] Ibid., 196.

[21] Ibid., 33-34.

[22] Ibid., 33.

[23] Edmund Gurney, Frederic W. H. Myers, and Frank Podmore, *Phantasms of the Living, Vol. 1* (Boston, MA: Elibron Classics, 2007); René Warcollier, *Mind to Mind* (Charlottesville, VA: Hampton Roads, 2001).

[24] Sinclair, *Mental Radio*, 43.

[25] Ibid., 7.

[26] Anthony Arthur, *Radical Innocent* (New York: Random House, 2006).

[27] "[O]ne must not rule out the possibility that in many tests, made across the width of a room, Mrs. Sinclair may have seen the wiggling of the top of a pencil, or arm movements, which would convey to her unconscious a rough notion of the drawing" (Martin Gardner, *Fads & Fallacies in the Name of Science* [Mineola, NY: Courier Dover Publications, 1957], 310-11).

[28] Sinclair, *Mental Radio*, xii. Like other debunkers that have pounced on psychical claims, Gardner often resorted to wild suppositions, sometimes without even reading the source material for the cases he attempted to debunk. See Greg Taylor, "How Martin Gardner Bamboozled the Skeptics," *Darklore* 5 (2010): 195-221.

[29] Wargo, *Time Loops*.

[30] Marcus Romondt was a pen-name for a Boer spy, propagandist, and writer on spiritualism and alternative medicine named Johanna Brandt. Upton's impression that *Patricia* was about South African religious cults is not correct: It is about a young Dutch woman who learns and practices the art of "magnetic" healing—she is a practitioner of mesmerism—in the years leading up to her emigration to South Africa sometime in the 19th century.

[31] Sinclair, *Mental Radio*, 36.

[32] Marcus Romondt, *Patricia, Vol I* (Johannesburg, South Africa: Author,

1923), 192.

[33] Ibid., 36-7.

[34] Richard Noakes, *Physics and Psychics* (Cambridge, UK: Cambridge University Press, 2019).

[35] Sinclair, *Mental Radio*, 37.

[36] Later research and application with remote viewing in the 1970s, first at Stanford Research Institute and then in the U.S. Department of Defense Star Gate program, was arguably muddled by the same confusion. Remote viewers were frequently accurate at describing geographic targets on the basis of no cuing information and with the experimenter blind to the assigned target chosen by a third party—meaning there was no way to know even what the intent of the task was without invoking either a divine guiding intelligence or else acknowledging that all the information—the "clairvoyantly" acquired information and the remote viewer's intuition that it was the right answer— came from the viewer's future in the form of feedback. See Eric Wargo, "Unknown Unknowns: Psi, Association, and the Physics of Information," *The Nightshirt*, July 5, 2015, http://www.thenightshirt.com/?p=3060; Eric Wargo, "Pat Price, Precognition, and 'Star Wars': A Reexamination of a Historic Remote Viewing Case," *EdgeScience* 42 (June, 2020): 10-21, https:// scientificexploration.s3.amazonaws.com/files/edgescience-42.pdf#page=10.

[37] Benedict Anderson, *Imagined Communities* (London: Verso, 1983).

[38] Luckhurst, *The Invention of Telepathy*.

[39] George Lakoff and Mark Johnson, *Metaphors We Live By* (Chicago, IL: The University of Chicago Press, 1980).

[40] There may be a bias here beyond the cultural. Humans seem to have a strong inclination to think spatially about complex causal relationships. To borrow a phrase from the Grail Knight Gurnemanz in Richard Wagner's opera *Parsifal*, we turn time into space. See Wargo, *Precognitive Dreamwork*.

[41] J. W. Dunne, *An Experiment with Time* (London: Faber and Faber, 1952).

[42] Ibid., 51

[43] Guy Inchbald, *The Man Who Dreamed Tomorrow* (Author, 2023).

[44] Sigmund Freud, "A Premonitory Dream Fulfilled," in *Psychoanalysis and the Occult*, ed. G. Devereux (London: Souvenir Press, 1974).

[45] Dunne, *An Experiment with Time*.

[46] Gerald Feinberg, "Precognition—A Memory of Things Future," in *Quantum Physics and Parapsychology*, ed. L. Oteri (New York: Parapsychology Foundation, Inc., 1975); Sean O'Donnell, *Future Memory and Time* (Galway, Ireland: PreCall Press, 1996); Jon Taylor, "The Nature of Precognition," *Journal of Parapsychology* 78 (2014): 19-38; Wargo, *Time Loops*.

47 Twain, "Mental Telegraphy."

48 Powers, *Mark Twain*, 373.

49 In a manuscript called "Why Are We Like This?" that was only published as an Appendix to a later edition of *Mental Radio*, Craig recorded one particularly vivid impression during her initial set of trials with Bob, which prompted her to call him immediately on the phone for confirmation instead of wait until their customary visit:

> One day, while I lay passively waiting for a "vision," a
> chair of a certain design floated before my mind. It was so
> vivid that I felt absolutely certain that this was the object
> my brother-in-law, thirty miles away, was visualizing for
> me. Other objects on other occasions had been vivid, but
> this one was not merely vivid; in some mysterious way,
> it carried absolute conviction with it. I knew positively
> that my mind was not deceiving me. I was so sure that
> this chair had come "on the air" from my brother-in-
> law's mind to mine, that I jumped up and went to the
> telephone and rang him up. His wife was in the room with
> him and my husband was in the room with me, and we
> called on them as witnesses—for we had set out on the
> experiment determined that there was to be no deception,
> of each other, nor of ourselves. ... My vision of the chair,
> and my drawing of it, were entirely correct. This was our
> first thrilling success. (Sinclair, *Mental Radio*, 196.)

An almost immediate reward, in other words—a "thrilling success." Its vividness in Craig's mind could have been a function of the fact that she would immediately confirm this "hit" via an excited phone call.

50 Kripal quips that Rhine effectively developed methods to "suppress psi and make it finally go away" (Kripal, *Authors of the Impossible*, 24).

51 Wargo, *Precognitive Dreamwork*.

52 Sinclair, *Mental Radio*, 25-6.

53 This amalgamating process is very similar to the dream-work process of "condensation" described by Sigmund Freud. See Sigmund Freud, *The Interpretation of Dreams* (New York: Avon Books, 1965).

54 In contrast, most dry expositions of telepathy experiments in psychical research journals then or ever omit any information about the feedback psychics received after the experiment, let alone the emotions they felt. But precognition of subsequent feedback may explain the pattern of results shown in at least some of these experiments. See Wargo, *Time Loops*.

55 Wargo, *Precognitive Dreamwork*.

[56] Kripal, *Authors of the Impossible.*

[57] Kripal, *Mutants and Mystics.*

[58] Another example from Myers and his colleagues illustrates how important such confirmatory scenes may be, however they are interpreted: A year after his young sister's tragic cholera death in Missouri, a Boston man on a business trip to that state thought he saw her sitting next to him, with a scratch on her cheek. So moved by this impossible vision, he canceled the rest of his trip and traveled home to tell his mother. At the detail about the scratch, the mother broke down and revealed that she had accidentally scratched the girl's cheek, in her grief, when preparing her body for burial, and had told nobody. The mother died a few weeks later, "happy she would rejoin her favorite daughter in a better world" (in Kripal, *Authors of the Impossible*, 78).

[59] The not-quite-simultaneity, and in some cases not-at-all simultaneity, of putative telepathic experiences has haunted the literature on telepathy from the start, causing writers to invoke something like precognition—or "thought forms" that take time to arrive—as a supplement to the theory, to make the data add up. See for instance Warcollier, *Mind to Mind.*

[60] Wargo, "Pat Price"; Wargo, *Time Loops.*

[61] Paul Smith, *Reading the Enemy's Mind* (New York: Forge, 2005).

[62] For instance, Kripal argues that cinematic images made possible by CGI are literally "changing the afterlife" by providing new, increasingly rich visual metaphors that feed into people's real near-death experiences. See Krohn and Kripal, *Changed in a Flash.*

[63] Price and Wharton, "Taming the Quantum Spooks."

[64] Charles H. Hinton, *A New Era of Thought* (London: Swan Sonnenschein & Co. Ltd., 1888).

[65] Octavio Paz, *Alternating Current* (New York: Arcade, 1990), 66.

[66] Calvin Tomkins, *Duchamp* (New York: The Museum of Modern Art, 2014), 113.

CHAPTER 3: No Backstory

[1] Freud, *The Interpretation of Dreams.*

[2] Ibid.

[3] Ibid.

[4] Salomon Resnik, *The Theatre of the Dream* (London: Tavistock Publications, 1987).

[5] Freud, *The Interpretation of Dreams*, 139.

[6] Wargo, *Time Loops*.

[7] Feinberg, "Precognition"; O'Donnell, *Future Memory and Time*; Taylor, "The Nature of Precognition"; Wargo, *Time Loops*.

[8] Krohn and Kripal, *Changed in a Flash*.

[9] Elizabeth G. Krohn, "The Eternal Life of Consciousness" (Essay submitted to Bigelow Institute for Consciousness Studies, July 21, 2021), accessed on January 22, 2024, https://theformulaforcreatingheavenonearth.com/wp-content/uploads/2022/04/04-RU-Elizabeth-Krohn.pdf; Elizabeth G. Krohn, Eyewitness to the Afterlife (King George, VA: The Mind & Meaning Institute, 2023).

[10] This is an important—crucial—observation made by Kripal in the book he co-authored with Krohn, *Changed in a Flash*.

[11] Wargo, *Precognitive Dreamwork*. See also Andrew Paquette, *Dreamer* (Winchester, UK: O Books, 2011).

[12] Vladimir Nabokov, *Insomniac Dreams* (Princeton, NJ: Princeton University Press, 2018).

[13] Ibid.

[14] Dunne, *An Experiment with Time*, 207.

[15] Wargo, *Time Loops*; Wargo, *Precognitive Dreamwork*.

[16] I discuss Freud's dream at length in *Time Loops*.

[17] Ingo Swann, *Your Nostradamus Factor* (New York: Swann-Ryder Productions, 2018).

[18] Wargo, *Precognitive Dreamwork*.

[19] Madeleine L'Engle, *A Wrinkle in Time* (New York: Farrar, Straus and Giroux, 2007).

[20] Christopher G. White, *Other Worlds* (Cambridge, MA: Harvard University Press, 2018).

[21] This has been supported experimentally. In 2011, physicist Seth Lloyd used a "quantum gun" to show that a photon "shot" a billionth of a second into its own past cannot interfere with its past self. See Seth Lloyd et al., "Closed Timelike Curves via Postselection: Theory and Experimental Test of Consistency," *Physical Review Letters* 106 (2011): 040403.

[22] Adam Frank, "There Is No Empirical, Scientific Evidence for the Multiverse," *Big Think*, February 3, 2022, https://bigthink.com/13-8/multiverse-no-evidence/. For the opposite viewpoint, see David Deutsch, *The Fabric of Reality* (New York: Penguin Books, 1998).

23 On quantum retrocausation, see Aharonov and Tollaksen, "New Insights on Time-Symmetry"; Price, "Does Time-Symmetry Imply Retrocausality?"; Price and Wharton, "A Live Alternative to Quantum Spooks"; Price and Wharton "Taming the Quantum Spooks." On the brain as a quantum computer, see Christian Matthias Kerskens and David López Pérez, "Experimental Indications of Non-Classical Brain Functions," *Journal of Physics Communications* 6(10) (2022): 105001, https://iopscience.iop.org/article/10.1088/2399-6528/ac94be.

24 Wargo, *Time Loops*.

25 Krohn and Kripal, *Changed in a Flash*, 178.

26 Krohn and Kripal, *Changed in a Flash*.

27 See D. W. Pasulka, *American Cosmic* (Oxford, UK: Oxford University Press, 2019).

28 Kripal, *Mutants and Mystics*, 330.

29 Gary Lachman, *Lost Knowledge of the Imagination* (Edinburgh, UK: Floris Books, 2018).

30 See, e.g., Michelle Karnes, "Marvels in the Medieval Imagination," *Speculum* 90(2) (April 2015), 327-65.

31 Psychiatrist Iain McGilchrist (*The Matter with Things* [London: Perspectiva Press, 2021], 774) writes, "My contention is that imagination, far from deceiving us, is the only means whereby we experience reality: it is the place where our individual creative consciousness meets the creative cosmos as a whole." It is a restatement of a position on the imagination articulated by Samuel Taylor Coleridge in his 1817 book *Biographia Literaria*—see Wargo, *Where Was It Before the Dream?*

32 Wargo, *Precognitive Dreamwork*. Dreams also put the dreamer in the seat of the action even when what is precognized is a picture, a news story, or a scene in a book or movie.

33 Cognitive scientist Donald Hoffman argues that perception is entirely illusory or imaginal, analogous to icons on a computer screen. See Donald D. Hoffman, *The Case Against Reality* (London: Penguin, 2020).

34 Stevenson, "A Review and Analysis"; Ian Stevenson, "Seven More Paranormal Experiences Associated with the Sinking of the Titanic," in *The Doomed Unsinkable Ship*, ed. W. H. Tantum (Riverside, Connecticut: 7 C's Press, 1974).

35 Sally Rhine Feather and Michael Schmicker, *The Gift* (New York: St. Martin's Press, 2005), 25.

36 In the 1960s, when playwright J. B. Priestley solicited viewers of a BBC television program for precognitive dream accounts, he was inundated with

letters from people all over Britain—more than 1,500. Many were from women who had experienced eye rolls and dismissiveness from their "no nonsense" spouses. J. B. Priestley, *Man & Time* (London: Bloomsbury Books, 1989).

[37] Kripal, *Comparing Religions*.

[38] David Sheff, *All We Are Saying* (New York: St. Martin's Griffin, 2000), 190.

[39] Ibid., 192.

[40] Ibid., 193 (emphasis in original).

[41] Lightman, *A Sense of the Mysterious*, 17.

[42] Max Brod, *Franz Kafka* (New York: Da Capo Press, 1995), 129.

[43] The term "autosymbolic" comes from early 20th century psychiatrist Herbert Silberer, who argued that hypnagogic images on the edge of sleep pictorially depicted verbal thoughts the individual was just then thinking. See Herbert Silberer, "Report on a Method of Eliciting and Observing Certain Symbolic Hallucination-Phenomena," in *Organization and Pathology of Thought*, ed. D. Rapaport (New York: Columbia University Press, 1959).

[44] Sacks, *The River of Consciousness*.

[45] King, *Bag of Bones*, 176. *The Peripheral* author William Gibson articulated something like this in an interview: "If the conscious part of me that thinks about story and motivation … were to sit down and outline something, it wouldn't be very good. I need the Stranger to sign in and give me the marching order" (quoted in Martel, *Reclaiming Art in the Age of Artifice*, 97).

[46] Neuroscientist and precognition researcher Julia Mossbridge argues that the idea that System 2 must be less biased than System 1 cannot be true: System 2 can only emerge from System 1, so the biases of the latter would be built into it (Julia Mossbridge, personal communication). See also Suzanne Kelly, "The Potential of Integrating Intelligence and Intuition," *The Cipher Brief*, June 10, 2022, https://www.thecipherbrief.com/the-potential-of-integrating-intelligence-and-intuition.

[47] Lehrer, *Imagine*, 6.

[48] Sheff, "All We Are Saying," 193.

[49] Chater, *The Mind Is Flat*.

[50] Powers, *Mark Twain*.

[51] "Decision augmentation" is a hypothesis offered by physicist and parapsychologist Edwin May to explain how precognition unintentionally and unconsciously skews experimental results. See Edwin C. May, "Experimenter Psi: A View of Decision Augmentation Theory," in *Extrasensory Perception Vol. 2*, ed. E. C. May & S. B. Marwaha (Santa Barbara, CA: Praeger, 2015).

[52] On the daimon (or daemon), see Matt Cardin, *What the Daemon Said* (New York: Hippocampus Press, 2022).

[53] Robert Kanigel, *The Man Who Knew Infinity* (New York: Washington Square Press, 1991).

[54] Kripal, *Mutants and Mystics*.

[55] Kripal, *Secret Body*.

[56] Pasulka, *American Cosmic*; D. W. Pasulka, *Encounters* (New York: St. Martin's Essentials, 2023).

[57] See Stuart Davis, "Man Meets Mantis" (2018 audio narrative), YouTube, accessed on January 22, 2024, https://youtu.be/Zi_8W0qCUH0; Kripal, *Authors of the Impossible*; Whitley Strieber and Jeffrey J. Kripal, *The Super Natural* (New York: Penguin Random House, 2016). That UFOs and related phenomena represent a nonhuman intervention in human affairs is an idea that goes back to the early-20th-century collector of unexplained events, Charles Fort, who expressed the rather gloomy opinion that "we are property."

[58] Peter K. Chadwick, *Borderline* (London: Routledge, 1992), 35-6.

[59] Andy Clark, *The Experience Machine* (New York: Pantheon Books, 2023).

[60] Peter K. Chadwick, "The Stepladder to the Impossible: A Firsthand Phenomenological Account of a Schizoaffective Psychotic Crisis," *Journal of Mental Health* 2 (1993): 239-50, 239.

[61] One must always be cautious when proposing the possible value or truth of psychotic experiences. There are many dark histories of minimizing the suffering of people with mental illness and their need for treatment through some nonmedicalized revaluation of their thought processes. The controversial approach of Scottish psychologist R. D. Laing in the 1960s comes to mind: His view of psychosis as a meaningful journey to be experienced, like an initiation, rather than treated within a standard psychiatric model, is widely regarded to have been a failure.

[62] Lennon would today be described as schizotypal. He described a lifelong facility with seeing visions and entering a trancelike state:

> Surrealism had a great effect on me because then I realized
> that the imagery in my mind wasn't insanity—that if
> it was insane, then I belonged to an exclusive club that
> sees the world in those terms. Surrealism to me is reality.
> Psychedelic vision is reality to me and always was. When
> I looked at myself in the mirror at twelve, thirteen … I
> would find myself seeing these hallucinatory images of my
> face changing, becoming cosmic and complete. I would
> start trancing out and the eyes would get bigger and the

room would vanish; I read the same description years later by a famous person who took opium. (Sheff, *All We Are Saying*, 158.)

[63] Layla Alexander-Garrett, *Andrei Tarkovsky* (London: Glagoslav Publications, 2013).

[64] Philip K. Dick, *The Exegesis of Philip K. Dick* (New York: Houghton Mifflin Harcourt, 2011).

[65] Wargo, *Precognitive Dreamwork*.

[66] Although *Let It Be* was released last, after the Beatles' breakup, the sessions in *Get Back* preceded the recording of *Abbey Road*.

[67] "Sour Milk Sea," The Beatles Bible, accessed on November 10, 2023, https://www.beatlesbible.com/songs/sour-milk-sea/

[68] The Beatles, *The Beatles: Get Back* (London: Callaway, 2021), 91.

CHAPTER 4: Falling from the Sky

[1] Werner Herzog, *A Guide for the Perplexed* (New York: Farrar, Straus and Giroux, 2014).

[2] Werner Herzog, *Scenarios* (Minneapolis, MN: University of Minnesota Press, 2017).

[3] Herzog, *A Guide for the Perplexed*, 111.

[4] "When I write a script, I often describe landscapes I have never seen. Although I had never been to Peru before I started making Aguirre, I imagined the atmosphere with strange precision, and when I arrived in the jungle for the first time everything was exactly as I had pictured it" (ibid., 97).

[5] Ibid.

[6] Juliane Koepcke, *When I Fell from the Sky* (Green Bay, WI: Title Town Publishing, 2011).

[7] Ibid.

[8] Herzog, *A Guide for the Perplexed*.

[9] Ibid. Herzog based his ship-in-a-tree on a mention in Cabeza de Vaca's *La Relacion*, about finding a rowboat from one of several ships lost in a storm on Hispaniola in some trees some distance from the water. David Carson (trans.), "Cabeza de Vaca's *La Relacion*," *TexasCounties*, accessed on September 22, 2023, http://www.texascounties.net/articles/discovery-of-texas/theaccount-cabezadevaca.htm. Herzog greatly altered this idea, making the

boat a brigantine ridiculously high atop a tree, from which dangles a single rowboat on a long rope. It seems like a condensed metaphoric dream image of Koepcke's row of seats falling from the Electra.

[10] Herzog, *A Guide for the Perplexed*, 255.

[11] Werner Herzog, *Every Man for Himself and God against All* (New York: Penguin Press, 2023), 103.

[12] Chris Heath, "Mad German Auteur, Now in 3-D!" *GQ*, April 29, 2011, https://www.gq.com/story/werner-herzog-profile-cave-of-forgotten-dreams.

[13] Dietmar Kammerer, "I've Never Stood Still: A Conversation with Werner Herzog," in W. Herzog, *Interviews* (Jackson, MI: University Press of Mississippi, 2014).

[14] The sublime and the beautiful were a highly gendered opposition in the aesthetics and philosophy of the Enlightenment. The most rarified philosophical/existential pleasure of conceptual self-destruction was reserved for men, believed to be more capable of experiencing it. Mere beauty, in contrast, was cozy and congenial, appealing (it was always asserted) to the feminine spirit with its love of comfort, prettiness, and pleasant domesticity.

[15] Sabina Spielrein, "Destruction as the Cause of Coming into Being," *Journal of Analytical Psychology* 39 (1994): 155-86.

[16] Some of the best children's literature and cinema is on this theme. A. E. Milne's *Winnie the Pooh* stories are stories about transitional objects—the melancholy tone of the stories coming from Christopher Robin's destined forgetting of his toys. Pixar's *Toy Story* films are similarly about children's loss, forgetting, and destruction of their transitional objects.

[17] Harold Bloom, *Agon* (Oxford, UK: Oxford University Press, 1983).

[18] Ariane Bazan and Sandrine Detandt, "On the Physiology of *Jouissance*: Interpreting the Mesolimbic Dopaminergic Reward Functions from a Psychoanalytic Perspective," *Frontiers in Human Neuroscience* 7 (2013): 709.

[19] Wargo, *Time Loops*.

[20] Four years later, Freud and Ernst would also endure the loss of Sophie's other son Heinerle, Ernst's brother, who had been Freud's favorite. Poor Ernst grew up in the shadow of these losses and the knowledge that, despite his central role in his grandfather's book, he was not seen as a remarkable child, and had not been foremost in his grandfather's eyes. He was raised by Anna Freud, in a household where his every behavior was psychoanalyzed, and not surprisingly, became a psychoanalyst himself.

[21] See Wargo, *Time Loops*.

[22] The term "time gimmick" was used originally by Jule Eisenbud in his book *Paranormal Foreknowledge* (New York: Human Sciences Press, 1982). On the

role played by time gimmicks in dreams, see Wargo, *Precognitive Dreamwork.*

[23] Jacques Lacan, *The Seminar of Jacques Lacan Book 1* (New York: W. W. Norton & Company, 1991).

[24] Similarly, J. F. Martel (*Reclaiming Art in the Age of Artifice*) discusses "rifts," points of rupture or eruption of the Real into a work that contains or embodies its prophetic power.

[25] I describe examples from Mary Shelley, J. R. R. Tolkien, and other writers in Wargo, *Where Was It Before the Dream?*

[26] Jonathan Culler, *Framing the Sign* (Norman, OK: University of Oklahoma Press, 1990).

[27] Sigmund Freud, *Civilization and Its Discontents* (New York: W. W. Norton & Company, 1961).

[28] Theodore Flournoy, *From India to the Planet Mars* (New York: Cosimo Classics, 2007).

[29] "The 'Face on Mars,'" NASA, accessed on January 22, 2024, https://mars.nasa.gov/resources/7493/the-face-on-mars/.

[30] Mac Tonnies, *After the Martian Apocalypse* (New York: Paraview Pocket Books, 2004).

[31] Richard C. Hoagland, *The Monuments of Mars* (Berkeley, CA: North Atlantic Books, 1992); Society for Planetary SETI Research, *The Case for the Face* (Kempton, IL: Adventures Unlimited Press, 1998). The Mars Anomaly community retains a belief that the Face is artificial and that NASA and/or its contractors have manipulated later images to make it look otherwise.

[32] Based on various pieces of evidence including an anomalous excess of the isotope Xenon 129 in the Martian atmosphere, author John E. Brandenburg, a former NASA plasma physicist, argues that the Red Planet's inhabitants perished about half a billion years ago in a nuclear attack. See John E. Brandenburg, *Death on Mars* (Kempton, IL: Adventures Unlimited Press, 2015).

[33] Carl Sagan, *Cosmos* (New York: Random House, 1980); Tonnies, *After the Martian Apocalypse.* The possibility of ET ruins in our solar system had also been expressed in a 1960 Brookings Institution Report: Donald N. Michael, "Proposed Studies on the Implications of Peaceful Space Activities for Human Affairs," NASA, accessed September 22, 2023, https://web.archive.org/web/20100514040440/http://ntrs.nasa.gov/archive/nasa/casi.ntrs.nasa.gov/19640053196_1964053196.pdf.

[34] Carl Sagan, *The Demon-Haunted World* (New York: Random House, 1997).

[35] Grant Morrison, "Grant Morrison: My Supergods from the Age of the Superhero," *The Guardian*, July 22, 2011, https://www.theguardian.com/

books/2011/jul/23/grant-morrison-supergods-superheroes.

36 "Jack Kirby," Wikipedia, accessed on November 12, 2023, https://en.wikipedia.org/wiki/Jack_Kirby.

37 Christopher Knowles, "The Sand Is Stained with the Blood of the Gods," *The Secret Sun*, December 29, 2011, https://secretsun.blogspot.com/2011/12/mindbomb-gulf-wars-and-gate-of-gods.html.

38 Christopher Knowles, "Mindbomb: John Carter, PKD and 'the Face on Mars,'" *The Secret Sun*, August 13, 2012, https://secretsun.blogspot.com/2012/08/mindbomb-john-carter-pkd-and-face-on.html.

39 Knowles, "The Sand Is Stained." Comics that seem to have prophesied world events is its own huge topic, even beyond the preternatural Jack Kirby. Comic artist John Byrne, for instance, may have prophesied the 1977 New York blackout, the death of Princess Diana, and the 1986 Challenger disaster in his comics for DC and Marvel in the 1970s and 1980s. See Maxwell Yezpitelok, "6 Eerily Specific World Events Predicted by Comics," *Cracked*, November 8, 2010, https://www.cracked.com/article_18836_6-eerily-specific-world-events-predicted-by-comics.html.

40 Hayden Herrera, *Listening to Stone* (New York: Farrar, Straus & Giroux, 2025).

41 Isamu Noguchi, *The Sculpture of Spaces* (New York: Whitney Museum of American Art, 1980), 18.

42 Herrera, *Listening to Stone*.

43 Besides being a significant year from the standpoint of the Cold War, 1947 is also considered the birth of the modern UFO phenomenon, including the first "flying saucer" sighting by Kenneth Arnold in Washington state and the crash, a week later, of an object near Roswell, New Mexico.

44 Martin Friedman, *Noguchi's Imaginary Landscapes* (Minneapolis, MN: Walker Art Center, 1978), 46.

45 Ron Walotsky, *Inner Visions* (London: Paper Tiger, 2000); Sagan, *Cosmos*.

46 Sonali Bhatt Marwaha and Edwin C. May, "The Multiphasic Model of Precognition," in *Extrasensory Perception Vol. 2*, ed. E. C. May & S. B. Marwaha (Santa Barbara, CA: Praeger, 2015).

47 Wargo, *Precognitive Dreamwork*.

48 Eric Wargo, "'But I Survived': Dream Premonitions and Survivor's Guilt" (paper presented at the 2021 annual meeting of the Society for Scientific Exploration-Parapsychology Association, July 24, 2021), YouTube, https://www.youtube.com/watch?v=bte-u-DIFwg; Wargo, *Precognitive Dreamwork*.

49 Ernest Becker, *The Denial of Death* (New York: Free Press, 1973).

50 Reiner Stach, *Kafka: The Years of Insight* (Princeton, NJ: Princeton

University Press, 2013).

[51] In *Where Was It Before the Dream?*, I argue that Kafka's *The Trial* was also a death-premonition.

[52] "A Final Interview with Ernest Becker, Author of The Pulitzer Prize Winning 'The Denial of Death,' And A Fond Farewell to the Wonderful Ernest Becker Foundation," *The Morbid Anatomy Online Journal*, December 19, 2023, https://www.patreon.com/posts/final-interview-94682299?l=fr.

[53] Pierre Bayard, *Demain est ecrit* (Paris: Les Éditions de Minuit, 2005). Bayard also shows that, although not quite "fatal," the descent into hedonism of the eponymous character in Oscar Wilde's 1891 novel *The Picture of Dorian Gray* is strikingly similar to the author's own life after he published his book. Wilde's affair with a young Lord Alfred Douglas, among various other scandals, resulted in Wilde's trial and imprisonment and hard labor in Reading Gaol from May 1895 to May 1897.

[54] Hundreds of people (350, by one count) were scheduled to fly on the four hijacked airliners but changed their plans at the last minute. A large number of prominent celebrities among them fueled later suspicions about insider knowledge prior to the attacks. See "Over 350 Passengers Canceled Their Reservations or Didn't Show Up for the Hijacked 9/11 Flights," *Shoestring 9/11*, August 22, 2014, https://shoestring911.blogspot.com/2014/08/over-350-passengers-canceled-their.html.

[55] Sam Knight, *The Premonitions Bureau* (New York: Penguin, 2022).

[56] Wargo, *Time Loops*.

[57] There is very often a dual valence about the outcomes precognized in dreams, some way in which we find ourselves relieved at the outcome of minor challenges, reflecting that things are not ideal but could have been worse (Wargo, *Precognitive Dreamwork*).

[58] Lopes, "Michael Richards' 'Winged.'"

[59] Richards described the tension in his art as expressing "the psychic conflict which results from the desire to belong to and resist a society which denies blackness even as it affirms" (Nonnenberg, "Stanford Presents").

[60] Deirdre A. Scott, *Passages: Contemporary Art in Transition* (New York: The Studio Museum in Harlem, 2000).

[61] Wargo, *Precognitive Dreamwork*.

[62] "Michelangelo's Prisoners or Slaves," Accademia, accessed on November 12, 2023, http://www.accademia.org/explore-museum/artworks/michelangelos-prisoners-slaves/.

[63] A web guide to the Accademia Gallery in Florence, where the Four Prisoners are displayed, describes:

They are some of the finest examples of Michelangelo's habitual working practice, referred to as "*non-finito*" (or incomplete), magnificent illustrations of the difficulty of the artist in carving out the figure from the block of marble and emblematic of the *struggle of man to free the spirit from matter*. These sculptures have been interpreted in many ways. As we see them, in various stages of completion, they evoke the enormous *strength of the creative concept* as they try to free themselves from the bonds and physical weight of the marble. It is now claimed that the artist deliberately left them incomplete to represent this *eternal struggle of human beings* to free themselves from their material trappings. ("Michelangelo's Prisoners or Slaves.")

[64] There have been many permutations of this fake quote: A Boston newspaper columnist in 1974 described an imaginary conversation in which "Mike" explained that he created his David thus: "All I did was chip away everything that didn't look like David." But there is a real basis for this idea in the sculptor's letters. In a letter to Benedetto Varchi, he wrote: "The sculptor arrives at his end by taking away what is superfluous." See "You Just Chip Away Everything That Doesn't Look like David," *Quote Investigator*, June 22, 2014, https://quoteinvestigator.com/2014/06/22/chip-away/; Nils Parker, "The Angel in the Marble," *Medium*, April 15, 2022, https://medium.com/@nilsaparker/the-angel-in-the-marble-f7aa43f333dc; "Michelangelo Quote Identification," *Ask MetaFilter*, accessed on September 22, 2023, https://ask.metafilter.com/267872/Michelangelo-quote-identification.

[65] Giorgio Vasari, *Lives of the Artists, Volume 1* (London: Penguin, 1987), 344.

[66] "Hall of the Prisoners by Michelangelo," Accademia, accessed on November 12, 2023, https://www.accademia.org/explore-museum/halls/hall-prisoners/.

CHAPTER 5: "They Have Been Here!"

[1] Gregory Curtis, *The Cave Painters* (New York: Anchor Books, 2006), 200.

[2] Jean-Marie Chauvet, Eliette Brunel Deschamps, and Christian Hillaire, *Dawn of Art* (New York: Harry N. Abrams, Inc., 1996), 41-2.

[3] Anita Quiles et al., "A High-Precision Chronological Model for the Decorated Upper Paleolithic Cave of Chauvet-Pont d'Arc, Ardèche, France," *Proceedings of the National Academy of Sciences* 113 (17) (2016): 4670–75, https://doi.org/10.1073/pnas.1523158113.

[4] Michael Balter, "Paintings in Italian Cave May Be Oldest Yet," Science 290 (5491) (October 20, 2000): 419–21.

[5] Brian Handwerk, "World's Oldest Known Figurative Paintings Discovered in Borneo Cave," *Smithsonian*, November 7, 2018, https://www.smithsonianmag.com/science-nature/worlds-oldest-known-figurative-paintings-discovered-borneo-cave-180970747/.

[6] Brian Handwerk, "45,000-Year-Old Pig Painting in Indonesia May Be Oldest Known Animal Art," *Smithsonian*, January 13, 2021, https://www.smithsonianmag.com/science-nature/45000-year-old-pig-painting-indonesia-may-be-oldest-known-animal-art-180976748/.

[7] Maxime Aubert et al., "Earliest Hunting Scene in Prehistoric Art, *Nature* 576 (December 19, 2019): 442-5, https://doi.org/10.1038/s41586-019-1806-y.

[8] Curtis, *The Cave Painters*.

[9] Michael Tucker, *Dreaming with Open Eyes* (London: Aquarian, 1992).

[10] Lysianna Ledoux and Myriam Boudadi-Maligne, "The Contribution of Geometric Morphometric Analysis to Prehistoric Ichnology: The Example of Large Canid Tracks and Their Implication for the Debate Concerning Wolf Domestication," *Journal of Archaeological Science* 61 (2015): 25-35, https://doi.org/10.1016/j.jas.2015.04.020.

[11] From their path through the cave, it is also clear that the child (or perhaps the wolf) took special interest in a block of limestone with a cave bear skull placed very deliberately on its upper surface—a feature that has invited much lay speculation about altars and controversial cave bear cults, along with academic finger-wags that it could just as easily have been some obsessive-compulsive visitor placing the skull like that because it looked nice. Perhaps it was even the child. No one knows.

[12] David Graeber and David Wengrow, *The History of Everything*. (London: Allen Lane, 2021).

[13] Michael Marshall, "70,000-Year-Old Remains Suggest Neanderthals Buried Their Dead," *New Scientist*, February 18, 2020, https://www.newscientist.com/article/2233918-70000-year-old-remains-suggest-neanderthals-buried-their-dead/.

[14] Ian Sample, "Neanderthals—Not Modern Humans—Were First Artists on Earth, Experts Claim," *The Guardian*, February 22, 2018, https://www.theguardian.com/science/2018/feb/22/neanderthals-not-humans-were-first-artists-on-earth-experts-claim.

[15] David Lewis-Williams, *The Mind in the Cave* (London: Thames & Hudson, 2002).

[16] "Werner Herzog's Cave Painting Documentary: 'the Birth of the Modern

Human Soul,'" *Der Spiegel*, February 16, 2011, https://www.spiegel.de/international/zeitgeist/werner-herzog-s-cave-painting-documentary-the-birth-of-the-modern-human-soul-a-745754.html. J. F. Martel puts this idea even more boldly: "the early humans didn't invent art. Art invented humanity" (Martel, *Reclaiming Art*, 9).

[17] Notably, representational art seems to have arisen "suddenly," and maturely: The very oldest paintings such as those in Chauvet Cave were as sophisticated, in some cases more sophisticated, than those in much younger caves like Lascaux—see Curtis, *The Cave Painters*; Jean Clottes, *What Is Paleolithic Art?* (Chicago, IL: The University of Chicago Press, 2016). "Apparently art did not begin clumsily," John Berger wrote; "There was a grace from the start" (John Berger, *Portraits* [London: Verso, 2021]). The fact that there is no identifiable prehistorical or evolutionary backstory to art—no prior evolution of childlike pictures—is, as Maria Popova puts it, a "meta-metaphor" for flashes of creative insight themselves, so often experienced as coming out of nowhere (Maria Popova, "How Creativity Works," *The Marginalian*, March 20, 2012, http://www.themarginalian.org/2012/03/20/jonah-lehrer-imagine-ho....).

[18] Graham Hancock, *Supernatural* (London: Arrow Books, 2006).

[19] Nick Longrich, "Evolution's 'Great Leap Forward': When Did Humans Cross the Intelligence Rubicon?," Genetic Literacy Project, November 4, 2020, https://geneticliteracyproject.org/2020/11/04/evolutions-great-leap-forward-when-did-humans-cross-the-intelligence-rubicon/

[20] Curtis, *The Cave Painters*; Clottes, *What Is Paleolithic Art?*

[21] Claude Lévi-Strauss, *Totemism* (Boston, MA: Beacon Press, 1963), 89.

[22] Kripal, *The Superhumanities*, 31.

[23] Krohn and Kripal, *Changed in a Flash*.

[24] Kripal, *The Superhumanities*.

[25] Some cave images may even be of UFOs: There are shapes highly suggestive of flying saucers. See Aime Michel, "Palaeolithic UFO-Shapes: Mysterious Drawings in the Stone Age Caves of France and Spain," *Flying Saucer Review* 15(6), November-December, 1969: 3-11, accessed February 21, 2024, http://www.ignaciodarnaude.com/avistamientos_ovnis/Michel,Palaeolithic%20UFO-Shapes,FSR69V15N6.pdf.

[26] "Trance" is an ill-defined term that some shamanism scholars like Richard Noll resist, finding it so vague as to be useless. I don't mind the vagueness, using it as a general synonym for any potentially visionary state in waking. Besides states of deep relaxation in meditation, it could include "flow" states experienced by athletes and artists, suggestible states under hypnosis, psychedelic experiences, and other waking ecstatic phenomena. For a classic

overview of the role of visions in shamanism, see Richard Noll, "Mental Imagery Cultivation as a Cultural Phenomenon: The Role of Visions in Shamanism," *Current Anthropology* 26(4) (1985): 443-461.

[27] J. David Lewis-Williams and Thomas A. Dowson, "The Signs of All Times: Entoptic Phenomena in Upper Paleolithic Art," *Current Anthropology* 29 (1988): 201-45.

[28] On the phenomenological trajectory of ayahuasca visions, for instance, see Stephan V. Beyer, *Singing to the Plants* (Albuquerque: University of New Mexico Press, 2009).

[29] It is partly an effect of the resolute cultural particularism (Kripal calls it "dogmatic localism") that has reigned in anthropology and its sister disciplines like paleoanthropology for the better part of a century, and it applies to long-vanished cultures as much as to living ones: You can't get into the head, or at least the experience, of the Other. Any attempt to do so is an imposition of one's own values or an appropriation, a kind of cognitive colonialism. See Sharma, "Why STEAM Needs the Humanities."

[30] Lewis-Williams, *The Mind in the Cave*. Lewis-Williams' cable metaphor is a useful one: Any particular evidential strand in a cable will necessarily have gaps in it, but when brought together, the different strands reinforce each other and make a larger, more interesting argument possible.

[31] Jean Clottes and David Lewis-Williams, *The Shamans of Prehistory* (New York: Harry N. Abrams, Inc., 1998). Clottes and Lewis-Williams expected that their book would be seen as a watershed contribution to the field, finally shedding at least some indirect light on the meanings of cave paintings after decades of scientific hesitation to interpret. Instead, they were baffled and depressed to find themselves either laughed at or ignored by many of their scientist peers. Prominent British archaeologist Paul Bahn contemptuously wrote in one review, "Membrane or Numb Brain," that the authors' "remarkable fantasies make one wonder if the authors themselves conjured up these visions out of an altered state of consciousness, like latter-day Edgar Cayces" (in Curtis, *The Cave Painters*, 226.). Another academic peer compared their book to Carlos Castaneda's "psychedelic ravings" (Ibid.). Essentially, they got a firsthand taste of the resistance and downright bullying that meet people in the postmodern academy who dare make bold comparative claims, especially if, in so doing, they accord validity to altered states of consciousness and mystical or supernormal experience. Nearly three decades later, their view is no longer so controversial.

[32] Clottes and Lewis-Williams, *The Shamans of Prehistory*.

[33] Ibid.

[34] Curtis, *The Cave Painters*.

[35] Verónica Fernández-Navarro, Edgard Camarós, and Diego Garate,

"Visualizing Childhood in Upper Palaeolithic Societies: Experimental and Archaeological Approach to Artists' Age Estimation through Cave Art Hand Stencils," *Journal of Archaeological Science* 140 (April, 2022): 105574, https://doi.org/10.1016/j.jas.2022.105574.

[36] Curtis, *The Cave Painters*.

[37] Ibid.

[38] Art historian Louise S. Milne calls hybrids a "master convention" for representing dual aspects of a person or other being. Although the fact that partial or complete transformations into animals are directly experienced in drug-induced altered states and dreams adds a dimension of possible experiential literalism to such images beyond any kind of conventional or ad hoc symbolic code. See Louise S. Milne, "A Storm in the Head: Animals, Dreams and Desire," *Cosmos* 27 (2011): 61-118, 63.

[39] Ibid., 61. Milne notes that later, in the Bronze Age, this iconographic complex took on additional meanings associated with the panic of warfare too.

[40] Michael Harner, *The Way of the Shaman* (New York: Harper & Row, 1990).

[41] Ustinova, *Caves*.

[42] Michael Harner, *Cave and Cosmos* (Berkeley, CA: North Atlantic Books, 2013), 18.

[43] Gil H. Renberg, *Where Dreams May Come* (Leiden: Brill, 2016).

[44] Rodney Castleden, *The Knossos Labyrinth* (London: Routledge, 1990).

[45] Ioan Couliano, *Out of This World* (Boston, MA: Shambhala, 1991).

[46] Ibid., 127.

[47] Richard M. Jones, *The Dream Poet* (Cambridge, MA: Schenkman Publishing Co, 1980).

[48] Curtis, *The Cave Painters*.

[49] Jean Stein, "William Faulkner, the Art of Fiction No. 12," *The Paris Review* 12 (Spring, 1956), https://www.theparisreview.org/interviews/4954/the-art-of-fiction-no-12-william-faulkner.

[50] Ewen Callaway, "'Cave of Forgotten Dreams' May Hold Earliest Painting of Volcanic Eruption," *Nature* (January 15, 2016), https://doi.org/10.1038/nature.2016.19177.

[51] Peter Kingsley, *In the Dark Places of Wisdom* (Point Reyes, CA: The Golden Sufi Center, 1999); Peter Kingsley, *Reality* (Point Reyes, CA: The Golden Sufi Center, 2004).

[52] Maxim W. Furek, *Sheppton* (Author, 2019).

[53] John Geiger, *The Third Man Factor* (New York: Hachette Books, 2010).

[54] Bill Schmeer, "The Entombed Miners' Staircase to Heaven," *Fate* 18(3) (March, 1965), 28-37.

[55] Furek, *Sheppton*, 166.

[56] William C. Kashatus, "Saint John XXIII's Second Miracle Might Have Occurred at Sheppton Mining Disaster," *Wilkes-Barre Citizens' Voice*, May 10, 2014, https://www.citizensvoice.com/lifestyles/saint-john-xxiiis-second-miracle-might-have-occurred-at-sheppton-mining-disaster/article_e76b2311-4d30-545b-a7da-f6f34ca51b7d.html.

[57] Wargo, *Precognitive Dreamwork*.

[58] Alexander Nicaise, "The Trapped Miners' Holy Visions: Investigating the Sheppton 'Miracle,'" *Skeptical Inquirer*, May 2, 2019, https://skepticalinquirer.org/2019/05/the-trapped-miners-holy-visions-investigating-the-sheppton-miracle/.

[59] Schmeer, "The Entombed Miners' Staircase."

[60] Wargo, *Precognitive Dreamwork*.

[61] Giorgio Samorini, "The Oldest Archeological Data Evidencing the Relationship of Homo Sapiens with Psychoactive Plants: A Worldwide Overview," *Journal of Psychedelic Studies* 3 (2) (2019): 63–80, https://doi.org/10.1556/2054.2019.008.

[62] Michael Winkelman, "Introduction: Evidence for Entheogen Use in Prehistory and World Religions," *Journal of Psychedelic Studies* 3 (Special Issue) (2019): 43–62, https://doi.org/10.1556/2054.2019.024.

[63] Brian Muraresku, *The Immortality Key* (New York: St. Martin's Press, 2020).

[64] Winkelman, "Introduction."

[65] Maxemiliano V. Vargas et al., "Psychedelics Promote Neuroplasticity through the Activation of Intracellular 5-HT2A Receptors, *Science* 379(6633) (2023): 700-6.

[66] David Luke, *Otherworlds* (London: Aeon Books Ltd., 2019); Dick Bierman, "The Effects of THC and Psilocybin on Paranormal Phenomena" (paper presented at Psychoactivity: A Multidisciplinary Conference on Plants, Shamanism, and States of Consciousness, Amsterdam, Netherlands, 1998), accessed on January 22, 2024, https://www.academia.edu/22937616/The_effects_of_THC_and_psilocybin_on_paranormal_phenomena.

[67] See Stanley Krippner, "The Cycle in Deaths among U.S. Presidents Elected at Twenty-Year Intervals," *International Journal of Parapsychology* 9(3) (Autumn 1967): 145-53.

[68] Stanislav Grof, "Varieties of Transpersonal Experiences: Observations from LSD Psychotherapy," in *Psychiatry and Mysticism*, ed. S. R. Dean (Chicago,

IL: Nelson-Hall, 1975).

69 Beyer, *Singing to the Plants*.

70 Ibid.; Kenneth M. Kensinger, "Banisteriopsis Usage Among the Peruvian Cashinahua," in *Hallucinogens and Shamanism*, ed. M. J. Harner (New York: Oxford University Press, 1973).

71 William S. Burroughs and Allen Ginsberg, *The Yage Letters* (San Francisco: City Lights Books, 1975), 54.

72 Ibid.

73 Allen Ginsberg, *South American Journals* (Minneapolis, MN: University of Minnesota Press, 2019), 226.

74 Burroughs and Ginsberg, *The Yage Letters*, 56.

75 "The Dendera Zodiac and the Panel of the Wounded Man at Lascaux," *Star Myths of the World*, September 6, 2011, https://www.starmythworld.com/mathisencorollary/2011/09/dendera-zodiac-and-panel-of-wounded-man.html.

76 See, e.g., Joan Halifax, *Shaman* (New York: Thames and Hudson, 1982).

77 Michel Jouvet, *The Paradox of Sleep* (Cambridge, MA: The MIT Press, 2001).

78 C. Fisher, J. Gross, J. Zuch, "Cycle of Penile Erection Synchronous With Dreaming (REM) Sleep: Preliminary Report," *Archives of General Psychiatry* 12(1) (1965): 29–45, doi:10.1001/archpsyc.1965.01720310031005.

79 Marques Redd, "The *Pyramid Texts* and The Origin of the Black Superhuman" (paper presented at the symposium Black Superhumanism, Esalen Center for Theory and Research, December, 2021).

80 Jeremy Naydler, *Shamanic Wisdom in the Pyramid Texts* (Rochester, VT: Inner Traditions, 2005); Algis Uždavinys, *Philosophy as a Rite of Rebirth* (Wiltshire, UK: The Prometheus Trust, 2008).

81 The similarity is noted by Jouvet, *The Paradox of Sleep*.

82 Lloyd D. Graham, "From Isis-kite to Nekhbet-vulture and Horus-falcon: Changes in the Identification of the Bird above Osiris's Phallus in Temple 'Conception of Horus' Scenes," *Birmingham Egyptology Journal* 8 (2020): 1-32, file:///Users/ericwargo/Downloads/From_Isis_kite_to_Nekhbet_vulture_and_Ho.pdf.

83 Eric Wargo, "The Great Work of Immortality: Astral Travel, Dreams, and Alchemy," *The Nightshirt*, May 16, 2015, https://www.thenightshirt.com/?p=2857.

84 Susan J. Blackmore, *Beyond the Body* (Chicago, Il: Academy Chicago Publishers, 1992); Michael Graziano, *Consciousness and the Social Brain*

(Oxford, UK: Oxford University Press, 2013); Evan Thompson, *Waking, Dreaming, Being* (New York: Columbia University Press, 2015).

I argue that some out-of-body-type experiences may be vivid previews of in-body experiences in the individual's future. If so, consciousness may not leave the body but, as J. W. Dunne argued, becomes detached from the temporal present—or as Kurt Vonnegut put it in *Slaughterhouse Five*, "unstuck in time." See Wargo, *Precognitive Dreamwork*.

[85] "Ancient Egypt and the Mystery of the Missing Phallus," Minneapolis Institute of Art, December 13, 2018, https://medium.com/minneapolis-institute-of-art/ancient-egypt-and-the-mystery-of-the-missing-phallus-97db0103ecdc.

[86] Redd, "The *Pyramid Texts*."

[87] See Algis Uždavinys, *Philosophy and Theurgy in Late Antiquity* (Kettering, OH: Angelico Press, 2014).

[88] Some (but not all) modern teachers extol masturbation as a precursor to lucid dreaming or out-of-body ("astral") travel. It may make some sense neurochemically: Orgasm releases serotonin, which interacts in the brain with some of the same neuronal receptors activated by hallucinogenic drugs; and serotonin metabolizes in the body to melatonin, the hormone that regulates sleep. Before you could purchase melatonin at your local drug or health food store, a person seeking rich, dream-filled slumber could use "Isis," if not sex with a partner, for the same purpose. In the myth, Osiris's dismemberment by Set could also reflect a kind of systematic focus of awareness on different parts of the body, a method also described in modern guides to inducing out-of-body experiences. See Robert Bruce, *Astral Dynamics* (Charlottesville, VA: Hampton Roads, 2009).

[89] Elizabeth Wayland Barber and Paul T. Barber, *When They Severed Earth from Sky* (Princeton, NJ: Princeton University Press, 2006).

[90] Ryan Hurd, "Unearthing the Paleolithic Mind in Lucid Dreams," in *Lucid Dreaming*, ed. R. Hurd & K. Bulkeley (Westport, Connecticut: Praeger/ABC-CLIO, 2014).

[91] Relatedly, Nobel-prize-winning physicist Roger Penrose and his collaborator Stuart Hameroff propose that consciousness arises from the so-called "collapse of the wavefunction" described in some interpretations of quantum mechanics, which they argue alters the very geometry of spacetime. See Stuart Hameroff and Roger Penrose, "Consciousness in the Universe: A Review of the 'Orch OR' Theory," *Physics of Life Reviews* 11(1) (2014): 39-78.

[92] On this question, I can't help but agreeing with Andrei Tarkovsky, who wrote in a 1970 diary entry:

It is meaningless, and therefore absurd, to make a
distinction between idealistic and materialistic philosophy
on the basis of a spurious watershed arbitrarily introduced
into the question of whether primacy lies with matter or
with consciousness. You might as well argue about which
came first—the chicken or the egg (Andrey Tarkovsky,
Time Within Time [London: Faber & Faber, 1994], 26).

[93] Ryan Hurd, "Unearthing the Paleolithic Mind."

[94] Harner, *Cave and Cosmos*.

[95] Redd, "The *Pyramid Texts*."

[96] Herzog, *A Guide for the Perplexed*.

[97] The book was probably a handsome volume with color images and text by
the French writer Georges Bataille, *Lascaux oder Die Geburt Der Kunst*, which
was put out in 1955 in multiple languages by the publisher Skira. It appeared
in English the same year with an identical cover: *Lascaux or the Birth of Art*.

[98] Kristoffer Hegnsvad, *Werner Herzog* (London: Reaktion Books, 2021), 18.

[99] Lila Moore, "From Cave to Screen: A Study of the Shamanic Origins of
Filmmaking," *Journal of Arts and Humanities* 8(12) (2019): 01-10, https://
doi.org/10.18533/journal.v8i12.1780.

[100] Jonathan Cott, "Werner Herzog: Signs of Life," *Rolling Stone*, November
18, 1976, https://www.rollingstone.com/movies/movie-features/werner-
herzog-signs-of-life-69852/.

[101] Judith Thurman, "First Impressions: What Does the World's Oldest Art
Say About Us?," *The New Yorker*, June 16, 2008, https://www.newyorker.
com/magazine/2008/06/23/first-impressions.

[102] Samuel Wigley, "Out of the Darkness: Werner Herzog's *Cave of Forgotten
Dreams*," in Herzog, *Interviews*.

[103] Ibid.

[104] Hegnsvad, *Werner Herzog*.

[105] Werner Herzog, *Cave of Forgotten Dreams* (film), History Films, Creative
Differences, 2010.

[106] "Alligator Spends Night in Cells," RFI, October 6, 2010, http://en.rfi.fr/
france/20101006-alligator-spends-night-cells; "French Police Seek Escaped
Gators," UPI, accessed September 22, 2023, https://www.upi.com/Odd_
News/2010/08/24/French-police-seek-escaped-gators/68971282669485/.

[107] Wigley, "Out of the Darkness."

[108] This, at least, is Werner Herzog's account—see Herzog, *A Guide for
the Perplexed*; Kraft Wetzel, "Interview with Werner Herzog," in Herzog,

Interviews.

[109] Ibid., 35.

CHAPTER 6: Life in the Deep C

[1] Robert J. Wallis, "Art and Shamanism: From Cave Paintings to the White Cube," *Religions* 10(54) (2019), https://www.mdpi.com/2077-1444/10/1/54/htm.

[2] Ibid.

[3] Mark Levy, *Technicians of Ecstasy* (Norfolk, Connecticut: Bramble Books, 1993); the expression comes from religion scholar Mircea Eliade.

[4] In Wallis, "Art and Shamanism," 2.

[5] Wallis, "Art and Shamanism."

[6] Jay Kinney, "Introduction," in P. K. Dick, *In Pursuit of VALIS* (Novato, CA: Underwood-Miller, 1991).

[7] Strieber and Kripal, *The Super Natural.*

[8] David Lynch, "I Am the Shaman" (Donovan music video), YouTube, accessed on September 22, 2023, https://www.youtube.com/watch?v=V5i98tfyGac.

[9] Tucker, *Dreaming with Open Eyes.*

[10] June O. Leavitt, *The Mystical Life of Franz Kafka* (Oxford, UK: Oxford University Press, 2012).

[11] Verlyn Flieger, *A Question of Time* (Kent, OH: Kent State University Press, 1997); Robert Tindall and Susana Bustos, *The Shamanic Odyssey* (Rochester, VT: Park Street Press).

[12] "The art life" is the philosophy Lynch adopted when he read *The Art Spirit*, by painter Robert Henri: "I loved that book ... and I had this idea that you drink coffee, you smoke cigarettes, and you paint, and that's it. Maybe girls come into it a *little* bit. But basically it's the incredible happiness of working and living that life." See Jon Nguyen, *David Lynch: The Art Life* (film), Duck Diver Films, 2016.

[13] Martel, *Reclaiming Art*, 98.

[14] Wargo, *Where Was It Before the Dream?*

[15] Noll, "Mental Imagery Cultivation"; see also Robert J. Wallis, "Exorcising 'Spirits': Approaching 'Shamans' and Rock Art Animically," in *Handbook of Contemporary Animism*, ed. G. Harvey (Durham, NC: Acumen, 2013).

[16] Stephen King, *On Writing* (New York: Scribner, 2010).

[17] Dick, *Exegesis*, 22.

[18] Chris O'Leary, *Rebel Rebel* (Winchester, UK: Zero Books, 2015).

[19] Brett Morgen, *Moonage Daydream* (film), BMG, Public Road Productions, Live Nation Productions, HBO Documentary Films, 2022.

[20] Social scientists over the decades have often played a kind of psychopathology whack-a-mole, "explaining" shamanism as this or that mental or brain disorder—autism, bipolar disorder, schizophrenia, take your pick. In more recent years, as appreciation of neuro-, sexual, and gender diversity has increased, along with recognition of the great diversity of shamans in different cultures, it has led to less reductive and pathologizing perspectives, and even to using the diversity-acceptance of non-Western societies as critical lens through which to view facile Western binarisms. See Robert G. Bednarik, "Brain Disorder and Rock Art," *Cambridge Archaeological Journal* 23(1) (2013): 69-81; Robert M. Kaplan, "The Neuropsychiatry of Shamanism," *Before Farming* 4 (2006), article 13.

[21] T. M. Luhrman, *How God Becomes Real* (Princeton, NJ: Princeton University Press, 2020); Noll, "Mental Imagery Cultivation."

[22] Cott, "Werner Herzog."

[23] Val Phoenix, "Embracing Otherness," *Cocteau Twins*, accessed on January 16, 2024, https://cocteautwins.com/embracing-otherness-alternative-press. html; Dave Simpson, "Elizabeth Fraser: The Cocteau Twins and Me," *The Guardian*, November 26, 2009, https://www.theguardian.com/music/2009/ nov/26/cocteau-twins-elizabeth-fraser-interview.

[24] See Christopher Knowles, "Laugh While You Still Can," *The Secret Sun*, October 17, 2020, https://secretsun.blogspot.com/2020/10/laugh-while-you-still-can.html; Christopher Knowles, "Songs of the Siren on the River Styx," *The Secret Sun*, September 26, 2014, https://secretsun.blogspot. com/2014/09/songs-of-siren-on-river-styx.html.
   With titles like "Sea, Swallow Me" (co-written with Harold Budd) and "Lorelei," water and sirens were frequent themes in songs Fraser recorded in the 1980s, although the song that is most uncannily prophetic of Jeff Buckley's drowning death, "Song to the Siren," was not written by her. First recorded by Jeff's father Tim Buckley in 1970, it was chosen by record producer Ivo Watts-Russell for the first album of his music collective This Mortal Coil in 1984, *It'll End in Tears*. The saga, as Knowles argues, is too weird not to be somehow paranormal, although Knowles' preferred idiom is synchronicity: Jeff Buckley heard Fraser's haunting cover of his dead father's song—with lyrics like "Hear me sing, swim to me, swim to me, let me enfold you"—and, like a mariner drawn to a siren, sought out the shy Scottish singer with the otherworldly voice. Fraser fell in love with him, which revitalized her emotionally after well over a decade in an unhappy codependent relationship with one of her Cocteau Twins bandmates. The love affair with Buckley didn't

last, however, and not long after parting ways, Fraser was in a Bristol, UK studio with the band Massive Attack recording a song she had written about Buckley called "Teardrop," when she got the news that he had disappeared while swimming in a channel of the Mississippi River. His body was found a few days later. She felt overwhelming guilt afterward, for not being more supportive of Buckley and for the missed opportunity their short relationship represented. For more on their relationship, see "Here Is One: The Story of Elizabeth Fraser & Jeff Buckley," *The Peeling*, November 12, 2021, https://thepeelingblog.com/2021/11/12/here-is-one-elizabeth-fraser-jeff-buckley/.

[25] Wargo, *Where Was It Before the Dream?* See also Leavitt, *The Mystical Life of Franz Kafka*.

[26] See also Wargo, *Where Was It Before the Dream?*

[27] Virginia Woolf, *Moments of Being* (Boston, MA: Mariner Books, 1985).

[28] Virginia Woolf, *The Diary of Virginia Woolf, Volume Three* (New York: Harvest/HBJ, 1980), 218.

[29] Manuela V. Boeira et al., "Virginia Woolf, Neuroprogression, and Bipolar Disorder," *Revista Brasileira de Psiquiatria* 39 (1) (2016): 69–71, https://doi.org/10.1590/1516-4446-2016-1962. A strangely bitter revisionist biography by anti-psychiatrist Thomas Szasz argues, contrarily, that she was merely a malingerer, feigning madness a la Hamlet, but it is largely unconvincing (even if it contains some interesting insights). See Thomas Szasz, *"My Madness Saved Me"* (London: Transaction Publishers, 2006).

[30] Guiseppe Scimeca et al., "Extrasensory Perception Experiences and Childhood Trauma: A Rorschach Investigation," Journal of Nervous and Mental Disorders 203(11) (2015): 856-63.

[31] Jeffrey J. Kripal, "The Traumatic Secret: Bataille and the Comparative Erotics of Mystical Literature," in *Negative Ecstasies*, eds. J. Biles and K. Brintnall (New York: Fordham University Press, 2015). See also Krohn and Kripal, *Changed in a Flash*, where precognitive dreamer Elizabeth Krohn describes her sexual abuse as a teen, which caused out-of-body experiences.

[32] This was very similar to Kafka's maturation as a writer—see Wargo, *Where Was It Before the Dream?*

[33] Woolf, *Moments of Being*, 81.

[34] Virginia Woolf, October 9, 1927 letter to Vita Sackville-West, in Ames Hawkins, *These Are Love(d) Letters* (Detroit, MI: Wayne State University Press, 2019), 230.

[35] Woolf, *Diary Volume Three*, 168.

[36] Neurologist Alice Weaver Flaherty, in her book *The Midnight Disease* (Boston, MA: Mariner Books, 2005), ties graphomania to temporal lobe epilepsy.

³⁷ William James, "The Stream of Consciousness," *Classics in the History of Psychology*, accessed on January 20, 2024, https://psychclassics.yorku.ca/James/jimmy11.htm. James writes:

> Consciousness, then, does not appear to itself chopped up in bits. Such words as 'chain' or 'train' do not describe it fitly as it presents itself in the first instance. It is nothing jointed; it flows. A 'river' or a 'stream' are the metaphors by which it is most naturally described. *In talking of it hereafter let us call it the stream of thought, of consciousness, or of subjective life.*

³⁸ See Christopher G. White, *Other Worlds* (Cambridge, MA: Harvard University Press, 2018).

³⁹ Julia Briggs, *Virginia Woolf* (New York: Houghton Mifflin Harcourt, 2005).

⁴⁰ In Briggs, *Virginia Woolf*, 130.

⁴¹ Virginia Woolf, *The Diary of Virginia Woolf, Volume One* (New York: Harvest/HBJ, 1977), 87.

⁴² Virginia Woolf, *The Diary of Virginia Woolf, Volume Two* (New York: Harvest/HBJ, 1978), 207.

⁴³ Briggs, *Virginia Woolf*. See also Anthony Curtis, "Kitty Maxse: The Real Mrs Dalloway," *PN Review* 24 (1) (1997), accessed on September 22, 2023, https://www.proquest.com/openview/222d7881941e47ac0cee907eda10a092/1?pq-origsite=gscholar&cbl=1817849.

⁴⁴ Curtis, "Kitty Maxse."

⁴⁵ Woolf, *Diary Volume Two*, 207.

⁴⁶ Briggs, *Virginia Woolf*.

⁴⁷ Woolf did however learn about Jungian psychotherapy from a palm reader named Charlotte Wolff who "analyzed" her in 1935—Wolff had undergone Jungian analysis.

⁴⁸ Steve Ellis, in his book *Virginia Woolf and the Victorians* (Cambridge, UK: Cambridge University Press, 2011) titles a chapter on Mrs. Dalloway, "Synchronicity," yet his discussion does not actually discuss Jung's theory or the novel's precognitive genesis. He's using the term just as a synonym for simultaneity.

⁴⁹ Carl Jung, *Synchronicity* (Princeton, NJ: Princeton University Press, 1973).

⁵⁰ Ibid., 19.

⁵¹ For instance, of letters that are preceded by a dream about the sender, Jung wrote "I have ascertained on several occasions that at the moment when the dream occurred the letter was already lying in the post-office of the addressee" (Ibid., 28). It seemed to matter to Jung that there was some

other scene like the post office, where the letter was sitting "at the moment," to help understand the occurrence. The era of electronic communications, of course, has shown that phone calls and emails can be preceded by dreams in exactly the same way as letters, obviating the need for such a scene, or the "meanwhile" it implies.

52 Vicente De Moura, "Learning from the Patient: The East, Synchronicity and Transference in the History of an Unknown Case of C.G. Jung," *Journal of Analytical Psychology* 59 (2014): 391-409.

53 Wargo, *Time Loops*.

54 Ibid.

55 De Moura, "Learning from the Patient."

56 Sergei Eisenstein, "From 'A Dialectic Approach to Film Form,'" in *Modernism*, ed. Vassiliki Kolocrotoni (Chicago, IL: The University of Chicago Press, 1998), 554-5.

57 And it was a two-way street. Synchronicity was not thinkable without cinema, but cinema also became essentially a Jungian, thoroughly synchronistic art form. Jung's influence on contemporary film and film language go way beyond *Star Wars* and other blockbusters of the 1970s, which were famously influenced by the Jungian scholar Joseph Campbell. Ever since screenwriting gurus of the time like Syd Field codified the principles of cinematic storytelling, movies largely follow an individuation template. In most Hollywood movies, the main character follows a Jungian mythic arc of development punctuated by the moments Campbell famously named ("belly of the beast," "dark night of the soul," etc.), while dense montage provides easy synchronicity after easy synchronicity to support both the realism and meaningfulness of the narrative. Movies are essentially synchronicity machines.

58 Woolf, *Diary Volume Two*, 206.

59 Ibid., 51.

60 Virginia Woolf, *Mrs. Dalloway* (New York: Warbler Classics, 2021), 169.

61 Wargo, *Time Loops*; Wargo, "'But I Survived.'"

62 Martel, *Reclaiming Art*, 91.

63 Virginia Woolf, *The Waves* (New York: Harcourt, 2006), 4.

64 "The Influential Science Fiction of Virginia Woolf," *Check Your Facts*, October 20, 2010, https://checkyourfacts.wordpress.com/2010/10/20/the-influential-science-fiction-of-virginia-woolf/.

65 Stephen Bitsoli, "Did Virginia Woolf Write Science Fiction? Not Really," *Bitsoli's Biblio Files*, accessed on October 2, 2022, http://bitsolisbibliofiles. blogspot.com/2013/09/did-virginia-woolf-write-science.html; Annalee

Newitz, "Introduction: The Radical Future of the Clockwork Man," in E. V. Odle, *The Clockwork Man* (Boston, MA: The MIT Press, 2022).

[66] See for instance Paul Tolliver Brown, "Relativity, Quantum Physics, and Consciousness in Virginia Woolf's *To the Lighthouse*," Journal of Modern Literature 32(3), 2009: 39-62; Ian Ettinger, "Relativity and Quantum Theory in Virginia Woolf's The Waves," *Zeteo*, accessed on January 10, 2024, file:/// Users/ericwargo/Downloads/Relativity_and_Quantum_Theory_in_Virgini-4. pdf; Holly Henry, *Virginia Woolf and the Discourse of Science* (Cambridge, UK: Cambridge University Press, 2003).

[67] Briggs, *Virginia Woolf.*

[68] Virginia Woolf, *To the Lighthouse* (Boston, MA: Mariner Books, 1981), 104-5.

[69] Virginia Woolf, *The Voyage Out* (London: Penguin Books, 1992), 44.

[70] In this, Woolf's writing perhaps anticipates what fellow Tavistock Square resident D. W. Winnicott would a couple decades later call "the place where we live," the liminal realm of transitional objects and play. Alison Bechdel highlights the overlaps of Woolf and Winnicott in her graphic novel *Are You My Mother* (Boston, MA: Mariner Books, 2013).

[71] Woolf, *Mrs. Dalloway*, 138. Clarissa also wonders whether "the unseen part of us, which spreads wide … might survive, be recovered somehow attached to this person or that, or even haunting certain places after death …" (Ibid.). See George M. Johnson, "'The Spirit of the Age': Virginia Woolf's Response to Second Wave Psychology," *Twentieth Century Literature* 40(2) (Summer, 1994): 139-64.

[72] In January 1924, Woolf reflected, "I've had some very curious visions in this room … lying in bed, mad, & seeing the sunlight quivering like gold water, on the wall. I've heard the voices of the dead here. And felt, through it all, exquisitely happy" (Woolf, *Diary Volume Two*, 283).

[73] Woolf, *Mrs. Dalloway*, 18.

[74] Julie Kane, "Varieties of Mystical Experience in the Writings of Virginia Woolf," *Twentieth Century Literature* 41(4) (1995), 328-9, 340.

[75] Woolf, *Diary Volume Three*, 114. It is interesting that in an essay on "The Cinema," she described the power of film in similar terms: "We behold [things in film] as they are when we are not there. We see life as it is when we have no part in it" (in Virginia Woolf, *Selected Essays* [Oxford, UK: Oxford University Press, 2009], 172-3).

[76] In Kane, "Varieties of Mystical Experience," 343.

[77] Richard Kennedy, *A Boy at the Hogarth Press* (Delray Beach, FL: Levenger Press, 2006), 29.

[78] Woolf, *Diary Volume Three*.

[79] James Jeans, *The Mysterious Universe* (Cambridge, UK: Cambridge University Press, 1930), 25.

[80] Ibid., 25-6.

[81] Ibid., 29.

[82] Ibid., 148.

[83] Kane, "Varieties of Mystical Experience," 345.

[84] Woolf, *Diary Volume Three*, 113.

[85] Ibid., 112

[86] In Briggs, *Virginia Woolf*, 243.

[87] Ibid. In *To the Lighthouse*, Woolf anticipates this image perhaps when she writes (p. 47): "She felt … how life, from being made up of little separate incidents which one lived one by one, became curled and whole like a wave which bore one up with it and threw one down with it, there, with a dash on the beach."

[88] Jeans, *Mysterious Universe*, 31.

[89] Ibid., 8.

[90] Jason Ā. Josephson-Storm, *The Myth of Disenchantment* (Chicago, IL: The University of Chicago Press, 2017).

[91] Art Historian E. H. Gombrich called the inference component of perception "the beholder's share."

[92] Slavoj Žižek, *The Sublime Object of Ideology* (London: Verso, 1989). See also Timothy Morton, "Sublime Objects," *Speculations* (2), 2011, 207-27.

[93] Here is the one place I disagree with my friend Jeffrey Kripal, who sees the reductive materialism of the neuroscientist as dismal nothing-but-ism. I've found in my own spiritual journey that it is precisely the flattest, most reductive or even "eliminative" scientific positions on consciousness that have the greatest potential, when intensely confronted and mulled over, to move one to epiphanies and even transcendence, whereas New Age writings promising a cozy meaning-saturated "conscious universe" leave me completely unmoved.

[94] Curtis, *The Cave Painters*.

[95] Georges Bataille, *Lascaux or the Birth of Art* (Lausanne, Switzerland: Skira, 1955).

[96] On the Overview Effect, see Pasulka, *Encounters*.

[97] Henry, *Virginia Woolf*.

[98] Woolf, *The Waves*, 198.

[99] In Henry, *Virginia Woolf*, 106.

[100] "The Science Fiction Writer Who Received Fan Mail from Virginia Woolf," *Gizmodo*, September 18, 2009, https://gizmodo.com/the-science-fiction-writer-who-received-fan-mail-from-v-5362291.

[101] Alvaro Zinos-Amaro, "Digging the Dirt: A Conversation with Kim Stanley Robinson," *Clarkesworld* 106 (2015), https://clarkesworldmagazine.com/robinson_interview/https://clarkesworldmagazine.com/robinson_interview/.

[102] Virginia Woolf, *Between the Acts*, Project Gutenberg Australia, accessed January 10, 2024, http://gutenberg.net.au/ebooks03/0301171h.html

[103] Bayard, *Demain est ecrit*.

[104] Arthur Koestler, *The Roots of Coincidence* (New York: Vintage Books, 1973), 98.

[105] Bernard Beitman, *Connecting with Coincidence* (Deerfield Beach, FL: Health Communications, Inc., 2016); Gary E. Schwartz, *Super Synchronicity* (Lumsden, SK, Canada: Waterfront Digital Press, 2017); David Wilcock, *The Synchronicity Key* (New York: Dutton, 2014).

[106] Christopher Knowles, with his popular *The Secret Sun* blog (https://secretsun.blogspot.com/) is one prominent example.

[107] Pasulka, *Encounters*.

[108] See Stephen E. Braude, *ESP and Psychokinesis* (Philadelphia, PA: Temple University Press, 1979).

[109] "Synchronicity (The Police album)," Wikipedia, accessed on January 14, 2024, https://en.wikipedia.org/wiki/Synchronicity_(The_Police_album).

CHAPTER 7: *Arise O Prophet! Work My Will*

[1] Wallis, "Art and Shamanism."

[2] Ronald Hutton, *Shamans* (London: Hambledon and London, 2001).

[3] Beyer, *Singing to the Plants*.

[4] See Wargo, *Where Was It Before the Dream?*

[5] Kripal, *The Superhumanities*.

[6] Ibid., 277.

[7] In his massive survey of 20th-century artists-who-are-shamans, Tucker (*Dreaming with Open Eyes*) does not discuss precognition or other ESP phenomena.

⁸ See Alexander-Garrett, *Andrei Tarkovsky*.

⁹ Ibid.

¹⁰ In his diary, the director recounted an amazing synchronicity, after he lost his only copy of the script for his film Andrei Rublev: "I left it in a taxi, and hours later the taxi-driver saw me walking along the street, in the crowd, at the same spot, and braked and handed me the folder. An unbelievable story" (Tarkovsky, *Time Within Time*, 122).

¹¹ Alexander-Garrett, *Andrei Tarkovsky*, 104.

¹² Wargo, *Precognitive Dreamwork*.

¹³ Darmon Richter, *Chernobyl* (London: FUEL Design & Publishing, 2020).

¹⁴ Markiyan Kamysh, *Stalking the Atomic City* (New York: Astra House, 2022).

¹⁵ Darren Orf, "The Mutant Wolves of Chernobyl Have Evolved to Survive Cancer," *Popular Mechanics*, February 17, 2024, https://www.popularmechanics.com/science/animals/a46799706/mutant-wolves-of-chernobyl/.

¹⁶ "Stalker (1979 Film)," Wikipedia, accessed on January 23, 2024, https://en.wikipedia.org/wiki/Stalker_(1979_film); Tarkovsky, *Time Within Time*.

¹⁷ Ibid.

¹⁸ Alexander-Garrett, *Andrei Tarkovsky*.

¹⁹ Sharun writes: "We were shooting near Tallinn in the area around the small river Jägala with a half-functioning hydroelectric station. Up the river was a chemical plant and it poured out poisonous liquids downstream. There is even this shot in Stalker: snow falling in the summer and white foam floating down the river. In fact it was some horrible poison. Many women in our crew got allergic reactions on their faces. Tarkovsky died from cancer of the right bronchial tube. And Tolya Solonitsyn too. That it was all connected to the location shooting for Stalker became clear to me when Larisa Tarkovskaya died from the same illness in Paris" ("Sharun—In Stalker Tarkovsky Foretold Chernobyl," *Nostalghia*, accessed on September 22, 2023, http://www.nostalghia.com/TheTopics/Stalker/sharun.html).

²⁰ It doesn't really matter which is true—that the cancer was from the toxicity of the shooting location or from assassination. What would matter is the connection Tarkovsky would have drawn between his friend's cancer and his own.

²¹ We also do not know how Tarkovsky reacted to the Chernobyl disaster. Unfolding as it did in the homeland he had escaped, he would have followed the news from the relative safety of Western Europe. It would not have been unlike the news stories of the *Titanic* disaster for readers in 1912 or 9/11 for American TV news audiences in 2001 outside of Manhattan or Washington,

DC, a calamity watched from a safe distance, a thing survived.

22 Tarkovsky, *Time Within Time*, 158-9.

23 "Sharun."

24 Alexander Pushkin, "The Prophet (trans. from Russian)," *Poems Found in Translation*, accessed on September 22, 2023, https://poemsintranslation. blogspot.com/2011/09/pushkin-prophet-from-russian.html.

25 Philip K. Dick, "April 4, 1974 letter to Claudia K. Bush," in P. K. Dick, *The Selected Letters of Philip K. Dick—1974* (Novato, CA: Underwood-Miller, 1991).

26 It is interesting that when Tarkovsky made *Stalker*, Castaneda had just introduced the faux-shamanic concept of "stalking" in his 1977 book *A Second Ring of Power*, and would elaborate on this idea in subsequent volumes. But Tarkovsky took the term for his shaman-like Zone guides from the 1972 Strugatsky brothers novel he was adapting.

27 Tarkovsky, *Time Within Time*. Vladimir Sharun claims that Tarkovsky himself saw a flying saucer, but is probably misremembering the 1975 encounter of his wife and son ("Sharun").

28 "Ninel Kulagina," Psi Encyclopedia, accessed on September 22, 2023, https://psi-encyclopedia.spr.ac.uk/articles/ninel-kulagina-0.

29 "Soviet Parapyschology Guru Is Back under Glasnost," UPI Archives, accessed on September 22, 2023, https://www.upi.com/ Archives/1988/04/17/Soviet-parapyschology-guru-is-back-under-glasnost/6071577252800/.

30 Alexander-Garrett, *Andrei Tarkovsky*.

31 "Nikolai Fyodorovich Fyodorov," Wikipedia, accessed on September 14, 2023, https://en.wikipedia.org/wiki/Nikolai_Fyodorovich_Fyodorov.

32 George Young, *The Russian Cosmists* (Oxford, UK: Oxford University Press, 2012).

33 Pavel Florensky, *Imaginaries in Geometry* (Sesto San Giovanni, Italy: Mimesis International, 2021).

34 Pavel Florensky, *Iconostasis* (Crestwood, NY: St. Vladimir's Seminary Press, 1996), 41.

35 Interestingly, the Holy Grail of Western European medieval romances had a similar logic. In one of the earliest romances, by Robert de Boron, the Grail was the vessel in which the communion meal at the Last Supper was celebrated, and then ended up being used to collect Christ's blood at the Deposition the next evening—implying that the vessel itself was either a time machine or that the Holy Blood travels backward in time—perhaps, as a physicist might now say, being made of tachyons.

36 The French psychoanalyst Jacques Lacan was, like Florensky, fascinated by hypertopologies like Moebius strips and Klein bottles. He was especially focused on the ways we overtake ourselves, pass through transitions and thresholds without experiencing them. Appropriately enough, of all major readers of Freud, Lacan came closest to arguing that the meanings of our dreams and symptoms come from our future. Florensky was in many ways a Lacanian before Lacan.

37 Robert Sheckley, *Store of the Worlds* (New York: NYRB, 2012).

38 James Gleick, *Time Travel* (New York: Pantheon, 2016).

39 Alexander-Garrett (*Andrei Tarkovsky*, 371) recalls that Andrei "had a fleeting thought that his illness was in fact an act of vengeance on the part of his wife; he saw in this a manifestation of some kind of supernatural power of hers."

40 In another draft version of "The Witch," it is simply learning to enjoy himself during the year he thinks he has left that miraculously cures the man of his disease.

41 According to Alexander-Garrett's research (*Andrei Tarkovsky*), this was a theme imported from another concept Tarkovsky had been working on since the early 1970s called "Two Saw the Vixen." *The Sacrifice* was a hybrid.

42 Alexander-Garrett (*Andrei Tarkovsky*, 30) claims that Tarkovsky himself collected "inexplicable events."

43 Andrey Tarkovsky, *Sculpting in Time* (Austin, TX: University of Texas Press, 1987).

44 A common response, even among Tarkovsky's friends, was perplexity at what was actually sacrificial about sex with a witch. Boris Strugatsky asked, "Is it because she is ugly? A hideous old hag? ... So where's the sacrifice?" (Alexander-Garrett, *Andrei Tarkovsky*, 130).

45 Alexander-Garrett, *Andrei Tarkovsky*.

46 Andrei Tarkovsky, *Collected Screenplays* (London: Faber & Faber, 2003), 531. The day before receiving his cancer diagnosis, Tarkovsky had a terrifying vision of his lungs eaten away. See Tarkovsky, *Time Within Time*.

CHAPTER 8: From Nothing

1 See, e.g., David Freedberg, *The Power of Images* (Chicago, IL: The University of Chicago Press, 1991).

2 Curtis, *The Cave Painters*.

‑

³ Daniel Lord Smail, *On Deep History and the Brain* (Berkeley, CA: University of California Press, 2007).

⁴ Kripal, *Mutants and Mystics*.

⁵ Martel, *Reclaiming Art*.

⁶ See also Clottes, *What Is Paleolithic Art?*

⁷ Nicholas Cullinan, "Nine Discourses on Commodus, or Cy Twombly's Beautiful 'Fiasco,'" in *Cy Twombly*, ed. J. Storsve (Munich: Sieveking Verlag, 2020); Joshua Rivkin, *Chalk* (Brooklyn, NY: Melville House, 2018).

⁸ Cullinan, "Nine Discourses."

⁹ "Commodus," Wikipedia, accessed on January 10, 2024, https://en.wikipedia.org/wiki/Commodus.

¹⁰ Cullinan, "Nine Discourses"; Theodore White, "Murder of the President: An Assassin Kills John F. Kennedy in Dallas," *Life* (November 29, 1963): 22-40.

¹¹ Donald Judd, "Cy Twombly," *Arts Magazine* 38(9) (May-June 1964): 38.

¹² Cullinan, "Nine Discourses." Castelli himself, although a supporter of Twombly's work, said the Commodus paintings were "not really very good. They were very sort of Europeanized and precious" (Ibid., 83).

¹³ "Nine Discourses on Commodus," Guggenheim Museum Bilbao, accessed on January 10, 2024, https://www.guggenheim-bilbao.eus/en/the-collection/works/nine-discourses-on-commodus.

¹⁴ Rivkin, *Chalk*.

¹⁵ William Tenn, "The Discovery of Morniel Mathaway," *Galaxy Science Fiction* 11(1) (October 1955): 44-59.

¹⁶ David Deutsch. "Quantum Mechanics Near Closed Timelike Lines," *Physical Review D* (44) (November 15, 1991): 3197-217.

¹⁷ Amanda Gefter, *Trespassing on Einstein's Lawn* (New York: Bantam Books, 2014).

¹⁸ Paul Nahin, *Time Machines* (New York: Springer-Verlag New York, Inc., 1999), 312.

¹⁹ Deutsch, "Quantum Mechanics," 3204.

²⁰ "One Is Art, One Is Vandalism—But Which Is Which?," *The Scotsman*, October 10, 2007, https://www.scotsman.com/whats-on/arts-and-entertainment/one-art-one-vandalism-which-which-2462004

²¹ "Woman Fined for Kissing Painting," *BBC*, November 16, 2007, http://news.bbc.co.uk/2/hi/entertainment/7098707.stm.

²² Ralph Blumenthal, "A Celebratory Splash for an Enigmatic Figure," *The New York Times*, June 4, 2005, https://www.nytimes.com/2005/06/04/arts/

design/a-celebratory-splash-for-an-enigmatic-figure.html; "The Painting that Took 22 Years to Finish," *Literary Hub*, October 26, 2018, https://lithub.com/the-painting-that-took-22-years-to-finish/.

[23] Catherine Lacey, "Say Goodbye, Catullus," *The Paris Review*, July 17, 2017, https://www.theparisreview.org/blog/2017/07/17/say-good-bye-catullus/.

[24] In my forthcoming *Where Was It Before the Dream?*, I apply this idea to literary interpretation, examining a number of classic works (including Mary Shelley's *Frankenstein*, J. R. R. Tolkien's *The Hobbit*, and Kafka's *The Metamorphosis*) that, I argue, were entirely self-caused in this way.

[25] Cy Twombly, *Fifty Days at Iliam* (Philadelphia, PA: Philadelphia Museum of Art, 2018).

[26] On Twombly's attitude of impatience at the public not understanding his work, see Rivkin, *Chalk*. The monumental *Fifty Days at Iliam*, with its name lists, which was made in the shadow of and certainly consciously inspired (in the usual linear way) by the Vietnam War and the Cold War more generally (e.g., the *A*s in ATHENA, ACHILLES, ACHAEANS, etc. are made to look like warheads) may be prophetic too. It has reminded many people of Maya Lin's Vietnam Veteran's Memorial on the National Mall in Washington, DC. The latter was completed and dedicated in 1982. Although it is also possible that Lin took direct, linear inspiration from Twombly's *Iliam* series, as the latter was first displayed in the U.S. at the Whitney in 1979, the year the Vietnam Veteran's Memorial Fund was established; the contest to design the memorial was announced the following year.

[27] Bankei, *The Unborn* (New York: North Point Press, 2000).

[28] Andy Clark, *Surfing Uncertainty* (Oxford, UK: Oxford University Press, 2016).

CHAPTER 9: Culture in Reverse

[1] Ralph Waldo Emerson, *Emerson's Essays* (New York: Harper Perennial, 1951), 32.

[2] Harold Bloom, *The Anxiety of Influence* (Oxford, UK: Oxford University Press, 1973).

[3] Harold Bloom, *A Map of Misreading* (Oxford, UK: Oxford University Press, 1975).

[4] Muireann Maguire and Timothy Langen, "Introduction: Countersense and Interpretation," in *Reading Backward*, ed. M. Maguire and T. Langen (Cambridge, UK: Open Book Publishers, 2021), accessed on January 10, 2024, https://books.openedition.org/obp/22430.

⁵ Pierre Bayard, *Le Plagiat par anticipation* (Paris: Les Éditions de Minuit, 2009).

⁶ See Wargo, *Time Loops.*

⁷ Slavoj Žižek, *Less than Zero* (London: Verso, 2013), 558.

⁸ Eric Naiman, "But Seriously Folks…," in *Reading Backward*, ed. M. Maguire and T. Langen (Cambridge, UK: Open Book Publishers, 2021), accessed on January 10, 2024, https://books.openedition.org/obp/22530.

⁹ Wargo, *Where Was It Before the Dream?*

¹⁰ Philippe Refabert points out one probable Talmudic influence, related secondhand from the third-century Christian theologian Origen, as something told to him by a Jewish scholar:

> [T]he Book, that is, the Law, is like a big house with many rooms, where each room has a door with a key, but the key in the lock is not the right one. The keys have been mixed up. The objective of study is to put them back in order. [But] the Law is made up of a great number of words, each word contains several letters, and each letter has six thousand faces, doors, entries. And the right key has been lost. Each face of each letter is intended for a single child of Israel. *Each one has a door destined only for him.* (In Philippe Refabert, *From Freud to Kafka* [London: Karnac, 2014] 70 [my emphasis].)

¹¹ Sigmund Freud, *On Metapsychology* (London: Penguin, 1984), 153.

¹² In Czech, *od-* is a prefix meaning "from," and the suffix *-ek* is a diminutive often attached affectionately to small objects or people. *Rad* means order, regulations, rules. Thus odradek has vague connotations both of something discarded—thrown away—as well as of something disordered, perhaps even removed or repressed from the orderly. The orthographically similar *rád* is a term that means "gladness," so an odradek could also be something ejected from bliss, or perhaps "dejected."

¹³ Franz Kafka, *The Complete Stories* (New York: Schocken Books, 1971), 429.

¹⁴ Ibid., 55.

¹⁵ Wargo, *Where Was It Before the Dream?*

¹⁶ Could there have been a reverse influence of Kafka upon Freud, either in the usual direction or precognitively? Probably not—at least, not directly. Frustratingly for the would-be literary biographer, there is seldom anywhere near a complete record of the things literary personages read during their lifetimes, and even when their libraries are preserved, their contents are only a fragment of the texts their owners' read. But compared to most famous writers, a great deal is known about Freud's reading habits, and he is not

known to have ever read Kafka. According to Michael Molnar, he does not seem to have followed modernist literary trends at all, even those that were clearly influenced by psychoanalysis. His tastes may have been too staid to appreciate avant-garde writers like Kafka; and by the time Kafka was becoming known, he may have been too old and tired to devote much energy to difficult literary experiments. See Michael Molnar, "The Bizarre Chair," in *Reading Freud's Reading*, ed. S. M. Gilman (New York: NYU Press, 1993).

[17] Robert Zemeckis' *Back to the Future* is the most obvious example: Marty McFly (Michael J. Fox) drives a time-machine back to the year his parents met, and must fend off the affections of own teenaged mother and introduce her instead to the man destined to be his father. See Andrew Gordon, "Back to the Future: Oedipus as Time Traveler," in *Liquid Metal*, ed. S. Redmond (New York: Wallflower Press, 2007).

[18] See Constance Penley, "Time Travel, Primal Scene and the Critical Dystopia," in *Liquid Metal*.

[19] Gerry Canavan, *Octavia E. Butler* (Urbana, IL: University of Illinois Press, 2016).

[20] Butler, who died in 2006, did not live long enough to see the Trump campaign and thus could not have been inspired by it precognitively—at least, not through the mechanism I propose. But the phrase had also been used by Ronald Reagan and Bill Clinton in their 1980 and 1992 presidential campaigns, respectively.

[21] Octavia E. Butler, *Kindred* (New York: Beacon Press, 2003).

[22] Larry McCaffery and Jim McMenamin, "An Interview with Octavia E. Butler," in *Conversations with Octavia Butler*, ed. C. Francis (Jackson, MS: University Press of Mississippi, 2010).

[23] Rasheedah Phillips, "[Black] Grandmother-Paradoxes," *Black Women Temporal*, accessed on January 19, 2024, https://www. blackwomentemporal.net/black-grandmother-paradoxes.

[24] James Cameron, "Terminator: A Treatment for a Feature Film Screenplay," *Daily Script*, accessed on January 19, 2024, https://www.dailyscript.com/scripts/T1.pdf.

[25] For more on this plagiarism saga and Ellison's own prophetic time-travel stories, see Eric Wargo, "Edges of Forever: Time Travel and the Stories That Might Have Been," *The Nightshirt*, February 21, 2019, http://www.thenightshirt.com/?p=4359.

[26] "Bright Tunes Music Corp. v. Harrisongs Music, Ltd.," Google Scholar, accessed on January 15, 2024, https://scholar.google.com/scholar_case?q=bright+tunes+v.+harrisongs&hl=en&as_sdt=400006&case=7721050309378220492&scilh=0; "My Sweet Lord," Wikipedia, accessed on January 15, 2024,

https://en.wikipedia.org/wiki/My_Sweet_Lord.

[27] "Determining the Extent of Plagiarism in Helen Keller's Writing 'The Frost King,'" *Scribd*, accessed on February 3, 2024, https://www.scribd.com/document/335664080/The-Frost-King.

[28] "The Frost King Incident," Perkins School for the Blind, April 29, 2019, https://www.perkins.org/the-frost-king-incident/.

[29] Helen Keller, *The Story of My Life* (Mineola, NY: Dover Publications, Inc., 1996), 34.

[30] Ibid.

[31] Anne Sullivan, "How Helen Keller Acquired Language," *American Annals of the Deaf* (April, 1892): 139-53, accessed on January 15, 2024, https://archive.org/details/helenkellernewsp01unkn/page/n131/mode/2up; Perkins Institute for the Blind, *Annual Report of the Trustees of the Perkins Institution and Massachusetts Asylum for the Blind to the Corporation* (Boston, MA: Wright & Potter Printing Co., 1889), 95, accessed on January 15, 2024, https://archive.org/details/annualreportoftr5860perk/page/94/mode/2up.

[32] Richard Noll, *The Aryan Christ* (New York: Random House, 1997), 27.

[33] Deirdre Bair, *Jung* (New York: Little, Brown, 2003).

[34] In Carl Jung, *Man and His Symbols* (New York: Doubleday Windfall, 1964), 311.

[35] Ibid.

[36] Ibid., 37.

[37] Theodore Flournoy, *From India to the Planet Mars* (New York: Cosimo Classics, 2007).

[38] Hilary Horn Ratner, Mary Ann Foley, and Nicole Gimpert, "Person Perspectives on Children's Memory and Learning: What Do Source-Monitoring Failures Reveal?," in *Children's Source Monitoring*, ed. K. P. Roberts and M. Blades (New York: Psychology Press, 2000).

[39] Wargo, *Time Loops*.

[40] Eric Wargo, "Stories Latent in the Landscape: Spirits, Time Slips, and 'Super-Psi,'" *The Nightshirt*, June 25, 2016, http://www.thenightshirt.com/?p=3874.

[41] Sullivan, "How Helen Keller," 145.

[42] Maria Popova, "All Ideas Are Second-Hand: Mark Twain's Magnificent Letter to Helen Keller about the Myth of Originality," *The Marginalian*, May 10, 2012, https://www.themarginalian.org/2012/05/10/mark-twain-helen-keller-plagiarism-originality/. But Interestingly, such musings did not prevent Twain from feeling the slight bitterness at his own belatedness in naming

and characterizing the phenomenon of mental telegraphy. He published his "Mental Telegraphy" article several years after Frederic W. H. Myers in England had coined the term "telepathy," but he prefaced his "rusty old manuscript" with a note to the editor not-too-subtly asserting his priority in hitting on the idea of such a mental connection between minds across great distances:

> By glancing over the inclosed bundle of rusty old manuscript, you will perceive that I once made a great discovery: the discovery that certain sorts of thing which, from the beginning of the world, had always been regarded as merely "curious coincidences"—that is to say, accidents—were no more accidental than is the sending and receiving of a telegram an accident. I made this discovery sixteen or seventeen years ago, and gave it a name—"Mental Telegraphy." It is the same thing around the outer edges of which the Psychical Society of England began to group (and play with) four or five years ago, and which they named "Telepathy" (Twain, "Mental Telegraphy").

[43] Arnold C. Brackman, *A Delicate Arrangement* (New York: Times Books, 1980).

[44] Ross A. Slotten, *The Heretic in Darwin's Court* (New York: Columbia University Press, 2006).

[45] Ibid., 153-4.

[46] Alfred Russel Wallace, *My Life, Vol. 1* (London: Forgotten Books, 2012).

[47] Mike Sutton, *Nullius in Verba* (Author, 2017).

[48] The fact that Darwin felt unhurried only until reading Wallace's essay suggests to me that he was indeed not consciously aware of Matthew, or Matthew would have been a greater source of influence anxiety and prod to completion of his own work.

CHAPTER 10: Aliens and Archetypes

[1] See Bruce MacLennan, "Evolution, Jung, and Theurgy: Their Role in Modern Neoplatonism," 2003, accessed March 23, 2024, https://web.eecs.utk.edu/~bmaclenn/papers/EJT/index.html.

[2] Richard Noll, *The Jung Cult* (Princeton, NJ: Princeton University Press, 1994).

[3] Leadbeater, who wrote about the Akashic Records in his 1899 book

Clairvoyance, described the ether and "etheric bodies" as a kind of intermediary between the physical and spiritual, or astral, plane. See C. W. Leadbeater, *Clairvoyance* (London: The Theosophical Publishing House, 1968).

[4] A. P. Sinnett, *Esoteric Buddhism* (London: The Theosophical Publishing House, 1972).

[5] James Gleick, *The Information* (New York: Vintage Books, 2012).

[6] Frederic W. H. Myers, "Fragments of Inner Life," Esalen, accessed March 15, 2024, https://www.esalen.org/ctr/fragments-of-inner-life; see also Kripal, *Authors of the Impossible*; Luckhurst, *The Invention of Telepathy*.

[7] Jung, *Synchronicity*, 23.

[8] Noll, *The Jung Cult*; Noll, *The Aryan Christ*.

[9] Noll, *The Jung Cult*; Noll, *The Aryan Christ*.

[10] According to Noll, the motif of a solar phallus could also be found in a 1903 book on Mithraic liturgy by Albrecht Dieterich and in an older, famous book of matriarchal theology, *Das Mutterecht* (or *Mother Right*) by Johann Jakob Bachofen. Schwyzer, who was interviewed not by Jung but by an assistant of his, had been in Burghölzli and other institutions much of his life; but many of his fellow patients were spiritually seeking neo-Pagans. One such individual was Otto Gross, a brilliant, drug-addicted young psychiatrist and manic proselytizer on all things matriarchal and specifically a fan of Bachofen's *Das Mutterecht*. Gross had been committed by his authoritarian father for his countercultural beliefs and lifestyle and was treated in Burghölzli by Jung just a year before this story was collected—in fact, their encounter was life-changing for Jung in many ways (see Noll, *The Aryan Christ*). Did Honegger get the solar-phallus image from Gross? (For more on Gross, whose life also intersected "synchronistically" with that of Franz Kafka, see Wargo, *Where Was It Before the Dream?*)

[11] This was a quarter century before the discovery of 40,000-year-old ivory fragments in the German cave of Hohlenstein Stadel that, when assembled in 1989, turned out to be a man with the head of a lion. See Warren Colman, *Act and Image* (London: Routledge, 2020).

[12] Noll, *The Aryan Christ*.

[13] Psychoanalytic clinics in Vienna and Zurich were mansplainy places, where female patients routinely had their own thoughts, bodies, and everything else explained to them by male medical authorities. I imagine Jung asked Maggy if she knew the symbolism of scarabs, and she shook her head politely so he could tell it to her.

[14] Wargo, *Precognitive Dreamwork*.

[15] Ibid.

[16] C. G. Jung, *The Red Book* (New York: W. W. Norton & Company, 2009).

[17] Sonu Shamdasani, *C. G. Jung—A Biography in Books* (New York: W. W. Norton & Company, 2012), 142.

[18] Ibid., 8.

[19] Ibid., 8-9.

[20] Ibid., 8.

[21] For an interesting reimagining of the Jungian collective unconscious as emergent product of the human symbolizing imagination, rather than a kind of Platonic realm outside history and materiality, see Colman, *Act and Image*.

[22] Carl Jung, *The Practice of Psychotherapy* (Princeton, NJ: Bollingen, 1985), 169.

[23] David Lynch, *Catching the Big Fish* (New York: Jeremy P. Tarcher/Penguin, 2006).

[24] "David Lynch," *Charlie Rose*, February 14, 1997, https://charlierose.com/videos/11971.

[25] David Lynch and Kristine McKenna, *Room to Dream* (New York: Random House, 2018), 95.

[26] Several sources on Giger and Lynch's reactions to Giger and his work were compiled by blogger Dominic Kulcsar. See especially Dominic Kulcsar, "Alien vs Eraserhead," *Alien Explorations*, accessed on September 22, 2023, http://alienexplorations.blogspot.com/2014/05/alien-vs-eraserhead.html; Dominic Kulcsar, "Giger Attempts to Board Lynch's Dune," *Alien Explorations*, accessed on September 22, 2023, https://alienexplorations.blogspot.com/1983/03/gigers-attempt-to-board-lynchs-dune.html.

[27] Giger is quoted in the film magazine *Cinefantastique* (14[4], [May, 1988]: 35) as saying:

> I was very eager to be [involved with Lynch's adaptation of *Dune*]. Through friends I asked Lynch if he was interested in my co- operation. I never heard from him. Later I came to know that he was upset because he thought we copied the chestburster in ALIEN from his monster baby in ERASERHEAD, which was not so. Ridley Scott and I hadn't even seen that film at the time. If one film influenced ALIEN it was THE TEXAS CHAINSAW MASSACRE. I would have loved to collaborate with Lynch on DUNE but apparently he wanted to do all the designs by himself. (In Kulcsar, "Alien vs Eraserhead.")

In another interview for *EasyReader* (July 14, 1988), Giger said that he had seen *Eraserhead* by the time they filmed *Alien*, but that Scott still had not:

[Lynch] was not pleased because he thought we had stolen his "Eraserhead" baby creature for "Alien." But it can't be true because Ridley Scott had never seen "Eraserhead." I saw it, but I don't know. Maybe he was jealous. But, I think, it's unnecessary for him to make such statements because he's so good. I like all of his films so much. I am a great admirer of David Lynch and I would very much like to work for him. (In Kulcsar, "Alien vs Eraserhead.")

[28] "ALIEN (project formerly titled STARBEAST)," *Daily Script*, accessed on January 16, 2024, https://www.dailyscript.com/scripts/alien_early.html.

[29] Lynch and McKenna, *Room to Dream*.

[30] Ibid., 164.

[31] Ibid.

[32] Frank Pavich, *Jodorowsky's Dune* (film), High Line Pictures, 2013.

[33] Stephen Mulhall, *On Film* (London: Routledge, 2002).

[34] Eric Wargo, "The Passion of the Space Jockey: Alienated Sentience and Endosymbiosis in the World of H. R. Giger," *Gnosis: Journal of Gnostic Studies* 5(1), 22-44.

[35] As Ian Nathan puts it in a book about the making of *Alien*: "The jockey possesses an air both elegiac and hopeful—the universe might yet offer nonlethal alien contact. Quite why he was (and is) considered benign is hard to pinpoint, yet everyone who saw him mourned his passing—a lost soul staring through his telescope at the unreachable heavens forevermore" (Ian Nathan, *Alien Vault* [Minneapolis, MN: Voyageur Press, 2011], 98).

[36] Wargo, *Where Was It Before the Dream?*

[37] Kulcsar, "Alien vs Eraserhead." Kulcsar, also a member of Lynch's fan site (as "wmmvrrvrrmm"), responded to Lynch's comment in the chatroom:

I thought about the comment you made last night that you once went to the place where Giger got his ideas from. But then Giger when he first saw Eraserhead thought it was a homage to his own paintings. Maybe you've been there more than you realised. although Giger's world has nothing to do with Philadelphia.

Giger replied: "Philadelphia is very close to Giger's world" (Ibid.).

[38] See Wargo, "The Passion of the Space Jockey."

[39] Kulcsar, "Alien vs Eraserhead."

[40] Another example is the anthropologist Claude Lévi-Strauss, who considered myth to be a language-like system that obeyed its own internal logic, a kind of mechanistic clockwork of culture, even a natural computer

in which animals and plants and other natural phenomena functioned as symbolic operators—what he called the "logic of the concrete." See Claude Lévi-Strauss, *The Savage Mind* (Chicago, IL: The University of Chicago Press, 1966).

[41] Elisabeth Roudinesco, *Jacques Lacan* (New York: Columbia University Press, 1997), 378-9.

[42] Eugene Wolters, "Noam Chomsky Calls Jacques Lacan a 'Charlatan,'" *Critical Theory*, February 28, 2013, https://www.critical-theory.com/noam-chomsky-calls-jacques-lacan-a-charlatan/.

[43] Raul Moncayo, *The Signifier Pointing at the Moon* (London: Karnac, 2012).

[44] Jacques Lacan, *The Four Fundamental Concepts of Psycho-Analysis* (New York: W. W. Norton & Co., 1981), 197-8.

[45] Wordplay has been important for many French writers and thinkers. The philosopher Jacques Derrida is a relatively recent example, but even the French alchemical tradition made much of double entendres and puns. The early 20th-century alchemist Fulcanelli's classic *The Mystery of the Cathedrals* couches hermetic philosophy in many-layered puns, for example. And pun-lover Marcel Duchamp made wordplay central to his art.

[46] Slavoj Žižek, *How to Read Lacan* (New York: W. W. Norton & Co., 2006).

[47] Mulhall, *On Film*.

[48] In my experience, nightmares are especially likely to be precognitive, even though the experience being foreseen may turn out to be very mundane. See Wargo, *Precognitive Dreamwork*.

[49] Wargo, *Precognitive Dreamwork*.

[50] Andrew Paquette, *Dreamer* (Winchester, UK: O Books, 2011).

[51] Owen Hewitson, "A Story from Lacan's Practice," LacanOnline.com, August 12, 2012, https://www.lacanonline.com/2012/08/a-story-from-lacans-practice/.

[52] I first became aware of this case through the writings of philosopher Slavoj Žižek, who, while a disbeliever in precognition or the collective unconscious, found the coincidence of imagery uncanny. In his earliest writings, before he became a sort of repetitious academic celebrity, Žižek developed an interesting and exciting Marxist-Lacanian critique of postmodern liberal capitalism using Lacan's concept of *jouissance*. Wherever power and Capital are operative, he argued, there is bound to be an unacknowledged, unspeakable "surplus enjoyment" lurking just under the surface, unsymbolizable—that is, unspeakable in language and disobeying our consensus iconographies—but represented in the collective imagination by some kind of monstrous, loathsome, fascinating *Thing*. The place to find such representations displayed openly is in popular culture, especially sci-fi/

horror. Žižek has often used *Alien* to illustrate his basic thesis. The protean Xenomorph represents the enjoyment underlying the class antagonisms characteristic of a postmodern military-industrial world (of which the *Nostromo* is a microcosm) and the sexual antagonisms that have, through the ages, given rise to horrific female-sexual and maternal archetypes—like the child-devouring Medea or Grendel's fearsome mother in *Beowulf* (who like the Xenomorph, had acid for blood). See Žižek, *The Sublime Object of Ideology*.

53 "Noosphere," Wikipedia, accessed on March 16, 2024, https://en.wikipedia.org/wiki/Noosphere. See also Young, *The Russian Cosmists*. There is some confusion about who originally came up with the term, with Vernadsky and Teilhard both saying they got the idea from the other.

54 Kripal, *Mutants and Mystics*; Pasulka, *Encounters*.

CHAPTER 11: VALIS-PM

1 Roy's upset and uncomprehending wife Ronnie (Teri Garr) ultimately takes their children to stay with her mother, unable to deal with her obsessed husband making a wreckage of their home and getting fired from his job for failing to show up to work. Roy makes his journey to Devil's Tower with a similarly lost witness, Jillian (Melinda Dillon) whose young boy was abducted by one of the UFOs.

2 To my knowledge, Dick is the only artist in any medium whose work has been systematically subjected to anything like the psychic deconstruction I am recommending in this book. For example, Anthony Peake's *A Life of Philip K. Dick: The Man Who Remembered the Future* is a catalog of Dick's literary prophecies and other precognitive experiences. I detail additional precognitive episodes in *Time Loops*. See also Apel, *Philip K. Dick*; Lawrence Sutin, *Divine Invasions* (New York: Carroll & Graf Publishers, 2005).

3 The "real" account appears in Dick's *Exegesis*.

4 Philip K. Dick, *Radio Free Albemuth* (New York: Arbor House, 1985), 23.

5 Ibid., 22.

6 Elsewhere I argue that the word "hobbit," which came to J. R. R. Tolkien out of nowhere while grading papers, was a similar premonitory word-object. It demanded its own exegesis, and grew into a novel that was prophetic of a significant turning point in its author's life. See Wargo, *Where Was It Before the Dream?* I imagine that the premonitory word-object "Odradek" came to Kafka in the same way.

7 Jacques Vallee, *The Invisible College* (New York: E. P. Dutton & Co., 1975). For more on Bergier, see Kripal, *Mutants and Mystics*.

[8] Dick, *Exegesis*.

[9] Wargo, *Time Loops*.

[10] Arthur Koestler, "Order from Disorder," *Harper's* 249(1490) (July 1974), 60.

[11] Ibid., 143.

[12] Wargo, *Time Loops*.

[13] Ibid.

[14] Philip K. Dick, *The Selected Letters of Philip K. Dick—1974* (Novato, CA: Underwood-Miller, 1991), 299.

[15] Jacques Vallee, *Forbidden Science, Volume 3* (San Francisco, CA: Documatica Research, LLC, 2016). In the same volume, he recounts a similar experience by his friend, French ufologist Aimé Michel. While working on writing a difficult article, Michel started humming an unfamiliar tune. He became obsessed with the melody and then went to play it on his piano. He then turned on the radio, and it was playing the same tune—he found out that it was Beethoven's 109th piano concerto.

[16] Writing about a 1978 discussion of the epistemology of ESP research with Puthoff and parapsychologists Charles Tart and Edwin May, he said, "How can one differentiate between clairvoyance and precognition? It always seems to me that the missing piece in all such debates is an adequate theory of time" (Jacques Vallee, *Forbidden Science, Volume 2* [San Francisco, CA: Documatica Research, LLC, 2011], 450). May went on to advance the "precognition only" theory of ESP, which I also tend to subscribe to.

[17] Vallee, *Forbidden Science, Volume 2*, 211-2.

[18] Jacques Vallee, *Messengers of Deception* (Brisbane, Australia: Daily Grail Publishing, 2008), 99.

[19] Ibid., 100.

[20] Vallee, *Forbidden Science Volume 2*, 328.

[21] Vallee, *Messengers*, 243.

[22] See Sue Llewellyn, "Such Stuff as Dreams Are Made On? Elaborative Encoding, the Ancient Art of Memory, and the Hippocampus," *Behavioral and Brain Sciences* 36 (2013): 589-607; Wargo, *Precognitive Dreamwork*.

[23] James Gleick, *The Information* (New York: Vintage Books, 2011).

[24] Vallee, *Forbidden Science, Volume 3*, 346.

[25] Ira Einhorn, "A Disturbing Communique …," *The CoEvolution Quarterly*, Winter 1977-78, 74-76.

[26] Philip K. Dick, *The Selected Letters of Philip K. Dick—1977-1979* (Novato, CA: Underwood-Miller, 1993), 144.

²⁷ Vallee, *Forbidden Science, Volume 3*. He writes: "Dick called it VALIS but he understood it only vaguely from the depths of his sacred delirium. Yet the quest could continue along rational lines" (Ibid., 346). Interestingly, Vallée also published an article in the same *CoEvolution* issue, "The Priest, the Well and the Pendulum," which contained an early iteration of the description of his Melchizedek experience and the idea of "traversing events by association" that was later published in *Messengers of Deception*. There is no indication from his letters that Dick read this article.

²⁸ In thinking of UFOs as a control system, Vallée may also have been drawing precognitively on the Strugatsky Brothers, whom he similarly named among his literary favorites. Their 1978 novel *Definitely Maybe* is about a mysterious, vaguely paranormal homeostatic control system placing limits on human innovation. See Arkady Strugatsky and Boris Strugatsky, *Definitely Maybe* (New York: Macmillan, 1978); Vallee, *Forbidden Science, Volume 2*.

²⁹ The following section was originally published, in slightly different form, as "Jeff Kripal and Jacques Vallee," in J. J. Kripal, E. Wargo, and J. L. Kripal, *A Space and Time* (privately printed, 2022).

³⁰ Dick, *Radio Free Albemuth*, 13.

³¹ May, "Experimenter Psi."

³² Jacques Vallee, *Forbidden Science, Volume 5* (San Francisco, CA: Documatica Research, LLC, 2023).

³³ Vallee also writes about his information singularity in *Forbidden Science, Volume 3*

³⁴ Kripal, *Authors of the Impossible*, 147.

³⁵ Barry Windsor-Smith, *Opus* (Seattle, WA: Fantagraphics Books, 1999).

³⁶ Ibid., 173-4.

³⁷ Jeffrey Kripal, "On Radar and Revelation: Connecting the Dots (and Each Other)" (address at Rice University Opening the Archives of the Impossible Conference, March 3, 2022), https://www.youtube.com/watch?v=u2rCtKGPwdo.

³⁸ Jeffrey Kripal, personal communication.

³⁹ Sigmund Freud, "Negation," in *On Metapsychology*, ed. J. Strachey (London: Penguin, 1984).

⁴⁰ Kripal writes, "The truth needs the trick, the fact the fantasy" (*Mutants and Mystics*, 2).

CHAPTER 12: Tradition and Tesseract

[1] Steven Pinker, "We Make Art Because We Can," *Steven Pinker*, 2016, https://stevenpinker.com/files/pinker/files/pinker_2016_we_make_art_because_we_can_mona_exhibit_by_steven_pinker.pdf.

[2] Martel, *Reclaiming Art*.

[3] Claude Lévi-Strauss, *The Savage Mind*.

[4] Wargo, *Time Loops*.

[5] Pasulka, *Encounters*, 69-70.

[6] Pasulka, *Encounters*.

[7] Harner, *Way of the Shaman*, 3.

[8] Ibid., 6.

[9] Ibid.

[10] Ibid.

[11] Ibid., 7.

[12] Harner writes that he had also learned in his vision that "the dragon-like creatures were … inside of all forms of life, including man" and in a footnote, noted that "In retrospect one could say [the dragons] were almost like DNA, although at that time, 1961, I knew nothing of DNA" (Ibid., 4). It was the following year that Watson and Crick would win the Nobel Prize for the discovery of the helical structure of DNA (a discovery that had been made possible by the X-ray photography work of the then-deceased Rosalind Franklin), and it was over the following decade that public awareness of DNA and genetics exploded. Had the drug brought Harner a preview of imminent scientific currents, bundled with his preview of the Book of Revelation?

[13] Ibid., 7.

[14] It was a path marked by similar precognitive experiences. For instance, three years later, among the Jivaro of Ecuador, Harner drank a local brew called *guayasa* and then saw reddish curvilinear patterns in the darkness. The next day, a Catholic missionary showed him a collection of ancient potsherds with patterns identical to what he had seen the previous night.

[15] Furek, *Sheppton*.

[16] Michael Lipka and Claire Gecewicz, "More Americans Now Say They're Spiritual but Not Religious," Pew Research Center, September 6, 2017, https://www.pewresearch.org/short-reads/2017/09/06/more-americans-now-say-theyre-spiritual-but-not-religious/.

[17] Noll, *The Jung Cult*.

---

[18] De Moura, "Learning from the Patient."

[19] Wargo, *Time Loops*.

[20] Donald Kalsched, *Trauma and the Soul* (London: Routledge, 2013).

[21] Pasulka, *Encounters*.

[22] Ibid.

[23] Hilarie M. Sheets, "David Lynch, Who Began as a Visual Artist, Gets a Museum Show," *The New York Times*, August 28, 2014, https://www.nytimes.com/2014/08/31/arts/design/museum-show-for-david-lynch-who-began-as-a-visual-artist.html.

[24] Also, the algorithms that increasingly guide our online behavior, news consumption, and purchasing produce constant synchronicities through non-paranormal methods that are nevertheless uncanny and potentially highly motivating.

[25] Hameroff and Penrose, "Consciousness in the Universe."

[26] Eric Wargo, "The Wyrd of the Early Earth: Cellular Pre-sense in the Primordial Soup," *The Nightshirt*, May 22, 2016, https://www.thenightshirt.com/?p=3840

[27] Hameroff and Penrose, "Consciousness in the Universe."

[28] Another slight head-scratcher is David Bowie's song "Valentine's Day," from his 2013 comeback album *The Next Day*, about a school shooter. Five years later, and almost exactly two years after Bowie died, a disturbed 19-year-old former student murdered 17 people at Marjory Stoneman Douglas High School in Parkland, Florida … on February 14, Valentine's Day. The shooter explained that he wanted to ruin the day for everyone because nobody loved him. The coincidence in this case is reduced somewhat by the law of large numbers: This was already the 18th school shooting in 2018 alone—they are such frequent occurrences now. Also, the shooter had researched school shootings for months, making it very possible he was consciously or unconsciously influenced by Bowie's song in the two years after it had been released. See Zahra Mulroy, "People Are Pointing Out Chilling Similarity Between Florida School Shooting and David Bowie's Valentine's Day," *Mirror*, February 15, 2018, https://www.mirror.co.uk/news/us-news/people-pointing-out-chilling-prediction-12030463.

[29] István Orosz, "The Book in the Mirror OR THE CASE OF THE EATEN SAILORS," *Hungarian Review* 12(4), March 16, 2022, https://hungarianreview.com/article/the-book-in-the-mirror-or-the-case-of-the-eaten-sailors/.

[30] The idea of art and religion as cultural systems comes from the anthropologist Clifford Geertz in his books *The Interpretation of Cultures* (New York: Basic Books, 1973) and *Local Knowledge* (New York: Basic Books,

1983).

[31] David Carrasco, *Quetzalcoatl and the Irony of Empire* (Chicago, IL: The University of Chicago Press, 1982).

[32] See Wargo, *Where Was It Before the Dream?*

[33] See Eric Wargo, "Altered States of Reading, Part 1: VALIS, Vallee, and Vaal," *The Nightshirt*, September 5, 2015, http://thenightshirt.com/?p=3329.

[34] Beyer, *Singing to the Plants*; Luis Eduardo Luna and Pablo Amaringo, *Ayahuasca Visions* (Berkeley, CA: North Atlantic Books, 1999).

[35] Shared visions are commonly reported among people taking ayahuasca together. Early researchers even called one of its active chemicals "telepathine" for this reason (see Beyer, *Singing to the Plants*). But there may be no way to readily distinguish genuine telepathy from precognition of later feedback or confirmation, people's drug experiences being shaped by conversations they would have right afterward. Such a process would produce the impression that they had coinhabited the same virtual or spiritual space.

[36] Gananath Obeyesekere, *The Apotheosis of Captain Cook* (Princeton, NJ: Princeton University Press, 1992).

[37] Marshall Sahlins, *How "Natives" Think* (Chicago, IL: The University of Chicago Press, 1995).

[38] Ibid.

[39] Paul Rydeen, "Philip K. Dick: The Other Side," *The Gnosis Archive*, accessed on January 8, 2024, http://gnosis.org/pkd.biography.html.

[40] See Wargo, *Time Loops*.

[41] Survival but at some cost is another meaning of Freudian "castration."

[42] Luna and Amaringo, *Ayahuasca Visions*.

[43] Krohn and Kripal, *Changed in a Flash*.

Afterword

[1] Rizwan Virk, *The Simulation Hypothesis* (San Francisco, CA: Bayview Books, 2019).

[2] Refaat Alareer, "If I Must Die," *If I Must Die…*, accessed on February 4, 2024, https://ifimustdie.net/.

[3] Refaat in Gaza, "If I must die, let it be a tale," X (Formerly Twitter), accessed on February 4, 2024, https://twitter.com/itranslate123/status/1719701312990830934.

[4] After encountering the flying blender, my fictional protagonist embarked

on a self-improvement program that included losing weight by making veggie smoothies. But Diana Pasulka describes a similar response in real UFO experiencers, a newfound entrainment to what really matters and the pursuit of more meaningful goals. And a similar response is reported by many people who take ayahuasca or other psychedelics in ritual settings: a feeling of being brought close to death and then returning to life with renewed clarity and purpose.

[5] Rainer Maria Rilke, "Archaic Torso of Apollo," *poets.org*, accessed on February 5, 2024, https://poets.org/poem/archaic-torso-apollo

[6] Wargo, *Precognitive Dreamwork*, 275.

[7] Myers, "Fragments of Inner Life."

Duchamp, Marcel, 69-70, 131, 209, 380n45
Dune (Herbert), 263, 312
Dune (Lynch), 259, 264
Dunne, J. W., 13, 60-63, 65-66, 68, 76, 78-80, 84-85, 87, 99, 171, 202, 242, 255, 358n84

Edison, Thomas, 1, 167, 215
Ehrlich, Max Simon, 309
Einhorn, Ira, 273, 287-288
Einstein, Albert, 35, 39, 40, 55, 69, 81, 177-178, 180, 181, 201, 312, 327
Eisenstein, Sergei, 172-173, 305
Elephant Man, The (David Lynch film), 16, 262-263, 265-266
Ellison, Harlan, 1, 236, 374n25
Emerson, Ralph Waldo, 225-226, 241, 261, 300
entanglement (see quantum entanglement)
Epimedes, 145, 153
Eraserhead (Lynch), 16, 257-259, 261-262, 264, 265-266, 271, 319, 378-379n26-27, 379n37
Esalen Institute, x, 68, 320-322
ESP (extrasensory perception), 18, 36, 37, 41, 58, 64, 68, 69, 88, 90, 109, 125, 148, 150, 165, 170, 189, 191, 233, 275, 277, 282, 290, 293, 313, 367n7, 382n16
Experiment with Time, An (Dunne), 61, 79, 84-85, 202
Eyes of Darkness, The (Koontz), 7
Ezekiel, 317-320, 326

Face on Mars, 14, 115-120
"Face on Mars, The" (Kirby), 116
Feather, Sally Rhine, 89
Fedorov, Nikolai, 201
Fellin, Dave, 148-149
Fifty Days at Iliam (Twombly), 209, 220, 372n26

Fishburne, Laurence, 322
Fitting, Peter, 73, 277, 279-280
Flatland (Abbott), 69-70
Florensky, Pavel, 201-202, 370n36
Flournoy, Theodore, 238-239, 241
Forbidden Science (Vallee), 223, 282, 382n15-16, 383n27-28
"fort-da" game, 110-111, 113, 115, 119, 231
Four Captives (Michelangelo), 128
"Fragments of Inner Life" (Myers), 252
Franketienne, 6-7, 99, 122
Fraser, Elizabeth, 164, 361-362n24, free will, 124, 125, 127, 128, 290
Freud, Sigmund, 3, 13, 15, 61, 74-76, 79-80, 83-84, 87, 93-97, 110-113, 121, 126, 127, 173, 174, 175, 189, 203, 221, 226-232, 242, 248, 252-253, 254, 267, 269, 285, 294, 340n53, 347n20, 370n36, 373n10, 373n16, 386n41
Friedrich, Caspar David, 9, 110, 121, 240
"Frost Fairies, The" (Canby), 237-238, 241-242, 249
"Frost King, The" (Keller), 237-238
Futility (Robertson), 5, 30
Future of the Body, The (Murphy), 68

Gardner, Martin, 32, 55, 329n9, 338n27-28
Get Back (Jackson), 100-101, 304, 346n66
"Get Back" (Beatles), 100, 248
Gibson, William, 35, 335n39, 344n45
Giger, H. R., ix, 16, 251, 259, 261, 263-266, 282, 378n26, 379n37
Ginsberg, Allen, 150-151, 300, 301
God Emperor of Dune (Herbert), 312
grandfather paradox, 81, 127, 234
Greene, Graham, 30

90, 96-97, 140, 165, 194, 272,
291-294, 298, 301, 305, 314-315,
320, 321, 322, 324, 327, 334n19,
340n50, 341n58, 341n62,
342n10, 345n57, 354n29,
362n31, 366n93
Krohn, Elizabeth, 77-78, 86, 124,
314, 362n31
Kubla Khan (Coleridge), 2, 92
Kubrick, Stanley, 79, 146, 258
Kuhn, Thomas, 34
Kulagina, Ninel, 200-201

L'Engle, Madeleine, 81
Lacan, Jacques, 111, 112, 121, 264,
267-270, 285, 288, 299, 307,
370n36, 380n52
"lamella" (Lacan term), 268-269,
288
LANSA Flight 508 crash, 107-109,
122
Large Hadron Collider (CERN),
155
Lascaux Cave, 14, 134-136, 145,
152-153, 156-157, 159, 186,
353n17
Lennon, John, 91--95, 101-102,
146, 162, 345n62
Lévi-Strauss, Claude, 140, 298,
379n40
Lewis-Williams, David, 140-143,
145, 149, 162, 179, 202, 354n30-
31
Lightman, Alan, 92
*Lives of the Most Eminent Painters,
Sculptors, and Architects* (Vasari),
2, 194
long self, the, 40, 67, 70-71, 83,
121, 173, 289, 294, 321, 324-327
Lower Manhattan Cultural Council (LMCC) (see World Views
Program)
Luke, David, 150, 302
Luna, Luis Eduardo, 315

Lynch, David, 16, 19, 92, 162, 251,
257-259, 261-266, 269, 271, 282,
304-305, 378n26-27, 379n37

Mailer, Norman, 5
Man and His Symbols (Jung), 241
Mandell, David, 33, 77, 124
Marooned (Caidin), 7-8, 330n22
Martel, J. F., 1, 18, 20, 162, 176,
344n45, 348n24, 352n16
Matrix, The (Wachovski sisters), 317,
322
Matthew, Patrick, 248-249, 376n48
Maxse, Kitty, 168-169, 174, 176,
219
May, Edwin, 290, 344n51, 383n16
McCartney, Paul, 100-102, 163
Melovivi (The Trap) (Frankétienne), 6
Menil Collection (Houston), 207,
217
Mental Radio (Sinclair), 55, 56, 64-
66, 337n16, 338n28, 340n49
"Mental Telegraphy" (Twain), 51,
375n42
Merrick, Joseph Carey ("John Mer-
rick"), 262-263, 265
Messengers of Deception (Vallee), 284,
383n27
Metamorphosis, The (Kafka), 15, 122,
258, 372n24
Meyrink, Gustav, 255-257
Michelangelo, 2, 128-129, 142, 161,
163, 209, 350n63, 351n64
microtubules, 306
Milne, Louise S., 143, 144, 164,
347n16, 355n38-39
Mind in the Cave, The (Lewis-Wil-
liams), 141, 354n30
Minkowski, Hermann, 39, 40, 147,
156, 178, 327
Minotaur, 143, 145
Moench, Doug, 67
Monney, Julien, 157
montage, 172-173, 299, 364n57

Moore, Alan, 39
Mount Pélee eruption, 60
Mrs. Dalloway (Woolf), 14, 165, 168-169, 170, 174-175, 179, 190, 210, 297, 319, 363n48, 365n71
"Mrs. Dalloway in Bond Street" (Woolf), 168, 176
Muraresku, Brian, 302
Mutants and Mystics (Kripal), ix, 67, 291, 292
"My Sweet Lord" (Harrison), 236-237
Myers, Frederic W. H., 48-49, 52, 59, 60, 64, 66, 67, 69, 80, 169, 171, 179, 252, 327, 341n58, 375n42
Mysterious Universe, The (Jeans), 181-184

Nabokov, Vladimir, 18, 78-79, 85
Narrative of Arthur Gordon Pym, The (Poe), 32, 306
Naumov, Eduard, 201
Neanderthals, 137-138
Nietzsche, Friedrich, 240-242, 312, 313
Nine Discourses on Commodus (Twombly), 210-211, 218, 219
Nkisi N'kondi figures, 27, 28, 208
Noguchi, Isamu, 116-120, 131
Noll, Richard, 253-254, 353n26
noösphere, 271-272
Novikov, Igor, 81-82
Nude Descending a Staircase, No. 2 (Duchamp), 70, 209

O'Bannon, Dan, 260, 264, 269, 271
Obeyesekere, Gananath, 310
Odle, E. V., 177
"Odradek" (see "The Cares of a Family Man"),
Oedipus (myth), 83-84, 126, 128, 227-228, 248, 373n16
Oedipus the King (Sophocles), 84,

227, 228
Ogotommeli, 310-311
Orlando (Woolf), 166, 177, 183
Orpheus and Eurydice (myth), 218
Osiris, 153-154, 358n88
Oulipo (group), 227
Overview Effect, 187
Owens, Richard, 236-237

Paleolithic art (see cave paintings)
Paquette, Andrew, 270
Paracelsus, 284-285
Parmenides, 147, 153, 220, 327
Pasulka, Diana W., 97, 187, 272, 299, 303, 304, 386n4
Patricia (Romondt), 57, 64, 66, 323, 338n30
Pennsylvania (steamboat), 51
Penrose, Roger, 358n91
Peripheral, The (Gibson), 35, 335n39, 344n45
Phaedrus (Plato), 216-219
Phantasms of the Living (Gurney, Podmore, Myers), 48, 171
Philadelphia Museum of Art, x, 209, 305, 320
Phillips, Rasheedah, 234
plagiarism, 15, 16, 225, 227-229, 231, 236, 237-239, 242-244, 246, 249, 259, 265-266, 267, 275, 374n25
Platform (Houellebecq), 6,
Plato, 34, 216-218, 251-252, 267, 269, 378n21
Poe, Edgar Allen, 228
Police, The (band), 288
Popper, Karl, 215
precognition,
    as alternative explanation for clairvoyance/remote viewing, 58-59, 62, 67-68, 282, 382n16
    as alternative explanation for mediumship, 62, 239, 242-243
    as alternative explanation for

telepathy, 60, 62-64, 66-68, 150, 340n54, 386n35
  as distinct from prediction, 7
  as form of memory, 37-38, 62, 65-66, 76-80, 83, 91, 242-243
  experimental evidence for, 12, 36-37, 64
  in dreams, 13, 33-34, 37-39, 41-42, 67, 70, 75-85, 87, 109, 112, 113, 124, 127, 149, 151, 156, 171-172, 173-174, 202, 218, 247-248, 255, 270-271, 275, 280-282, 289, 299-301, 303-305, 308-309, 311-312, 321-322, 324-325, 327, 334n31
  in waking visions, 18, 87-91, 125, 148, 189, 255, 262-263, 276, 294, 299, 301, 304-305, 313, 321
Preiswerk, Hélène ("Helly"), 239
presentiment, experimental evidence for, 36-37
primary process (Freud concept), 75, 143, 174, 189, 265, 324
Producers, The (Brooks), 323-324
prophecy (see precognition)
"Prophet, The" (Pushkin), 200
Psychopathology of Everyday Life (Freud), 87, 112
Pushkin, Alexander, 123, 200, 204
Puthoff, Hal, 282, 285, 290, 299, 382n16

quantum computing, 35, 56, 213, 284
quantum entanglement, 56, 68
quantum physics, 14-15, 125, 170, 180, 183-185

Quarles, Maggy, 170-173, 253-255, 303, 377n13
Quetzalcoatl, 308, 310

Radin, Dean, 36
Radio Free Albemuth (Dick), 275,

278, 281, 289, 292
Reclaiming Art in the Age of Artifice (Martel), 1, 18, 344n45, 348n24, 352n16
"Red Book" (*Liber Novus*) (Jung), 255
Redd, Marques, 156
Reiner, Rob, 10
retrocausation (see also teleology, time loops), 34, 36, 43, 68, 82, 83, 156, 170, 180, 286, 299-300, 306
Rhine, J. B., 64, 89, 170, 340n90
Rhine, Louisa, 64, 82, 89, 170
Richards, Michael Rolando, 13, 25-29, 31, 38, 123-128, 208, 333n17, 350n59
Rilke, Rainer Maria, 317, 327
Roadside Picnic (Strugatsky bros. novel), 198, 219
Robertson, Morgan, 5, 8, 11, 30, 331n27
Robinson, Kim Stanley, 188, 330n23,
Romondt, Marcus, 57, 66, 338n30
Roots of Coincidence, The (Koestler), 189-191, 299

Sackville-West, Vita, vii, 166, 189
Sacrifice, The (Tarkovsky), 123, 195, 204, 205-206, 370n41
Sagan, Carl, 115, 119, 181, 187, 348n33
Sahlins, Marshall, 310
Sam, Rindy, 216-217
Saussure, Ferdinand de, 267
Sheckley, Robert, 202
Schrödinger, Erwin, 110, 181
Schwyzer, Emile, 253, 255, 377n10
Scott, Ridley, 16, 259, 261, 264, 265, 268, 269, 378n27
Sculpture To Be Seen from Mars (Noguchi), 116-117
Sea of Ice, The (Friedrich), 9, 110

Printed in Great Britain
by Amazon

42558745R00233